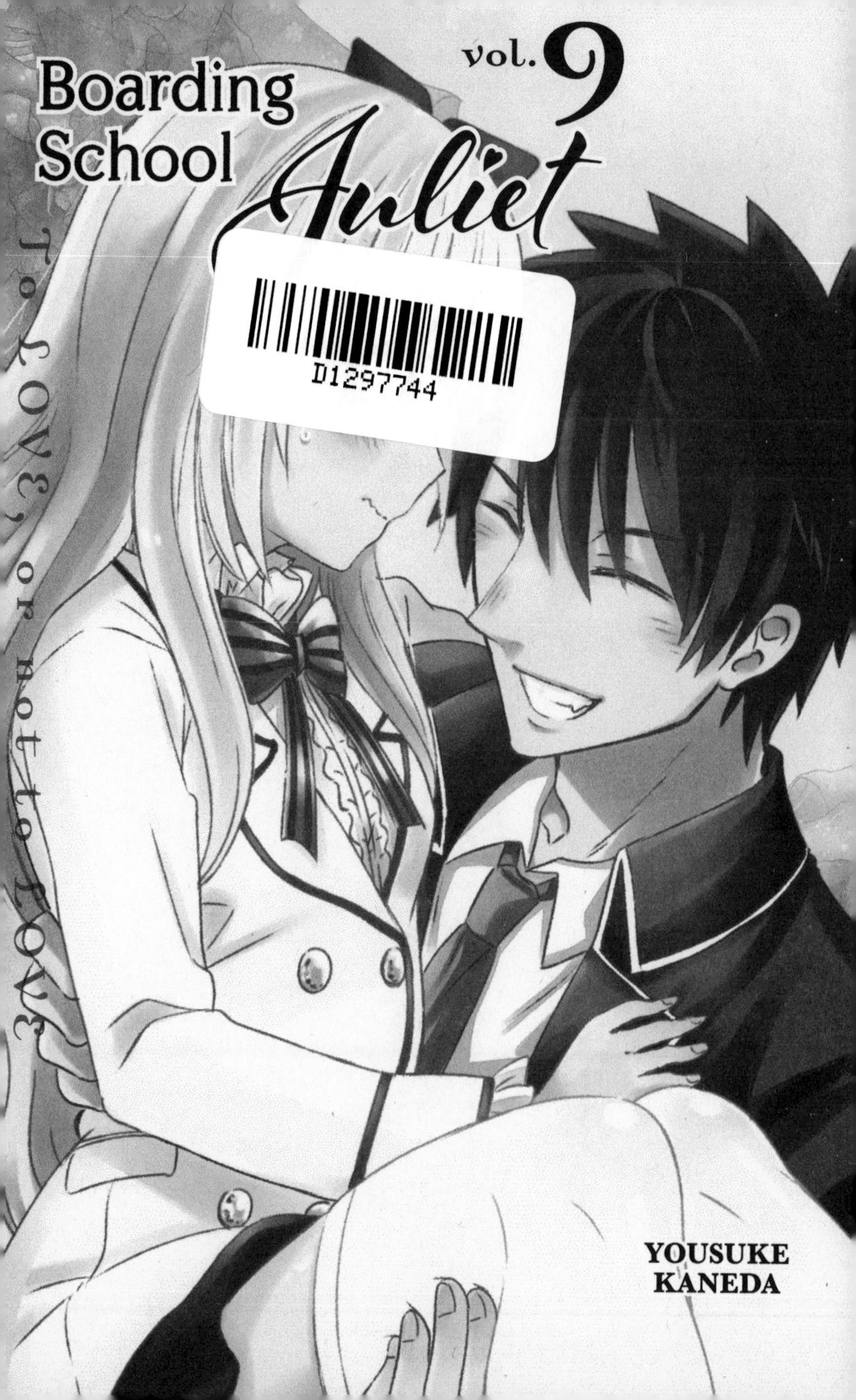
Boarding School
Juliet
vol. 9
To LOVE, or not to LOVE
YOUSUKE KANEDA

THE PLAYERS

character

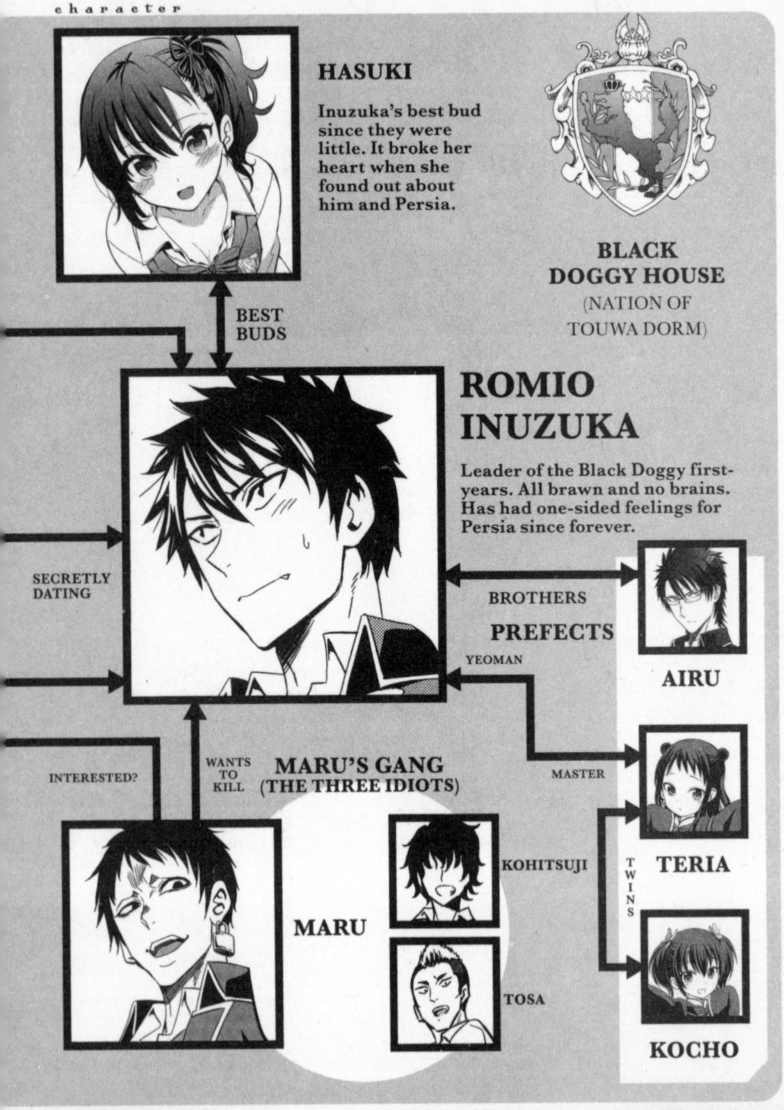
HASUKI
Inuzuka's best bud since they were little. It broke her heart when she found out about him and Persia.
BLACK DOGGY HOUSE
(NATION OF TOUWA DORM)
BEST BUDS
ROMIO INUZUKA
Leader of the Black Doggy first-years. All brawn and no brains. Has had one-sided feelings for Persia since forever.
SECRETLY DATING
BROTHERS
PREFECTS
YEOMAN
AIRU
MASTER
WANTS TO KILL
MARU'S GANG (THE THREE IDIOTS)
INTERESTED?
TERIA
TWINS
KOHITSUJI
MARU
TOSA
KOCHO

BOARDING SCHOOL JULIE[T]

To LOVE, or not to LOVE

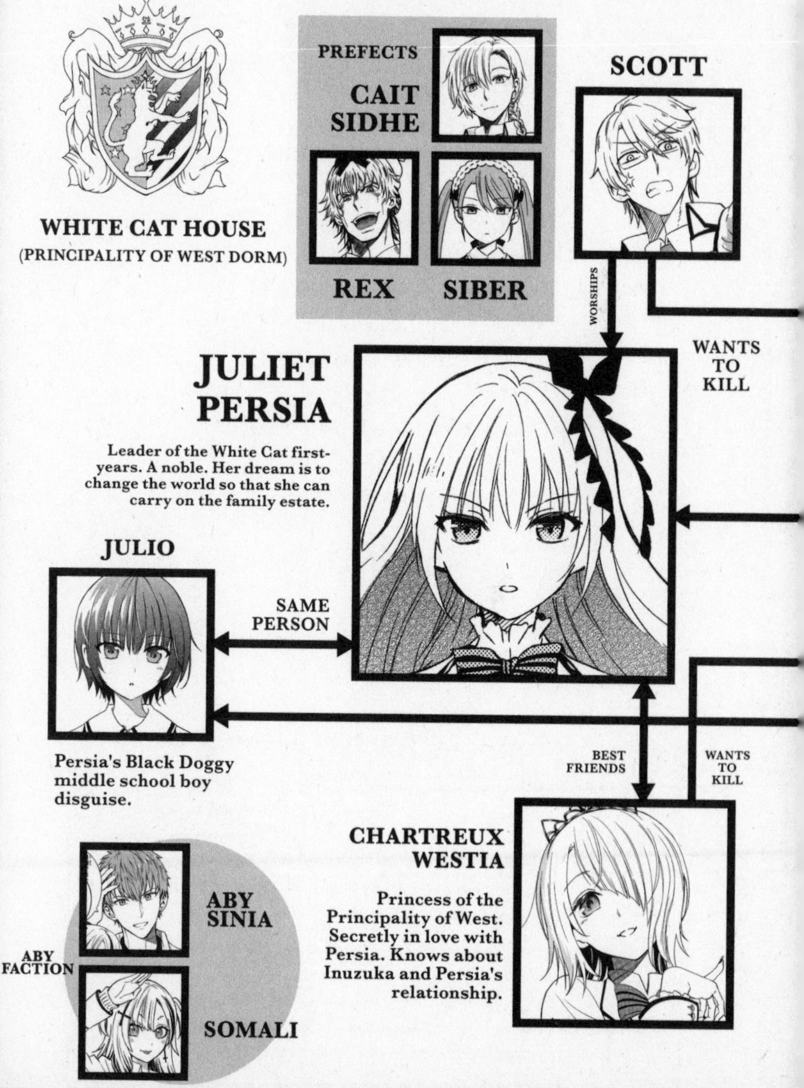

WHITE CAT HOUSE
(PRINCIPALITY OF WEST DORM)
PREFECTS
CAIT SIDHE
REX
SIBER
SCOTT
WORSHIPS
WANTS TO KILL
JULIET PERSIA
Leader of the White Cat first-years. A noble. Her dream is to change the world so that she can carry on the family estate.
JULIO
SAME PERSON
Persia's Black Doggy middle school boy disguise.
BEST FRIENDS
WANTS TO KILL
CHARTREUX WESTIA
Princess of the Principality of West. Secretly in love with Persia. Knows about Inuzuka and Persia's relationship.
ABY SINIA
ABY FACTION
SOMALI

contents

story

At boarding school Dahlia Academy, attended by students from two feuding countries, one first-year longs for a forbidden love. His name: Romio Inuzuka, leader of the Black Doggy House first-years. The apple of his eye: Juliet Persia, leader of the White Cat House first-years. It all begins when Inuzuka confesses his feelings to her. This is Inuzuka and Persia's star-crossed, secret love story...

Inuzuka goes home to Touwa for winter vacation, with Persia, disguised as Julio, in tow. However, awaiting them at Inuzuka's place is his "little sister" Shuna—who's bent on ejecting any and all women who come anywhere near him! To sweep Shuna's suspicions of Julio's gender under the rug, our secret sweethearts have no choice but to bathe together...!

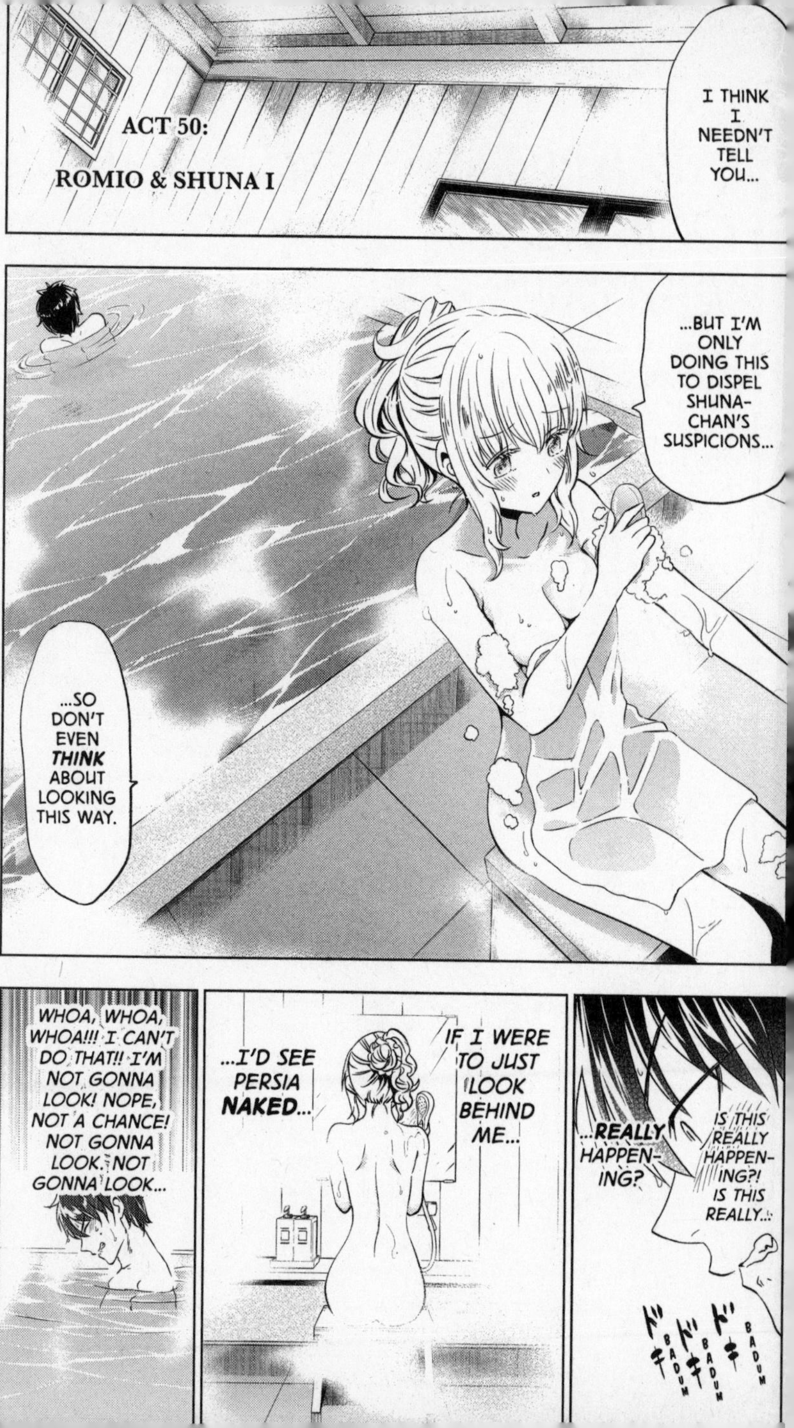
I THINK I NEEDN'T TELL YOU...
ACT 50:
ROMIO & SHUNA I
...BUT I'M ONLY DOING THIS TO DISPEL SHUNA-CHAN'S SUSPICIONS...
...SO DON'T EVEN **THINK** ABOUT LOOKING THIS WAY.
IS THIS REALLY HAPPEN-ING?! IS THIS REALLY...
...**REALLY** HAPPEN-ING?
ドキ BADUM
ドキ BADUM
ドキ BADUM
IF I WERE TO JUST LOOK BEHIND ME...
...I'D SEE PERSIA **NAKED**...
WHOA, WHOA, WHOA!!! I CAN'T DO THAT!! I'M NOT GONNA LOOK! NOPE, NOT A CHANCE! NOT GONNA LOOK. NOT GONNA LOOK...

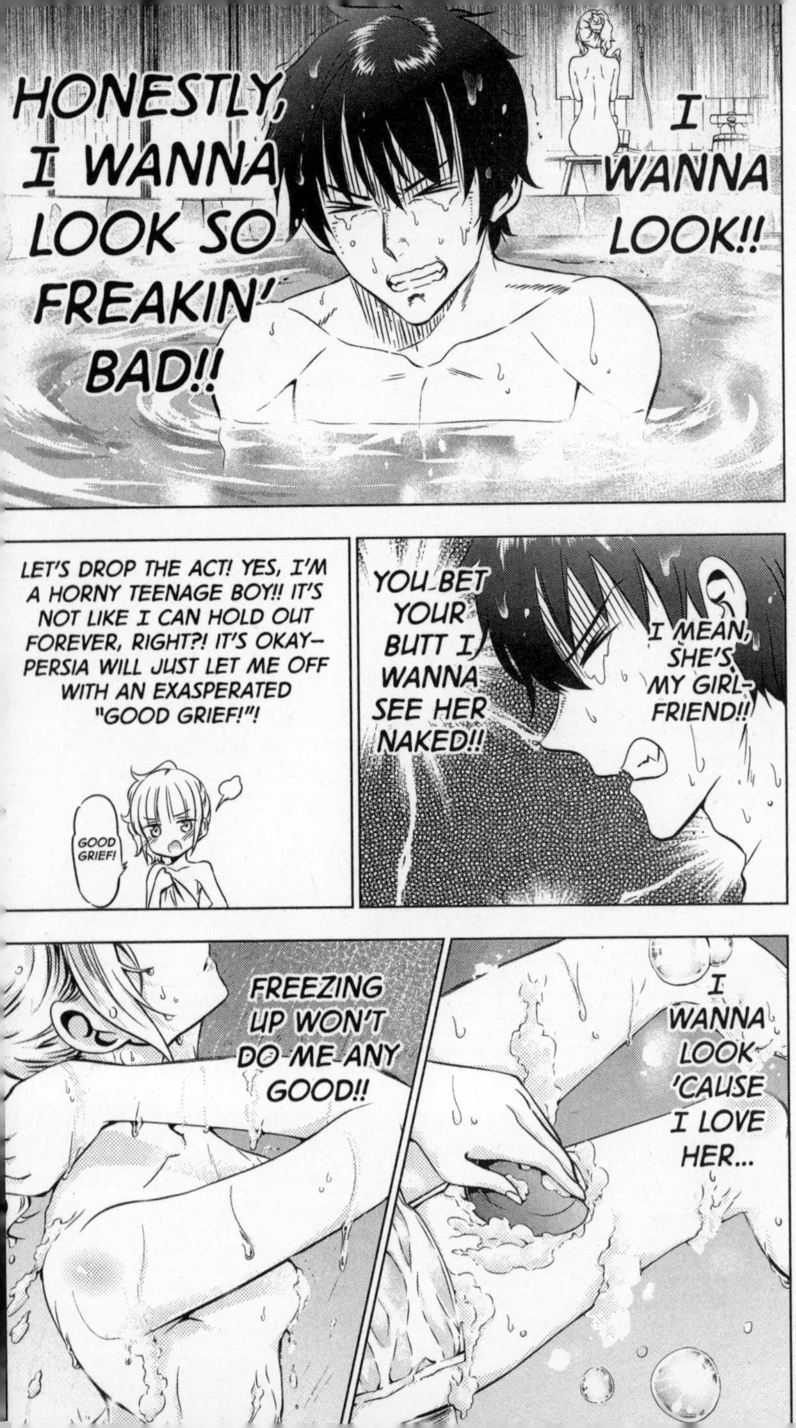
I WANNA LOOK!!
HONESTLY, I WANNA LOOK SO FREAKIN' BAD!!
I MEAN, SHE'S MY GIRL-FRIEND!!
YOU BET YOUR BUTT I WANNA SEE HER NAKED!!
LET'S DROP THE ACT! YES, I'M A HORNY TEENAGE BOY!! IT'S NOT LIKE I CAN HOLD OUT FOREVER, RIGHT?! IT'S OKAY—PERSIA WILL JUST LET ME OFF WITH AN EXASPERATED "GOOD GRIEF!"!
GOOD GRIEF!
I WANNA LOOK 'CAUSE I LOVE HER...
FREEZING UP WON'T DO ME ANY GOOD!!

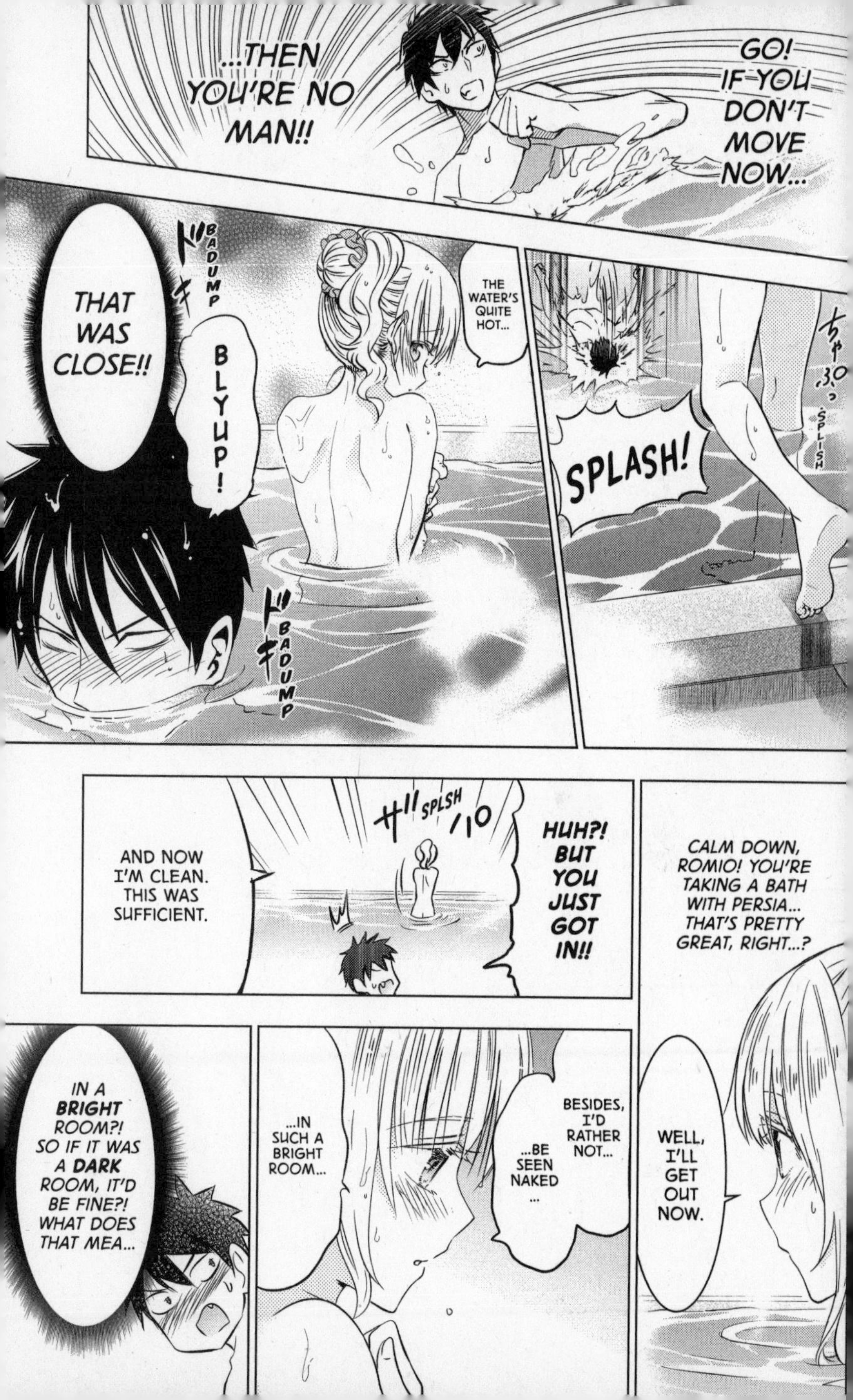
GO! IF YOU DON'T MOVE NOW...
...THEN YOU'RE NO MAN!!
ちゃぷっ
SPLISH
SPLASH!
THE WATER'S QUITE HOT...
ドキ BADUMP
BLYUP!
THAT WAS CLOSE!!
ドキ BADUMP
CALM DOWN, ROMIO! YOU'RE TAKING A BATH WITH PERSIA... THAT'S PRETTY GREAT, RIGHT...?
HUH?! BUT YOU JUST GOT IN!!
SPLSH
AND NOW I'M CLEAN. THIS WAS SUFFICIENT.
WELL, I'LL GET OUT NOW.
BESIDES, I'D RATHER NOT...
...BE SEEN NAKED...
...IN SUCH A BRIGHT ROOM...
IN A **BRIGHT** ROOM?! SO IF IT WAS A **DARK** ROOM, IT'D BE FINE?! WHAT DOES THAT MEA...

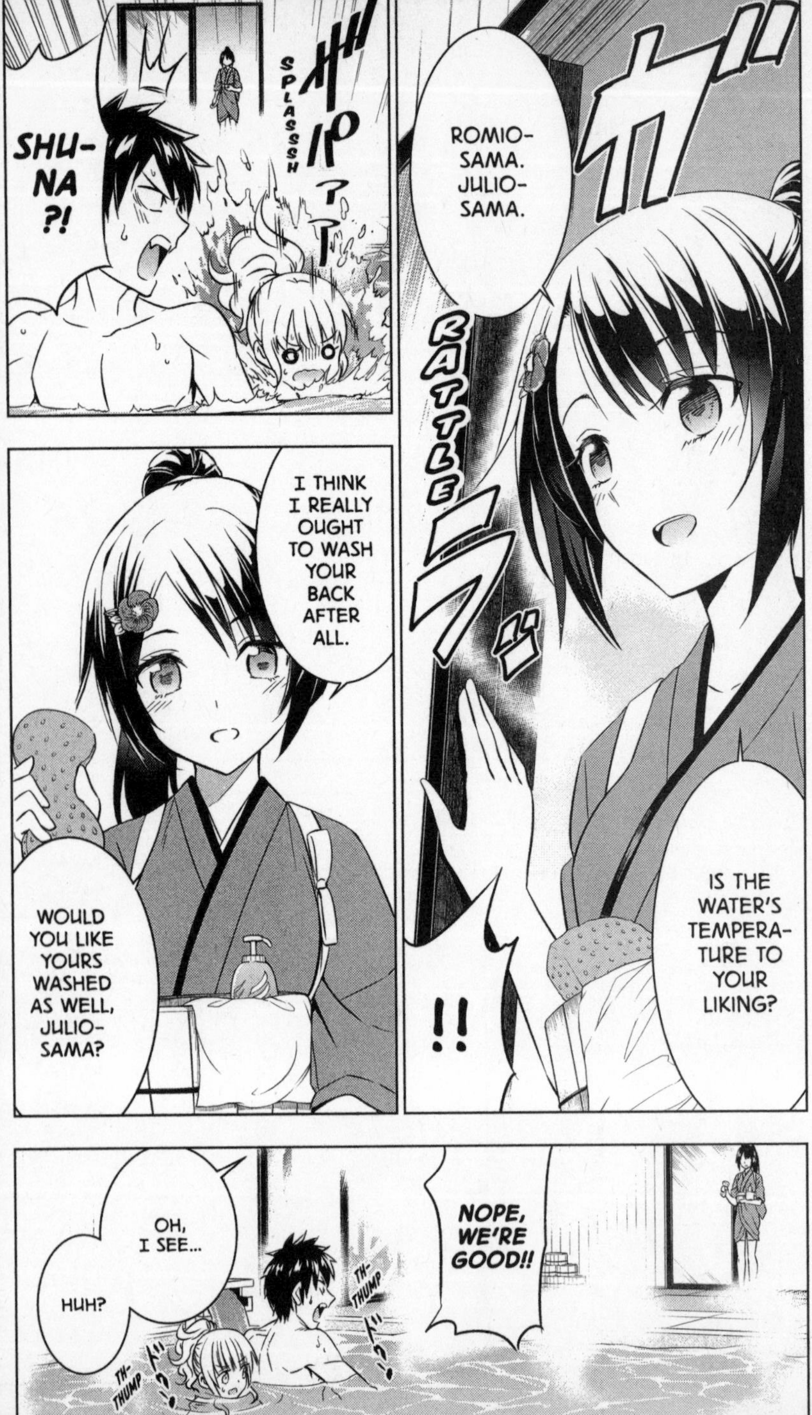
RATTLE
ROMIO-SAMA. JULIO-SAMA.
IS THE WATER'S TEMPERA-TURE TO YOUR LIKING?
!!
SPLASSSH
SHU-NA?!
I THINK I REALLY OUGHT TO WASH YOUR BACK AFTER ALL.
WOULD YOU LIKE YOURS WASHED AS WELL, JULIO-SAMA?
NOPE, WE'RE GOOD!!
OH, I SEE...
HUH?
TH-THUMP
TH-THUMP

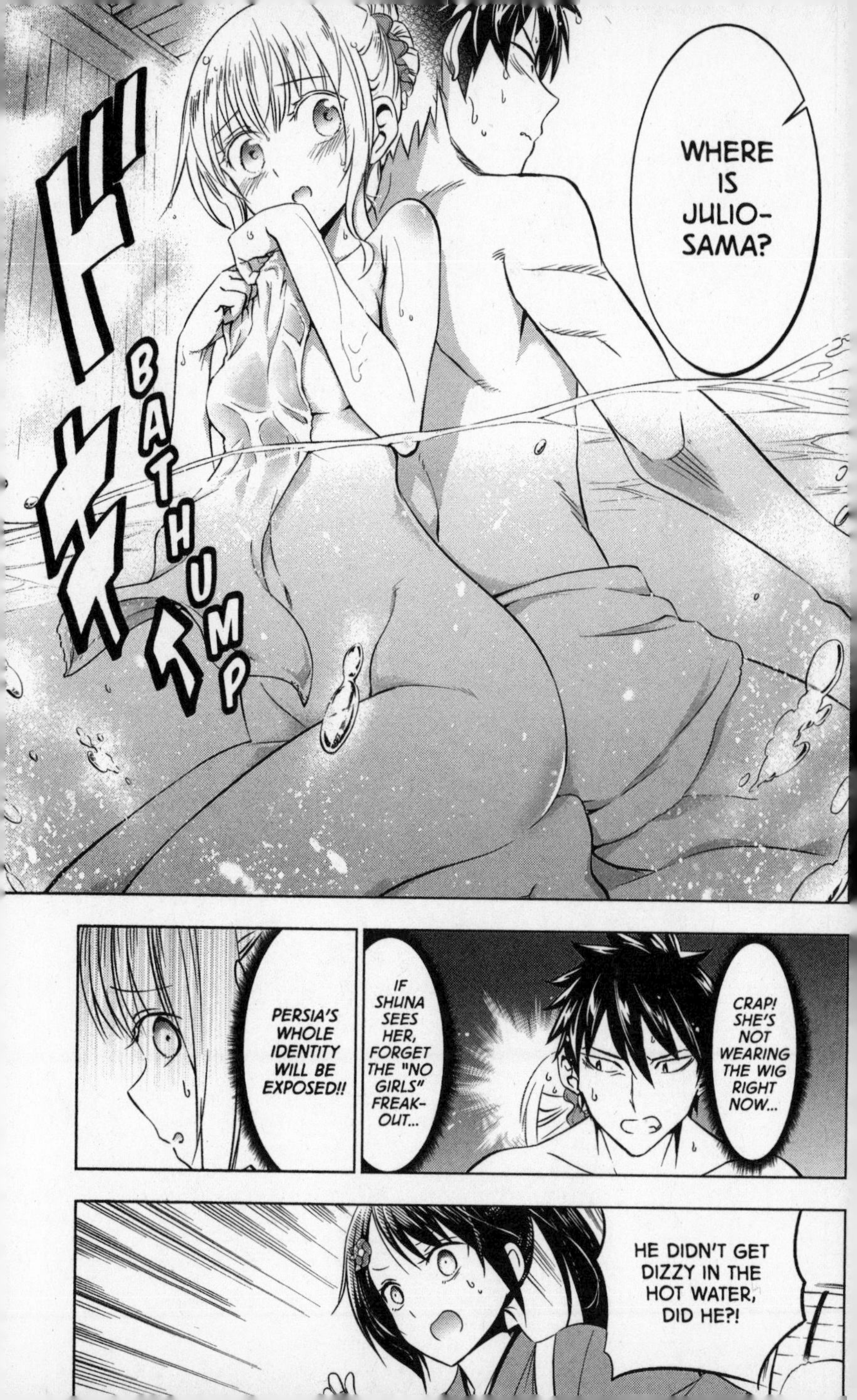
WHERE IS JULIO-SAMA?
BATHUMP
CRAP! SHE'S NOT WEARING THE WIG RIGHT NOW...
IF SHUNA SEES HER, FORGET THE "NO GIRLS" FREAK-OUT...
PERSIA'S WHOLE IDENTITY WILL BE EXPOSED!!
HE DIDN'T GET DIZZY IN THE HOT WATER, DID HE?!

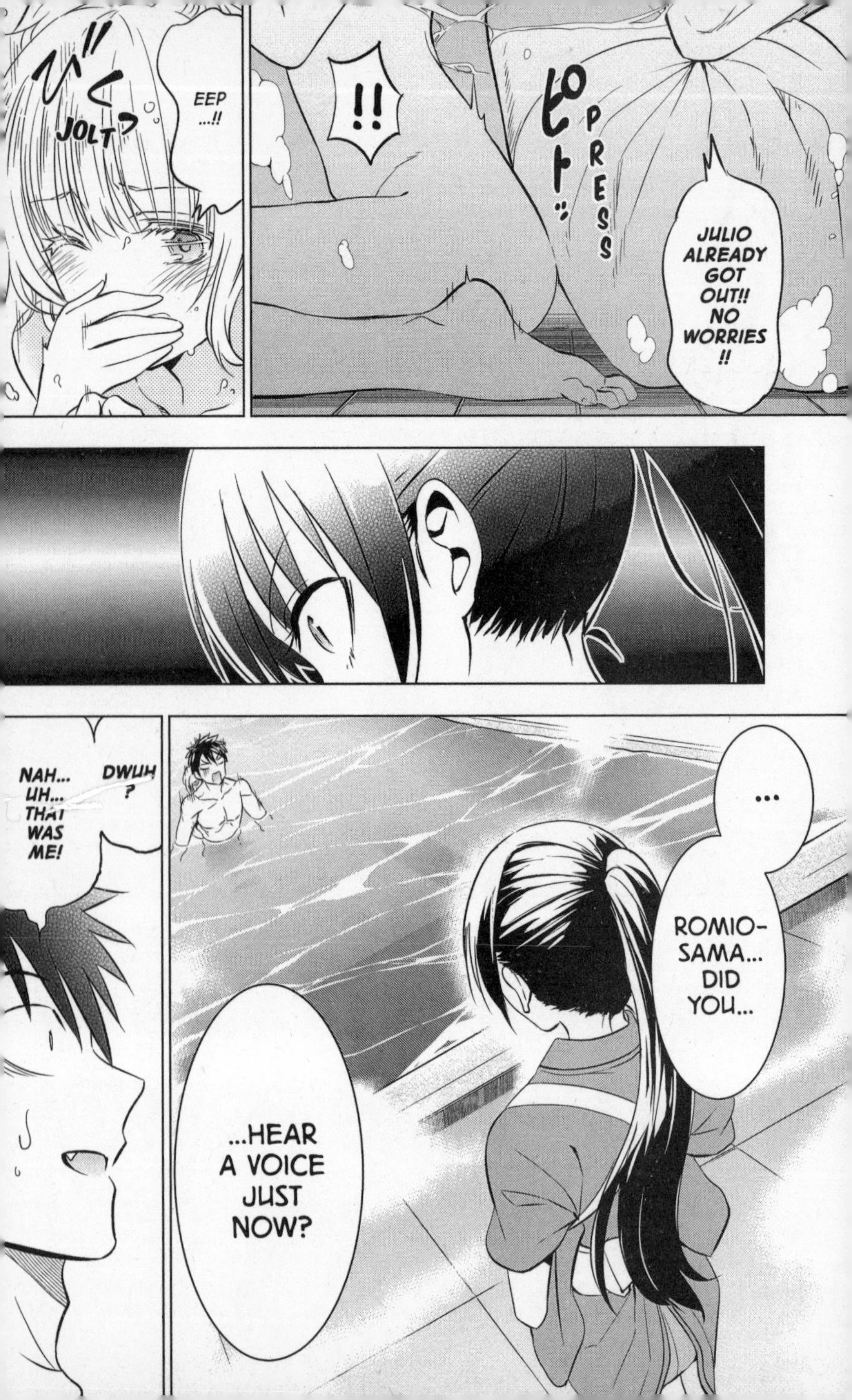
!!
ピト PRESS
JULIO ALREADY GOT OUT!! NO WORRIES!!
びくっ JOLT
EEP ...!!
...
ROMIO-SAMA... DID YOU...
...HEAR A VOICE JUST NOW?
DWUH?
NAH... UH... THAT WAS ME!

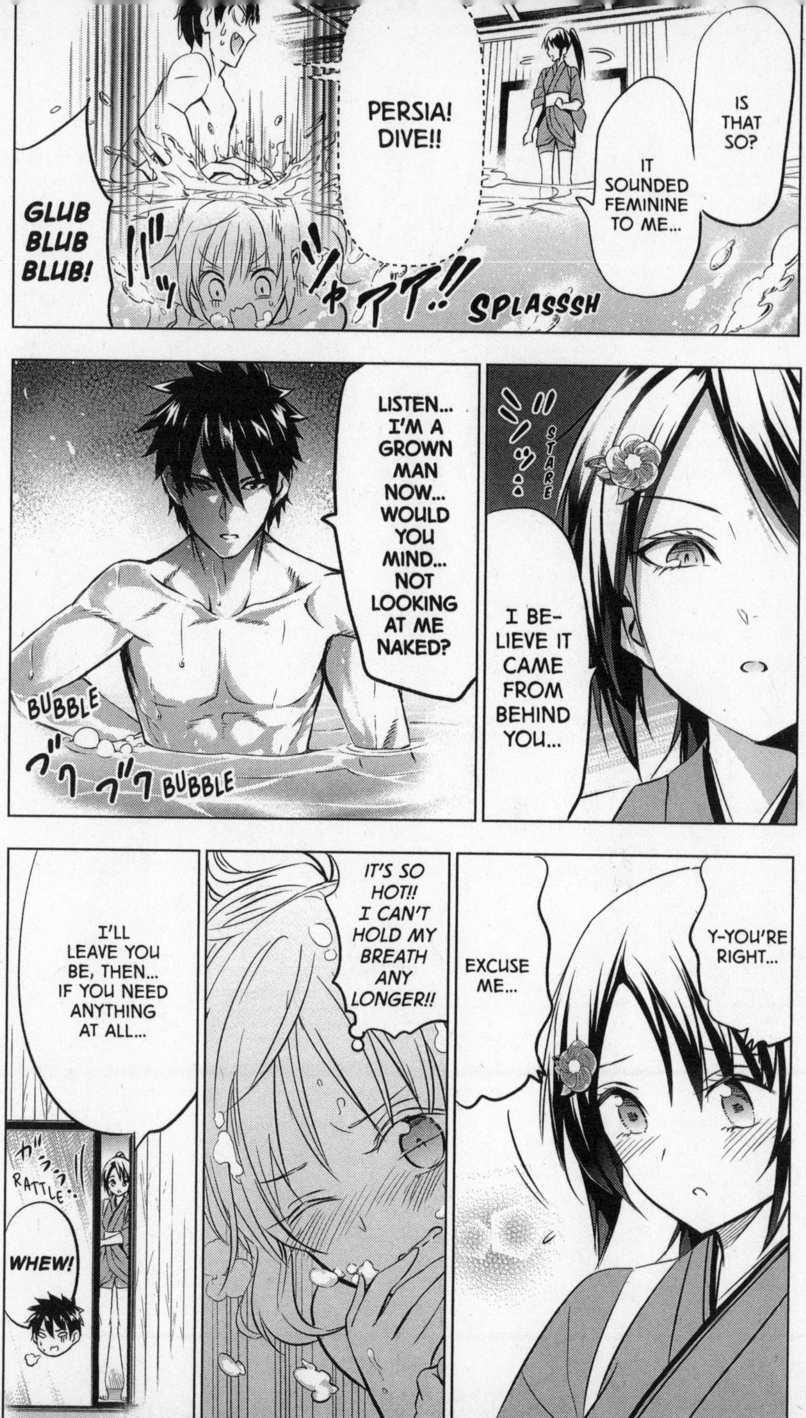
IS THAT SO?
IT SOUNDED FEMININE TO ME...
PERSIA! DIVE!!
SPLASSSH
GLUB BLUB BLUB!
STARE
I BE-LIEVE IT CAME FROM BEHIND YOU...
LISTEN... I'M A GROWN MAN NOW... WOULD YOU MIND... NOT LOOKING AT ME NAKED?
BUBBLE
BUBBLE
Y-YOU'RE RIGHT...
EXCUSE ME...
IT'S SO HOT!! I CAN'T HOLD MY BREATH ANY LONGER!!
I'LL LEAVE YOU BE, THEN... IF YOU NEED ANYTHING AT ALL...
RATTLE
WHEW!

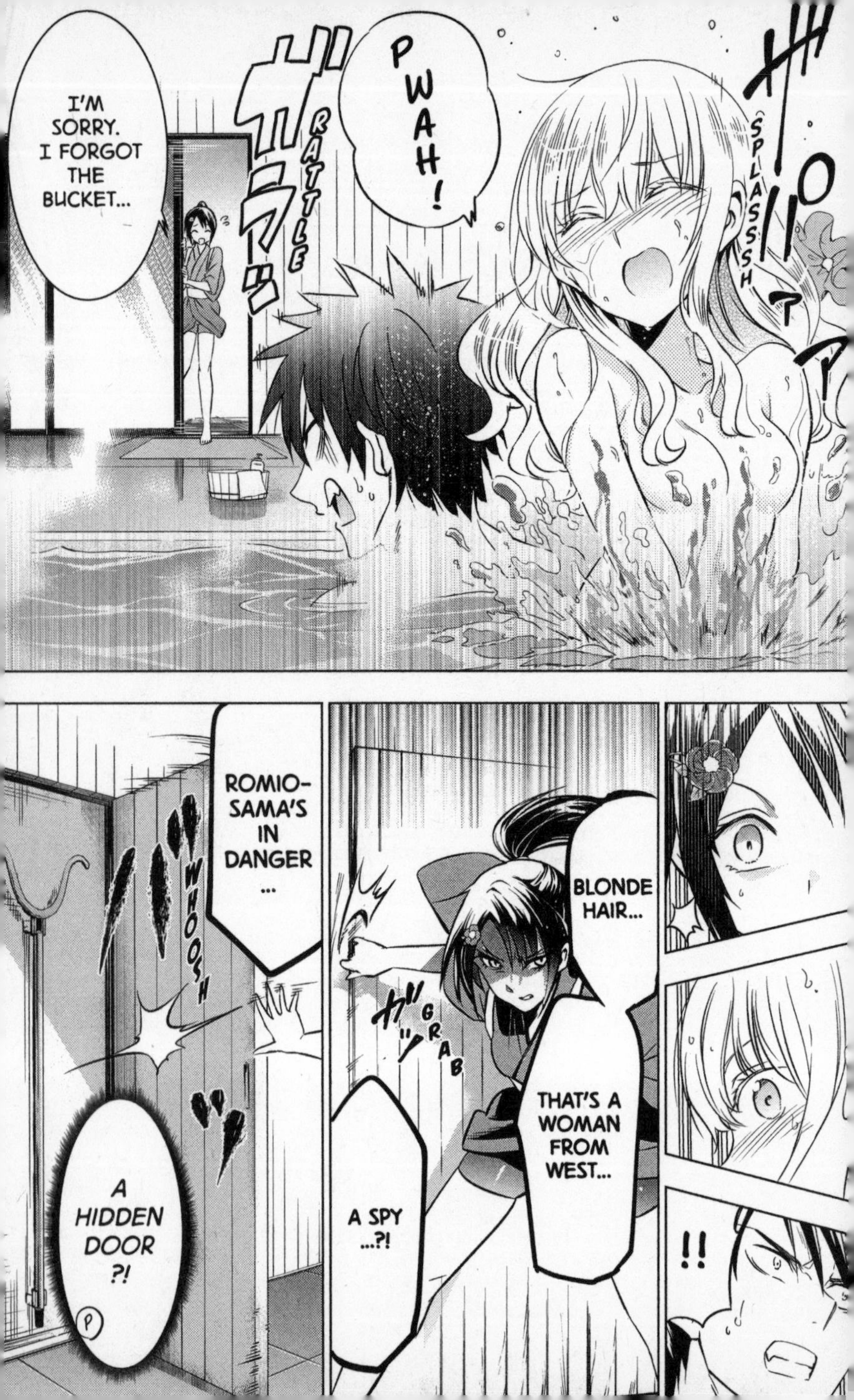
SPLASSSH
PWAH!
RATTLE
I'M SORRY. I FORGOT THE BUCKET...
!!
BLONDE HAIR...
THAT'S A WOMAN FROM WEST...
GRAB
A SPY ...?!
ROMIO-SAMA'S IN DANGER ...
WHOOOSH
A HIDDEN DOOR ?!

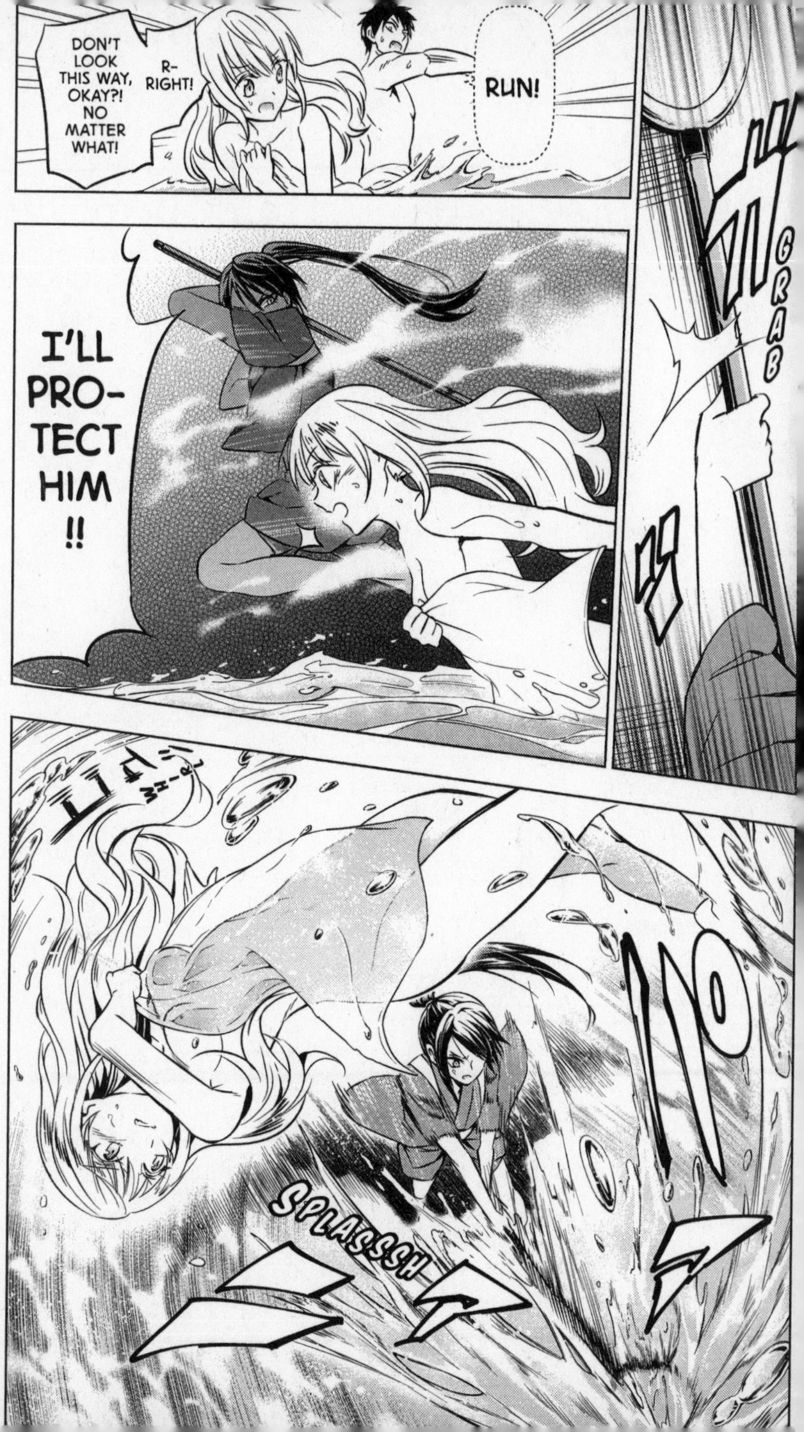

GRAB
RUN!
R-RIGHT!
DON'T LOOK THIS WAY, OKAY?! NO MATTER WHAT!
I'LL PROTECT HIM!!
WHIR
SPLASSSH

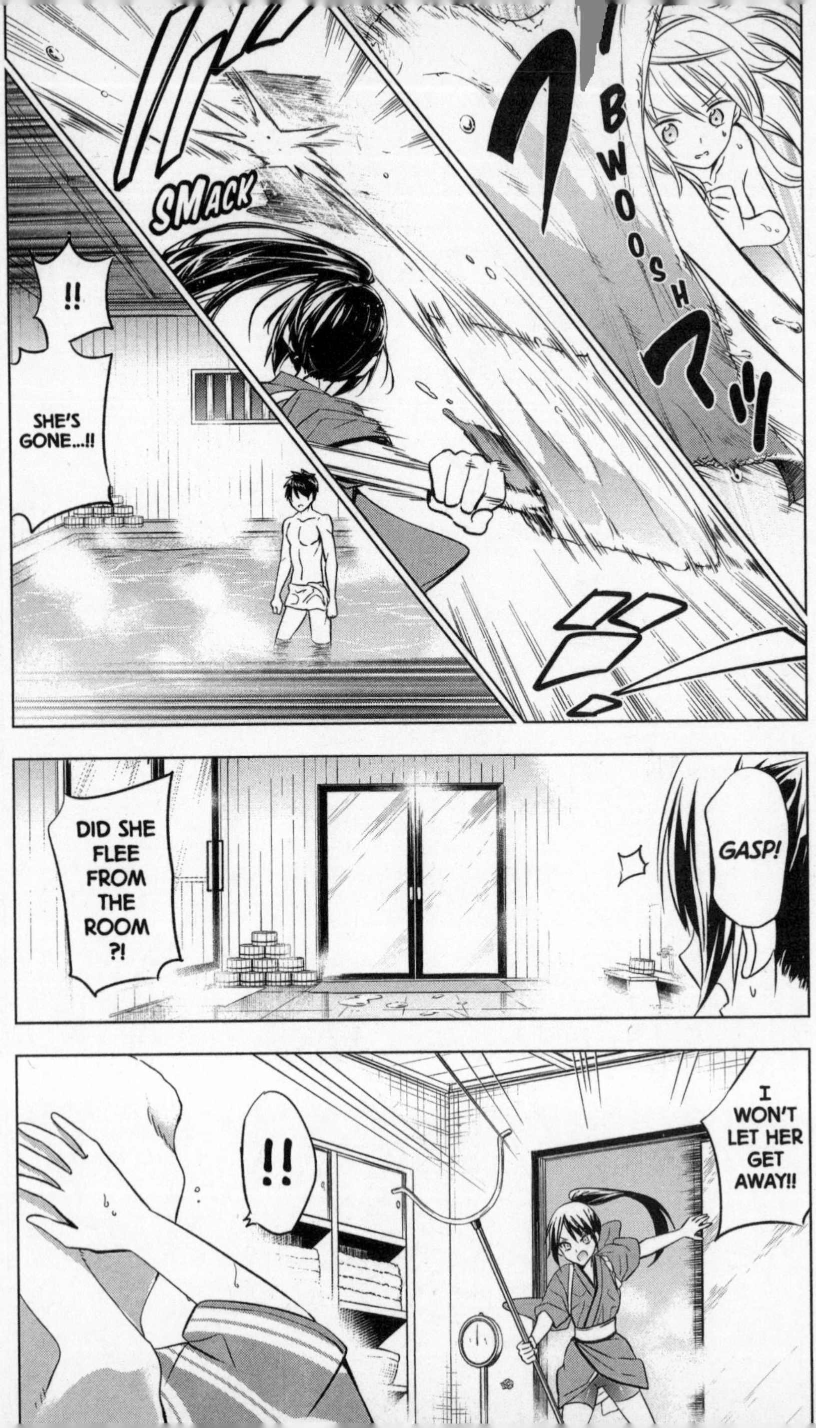
BWOOSH
SMACK
!!
SHE'S GONE...!!
GASP!
DID SHE FLEE FROM THE ROOM?!
I WON'T LET HER GET AWAY!!
!!

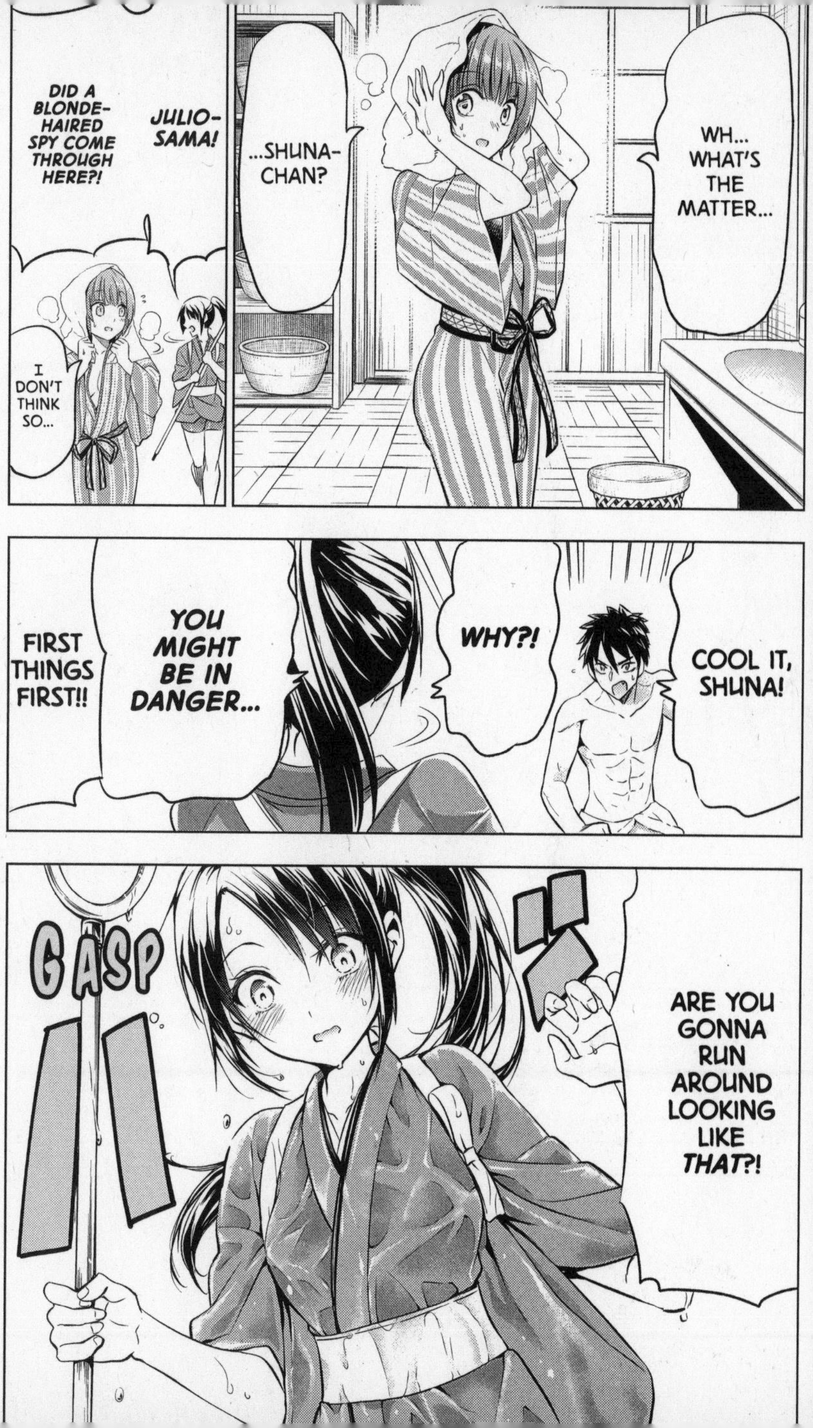
WH... WHAT'S THE MATTER...
...SHUNA-CHAN?
JULIO-SAMA!
DID A BLONDE-HAIRED SPY COME THROUGH HERE?!
I DON'T THINK SO...
COOL IT, SHUNA!
WHY?!
YOU MIGHT BE IN DANGER...
FIRST THINGS FIRST!!
ARE YOU GONNA RUN AROUND LOOKING LIKE *THAT*?!
GASP

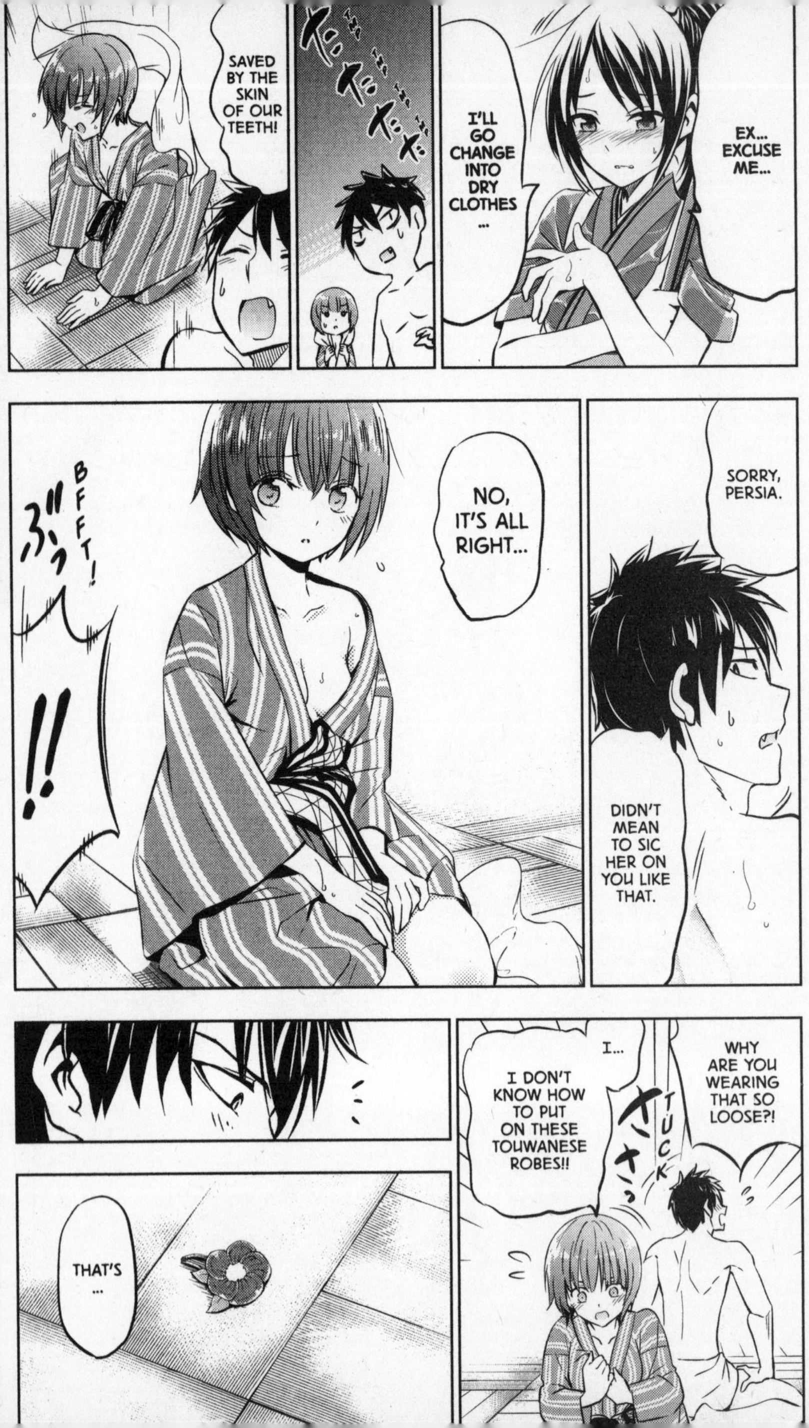
EX... EXCUSE ME...
I'LL GO CHANGE INTO DRY CLOTHES ...
SAVED BY THE SKIN OF OUR TEETH!
SORRY, PERSIA.
DIDN'T MEAN TO SIC HER ON YOU LIKE THAT.
NO, IT'S ALL RIGHT...
BFFT!
!!
WHY ARE YOU WEARING THAT SO LOOSE?!
I...
I DON'T KNOW HOW TO PUT ON THESE TOUWANESE ROBES!!
TUCK
THAT'S ...

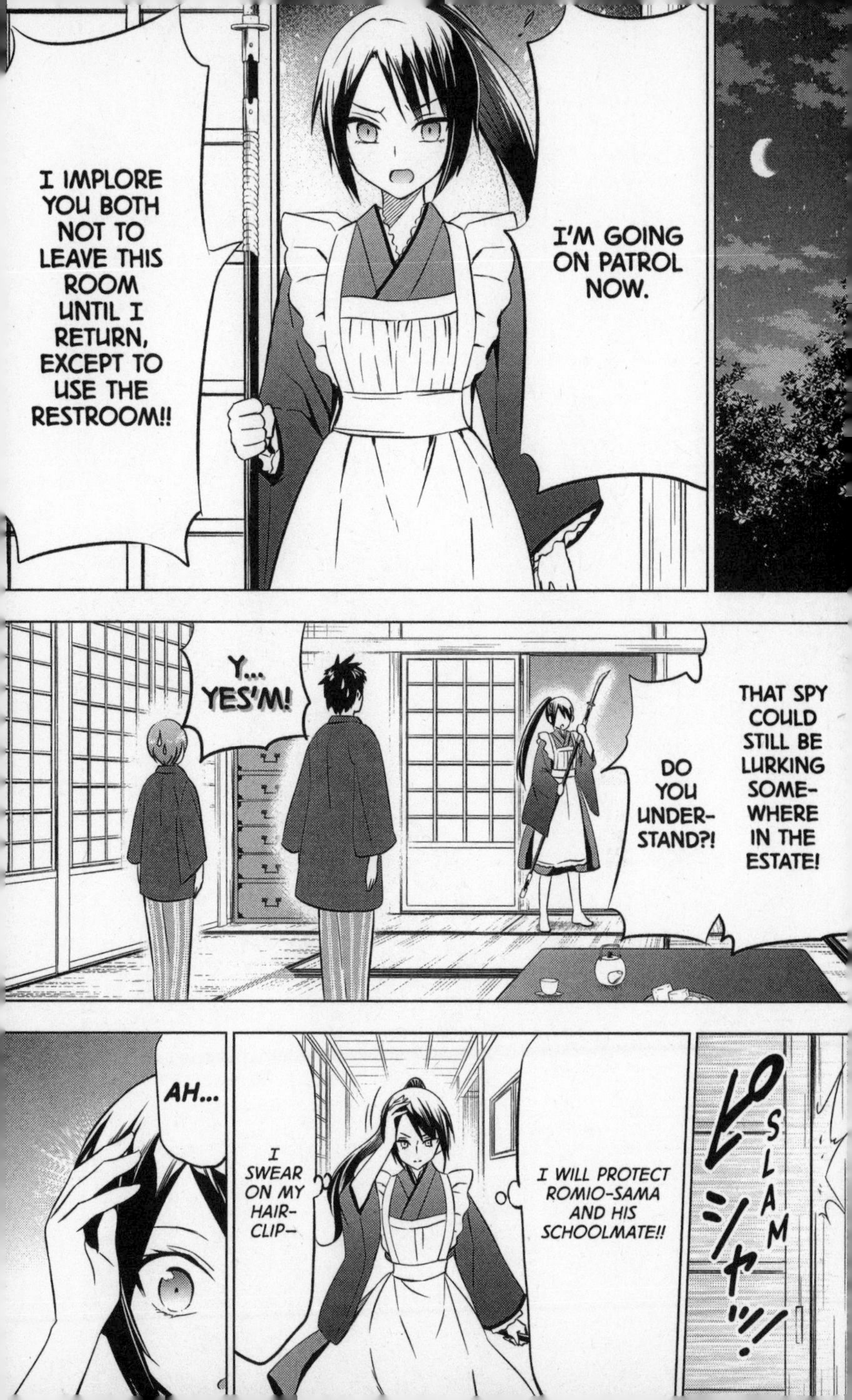
I'M GOING ON PATROL NOW.
I IMPLORE YOU BOTH NOT TO LEAVE THIS ROOM UNTIL I RETURN, EXCEPT TO USE THE RESTROOM!!
THAT SPY COULD STILL BE LURKING SOME-WHERE IN THE ESTATE!
DO YOU UNDER-STAND?!
Y... YES'M!
ピシャッ!!
SLAM
I WILL PROTECT ROMIO-SAMA AND HIS SCHOOLMATE!!
I SWEAR ON MY HAIR-CLIP—
AH...

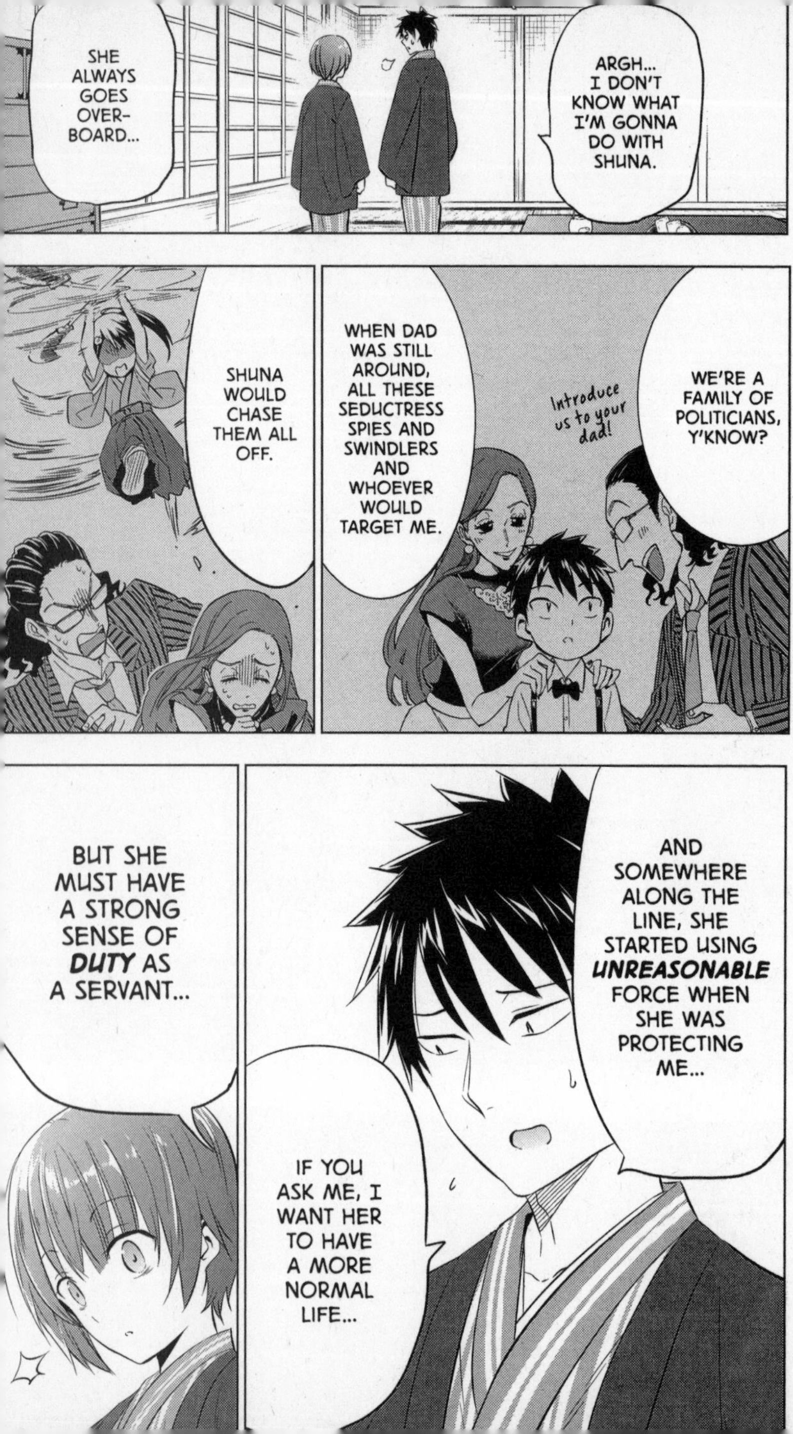
ARGH... I DON'T KNOW WHAT I'M GONNA DO WITH SHUNA.
SHE ALWAYS GOES OVER-BOARD...
WE'RE A FAMILY OF POLITICIANS, Y'KNOW?
Introduce us to your dad!
WHEN DAD WAS STILL AROUND, ALL THESE SEDUCTRESS SPIES AND SWINDLERS AND WHOEVER WOULD TARGET ME.
SHUNA WOULD CHASE THEM ALL OFF.
AND SOMEWHERE ALONG THE LINE, SHE STARTED USING ***UNREASONABLE*** FORCE WHEN SHE WAS PROTECTING ME...
IF YOU ASK ME, I WANT HER TO HAVE A MORE NORMAL LIFE...
BUT SHE MUST HAVE A STRONG SENSE OF ***DUTY*** AS A SERVANT...

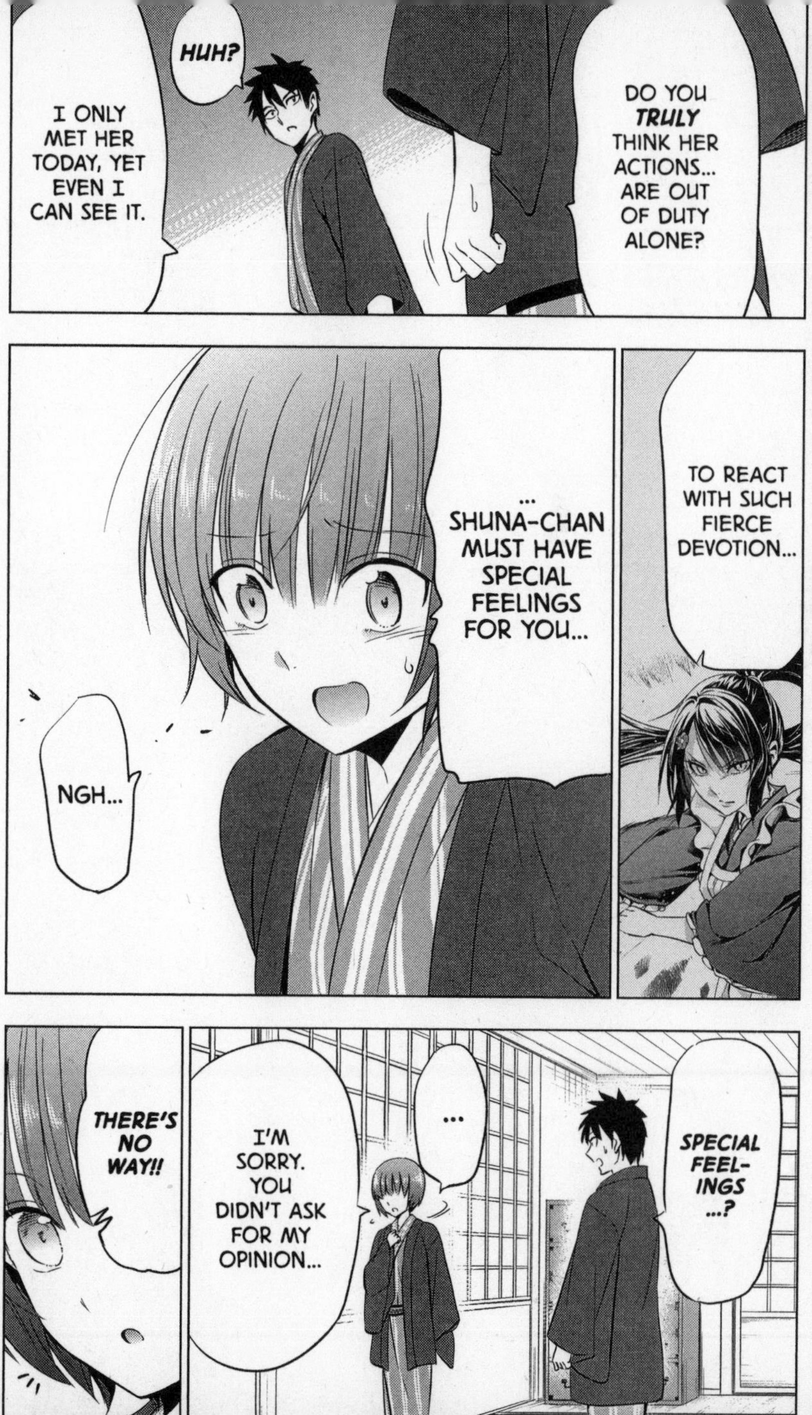
DO YOU TRULY THINK HER ACTIONS... ARE OUT OF DUTY ALONE?
HUH?
I ONLY MET HER TODAY, YET EVEN I CAN SEE IT.
TO REACT WITH SUCH FIERCE DEVOTION...
...SHUNA-CHAN MUST HAVE SPECIAL FEELINGS FOR YOU...
NGH...
SPECIAL FEEL-INGS...?
...
I'M SORRY. YOU DIDN'T ASK FOR MY OPINION...
THERE'S NO WAY!!

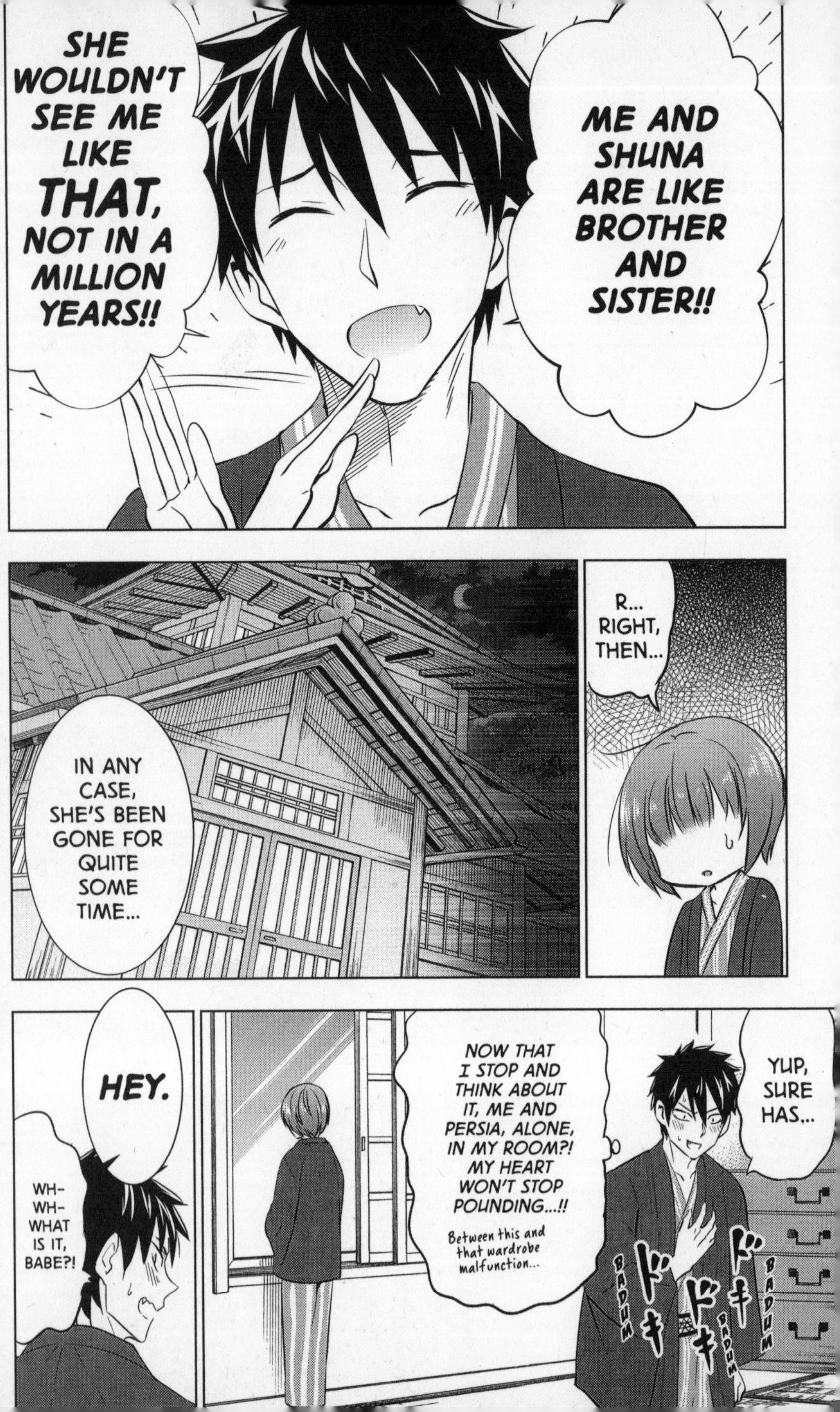
ME AND SHUNA ARE LIKE BROTHER AND SISTER!!
SHE WOULDN'T SEE ME LIKE THAT, NOT IN A MILLION YEARS!!
R... RIGHT, THEN...
IN ANY CASE, SHE'S BEEN GONE FOR QUITE SOME TIME...
YUP, SURE HAS...
ドキ ドキ
BADUM BADUM
ドキ ドキ
BADUM BADUM
NOW THAT I STOP AND THINK ABOUT IT, ME AND PERSIA, ALONE, IN MY ROOM?! MY HEART WON'T STOP POUNDING...!!
Between this and that wardrobe malfunction...
HEY.
WH-WH-WHAT IS IT, BABE?!

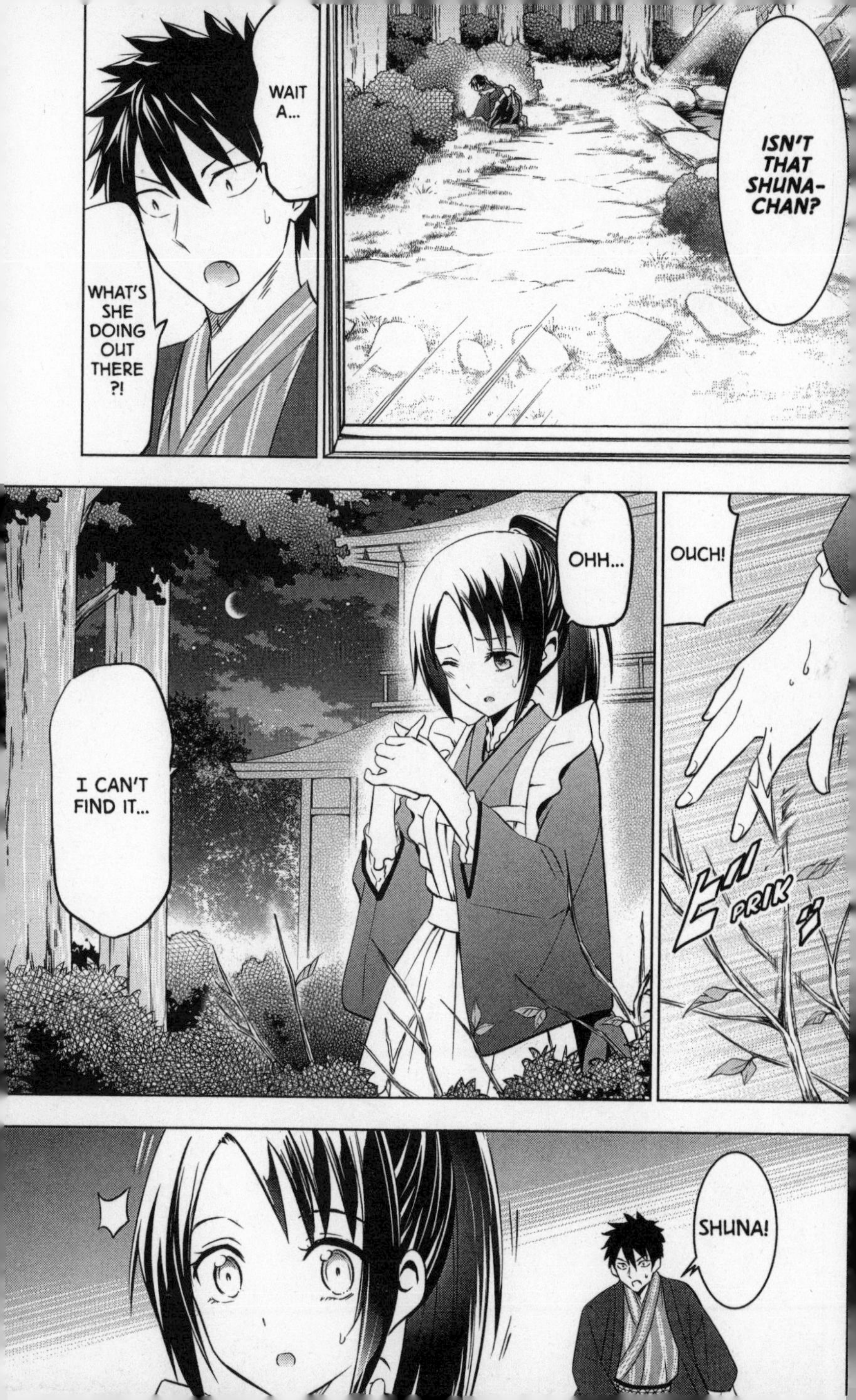
ISN'T THAT SHUNA-CHAN?
WAIT A...
WHAT'S SHE DOING OUT THERE ?!
OUCH!
PRIK
OHH...
I CAN'T FIND IT...
SHUNA!

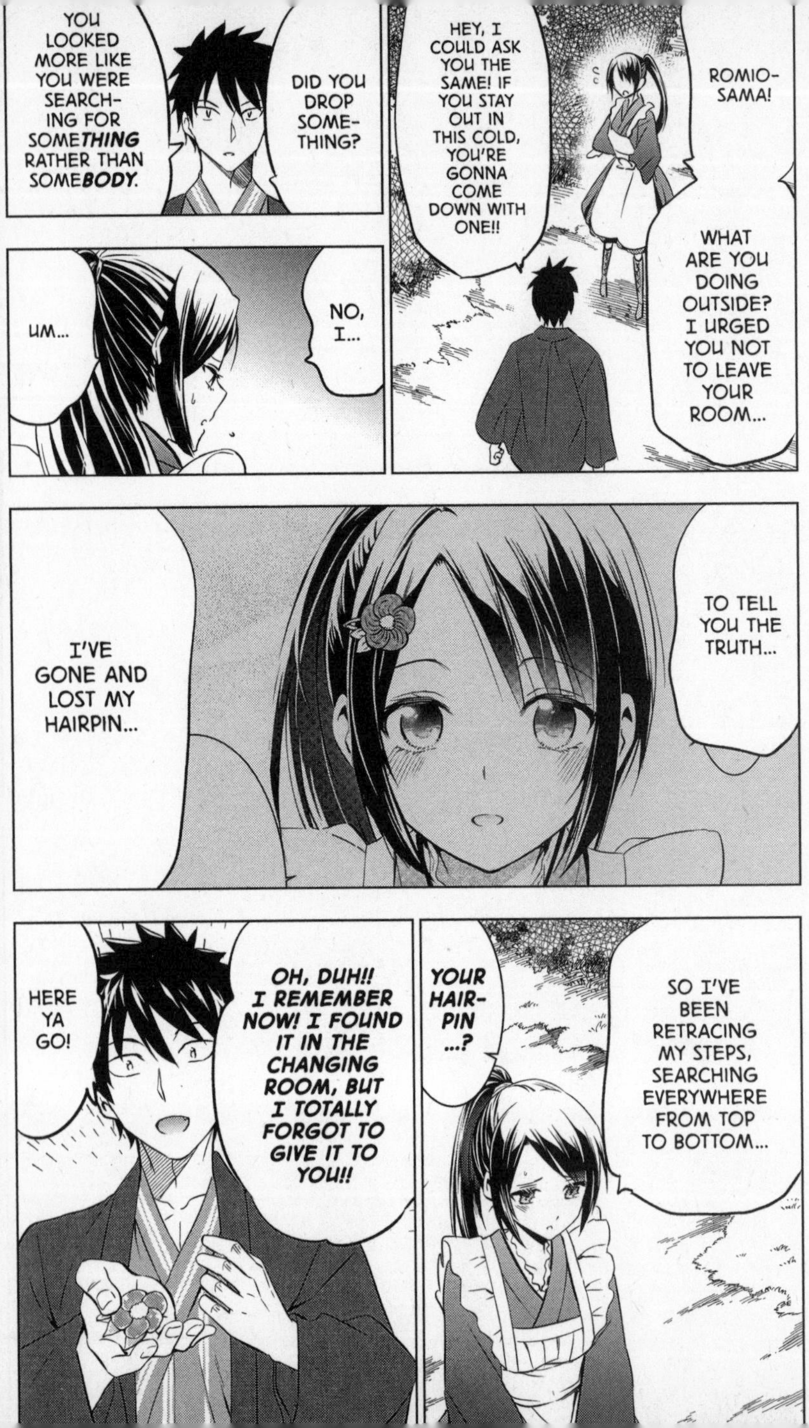
ROMIO-SAMA!
WHAT ARE YOU DOING OUTSIDE? I URGED YOU NOT TO LEAVE YOUR ROOM...
HEY, I COULD ASK YOU THE SAME! IF YOU STAY OUT IN THIS COLD, YOU'RE GONNA COME DOWN WITH ONE!!
DID YOU DROP SOMETHING?
YOU LOOKED MORE LIKE YOU WERE SEARCHING FOR SOME*THING* RATHER THAN SOME*BODY*.
NO, I...
UM...
TO TELL YOU THE TRUTH...
I'VE GONE AND LOST MY HAIRPIN...
SO I'VE BEEN RETRACING MY STEPS, SEARCHING EVERYWHERE FROM TOP TO BOTTOM...
YOUR HAIRPIN...?
OH, DUH!! I REMEMBER NOW! I FOUND IT IN THE CHANGING ROOM, BUT I TOTALLY FORGOT TO GIVE IT TO YOU!!
HERE YA GO!

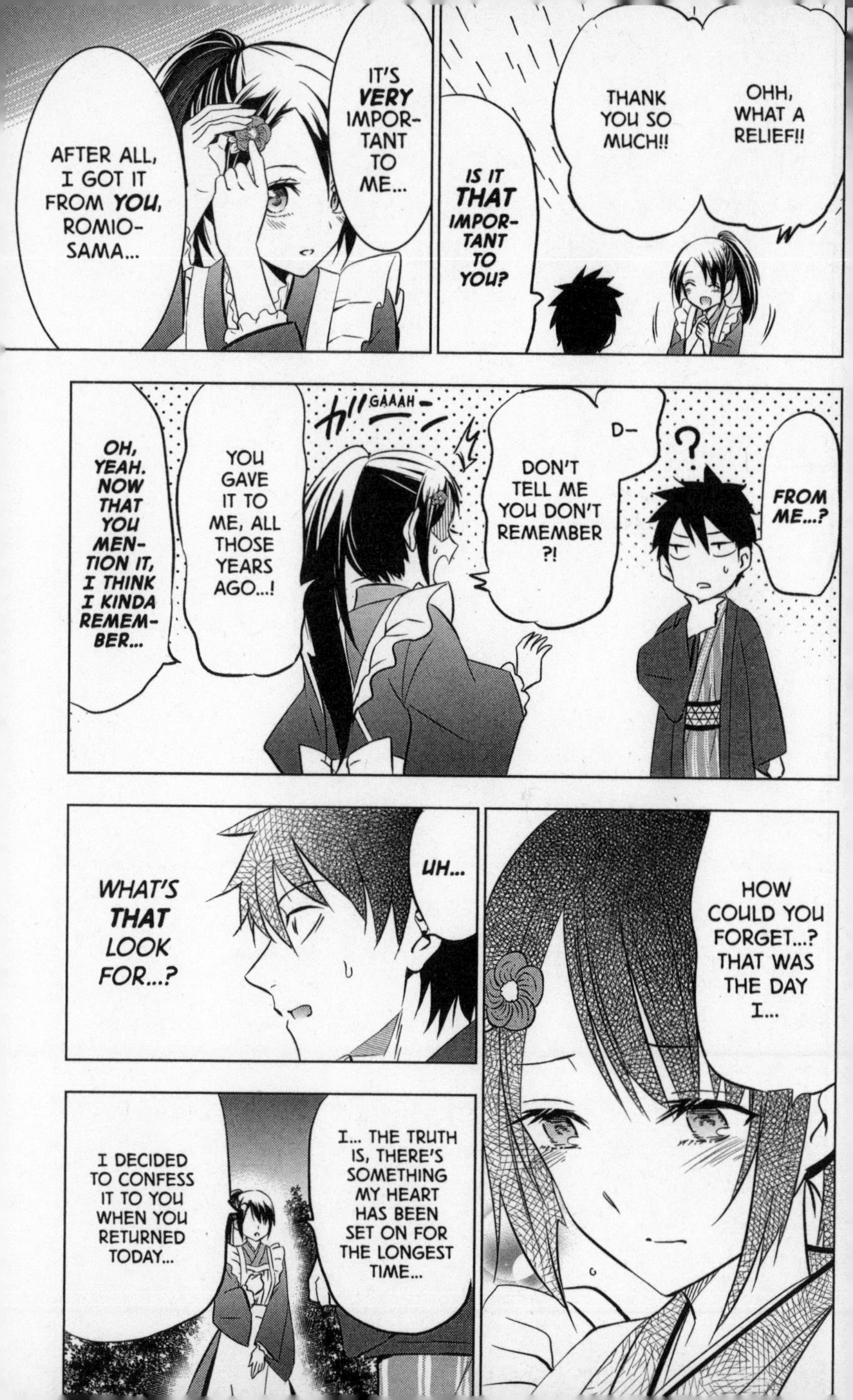
OHH, WHAT A RELIEF!!
THANK YOU SO MUCH!!
IS IT THAT IMPORTANT TO YOU?
IT'S VERY IMPORTANT TO ME...
AFTER ALL, I GOT IT FROM YOU, ROMIO-SAMA...
FROM ME...?
D-
DON'T TELL ME YOU DON'T REMEMBER?!
GAAAH
YOU GAVE IT TO ME, ALL THOSE YEARS AGO...!
OH, YEAH. NOW THAT YOU MENTION IT, I THINK I KINDA REMEMBER...
HOW COULD YOU FORGET...? THAT WAS THE DAY I...
UH...
WHAT'S THAT LOOK FOR...?
I... THE TRUTH IS, THERE'S SOMETHING MY HEART HAS BEEN SET ON FOR THE LONGEST TIME...
I DECIDED TO CONFESS IT TO YOU WHEN YOU RETURNED TODAY...

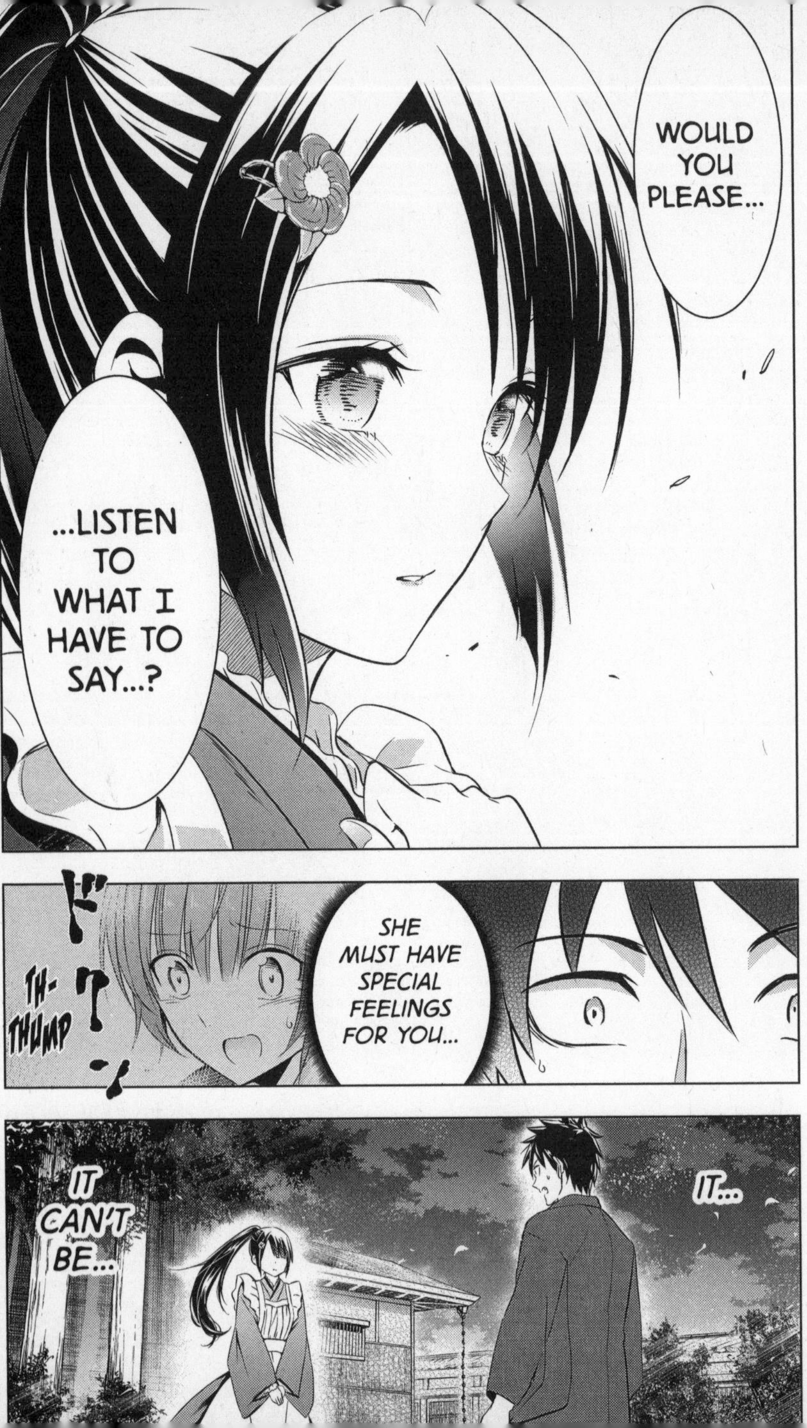
WOULD YOU PLEASE...
...LISTEN TO WHAT I HAVE TO SAY...?
SHE MUST HAVE SPECIAL FEELINGS FOR YOU...
TH-THUMP
IT...
IT CAN'T BE...

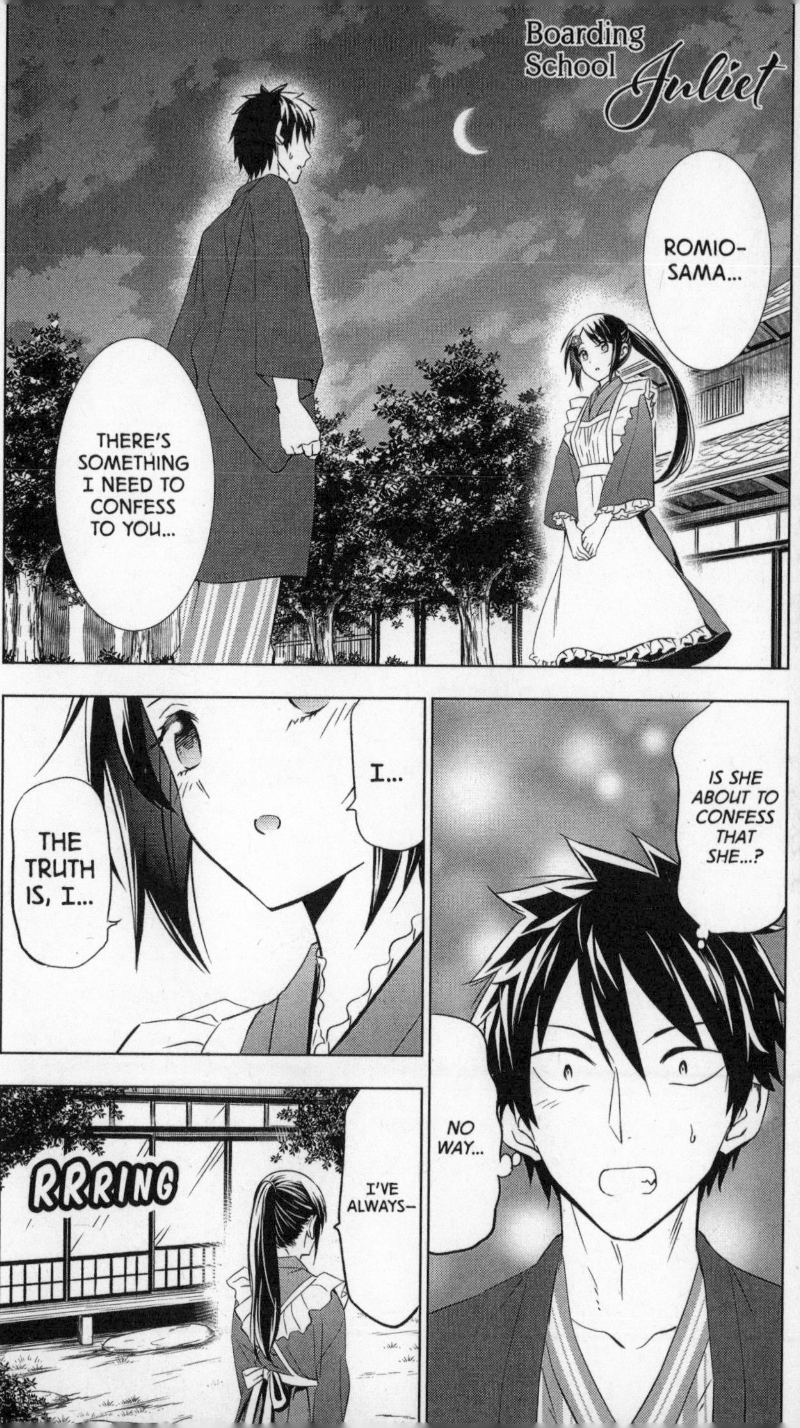
Boarding School Juliet
ROMIO-SAMA...
THERE'S SOMETHING I NEED TO CONFESS TO YOU...
IS SHE ABOUT TO CONFESS THAT SHE...?
NO WAY...
I...
THE TRUTH IS, I...
I'VE ALWAYS—
RRRING

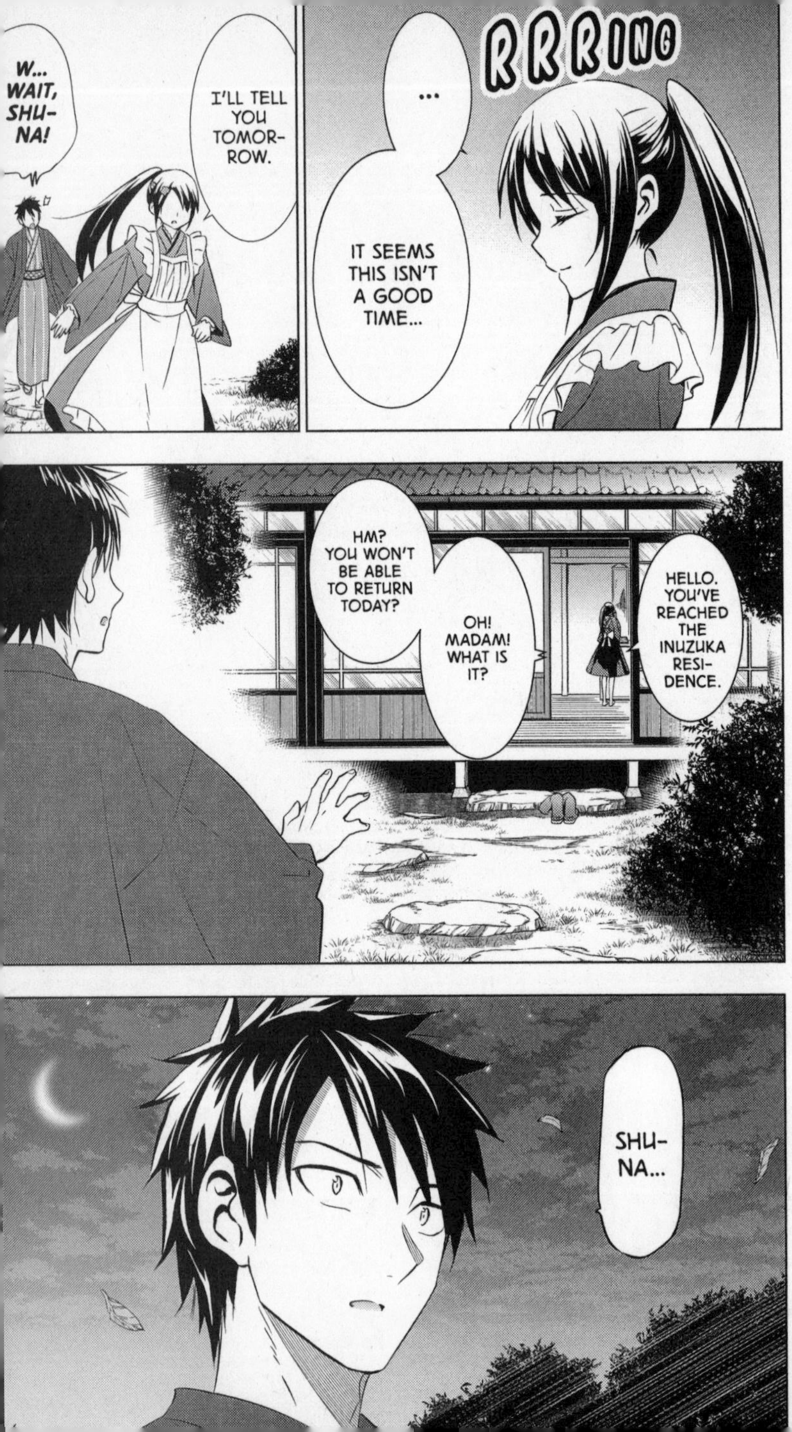
RRRING
...
IT SEEMS THIS ISN'T A GOOD TIME...
I'LL TELL YOU TOMORROW.
W... WAIT, SHUNA!
HELLO. YOU'VE REACHED THE INUZUKA RESIDENCE.
OH! MADAM! WHAT IS IT?
HM? YOU WON'T BE ABLE TO RETURN TODAY?
SHUNA...

ACT 51:

ROMIO & SHUNA II

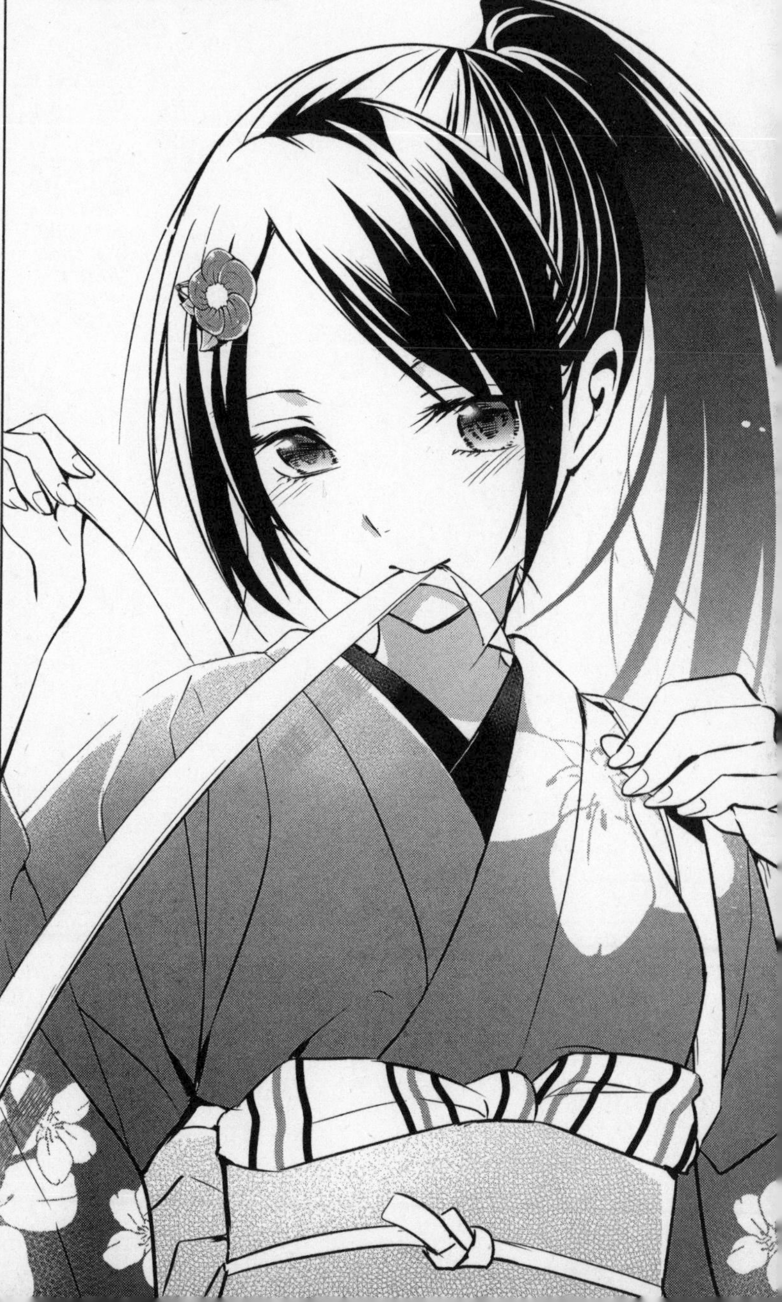

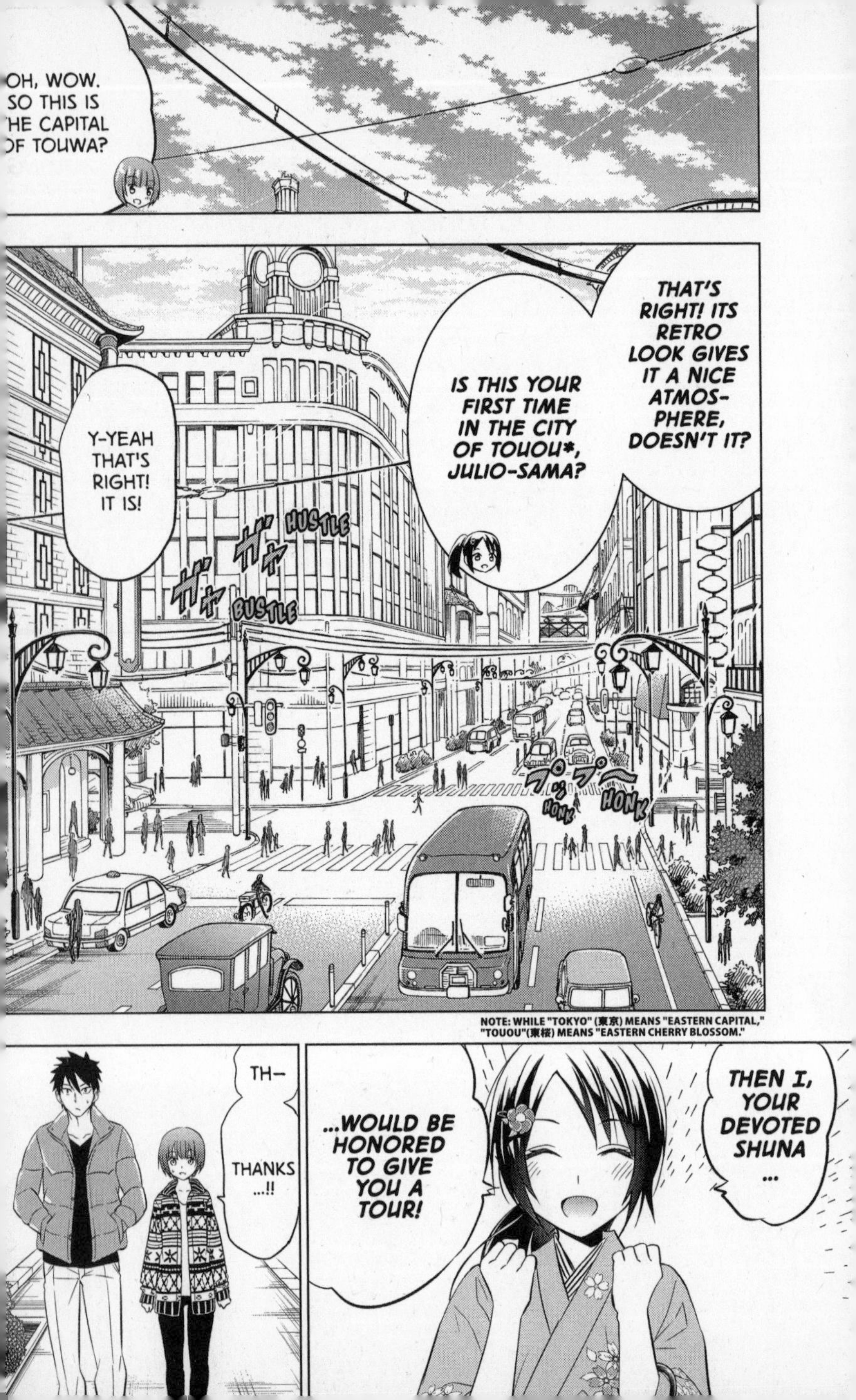
OH, WOW. SO THIS IS THE CAPITAL OF TOUWA?
THAT'S RIGHT! ITS RETRO LOOK GIVES IT A NICE ATMOS-PHERE, DOESN'T IT?
IS THIS YOUR FIRST TIME IN THE CITY OF TOUOU*, JULIO-SAMA?
Y-YEAH THAT'S RIGHT! IT IS!
HUSTLE
BUSTLE
HONK
HONK
THEN I, YOUR DEVOTED SHUNA ...
...WOULD BE HONORED TO GIVE YOU A TOUR!
TH-
THANKS ...!!
NOTE: WHILE "TOKYO" (東京) MEANS "EASTERN CAPITAL," "TOUOU"(東桜) MEANS "EASTERN CHERRY BLOSSOM."

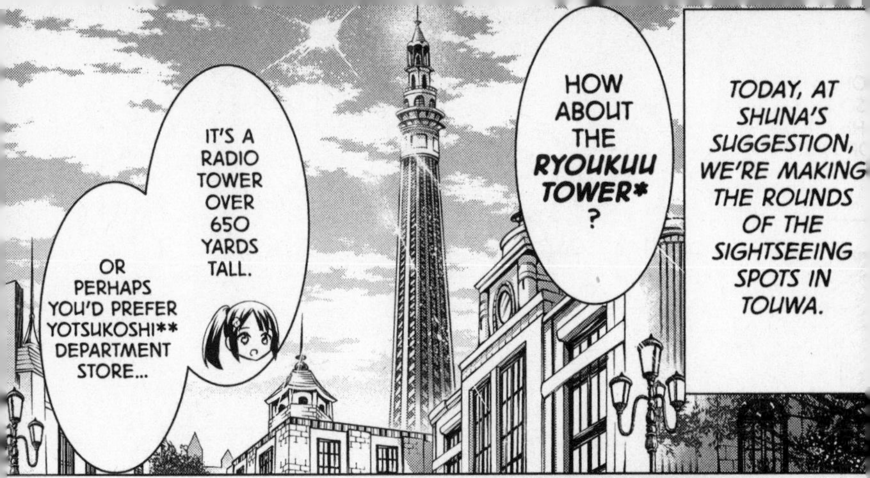
TODAY, AT SHUNA'S SUGGESTION, WE'RE MAKING THE ROUNDS OF THE SIGHTSEEING SPOTS IN TOUWA.
HOW ABOUT THE RYOUKUU TOWER* ?
IT'S A RADIO TOWER OVER 650 YARDS TALL.
OR PERHAPS YOU'D PREFER YOTSUKOSHI** DEPARTMENT STORE...

NOTE: THIS IS LIKELY BASED ON THE TOKYO SKYTREE TOWER, THOUGH T
IS ALSO ANOTHER FAMOUS TOWER IN TOKYO (TOKYO TOWER).

NOTE: A TAKEOFF ON MITSUKOSHI DEPARTMENT STORES.

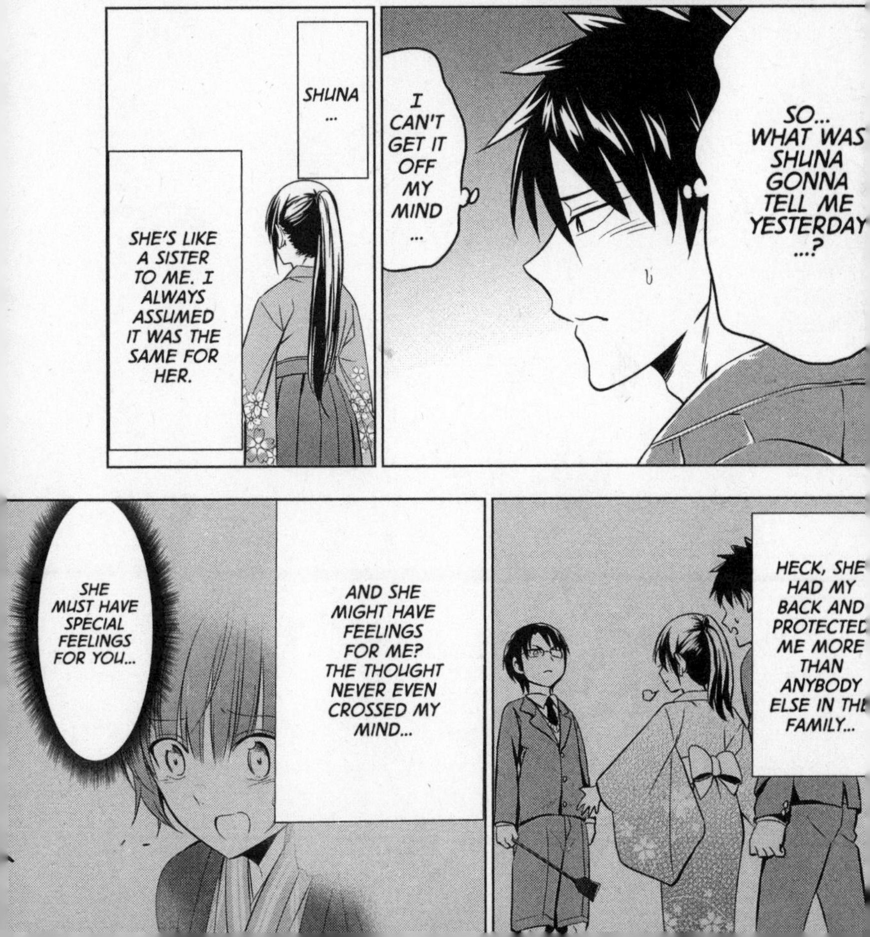
SO... WHAT WAS SHUNA GONNA TELL ME YESTERDAY ...?
I CAN'T GET IT OFF MY MIND ...
SHUNA ...
SHE'S LIKE A SISTER TO ME. I ALWAYS ASSUMED IT WAS THE SAME FOR HER.
HECK, SHE HAD MY BACK AND PROTECTE ME MORE THAN ANYBODY ELSE IN TH FAMILY...
AND SHE MIGHT HAVE FEELINGS FOR ME? THE THOUGHT NEVER EVEN CROSSED MY MIND...
SHE MUST HAVE SPECIAL FEELINGS FOR YOU...

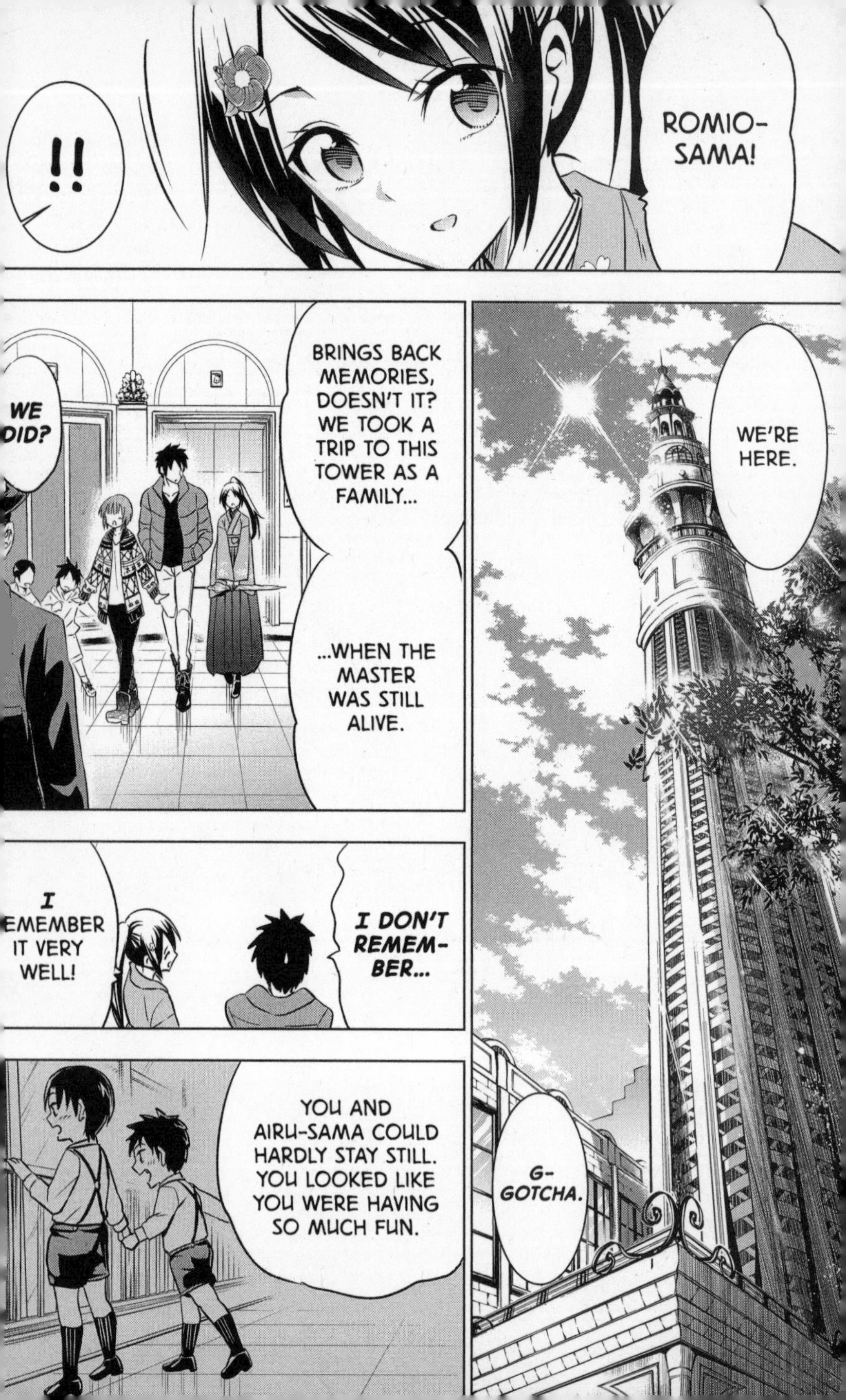
ROMIO-SAMA!
!!
WE'RE HERE.
G-GOTCHA.
BRINGS BACK MEMORIES, DOESN'T IT? WE TOOK A TRIP TO THIS TOWER AS A FAMILY...
...WHEN THE MASTER WAS STILL ALIVE.
WE DID?
I DON'T REMEM-BER...
I EMEMBER IT VERY WELL!
YOU AND AIRU-SAMA COULD HARDLY STAY STILL. YOU LOOKED LIKE YOU WERE HAVING SO MUCH FUN.

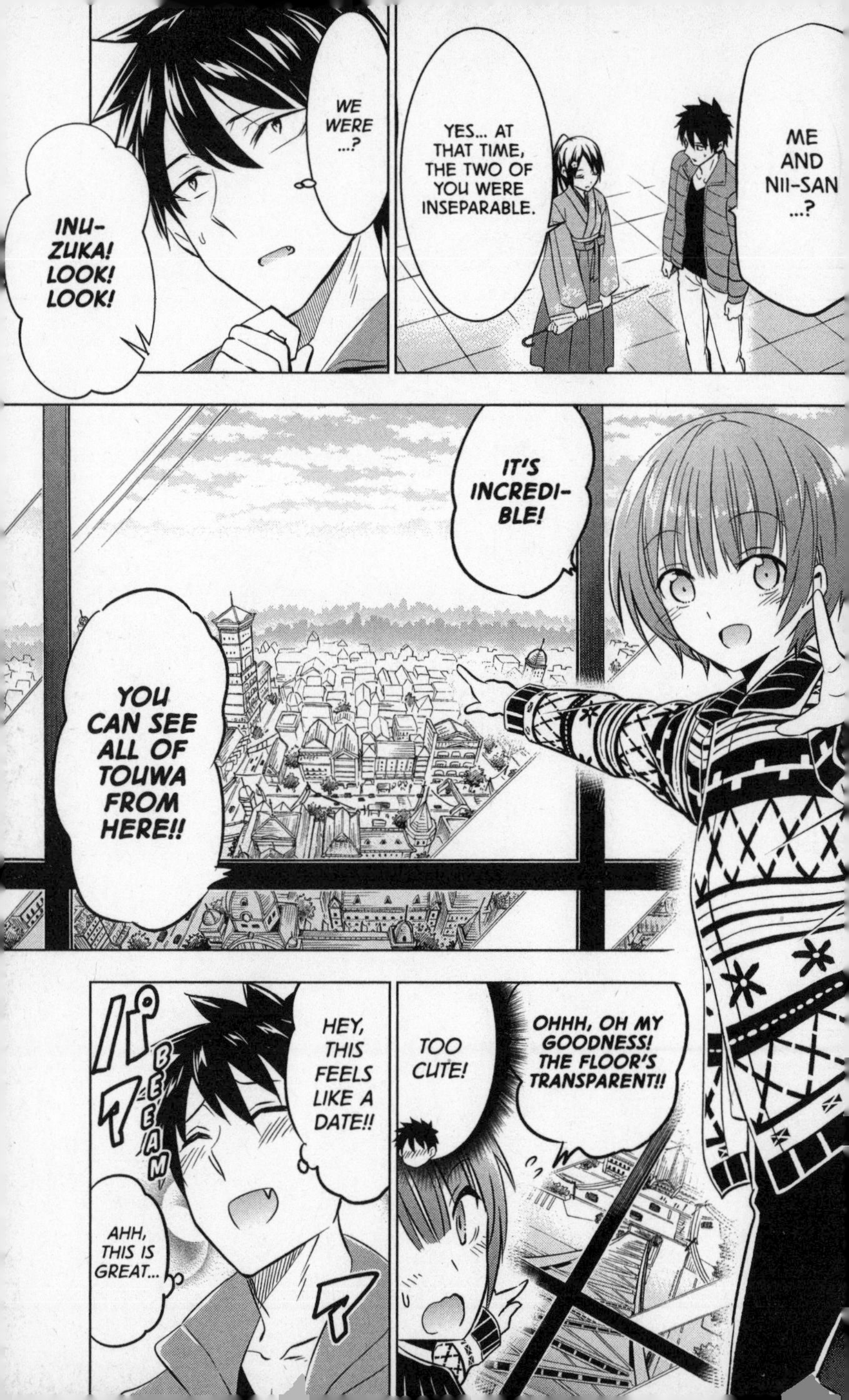
ME AND NII-SAN ...?
YES... AT THAT TIME, THE TWO OF YOU WERE INSEPARABLE.
WE WERE ...?
INU-ZUKA! LOOK! LOOK!
IT'S INCREDI-BLE!
YOU CAN SEE ALL OF TOUWA FROM HERE!!
OHHH, OH MY GOODNESS! THE FLOOR'S TRANSPARENT!!
TOO CUTE!
HEY, THIS FEELS LIKE A DATE!!
BEEEAM
AHH, THIS IS GREAT...

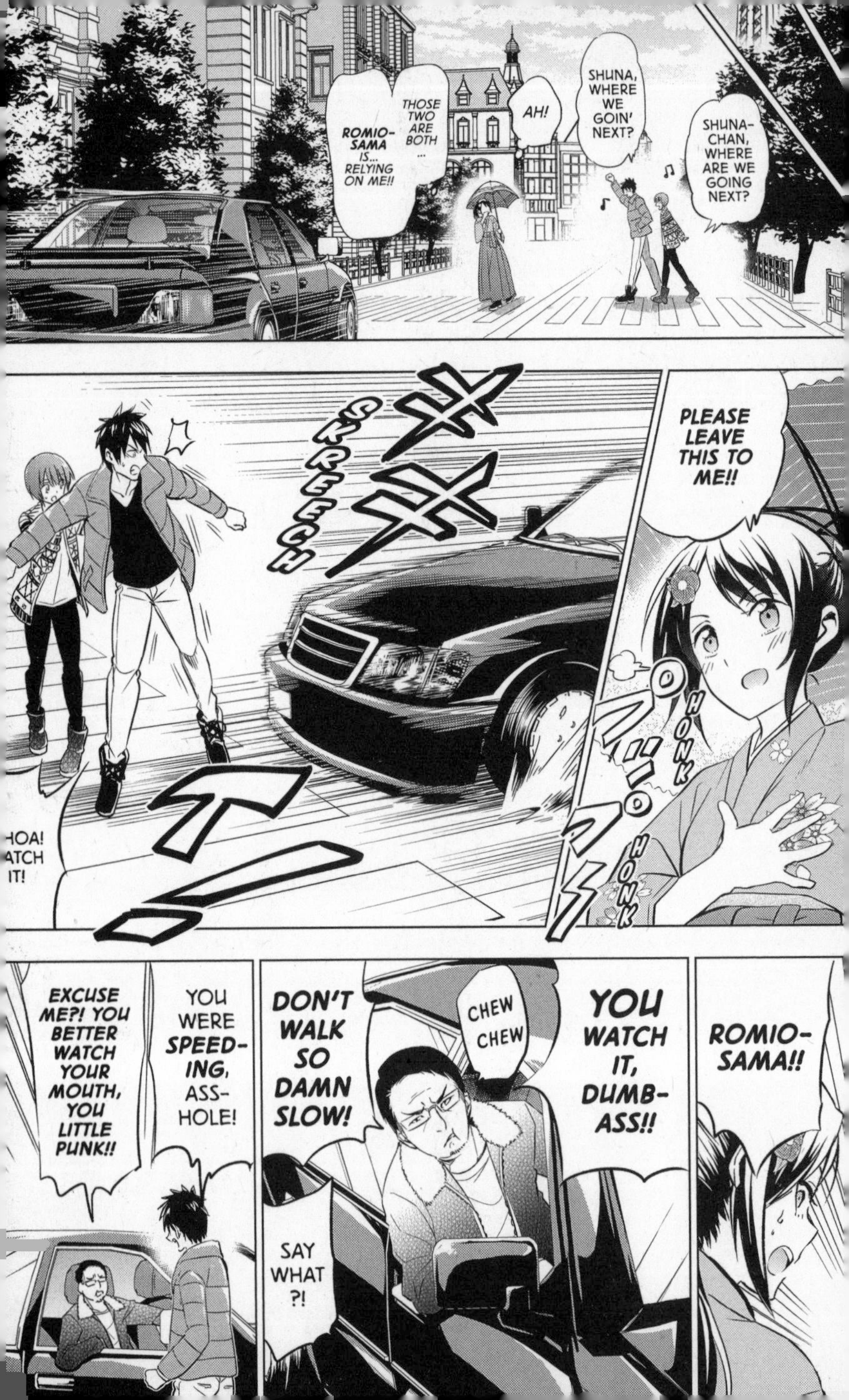
SHUNA-CHAN, WHERE ARE WE GOING NEXT?
SHUNA, WHERE WE GOIN' NEXT?
AH!
THOSE TWO ARE BOTH ...
ROMIO-SAMA IS... RELYING ON ME!!
PLEASE LEAVE THIS TO ME!!
HONK
HONK
SKREECH
HOA! ATCH IT!
ROMIO-SAMA!!
YOU WATCH IT, DUMB-ASS!!
CHEW CHEW
DON'T WALK SO DAMN SLOW!
SAY WHAT ?!
YOU WERE SPEED-ING, ASS-HOLE!
EXCUSE ME?! YOU BETTER WATCH YOUR MOUTH, YOU LITTLE PUNK!!

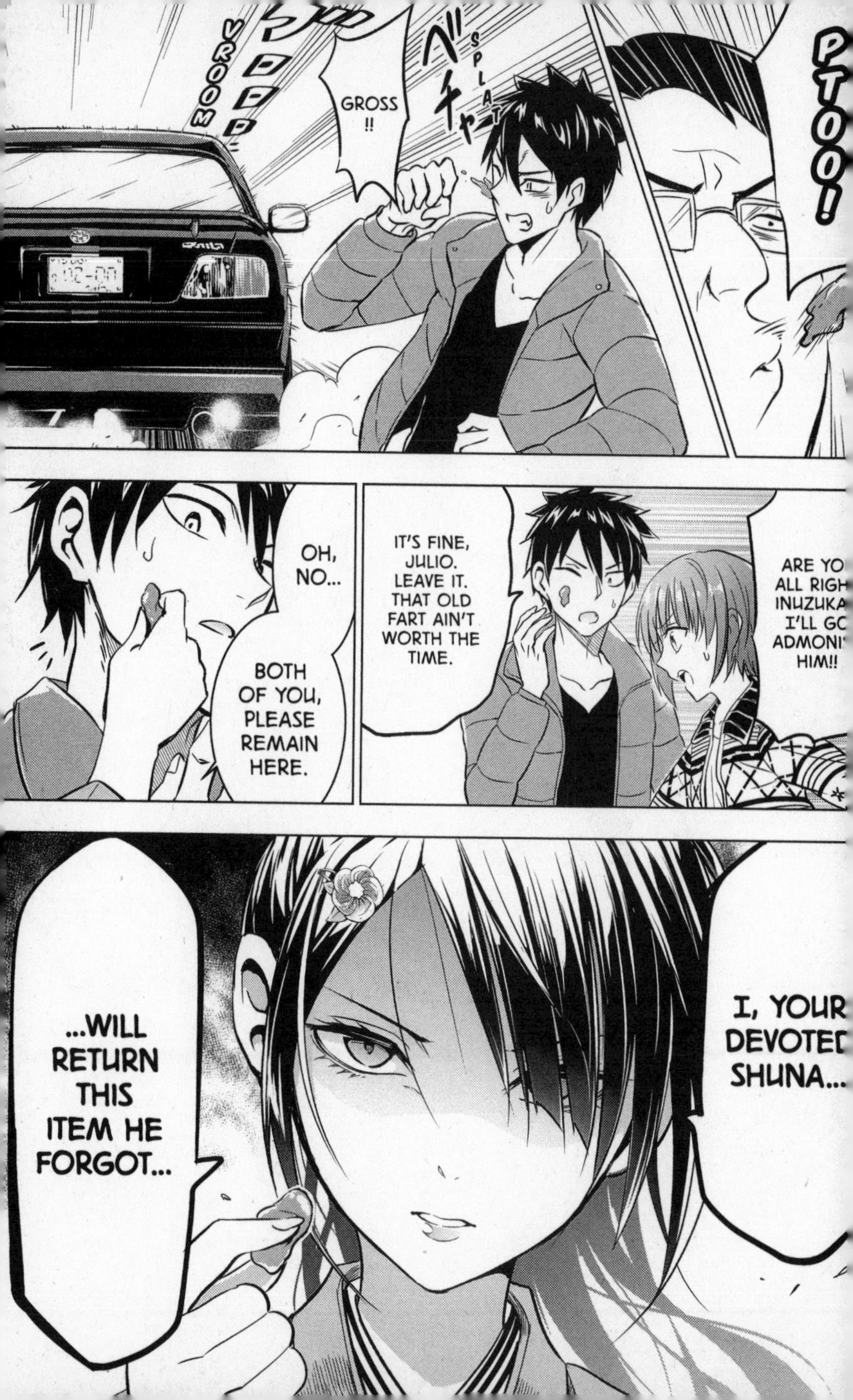
PTOOO!
べチャ
SPLAT
GROSS!!
VROOM
ARE YO ALL RIGH INUZUKA I'LL GO ADMONI HIM!!
IT'S FINE, JULIO. LEAVE IT. THAT OLD FART AIN'T WORTH THE TIME.
OH, NO...
BOTH OF YOU, PLEASE REMAIN HERE.
I, YOUR DEVOTED SHUNA...
...WILL RETURN THIS ITEM HE FORGOT...

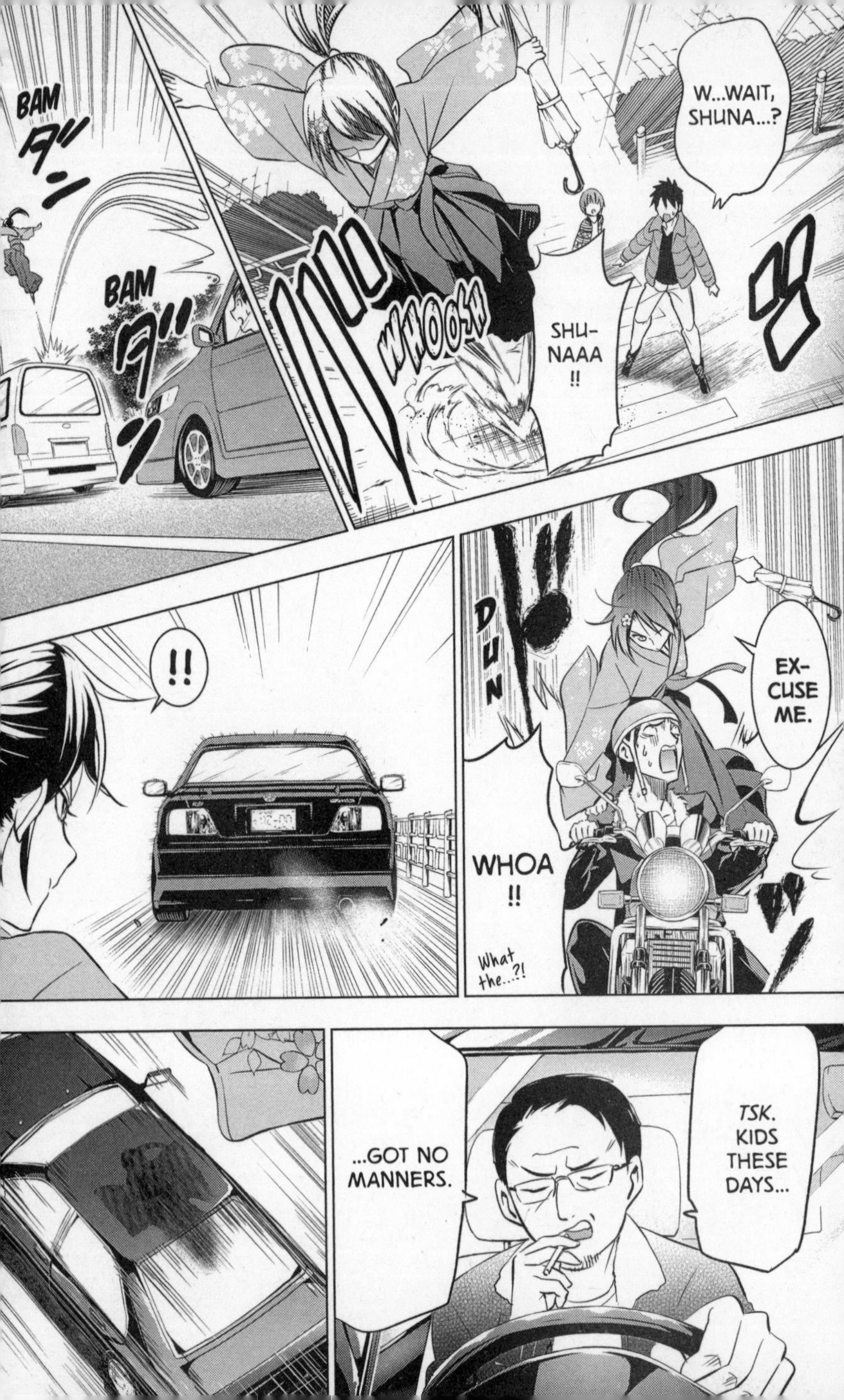
W...WAIT, SHUNA...?
SHU-NAAA !!
WHOOSH
BAM
ダン
BAM
ダッ
DUN
EX-CUSE ME.
WHOA !!
What the...?!
!!
TSK. KIDS THESE DAYS...
...GOT NO MANNERS.

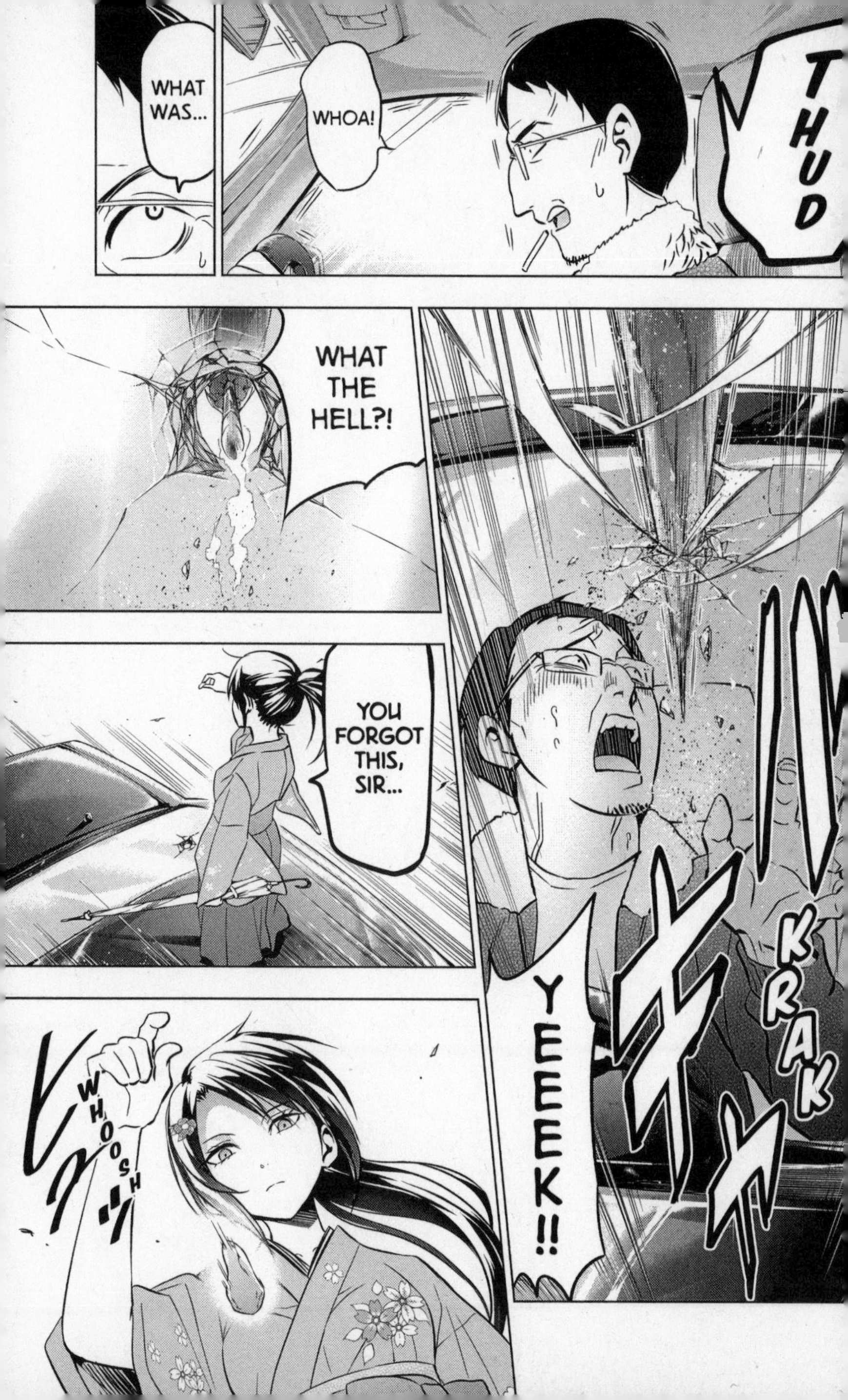
THUD
WHOA!
WHAT WAS...
KRAK
YEEEK!!
WHAT THE HELL?!
YOU FORGOT THIS, SIR...
WHOOSH

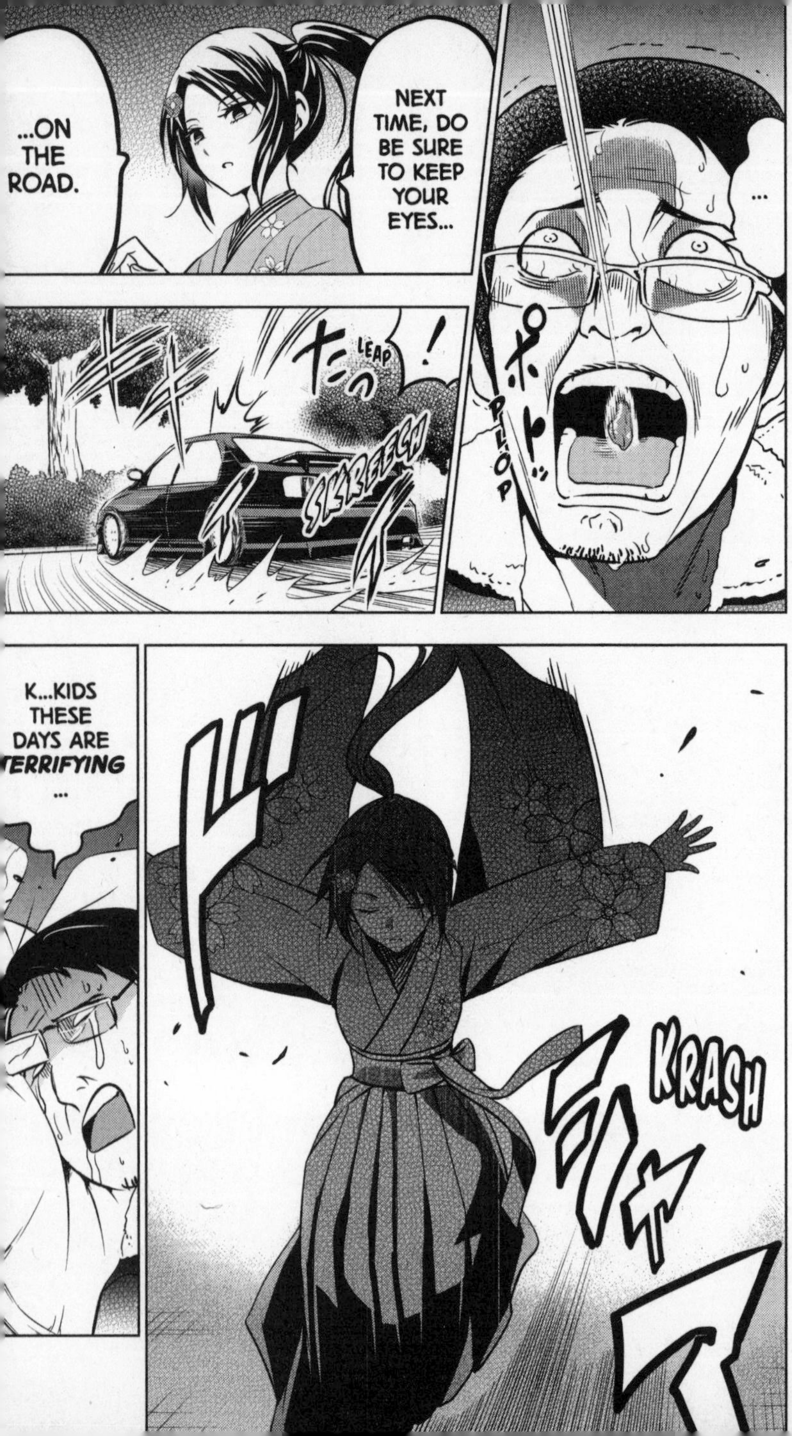
...
PLOP
NEXT TIME, DO BE SURE TO KEEP YOUR EYES...
...ON THE ROAD.
!
LEAP
SKREEECH
KRASH
K...KIDS THESE DAYS ARE TERRIFYING ...

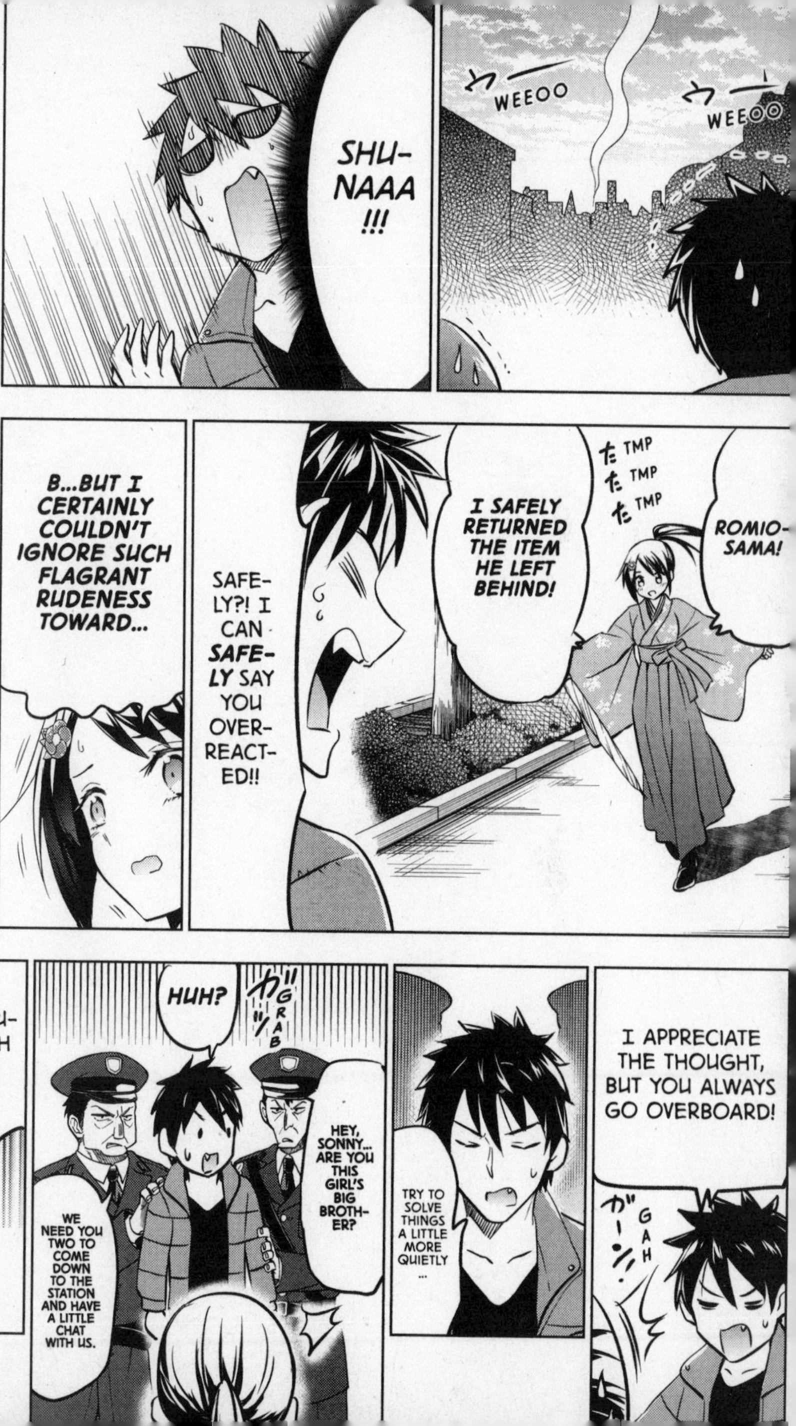
ウー WEEOO
ウー WEEOO
SHU-NAAA!!!
ROMIO-SAMA!
た TMP
た TMP
た TMP
I SAFELY RETURNED THE ITEM HE LEFT BEHIND!
SAFE-LY?! I CAN SAFE-LY SAY YOU OVER-REACT-ED!!
B...BUT I CERTAINLY COULDN'T IGNORE SUCH FLAGRANT RUDENESS TOWARD...
I APPRECIATE THE THOUGHT, BUT YOU ALWAYS GO OVERBOARD!
ガーン GAH
TRY TO SOLVE THINGS A LITTLE MORE QUIETLY...
HUH?
ガッ GRAB
HEY, SONNY... ARE YOU THIS GIRL'S BIG BROTHER?
WE NEED YOU TWO TO COME DOWN TO THE STATION AND HAVE A LITTLE CHAT WITH US.
WHU-UUH?!

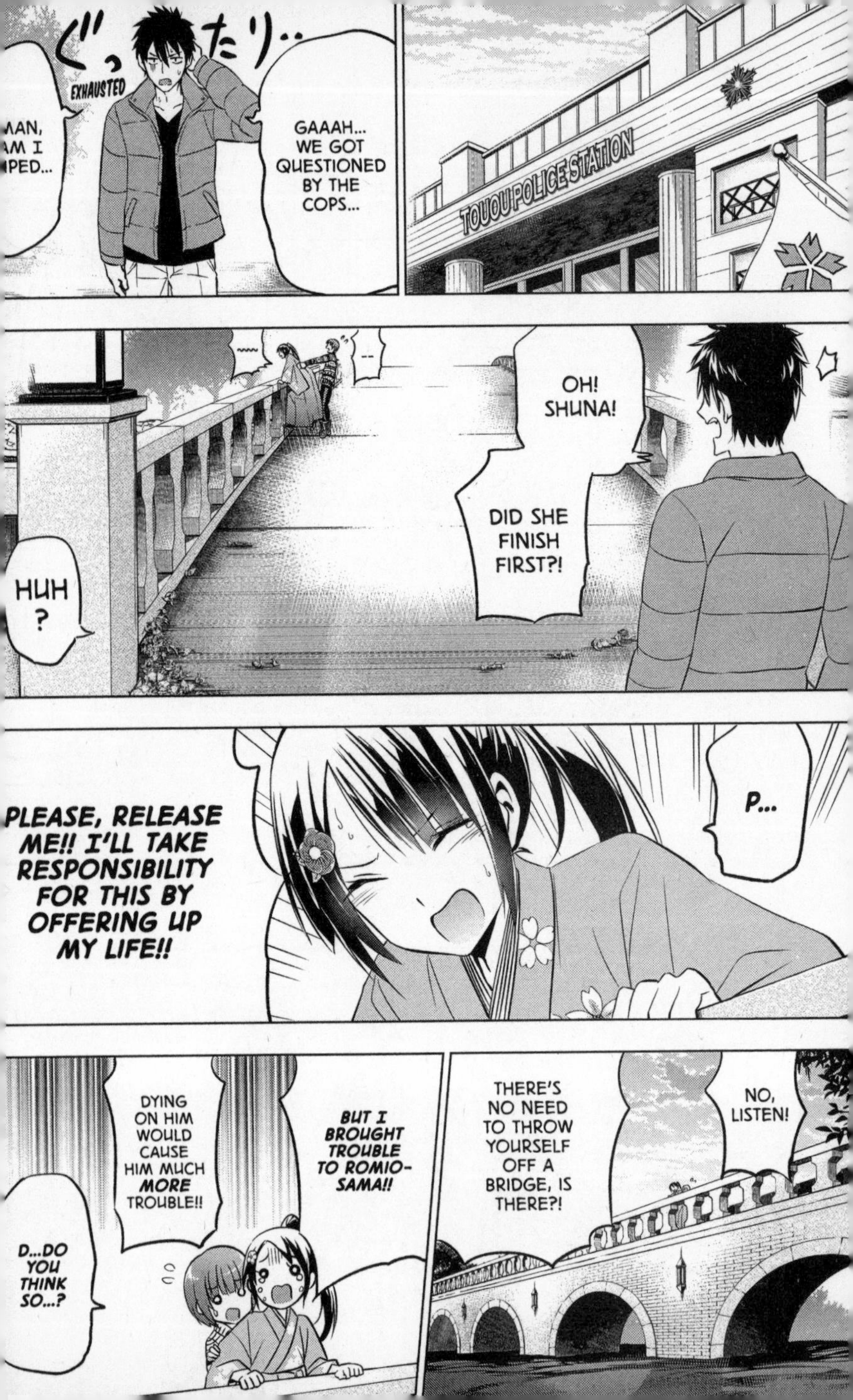
TOUOU POLICE STATION
ぐったり..
EXHAUSTED
GAAAH... WE GOT QUESTIONED BY THE COPS...
MAN, AM I
OH! SHUNA!
DID SHE FINISH FIRST?!
HUH?
P...
PLEASE, RELEASE ME!! I'LL TAKE RESPONSIBILITY FOR THIS BY OFFERING UP MY LIFE!!
NO, LISTEN!
THERE'S NO NEED TO THROW YOURSELF OFF A BRIDGE, IS THERE?!
BUT I BROUGHT TROUBLE TO ROMIO-SAMA!!
DYING ON HIM WOULD CAUSE HIM MUCH MORE TROUBLE!!
D...DO YOU THINK SO...?

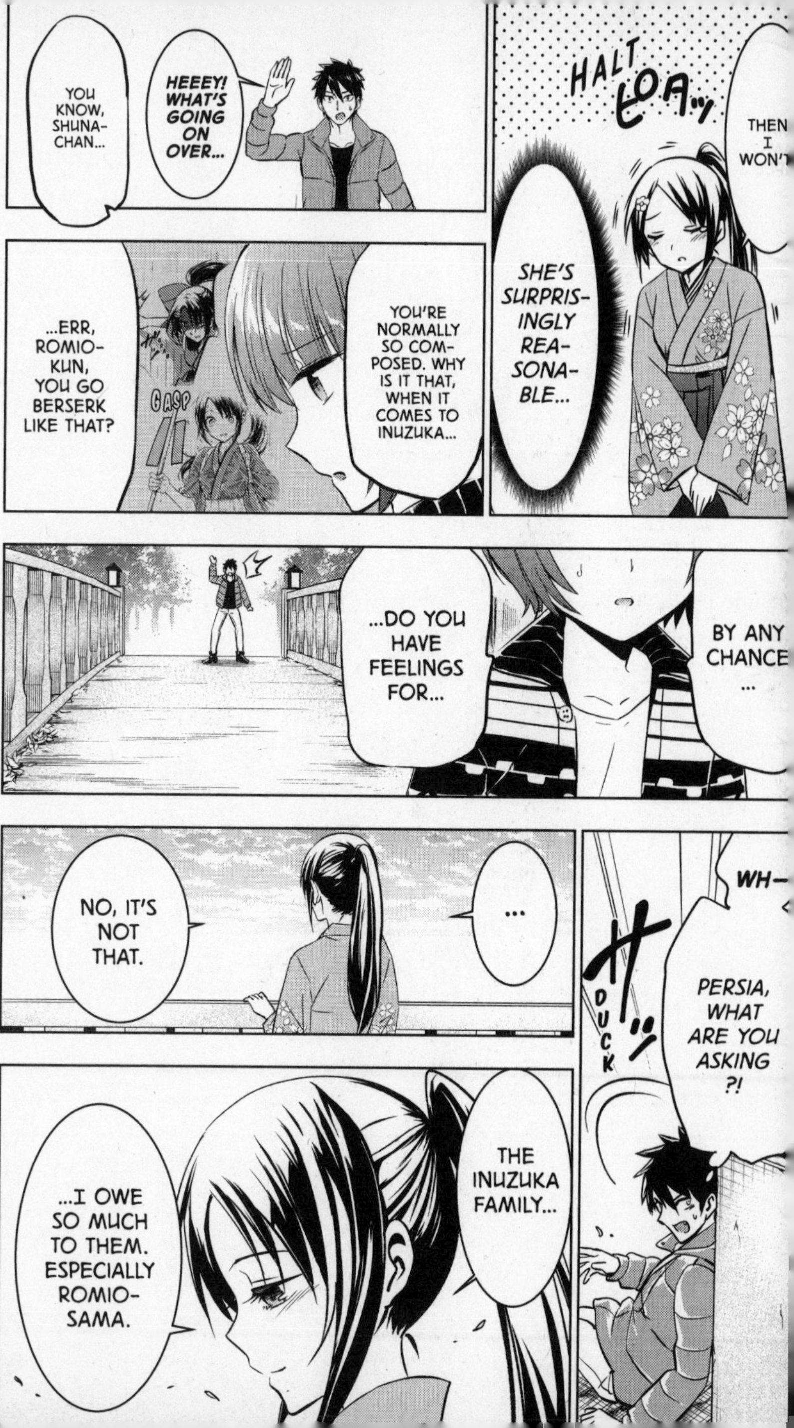
THEN I WON'T
HALT
SHE'S SURPRISINGLY REASONABLE...
HEEEY! WHAT'S GOING ON OVER...
YOU KNOW, SHUNA-CHAN...
YOU'RE NORMALLY SO COMPOSED. WHY IS IT THAT, WHEN IT COMES TO INUZUKA...
...ERR, ROMIO-KUN, YOU GO BERSERK LIKE THAT?
GASP
BY ANY CHANCE...
...DO YOU HAVE FEELINGS FOR...
WH-
DUCK
PERSIA, WHAT ARE YOU ASKING?!
...
NO, IT'S NOT THAT.
THE INUZUKA FAMILY...
...I OWE SO MUCH TO THEM. ESPECIALLY ROMIO-SAMA.

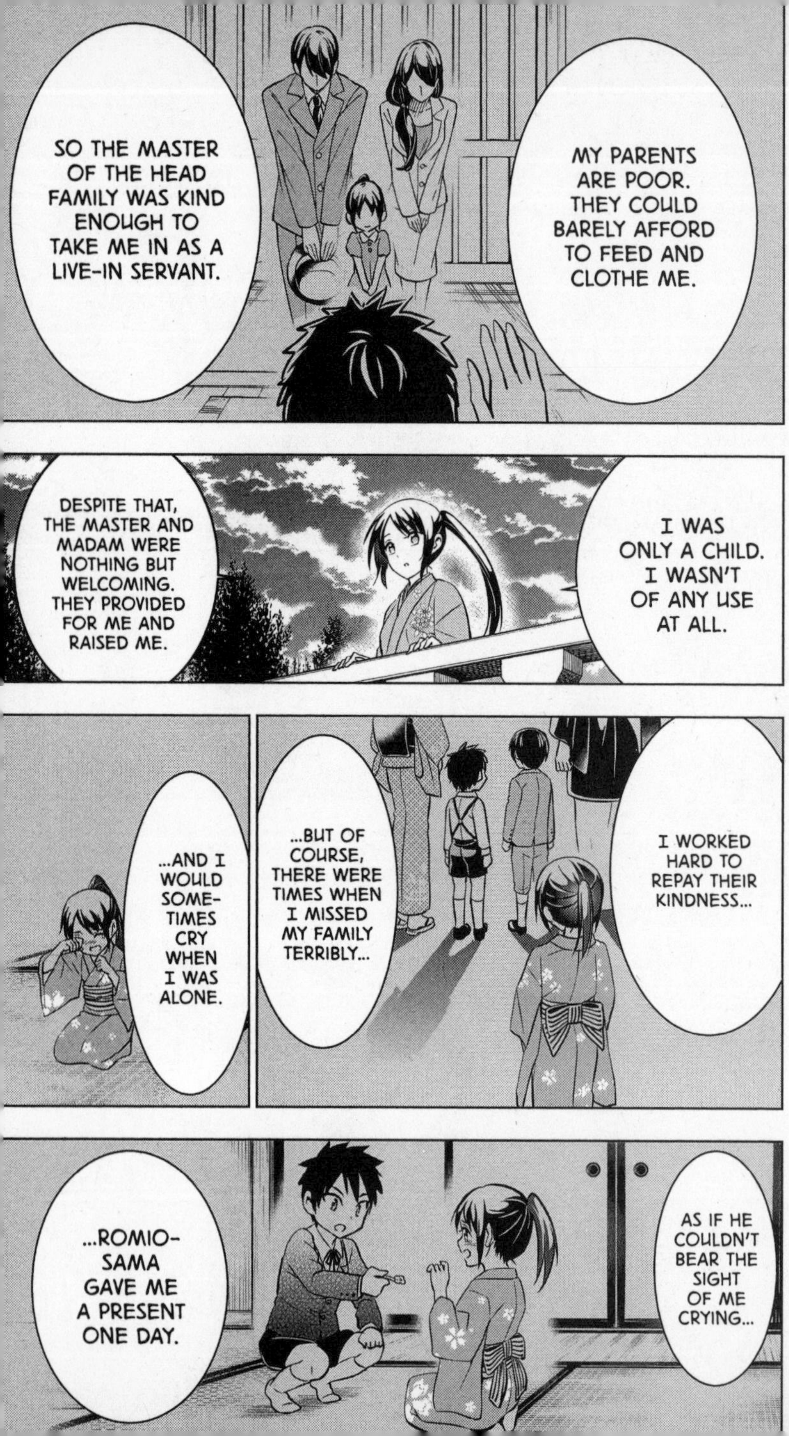
MY PARENTS ARE POOR. THEY COULD BARELY AFFORD TO FEED AND CLOTHE ME.
SO THE MASTER OF THE HEAD FAMILY WAS KIND ENOUGH TO TAKE ME IN AS A LIVE-IN SERVANT.
I WAS ONLY A CHILD. I WASN'T OF ANY USE AT ALL.
DESPITE THAT, THE MASTER AND MADAM WERE NOTHING BUT WELCOMING. THEY PROVIDED FOR ME AND RAISED ME.
I WORKED HARD TO REPAY THEIR KINDNESS...
...BUT OF COURSE, THERE WERE TIMES WHEN I MISSED MY FAMILY TERRIBLY...
...AND I WOULD SOME-TIMES CRY WHEN I WAS ALONE.
AS IF HE COULDN'T BEAR THE SIGHT OF ME CRYING...
...ROMIO-SAMA GAVE ME A PRESENT ONE DAY.

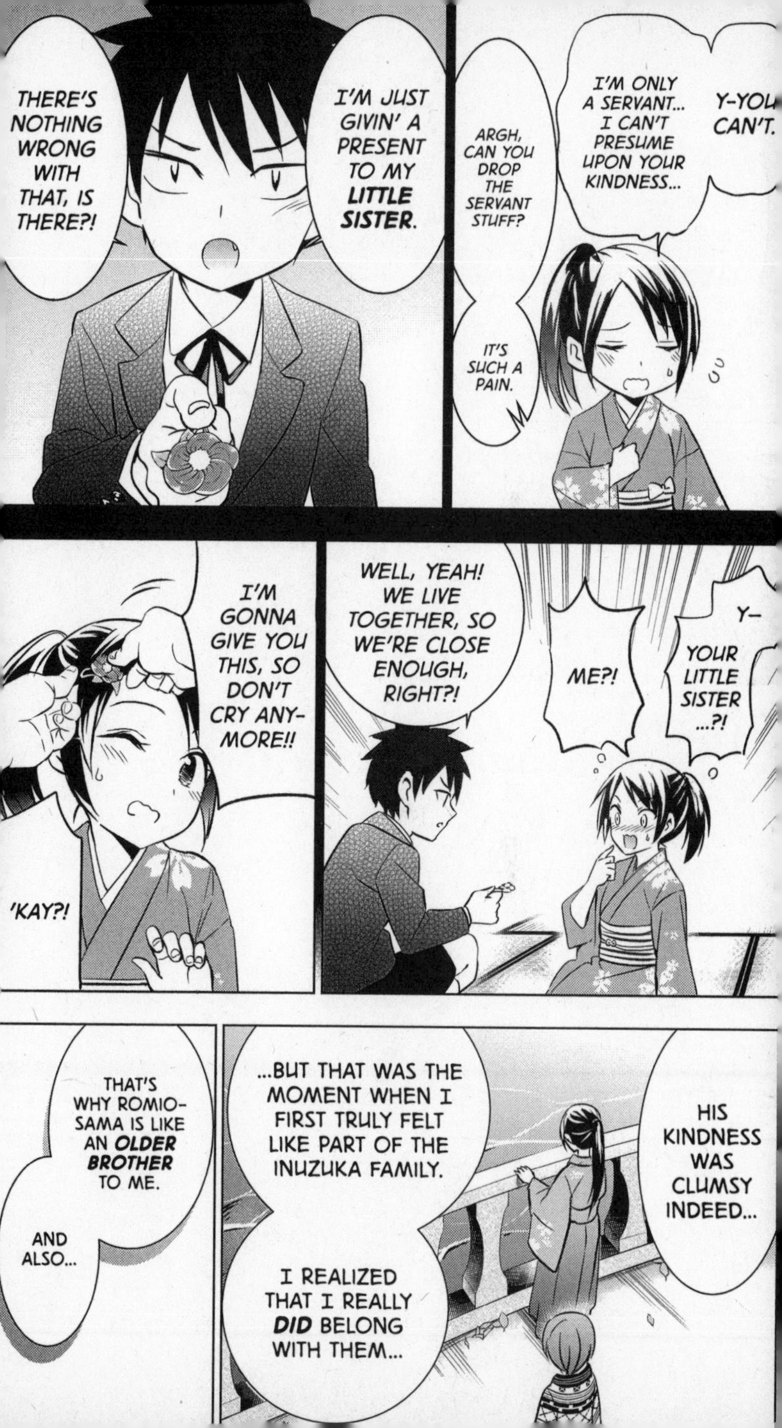
Y-YOU CAN'T.
I'M ONLY A SERVANT... I CAN'T PRESUME UPON YOUR KINDNESS...
ARGH, CAN YOU DROP THE SERVANT STUFF?
IT'S SUCH A PAIN.
I'M JUST GIVIN' A PRESENT TO MY LITTLE SISTER.
THERE'S NOTHING WRONG WITH THAT, IS THERE?!
Y—
YOUR LITTLE SISTER ...?!
ME?!
WELL, YEAH! WE LIVE TOGETHER, SO WE'RE CLOSE ENOUGH, RIGHT?!
I'M GONNA GIVE YOU THIS, SO DON'T CRY ANY-MORE!!
'KAY?!
HIS KINDNESS WAS CLUMSY INDEED...
...BUT THAT WAS THE MOMENT WHEN I FIRST TRULY FELT LIKE PART OF THE INUZUKA FAMILY.
I REALIZED THAT I REALLY DID BELONG WITH THEM...
THAT'S WHY ROMIO-SAMA IS LIKE AN OLDER BROTHER TO ME.
AND ALSO...

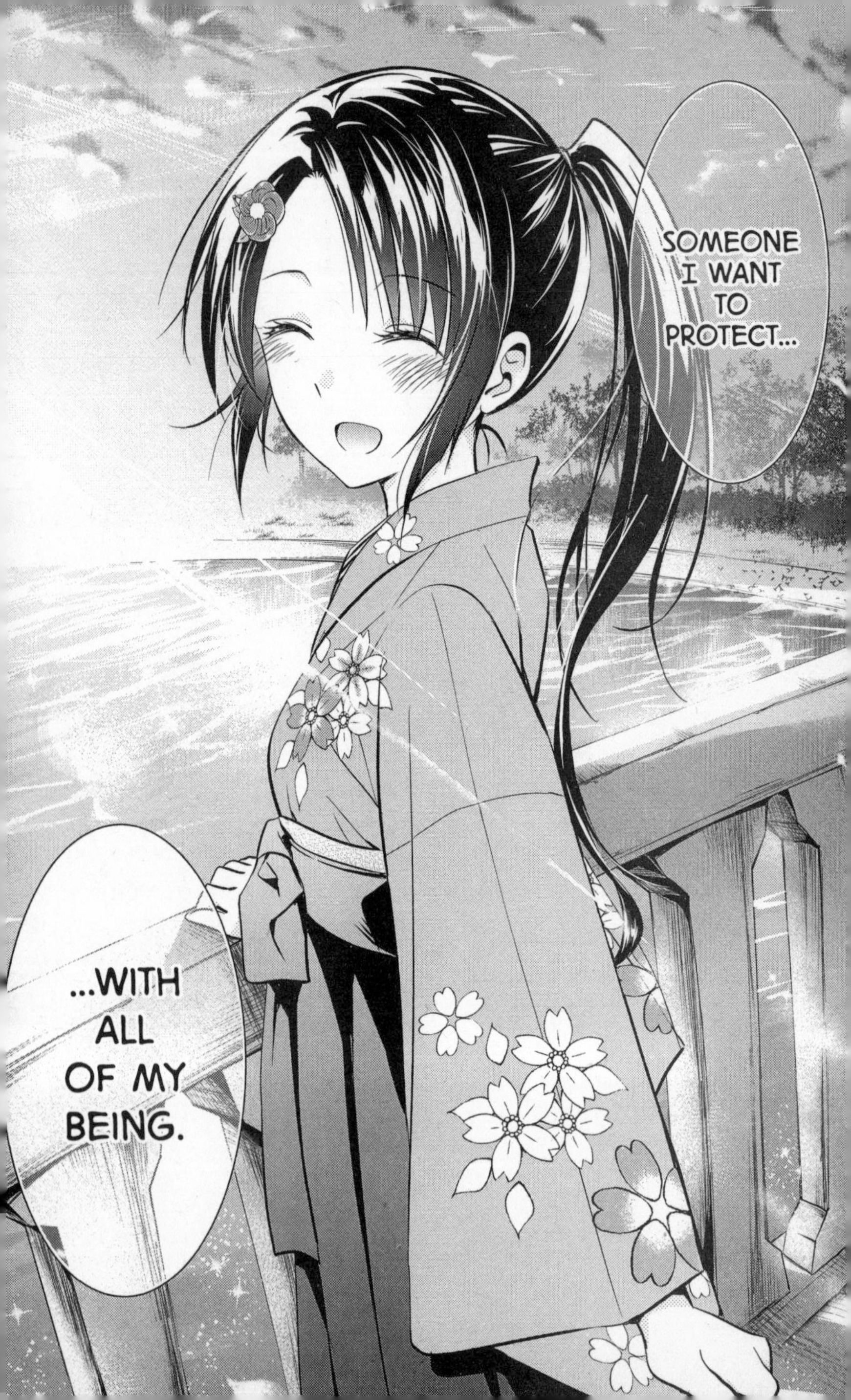
SOMEONE I WANT TO PROTECT...
...WITH ALL OF MY BEING.

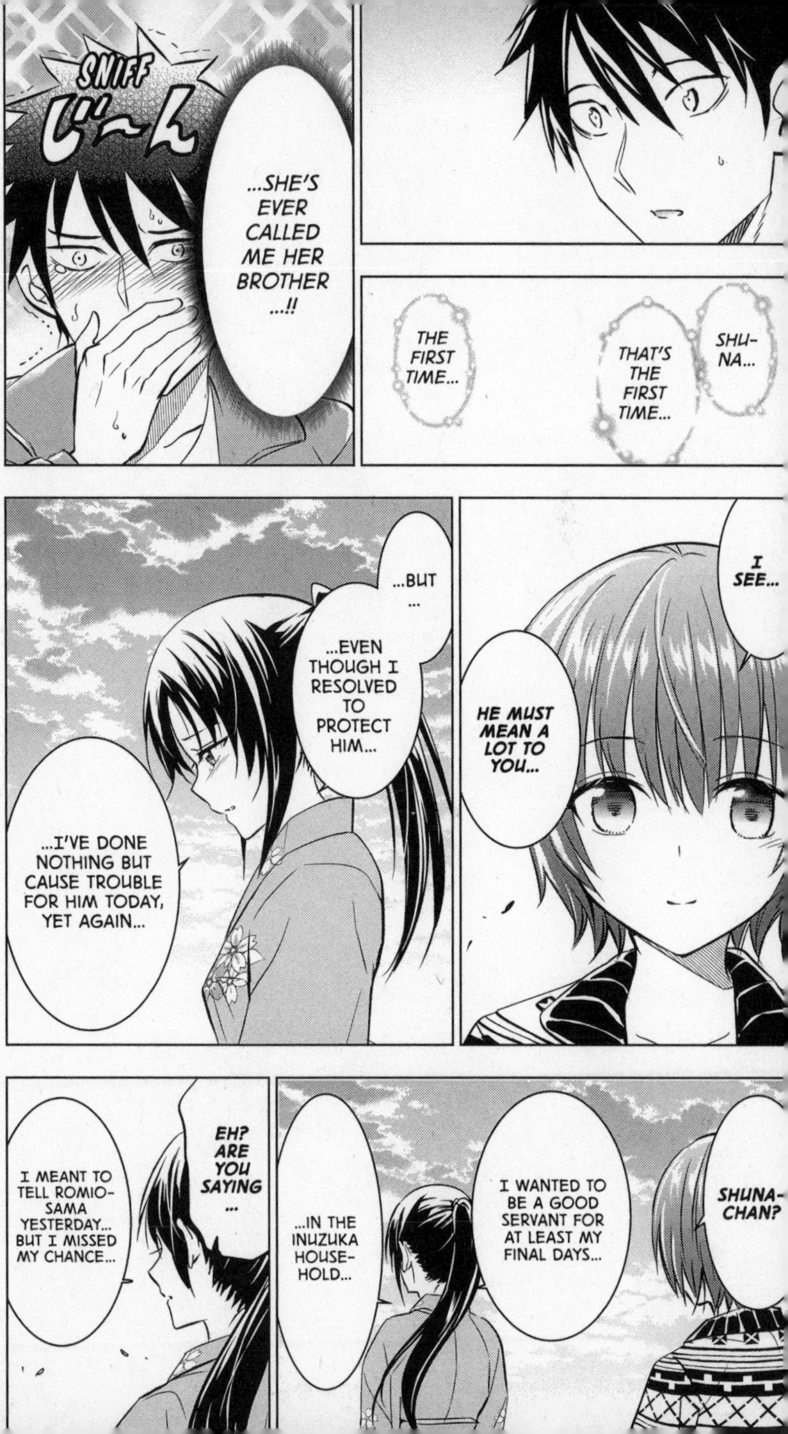
SHU-NA...
THAT'S THE FIRST TIME...
THE FIRST TIME...
SNIFF
じ~ん
...SHE'S EVER CALLED ME HER BROTHER ...!!
I SEE...
HE MUST MEAN A LOT TO YOU...
...BUT ...
...EVEN THOUGH I RESOLVED TO PROTECT HIM...
...I'VE DONE NOTHING BUT CAUSE TROUBLE FOR HIM TODAY, YET AGAIN...
SHUNA-CHAN?
I WANTED TO BE A GOOD SERVANT FOR AT LEAST MY FINAL DAYS...
...IN THE INUZUKA HOUSE-HOLD...
EH? ARE YOU SAYING ...
I MEANT TO TELL ROMIO-SAMA YESTERDAY... BUT I MISSED MY CHANCE...

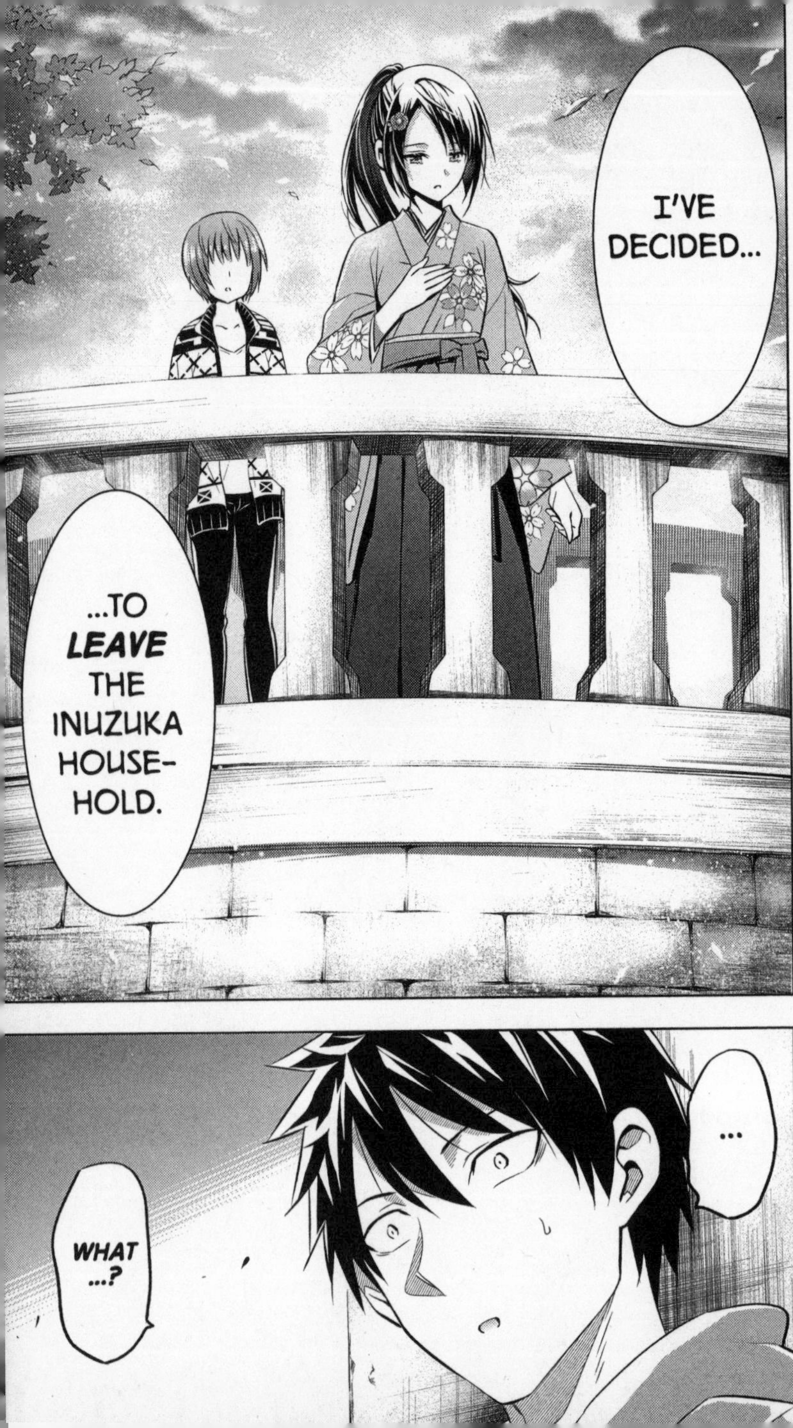
I'VE DECIDED...
...TO LEAVE THE INUZUKA HOUSE-HOLD.
...
WHAT ...?

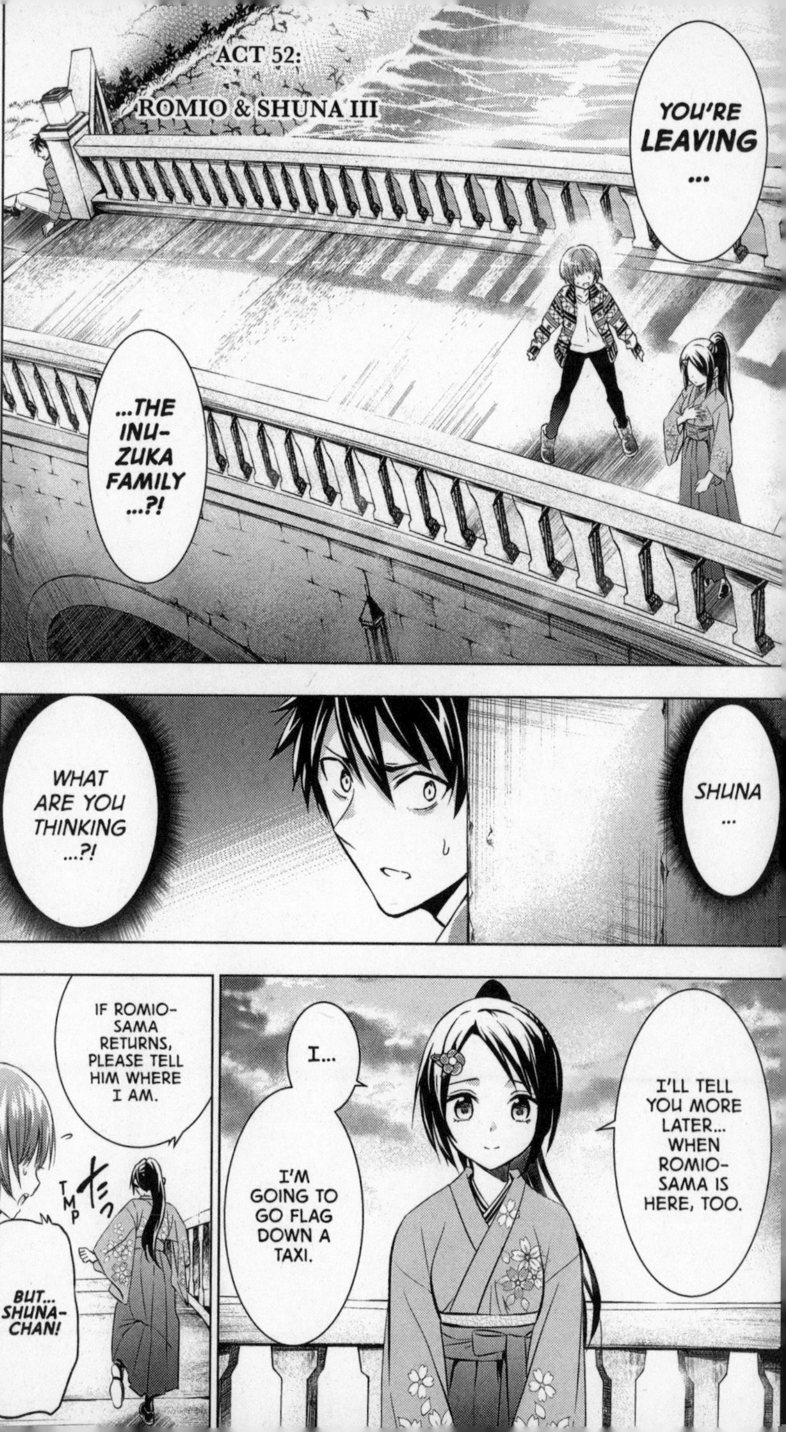
ACT 52:
ROMIO & SHUNA III
YOU'RE LEAVING ...
...THE INU-ZUKA FAMILY ...?!
SHUNA ...
WHAT ARE YOU THINKING ...?!
I'LL TELL YOU MORE LATER... WHEN ROMIO-SAMA IS HERE, TOO.
I...
I'M GOING TO GO FLAG DOWN A TAXI.
IF ROMIO-SAMA RETURNS, PLEASE TELL HIM WHERE I AM.
TMP
BUT... SHUNA-CHAN!

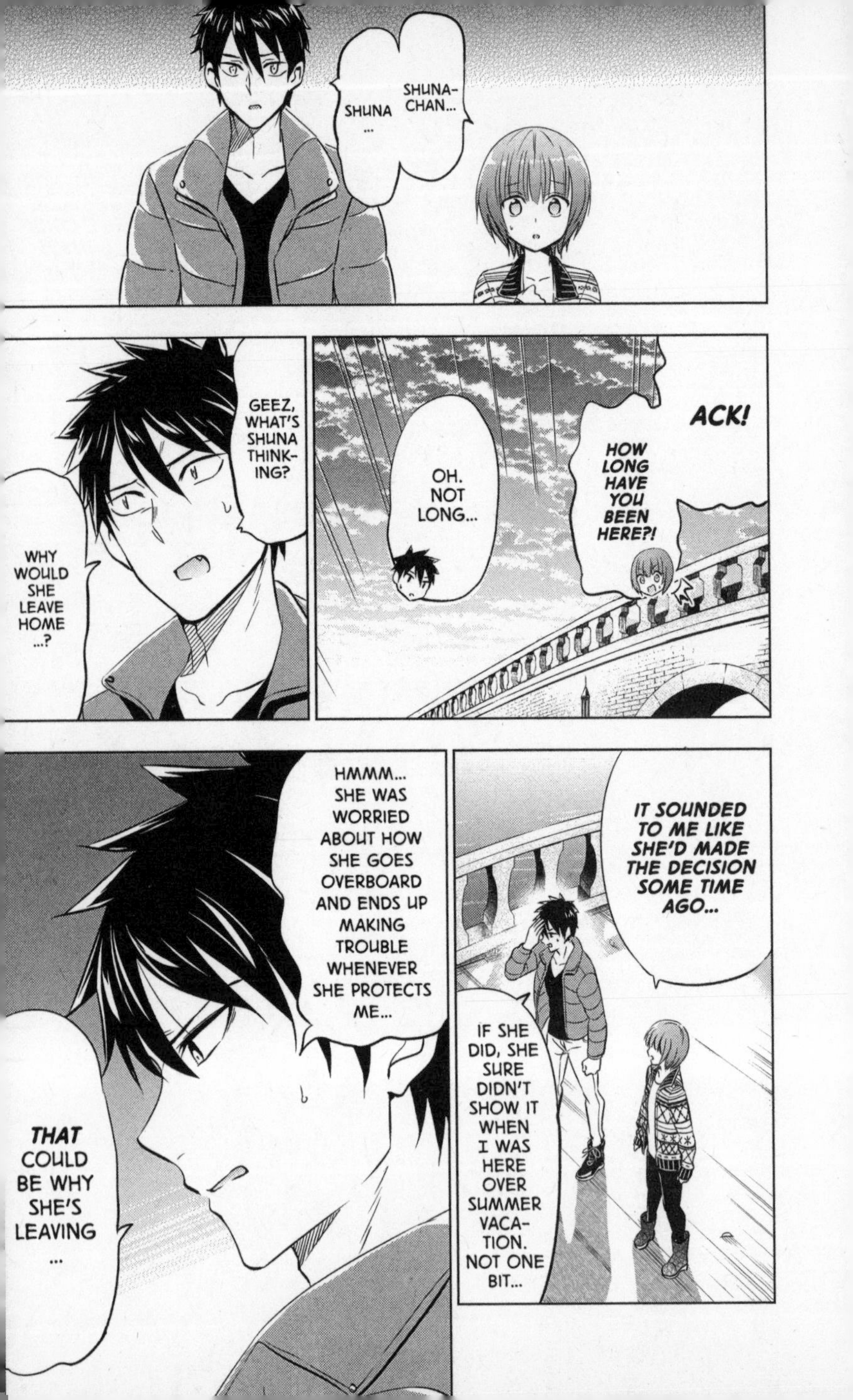
SHUNA-CHAN...
SHUNA ...
ACK!
HOW LONG HAVE YOU BEEN HERE?!
OH. NOT LONG...
GEEZ, WHAT'S SHUNA THINKING?
WHY WOULD SHE LEAVE HOME ...?
IT SOUNDED TO ME LIKE SHE'D MADE THE DECISION SOME TIME AGO...
IF SHE DID, SHE SURE DIDN'T SHOW IT WHEN I WAS HERE OVER SUMMER VACATION. NOT ONE BIT...
HMMM... SHE WAS WORRIED ABOUT HOW SHE GOES OVERBOARD AND ENDS UP MAKING TROUBLE WHENEVER SHE PROTECTS ME...
THAT COULD BE WHY SHE'S LEAVING ...

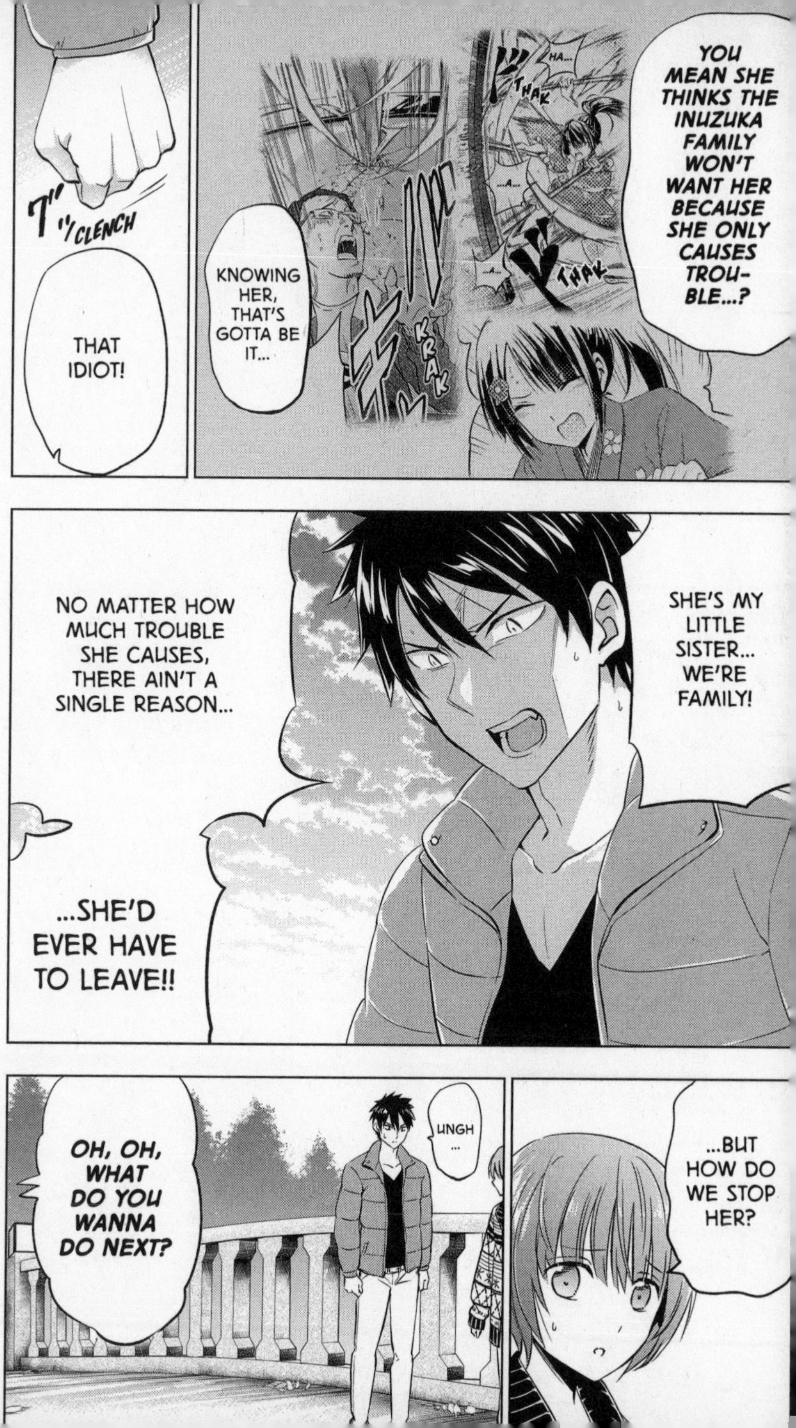
YOU MEAN SHE THINKS THE INUZUKA FAMILY WON'T WANT HER BECAUSE SHE ONLY CAUSES TROU-BLE...?
HA...
THAK
...A...
...A...
THAK
KRAK
KNOWING HER, THAT'S GOTTA BE IT...
CLENCH
THAT IDIOT!
SHE'S MY LITTLE SISTER... WE'RE FAMILY!
NO MATTER HOW MUCH TROUBLE SHE CAUSES, THERE AIN'T A SINGLE REASON...
...SHE'D EVER HAVE TO LEAVE!!
...BUT HOW DO WE STOP HER?
UNGH ...
OH, OH, WHAT DO YOU WANNA DO NEXT?

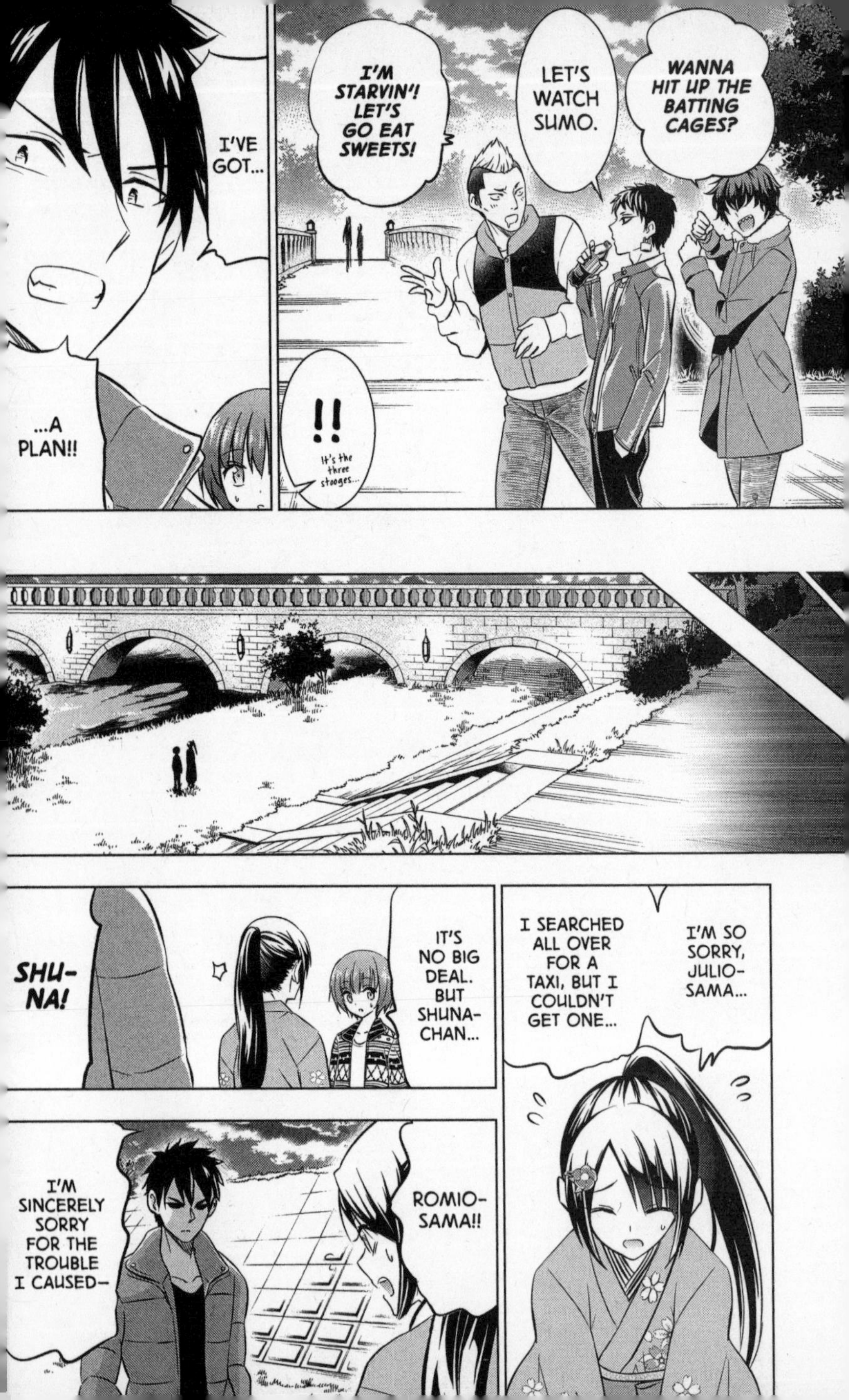
WANNA HIT UP THE BATTING CAGES?
LET'S WATCH SUMO.
I'M STARVIN'! LET'S GO EAT SWEETS!
!!
It's the three stooges...
I'VE GOT...
...A PLAN!!
I'M SO SORRY, JULIO-SAMA...
I SEARCHED ALL OVER FOR A TAXI, BUT I COULDN'T GET ONE...
IT'S NO BIG DEAL. BUT SHUNA-CHAN...
SHU-NA!
ROMIO-SAMA!!
I'M SINCERELY SORRY FOR THE TROUBLE I CAUSED–

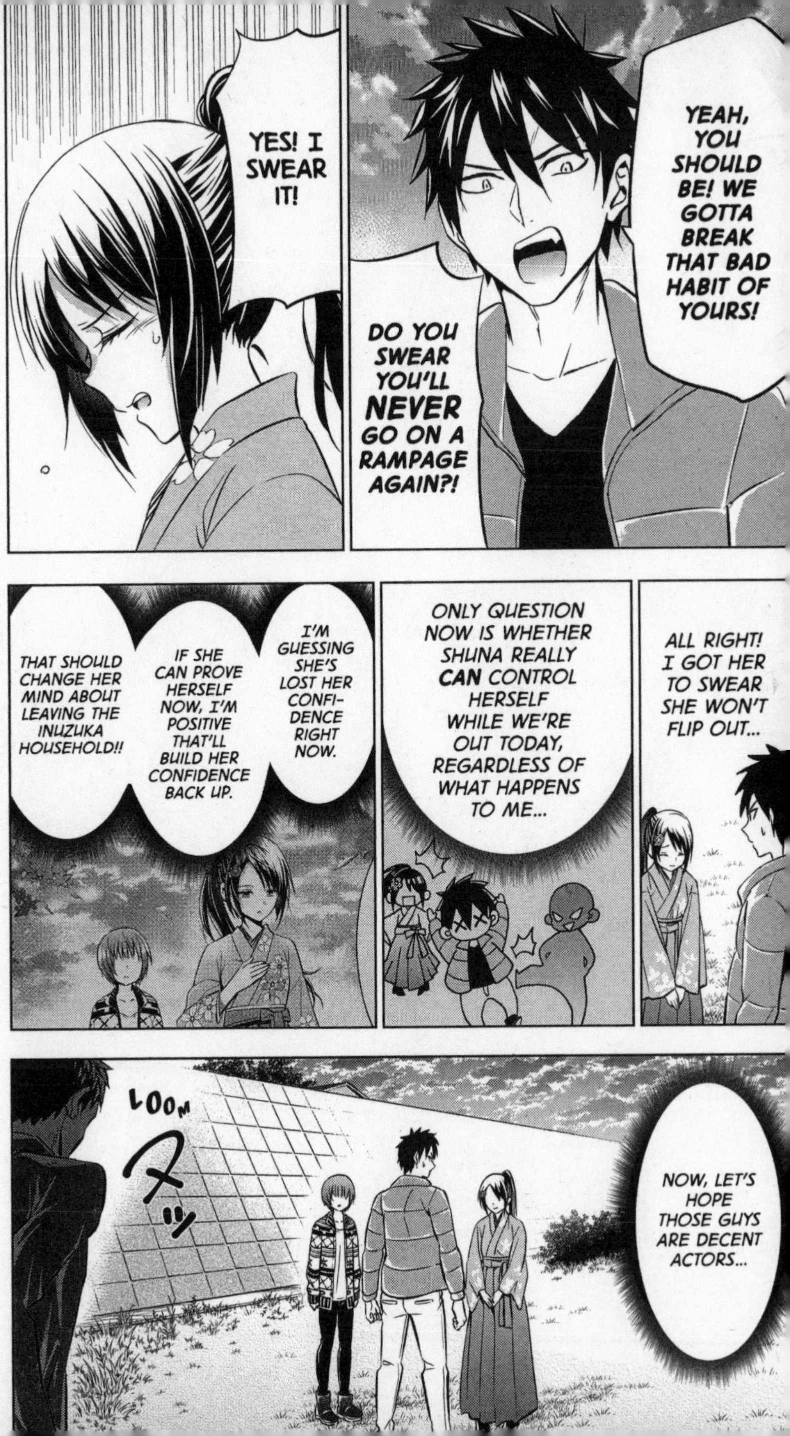
YEAH, YOU SHOULD BE! WE GOTTA BREAK THAT BAD HABIT OF YOURS!
DO YOU SWEAR YOU'LL NEVER GO ON A RAMPAGE AGAIN?!
YES! I SWEAR IT!
ALL RIGHT! I GOT HER TO SWEAR SHE WON'T FLIP OUT...
ONLY QUESTION NOW IS WHETHER SHUNA REALLY CAN CONTROL HERSELF WHILE WE'RE OUT TODAY, REGARDLESS OF WHAT HAPPENS TO ME...
I'M GUESSING SHE'S LOST HER CONFI-DENCE RIGHT NOW.
IF SHE CAN PROVE HERSELF NOW, I'M POSITIVE THAT'LL BUILD HER CONFIDENCE BACK UP.
THAT SHOULD CHANGE HER MIND ABOUT LEAVING THE INUZUKA HOUSEHOLD!!
NOW, LET'S HOPE THOSE GUYS ARE DECENT ACTORS...
LOOM

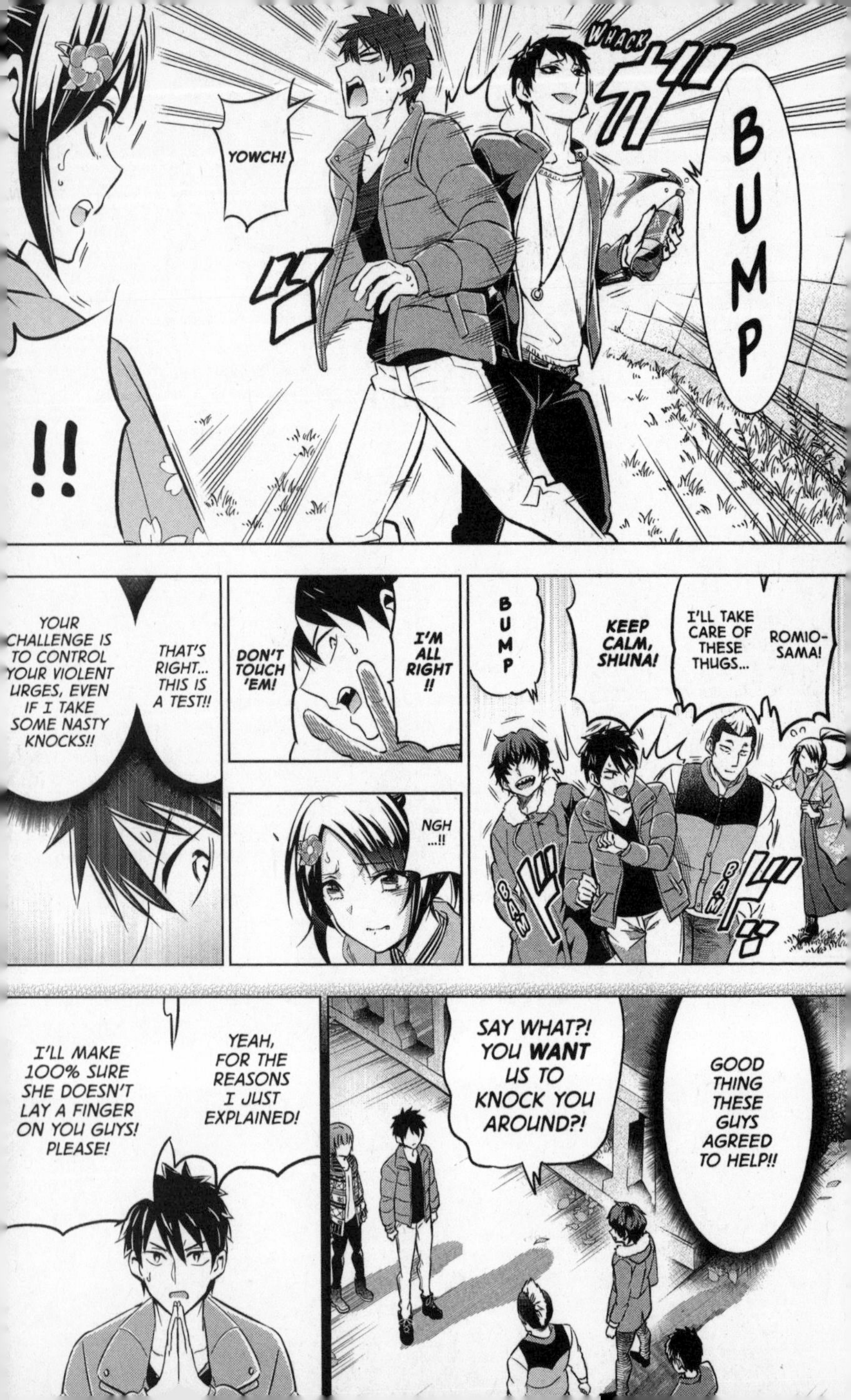
BUMP
WHACK
YOWCH!
!!
ROMIO-SAMA!
I'LL TAKE CARE OF THESE THUGS...
KEEP CALM, SHUNA!
BUMP
BAM
BAM
I'M ALL RIGHT!!
DON'T TOUCH 'EM!
NGH...!!
THAT'S RIGHT... THIS IS A TEST!!
YOUR CHALLENGE IS TO CONTROL YOUR VIOLENT URGES, EVEN IF I TAKE SOME NASTY KNOCKS!!
GOOD THING THESE GUYS AGREED TO HELP!!
SAY WHAT?! YOU WANT US TO KNOCK YOU AROUND?!
YEAH, FOR THE REASONS I JUST EXPLAINED!
I'LL MAKE 100% SURE SHE DOESN'T LAY A FINGER ON YOU GUYS! PLEASE!

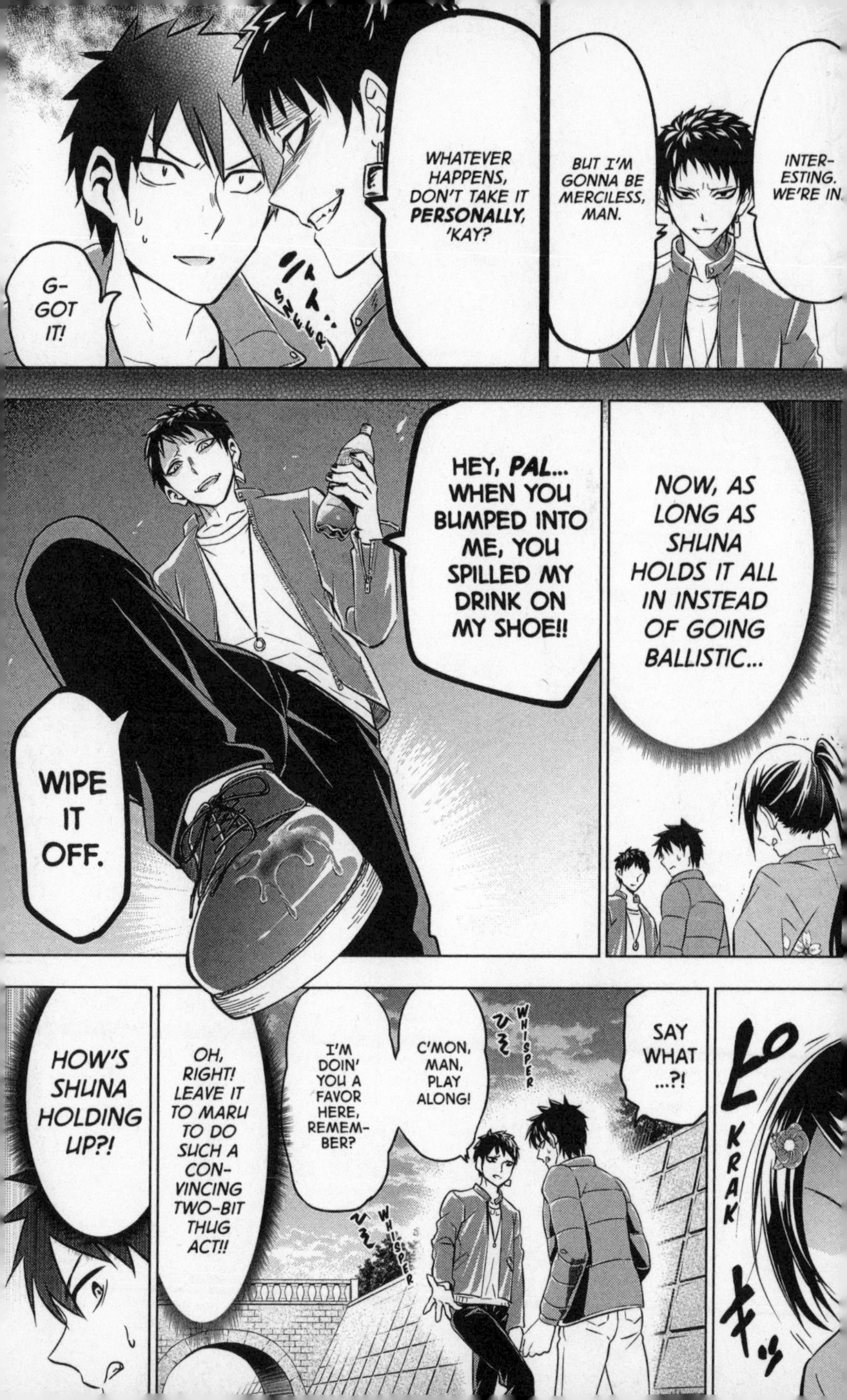
INTER-ESTING. WE'RE IN.
BUT I'M GONNA BE MERCILESS, MAN.
WHATEVER HAPPENS, DON'T TAKE IT **PERSONALLY**, 'KAY?
SNEER
G-GOT IT!
NOW, AS LONG AS SHUNA HOLDS IT ALL IN INSTEAD OF GOING BALLISTIC...
HEY, ***PAL***... WHEN YOU BUMPED INTO ME, YOU SPILLED MY DRINK ON MY SHOE!!
WIPE IT OFF.
KRAK
SAY WHAT ...?!
WHISPER
C'MON, MAN, PLAY ALONG!
I'M DOIN' YOU A FAVOR HERE, REMEMBER?
WHISPER
OH, RIGHT! LEAVE IT TO MARU TO DO SUCH A CONVINCING TWO-BIT THUG ACT!!
HOW'S SHUNA HOLDING UP?!

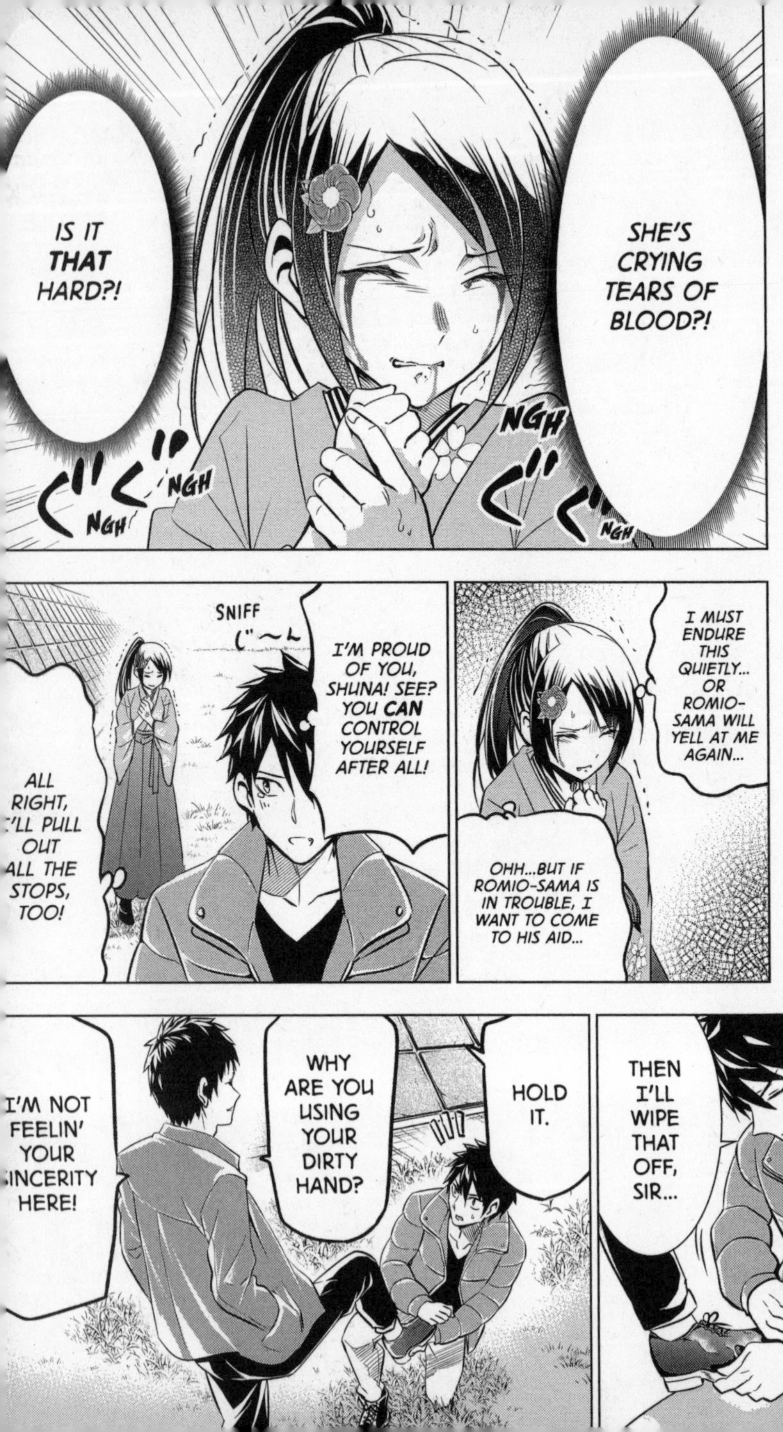
SHE'S CRYING TEARS OF BLOOD?!
IS IT THAT HARD?!
NGH
NGH
NGH
NGH
I MUST ENDURE THIS QUIETLY... OR ROMIO-SAMA WILL YELL AT ME AGAIN...
OHH...BUT IF ROMIO-SAMA IS IN TROUBLE, I WANT TO COME TO HIS AID...
SNIFF
I'M PROUD OF YOU, SHUNA! SEE? YOU **CAN** CONTROL YOURSELF AFTER ALL!
ALL RIGHT, 'LL PULL OUT ALL THE STOPS, TOO!
THEN I'LL WIPE THAT OFF, SIR...
HOLD IT.
WHY ARE YOU USING YOUR DIRTY HAND?
I'M NOT FEELIN' YOUR INCERITY HERE!

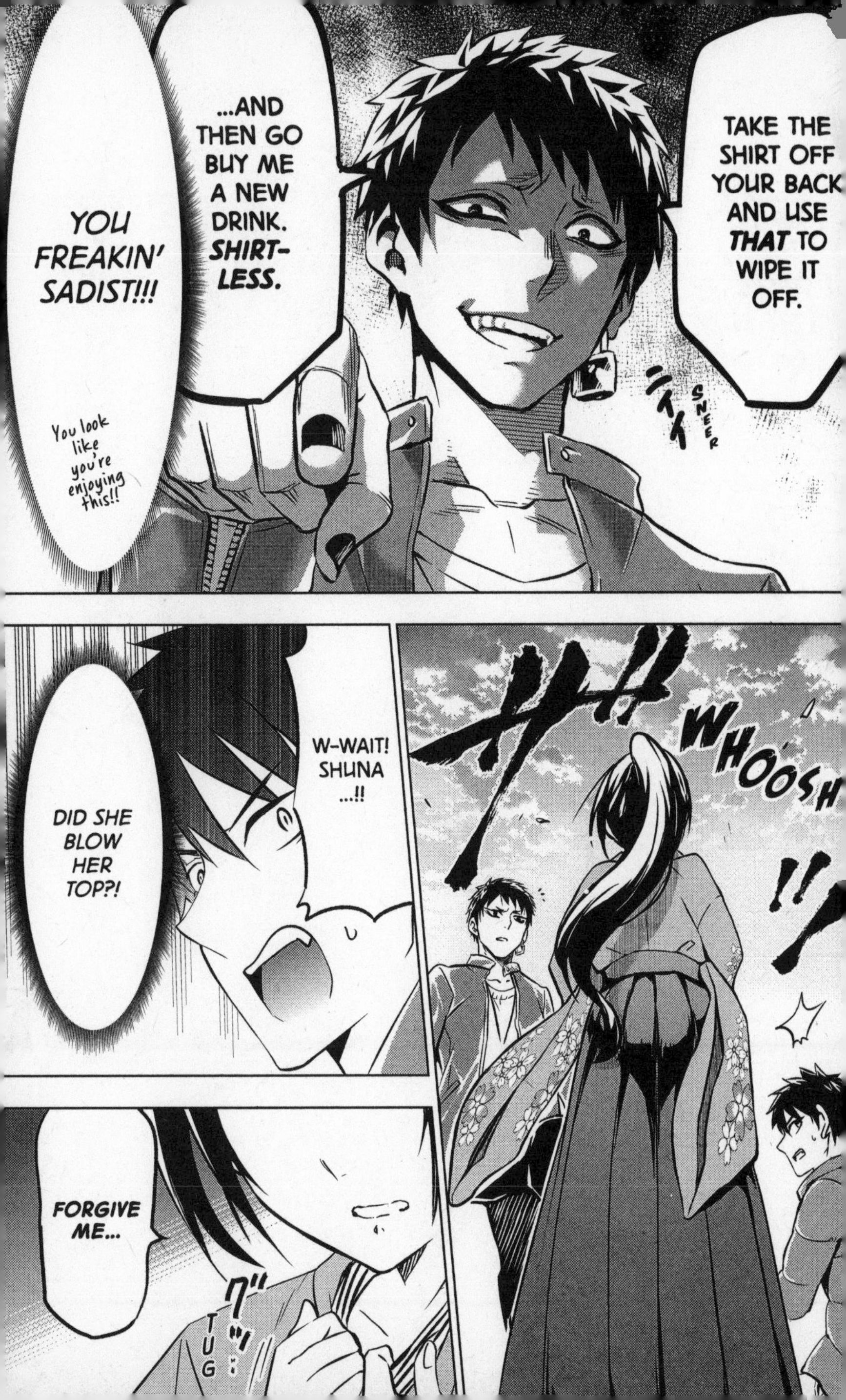

TAKE THE SHIRT OFF YOUR BACK AND USE *THAT* TO WIPE IT OFF.
SNEER
...AND THEN GO BUY ME A NEW DRINK. **SHIRT-LESS.**
YOU FREAKIN' SADIST!!!
You look like you're enjoying this!!
WHOOSH
!!
W-WAIT! SHUNA ...!!
DID SHE BLOW HER TOP?!
FORGIVE ME...
TUG

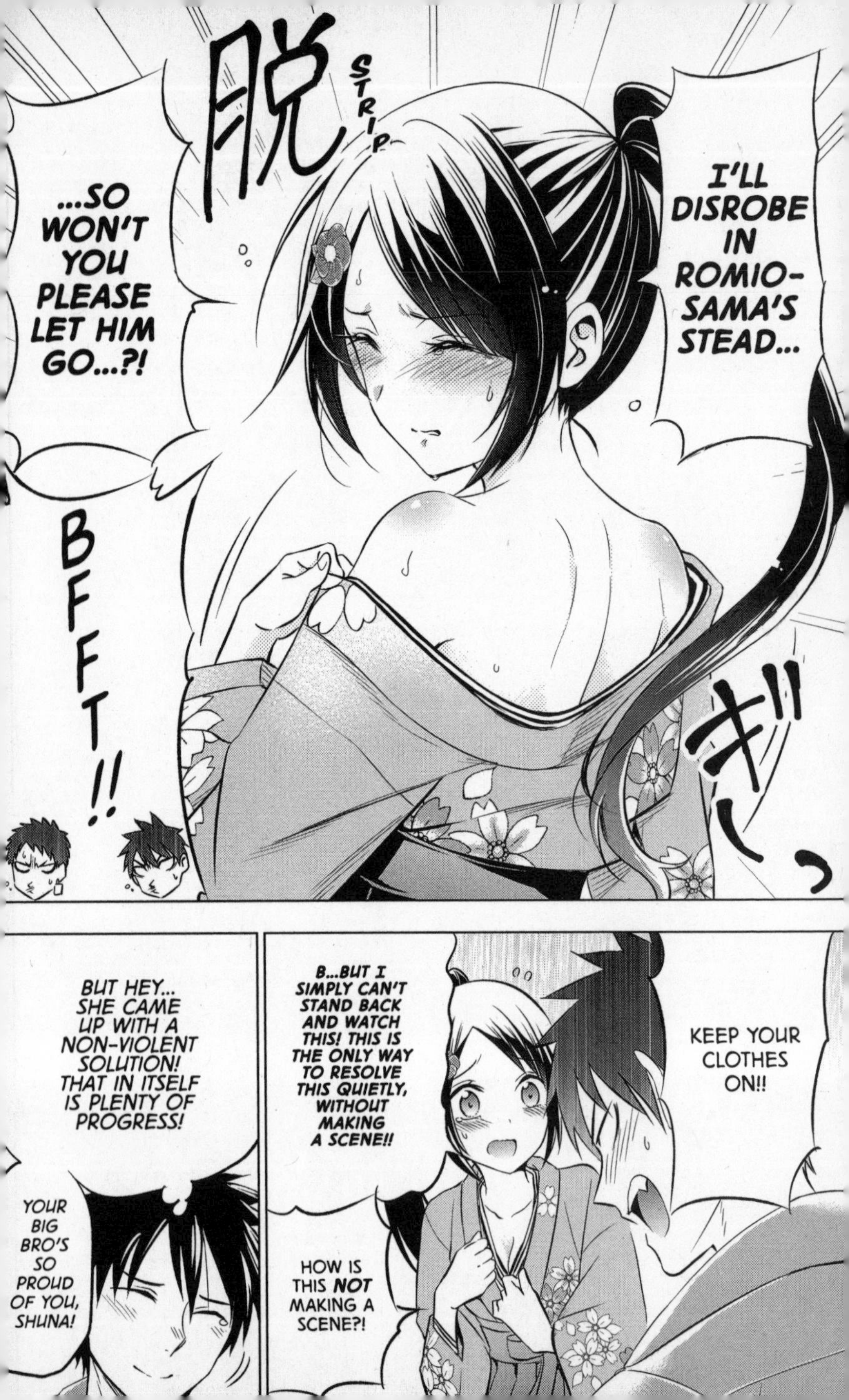
脱
STRIP
I'LL DISROBE IN ROMIO-SAMA'S STEAD...
...SO WON'T YOU PLEASE LET HIM GO...?!
BFFT!!
KEEP YOUR CLOTHES ON!!
B...BUT I SIMPLY CAN'T STAND BACK AND WATCH THIS! THIS IS THE ONLY WAY TO RESOLVE THIS QUIETLY, WITHOUT MAKING A SCENE!!
HOW IS THIS **NOT** MAKING A SCENE?!
BUT HEY... SHE CAME UP WITH A NON-VIOLENT SOLUTION! THAT IN ITSELF IS PLENTY OF PROGRESS!
YOUR BIG BRO'S SO PROUD OF YOU, SHUNA!

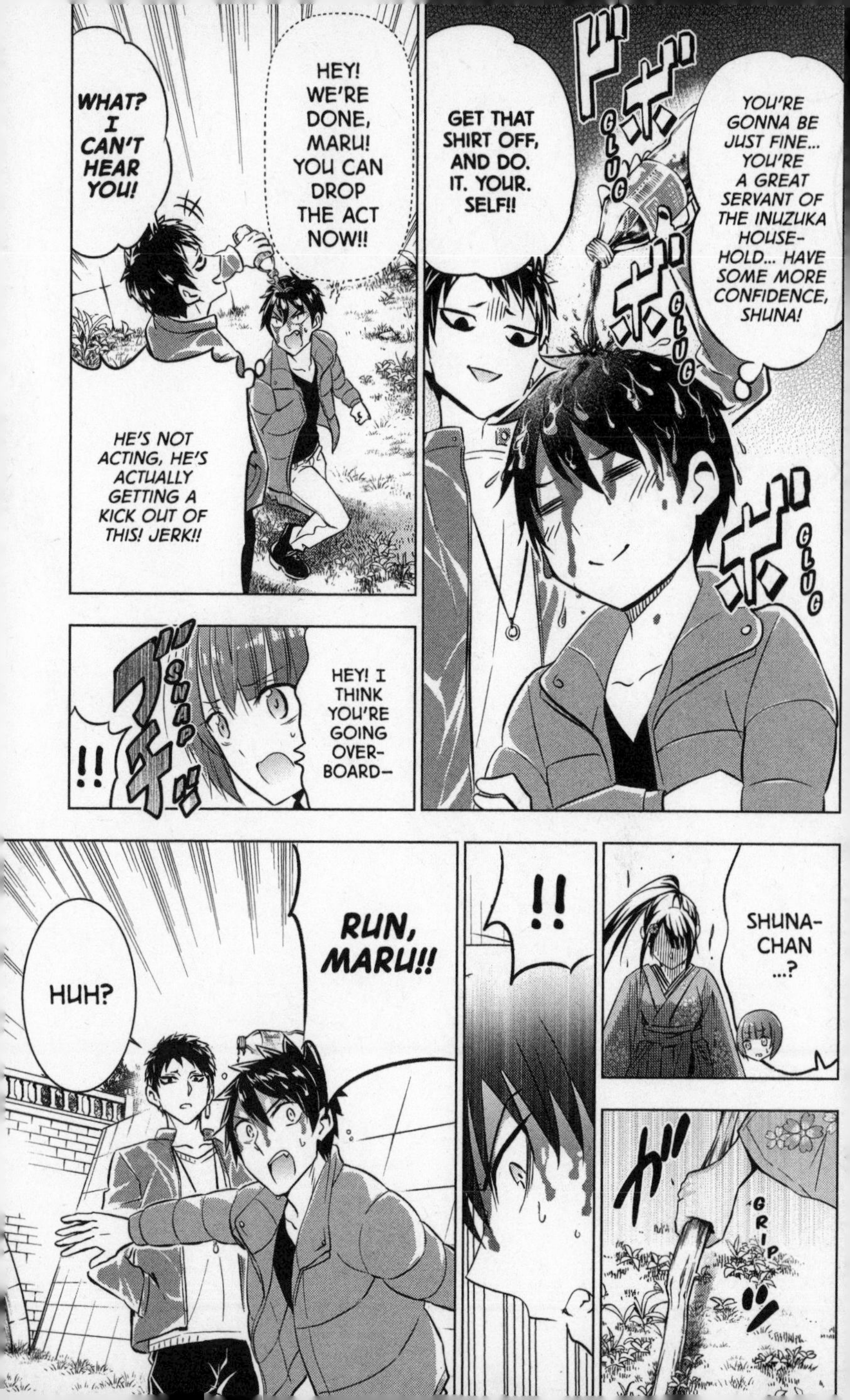
GLUG GLUG
YOU'RE GONNA BE JUST FINE... YOU'RE A GREAT SERVANT OF THE INUZUKA HOUSE-HOLD... HAVE SOME MORE CONFIDENCE, SHUNA!
GET THAT SHIRT OFF, AND DO. IT. YOUR. SELF!!
GLUG
HEY! WE'RE DONE, MARU! YOU CAN DROP THE ACT NOW!!
WHAT? I CAN'T HEAR YOU!
HE'S NOT ACTING, HE'S ACTUALLY GETTING A KICK OUT OF THIS! JERK!!
HEY! I THINK YOU'RE GOING OVER-BOARD—
SNAP
!!
SHUNA-CHAN ...?
GRIP
!!
RUN, MARU!!
HUH?

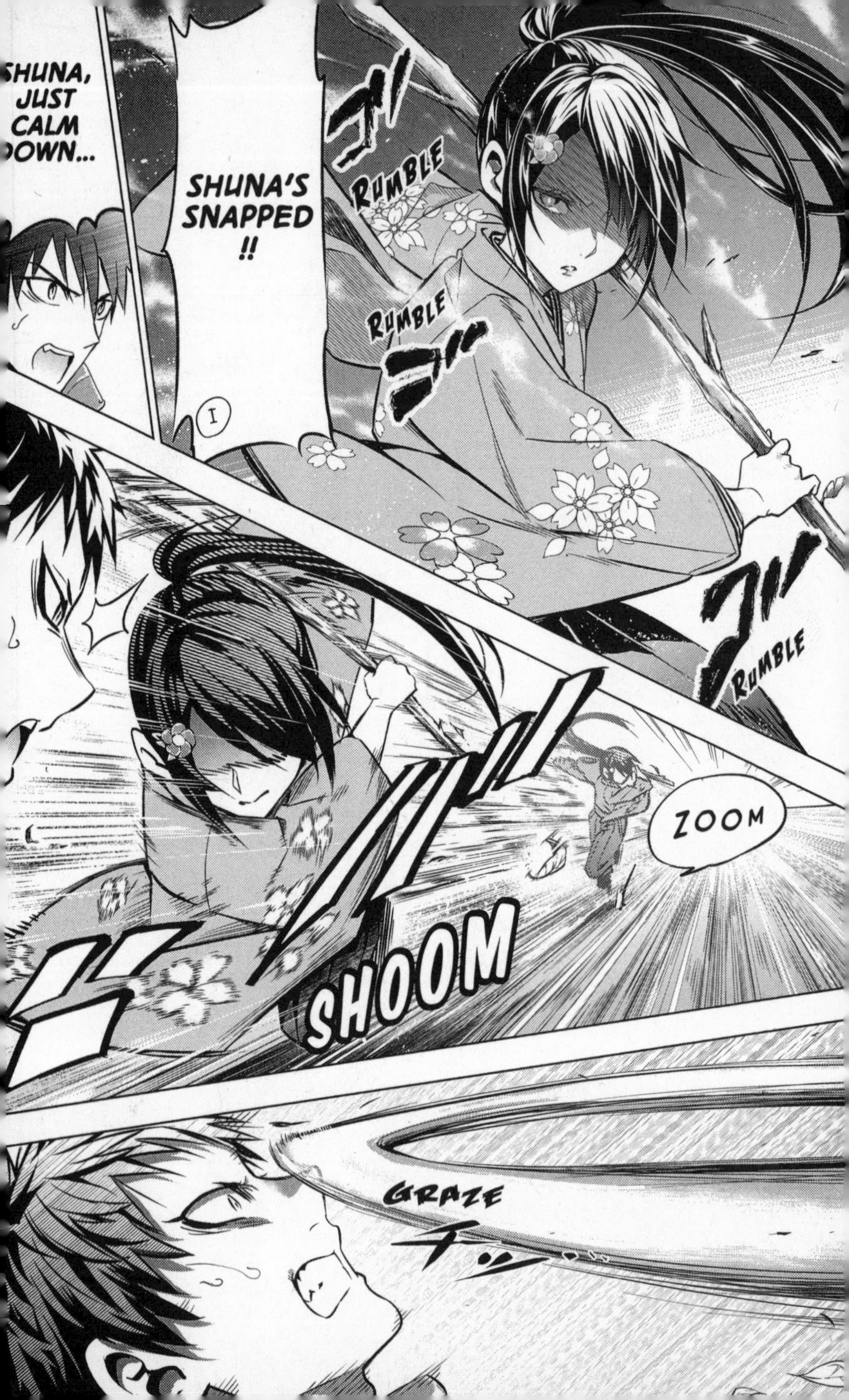
RUMBLE
RUMBLE
SHUNA'S SNAPPED !!
RUMBLE
SHUNA, JUST CALM DOWN...
I
ZOOM
SHOOM
GRAZE

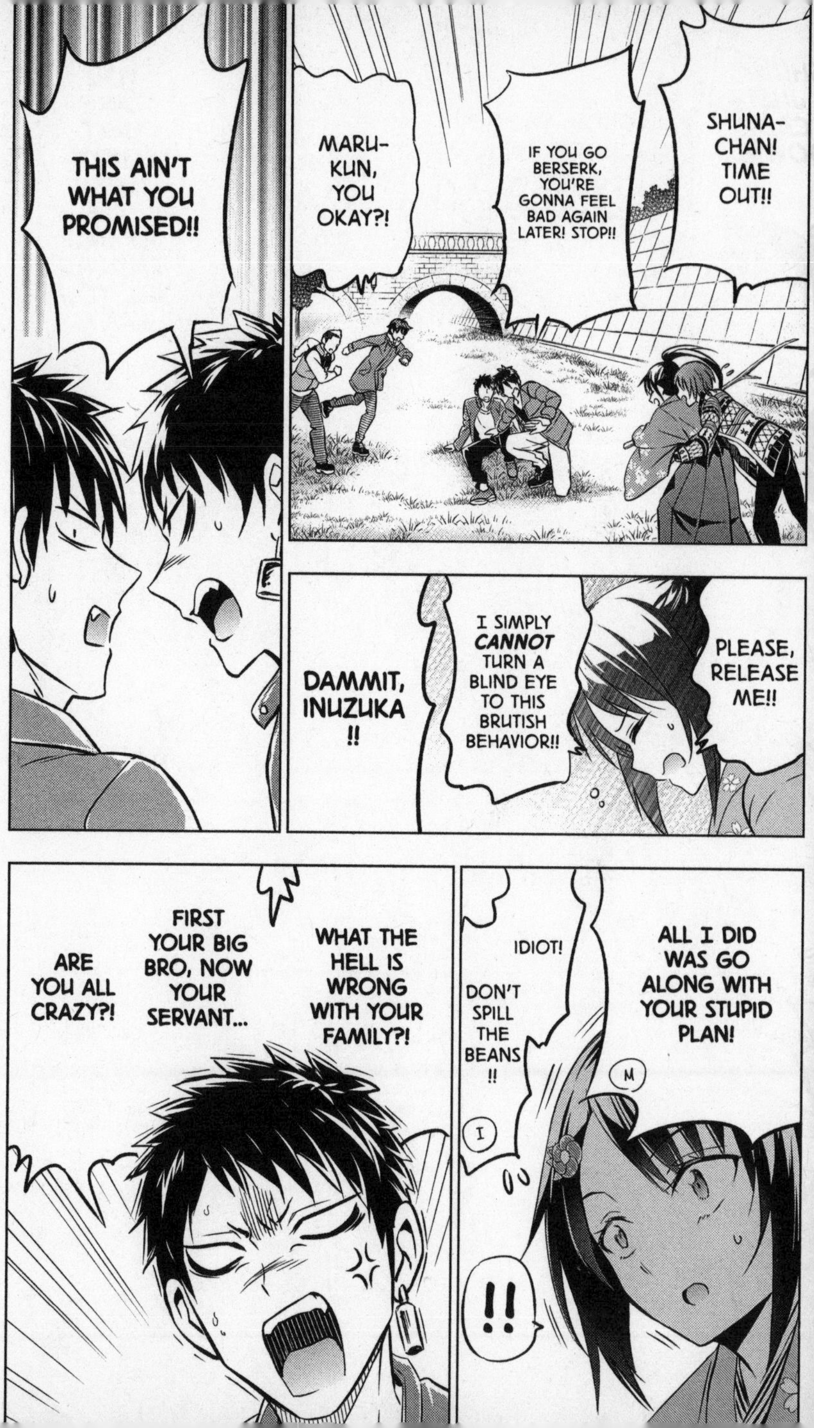
SHUNA-CHAN! TIME OUT!!
IF YOU GO BERSERK, YOU'RE GONNA FEEL BAD AGAIN LATER! STOP!!
MARU-KUN, YOU OKAY?!
PLEASE, RELEASE ME!!
I SIMPLY *CANNOT* TURN A BLIND EYE TO THIS BRUTISH BEHAVIOR!!
DAMMIT, INUZUKA!!
THIS AIN'T WHAT YOU PROMISED!!
ALL I DID WAS GO ALONG WITH YOUR STUPID PLAN!
IDIOT!
DON'T SPILL THE BEANS!!
M
I
!!
WHAT THE HELL IS WRONG WITH YOUR FAMILY?!
FIRST YOUR BIG BRO, NOW YOUR SERVANT...
ARE YOU ALL CRAZY?!

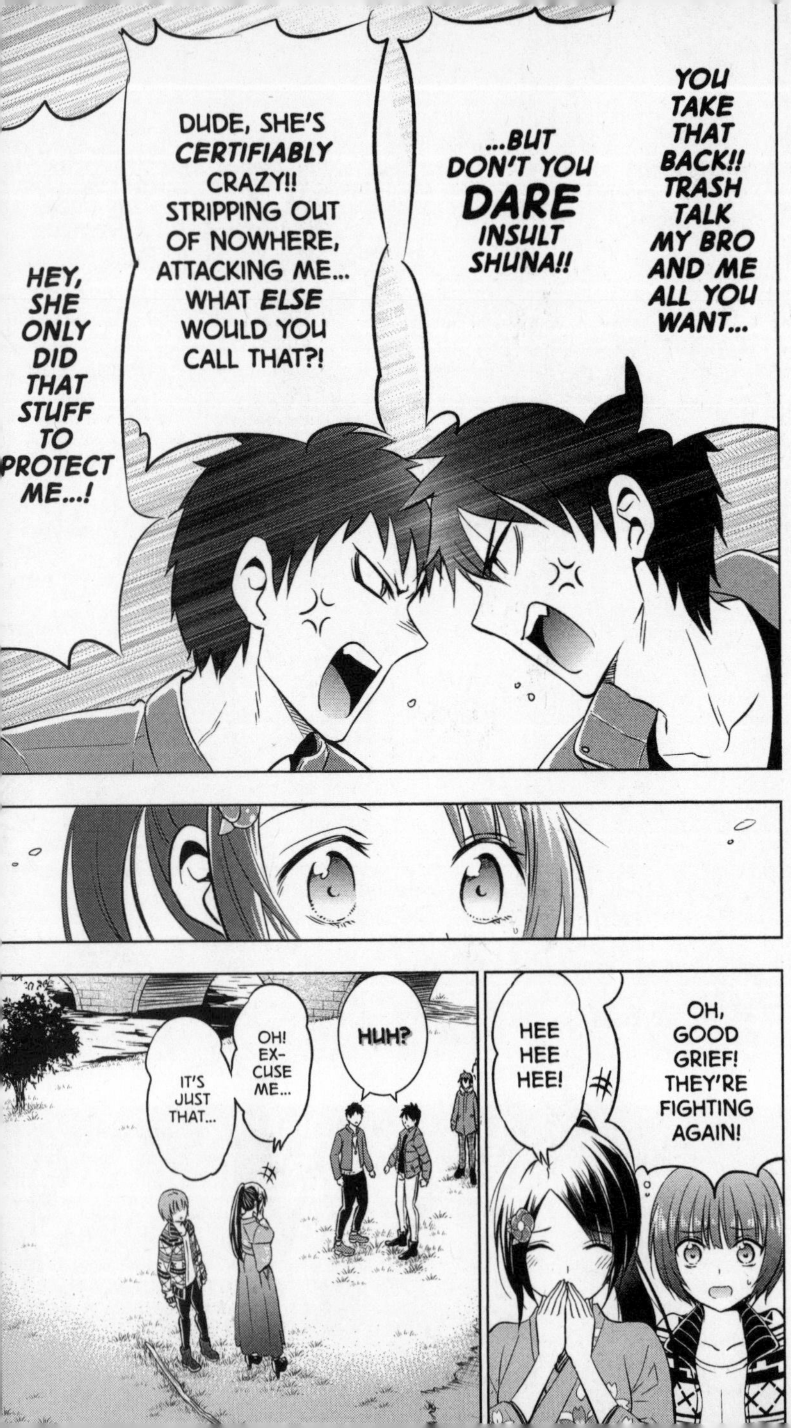
YOU TAKE THAT BACK!! TRASH TALK MY BRO AND ME ALL YOU WANT...
...BUT DON'T YOU DARE INSULT SHUNA!!
DUDE, SHE'S CERTIFIABLY CRAZY!! STRIPPING OUT OF NOWHERE, ATTACKING ME... WHAT ELSE WOULD YOU CALL THAT?!
HEY, SHE ONLY DID THAT STUFF TO PROTECT ME...!
OH, GOOD GRIEF! THEY'RE FIGHTING AGAIN!
HEE HEE HEE!
HUH?
OH! EX-CUSE ME...
IT'S JUST THAT...

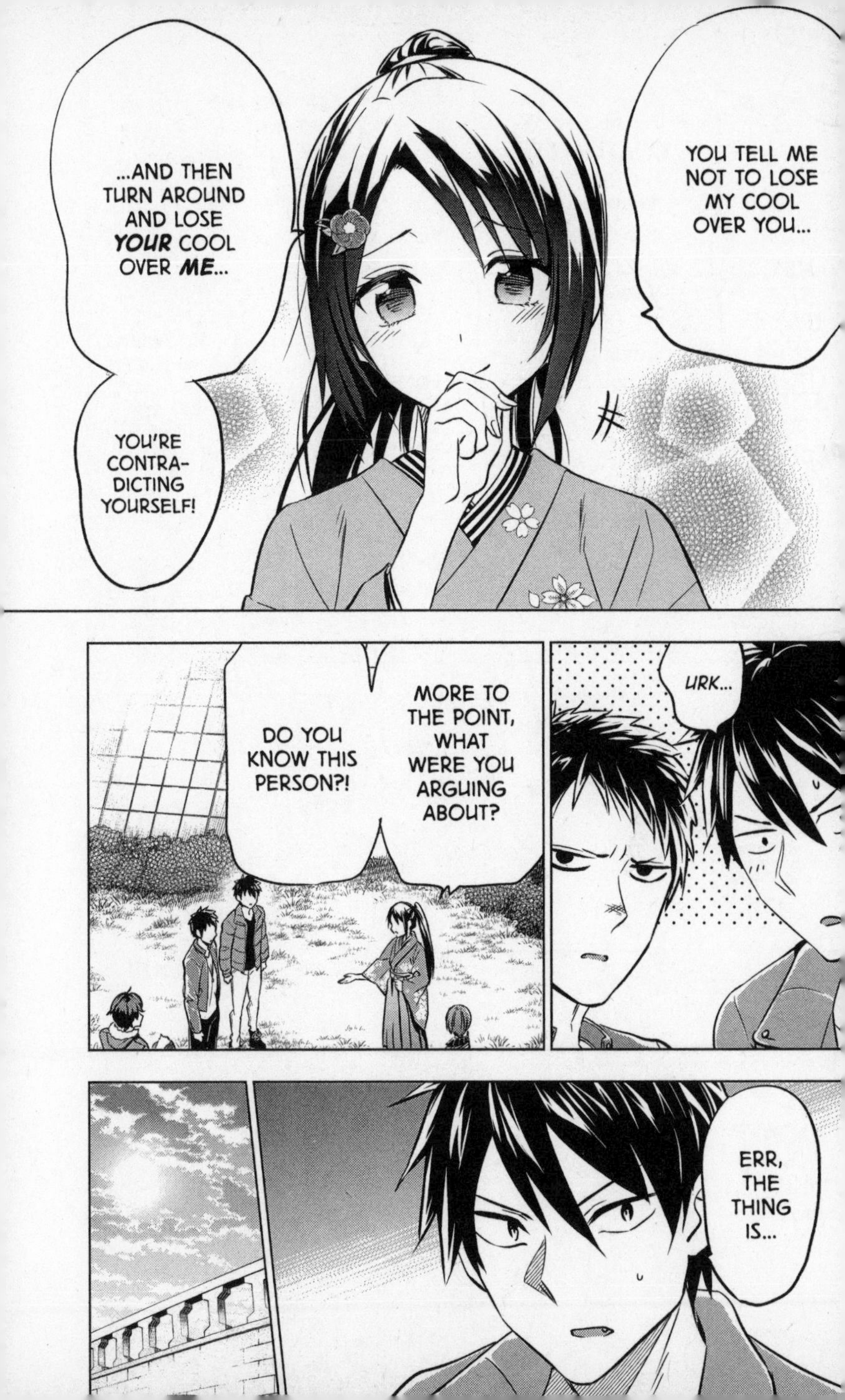
YOU TELL ME NOT TO LOSE MY COOL OVER YOU...
...AND THEN TURN AROUND AND LOSE *YOUR* COOL OVER *ME*...
YOU'RE CONTRA-DICTING YOURSELF!
URK...
DO YOU KNOW THIS PERSON?!
MORE TO THE POINT, WHAT WERE YOU ARGUING ABOUT?
ERR, THE THING IS...

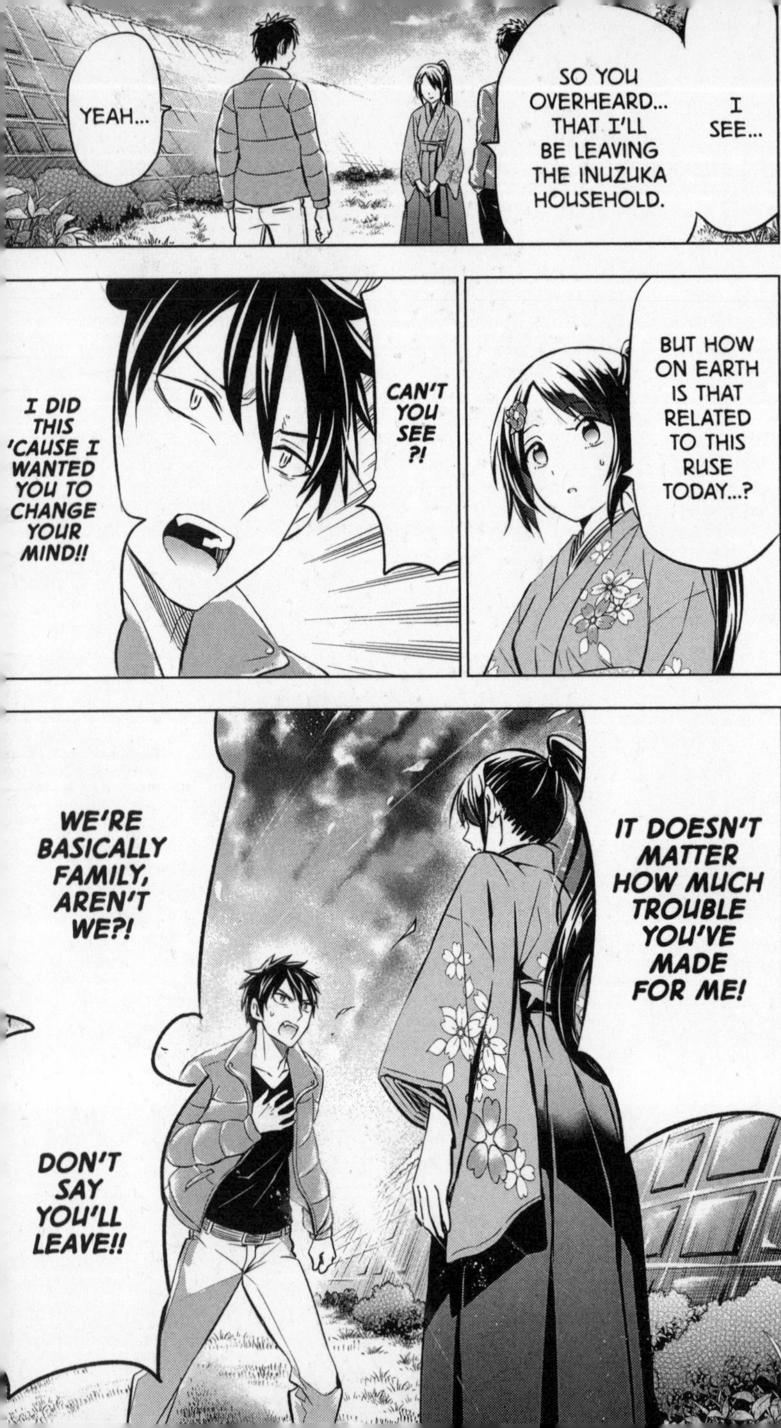
I SEE...
SO YOU OVERHEARD... THAT I'LL BE LEAVING THE INUZUKA HOUSEHOLD.
YEAH...
BUT HOW ON EARTH IS THAT RELATED TO THIS RUSE TODAY...?
CAN'T YOU SEE?!
I DID THIS 'CAUSE I WANTED YOU TO CHANGE YOUR MIND!!
IT DOESN'T MATTER HOW MUCH TROUBLE YOU'VE MADE FOR ME!
WE'RE BASICALLY FAMILY, AREN'T WE?!
DON'T SAY YOU'LL LEAVE!!

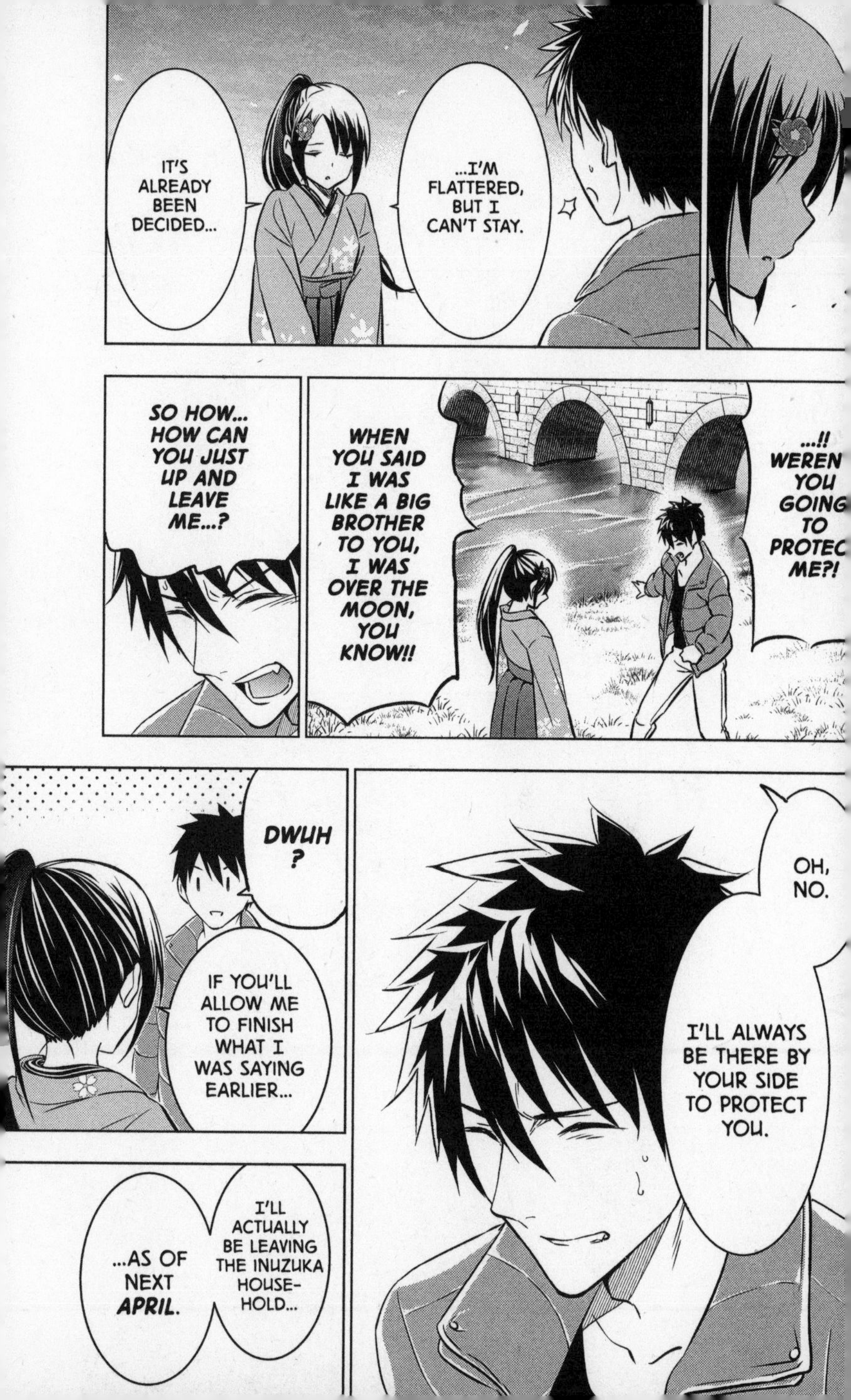

...I'M FLATTERED, BUT I CAN'T STAY.
IT'S ALREADY BEEN DECIDED...
...!! WEREN YOU GOING TO PROTEC ME?!
WHEN YOU SAID I WAS LIKE A BIG BROTHER TO YOU, I WAS OVER THE MOON, YOU KNOW!!
SO HOW... HOW CAN YOU JUST UP AND LEAVE ME...?
OH, NO.
I'LL ALWAYS BE THERE BY YOUR SIDE TO PROTECT YOU.
DWUH ?
IF YOU'LL ALLOW ME TO FINISH WHAT I WAS SAYING EARLIER...
I'LL ACTUALLY BE LEAVING THE INUZUKA HOUSE-HOLD...
...AS OF NEXT APRIL.

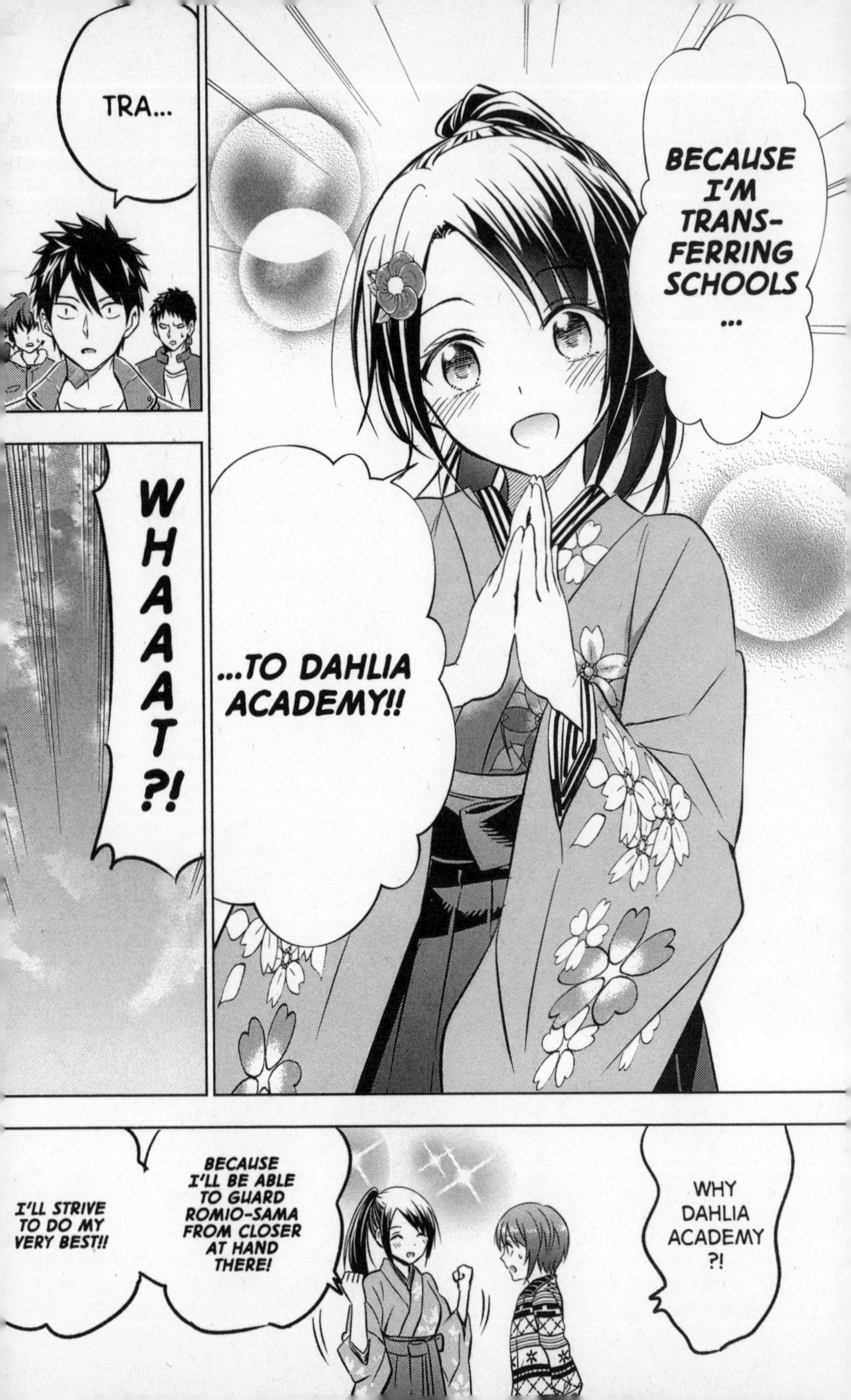
BECAUSE I'M TRANS-FERRING SCHOOLS...
...TO DAHLIA ACADEMY!!
TRA...
WHAAAAT?!
WHY DAHLIA ACADEMY?!
BECAUSE I'LL BE ABLE TO GUARD ROMIO-SAMA FROM CLOSER AT HAND THERE!
I'LL STRIVE TO DO MY VERY BEST!!

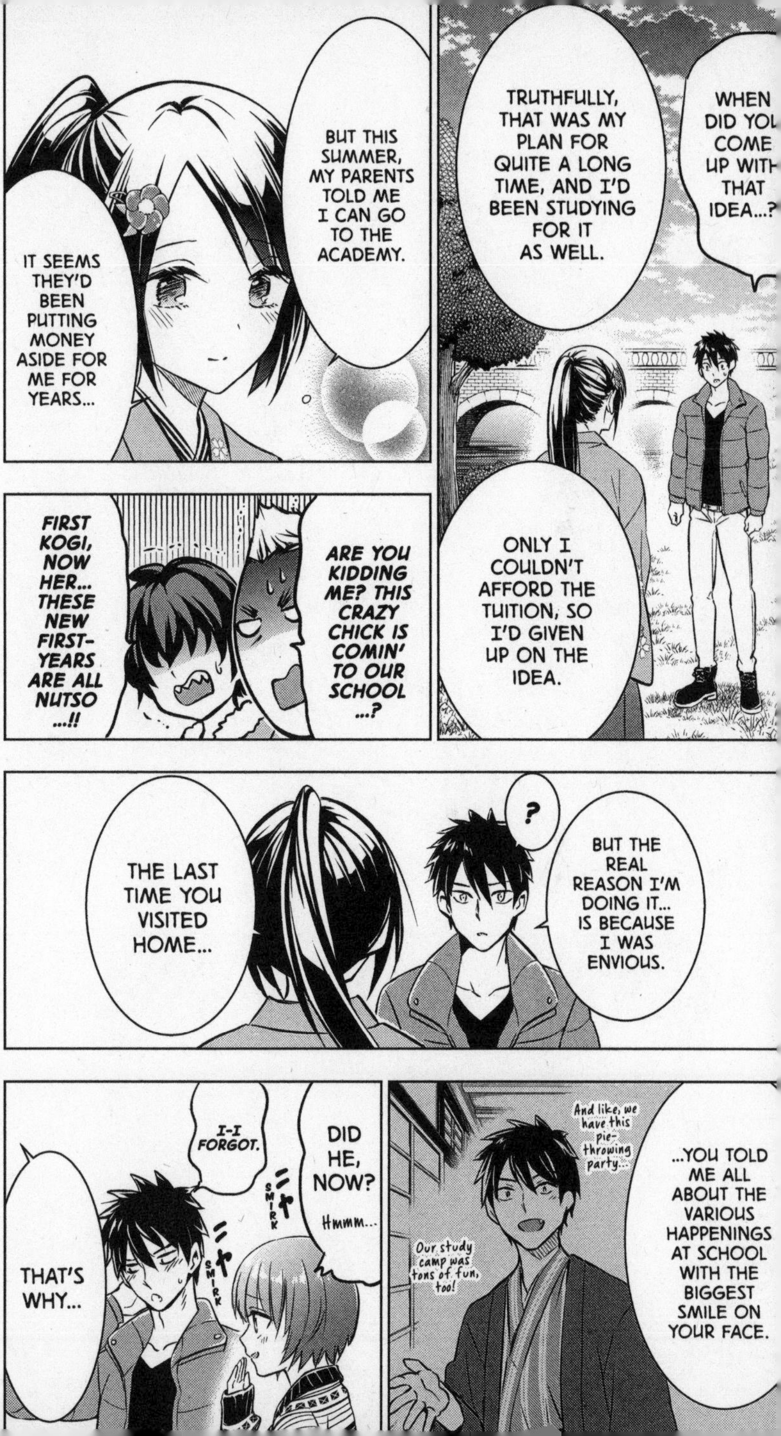
WHEN DID YOU COME UP WITH THAT IDEA...?
TRUTHFULLY, THAT WAS MY PLAN FOR QUITE A LONG TIME, AND I'D BEEN STUDYING FOR IT AS WELL.
ONLY I COULDN'T AFFORD THE TUITION, SO I'D GIVEN UP ON THE IDEA.
BUT THIS SUMMER, MY PARENTS TOLD ME I CAN GO TO THE ACADEMY.
IT SEEMS THEY'D BEEN PUTTING MONEY ASIDE FOR ME FOR YEARS...
ARE YOU KIDDING ME? THIS CRAZY CHICK IS COMIN' TO OUR SCHOOL ...?
FIRST KOGI, NOW HER... THESE NEW FIRST-YEARS ARE ALL NUTSO ...!!
?
BUT THE REAL REASON I'M DOING IT... IS BECAUSE I WAS ENVIOUS.
THE LAST TIME YOU VISITED HOME...
...YOU TOLD ME ALL ABOUT THE VARIOUS HAPPENINGS AT SCHOOL WITH THE BIGGEST SMILE ON YOUR FACE.
And like, we have this pie-throwing party...
Our study camp was tons of fun, too!
DID HE, NOW?
Hmmm...
SMIRK
SMIRK
I-I FORGOT.
THAT'S WHY...

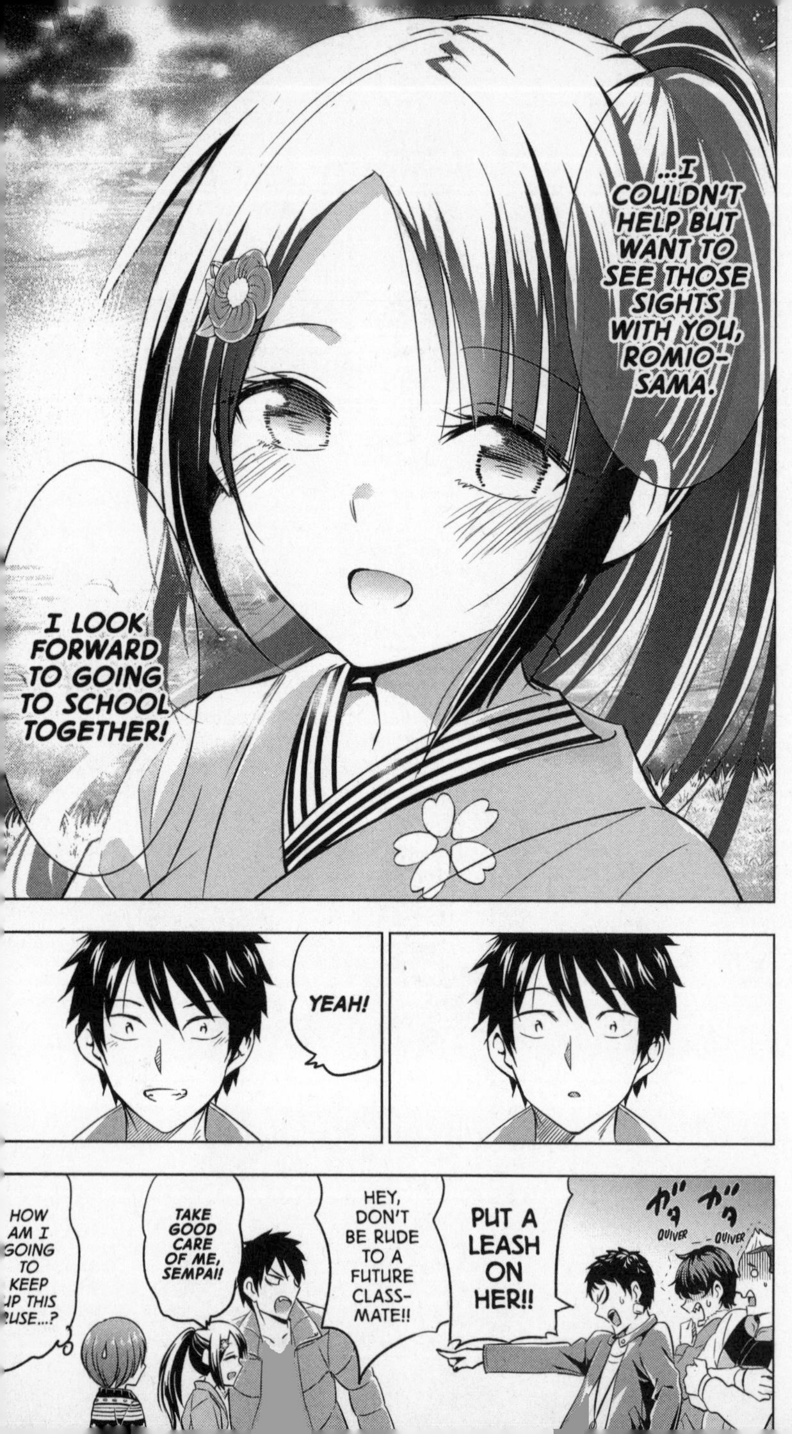

...I COULDN'T HELP BUT WANT TO SEE THOSE SIGHTS WITH YOU, ROMIO-SAMA.
I LOOK FORWARD TO GOING TO SCHOOL TOGETHER!
YEAH!
QUIVER QUIVER
PUT A LEASH ON HER!!
HEY, DON'T BE RUDE TO A FUTURE CLASS-MATE!!
TAKE GOOD CARE OF ME, SEMPAI!
HOW AM I GOING TO KEEP UP THIS RUSE...?

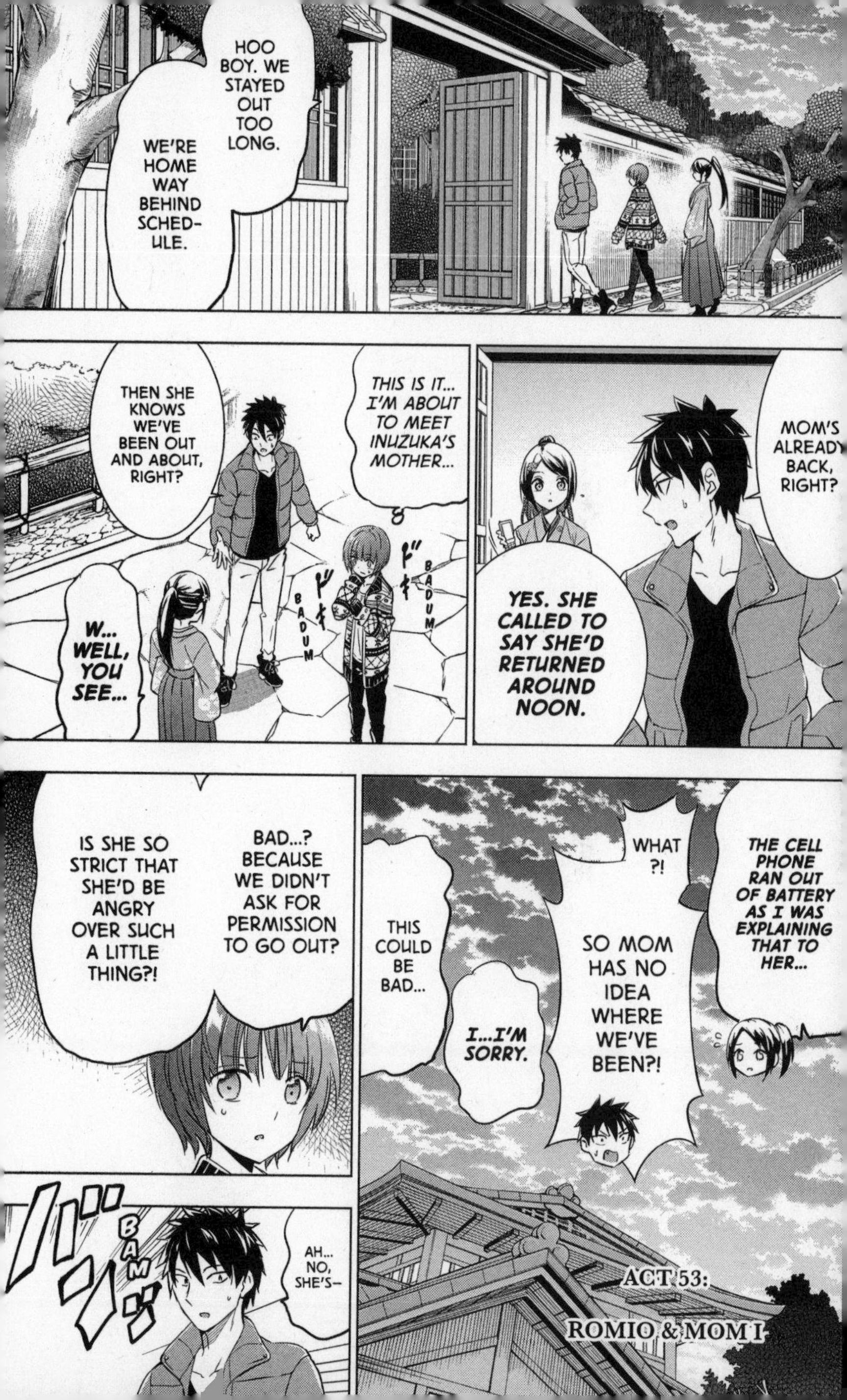
HOO BOY. WE STAYED OUT TOO LONG.
WE'RE HOME WAY BEHIND SCHED-ULE.
MOM'S ALREADY BACK, RIGHT?
YES. SHE CALLED TO SAY SHE'D RETURNED AROUND NOON.
THIS IS IT... I'M ABOUT TO MEET INUZUKA'S MOTHER...
BADUM
BADUM
THEN SHE KNOWS WE'VE BEEN OUT AND ABOUT, RIGHT?
W... WELL, YOU SEE...
THE CELL PHONE RAN OUT OF BATTERY AS I WAS EXPLAINING THAT TO HER...
WHAT?!
SO MOM HAS NO IDEA WHERE WE'VE BEEN?!
I...I'M SORRY.
THIS COULD BE BAD...
ACT 53:
ROMIO & MOM I
BAD...? BECAUSE WE DIDN'T ASK FOR PERMISSION TO GO OUT?
IS SHE SO STRICT THAT SHE'D BE ANGRY OVER SUCH A LITTLE THING?!
AH... NO, SHE'S–
BAM

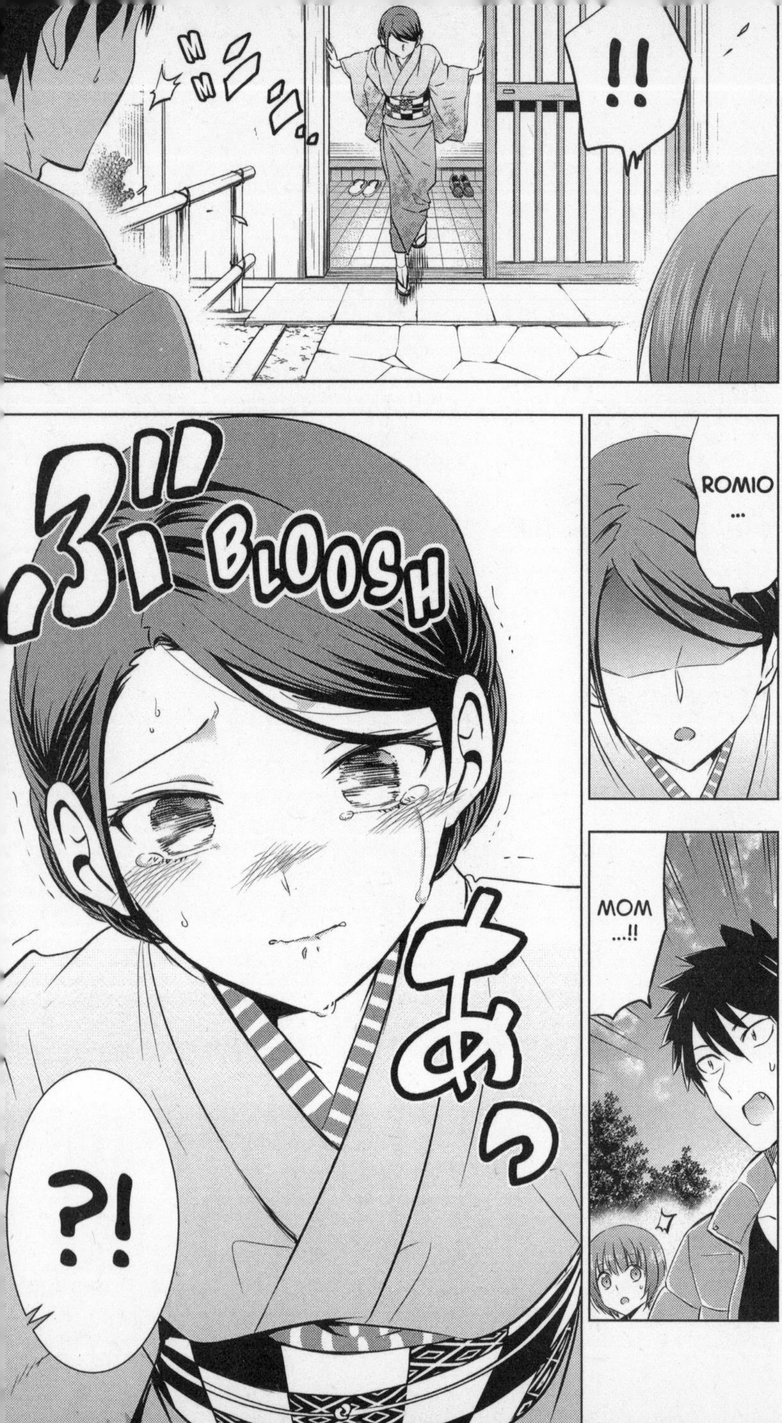
!!
MM
ROMIO ...
MOM ...!!
ぶ
BLOOSH
あっ
?!

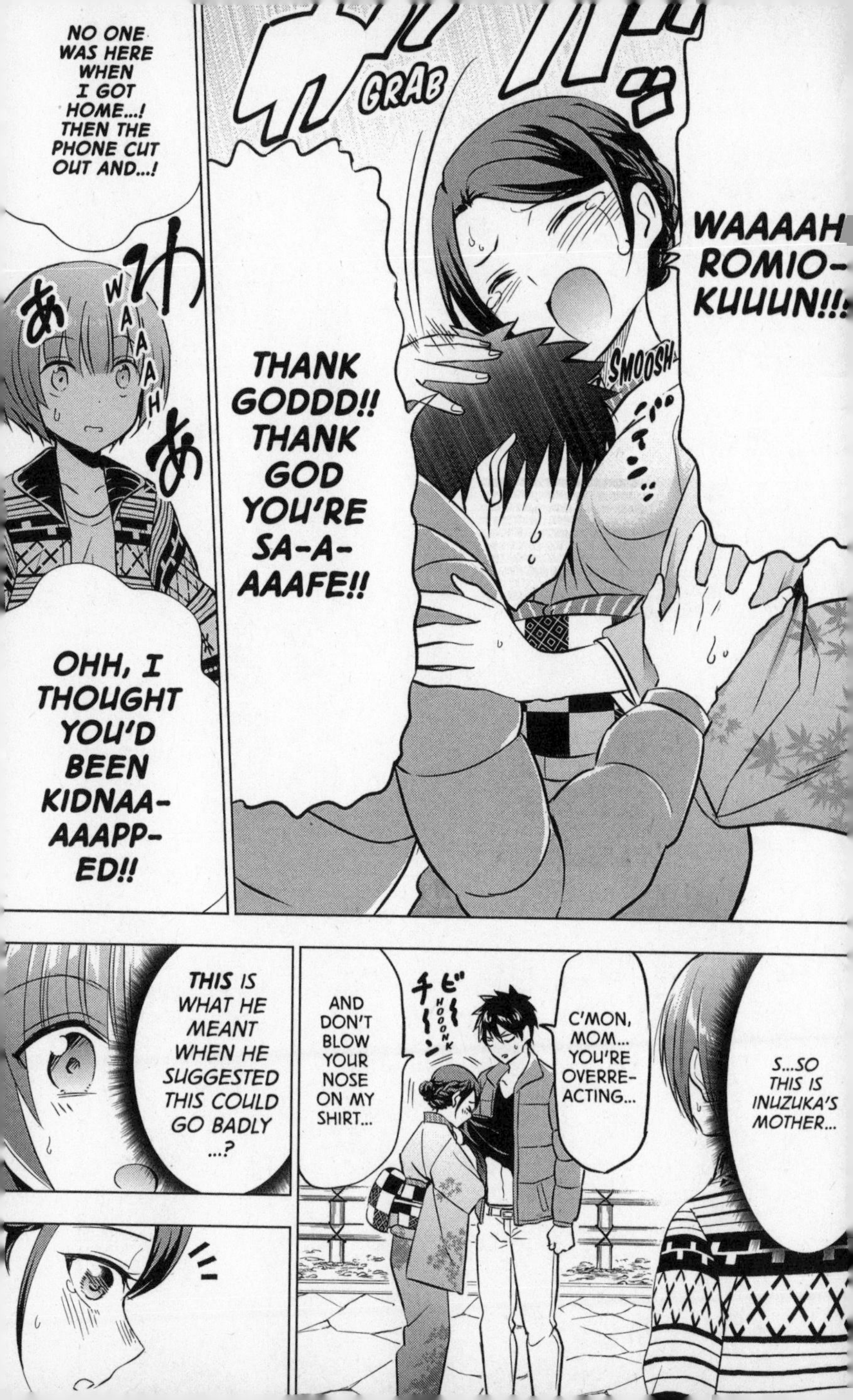
GRAB
WAAAAH ROMIO-KUUUN!!!
SMOOSH
THANK GODDD!! THANK GOD YOU'RE SA-A-AAAFE!!
NO ONE WAS HERE WHEN I GOT HOME...! THEN THE PHONE CUT OUT AND...!
WAAAAH
OHH, I THOUGHT YOU'D BEEN KIDNAA-AAAPP-ED!!
S...SO THIS IS INUZUKA'S MOTHER...
C'MON, MOM... YOU'RE OVERRE-ACTING...
HOOONK
AND DON'T BLOW YOUR NOSE ON MY SHIRT...
THIS IS WHAT HE MEANT WHEN HE SUGGESTED THIS COULD GO BADLY ...?

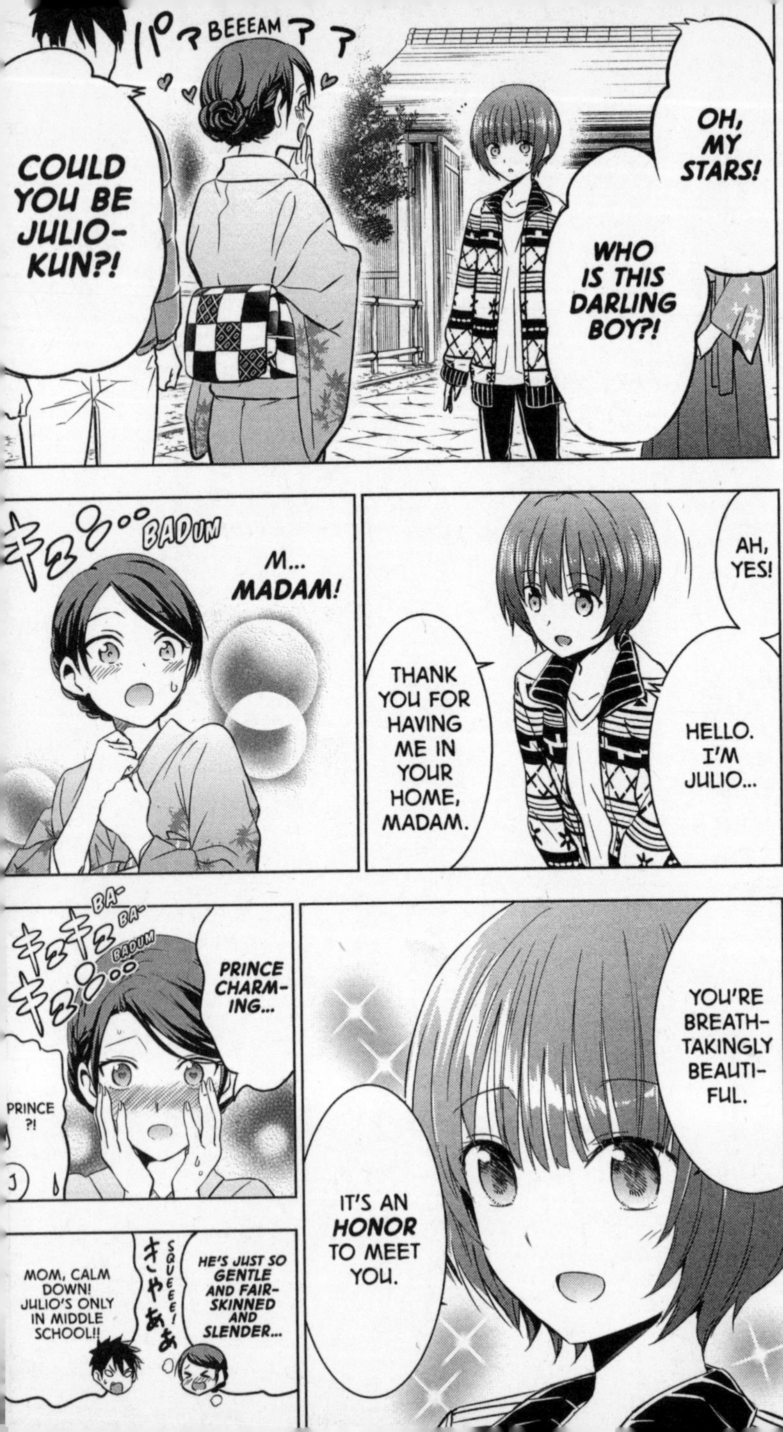
OH, MY STARS!
WHO IS THIS DARLING BOY?!
BEEEAM
COULD YOU BE JULIO-KUN?!
AH, YES!
HELLO. I'M JULIO...
THANK YOU FOR HAVING ME IN YOUR HOME, MADAM.
BADUM
M... MADAM!
YOU'RE BREATH-TAKINGLY BEAUTI-FUL.
IT'S AN HONOR TO MEET YOU.
BA- BA- BADUM
PRINCE CHARM-ING...
PRINCE ?!
HE'S JUST SO GENTLE AND FAIR-SKINNED AND SLENDER...
SQUEEEE!
MOM, CALM DOWN! JULIO'S ONLY IN MIDDLE SCHOOL!!

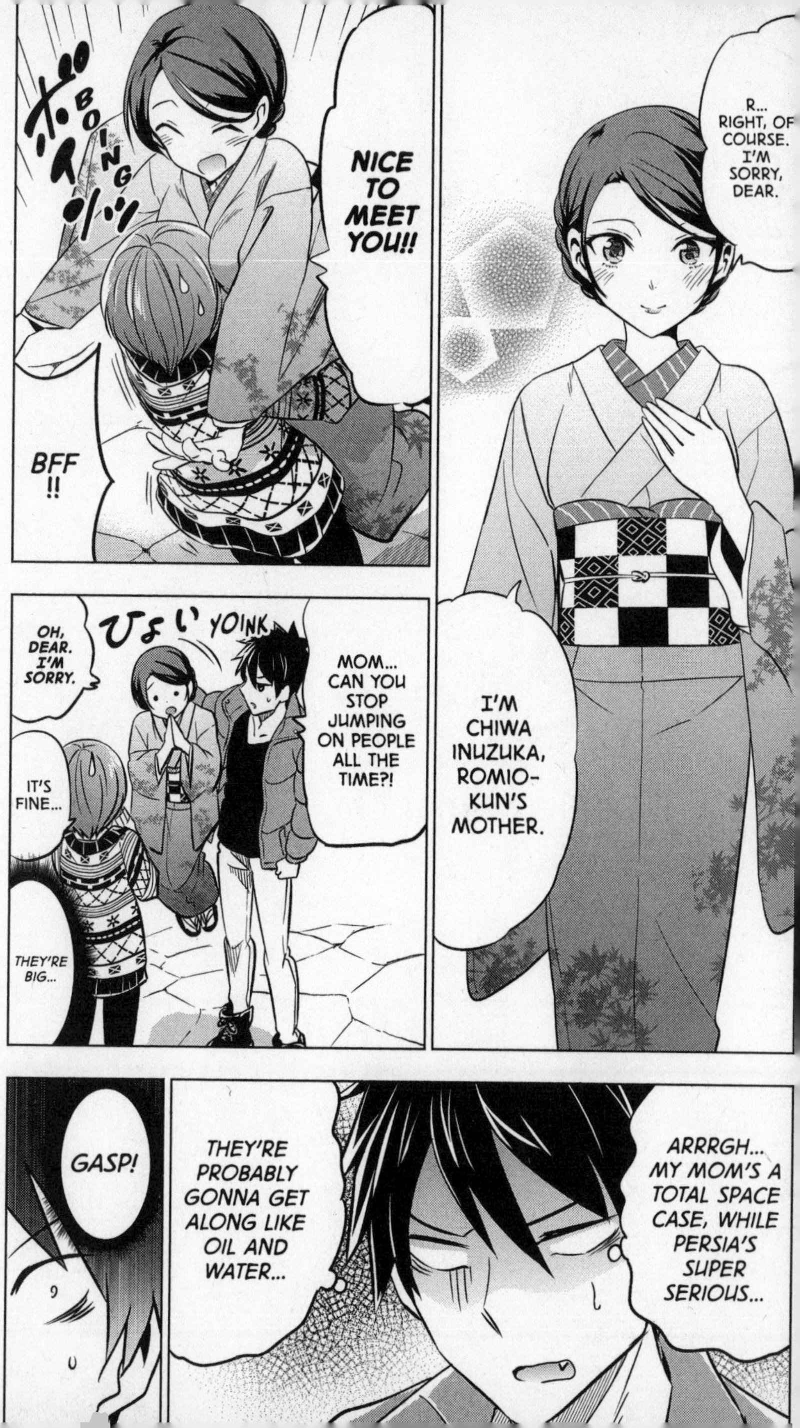
R... RIGHT, OF COURSE. I'M SORRY, DEAR.
I'M CHIWA INUZUKA, ROMIO-KUN'S MOTHER.
ボイン
BOING
NICE TO MEET YOU!!
BFF !!
MOM... CAN YOU STOP JUMPING ON PEOPLE ALL THE TIME?!
ひょい
YOINK
OH, DEAR. I'M SORRY.
IT'S FINE...
THEY'RE BIG...
ARRRGH... MY MOM'S A TOTAL SPACE CASE, WHILE PERSIA'S SUPER SERIOUS...
THEY'RE PROBABLY GONNA GET ALONG LIKE OIL AND WATER...
GASP!

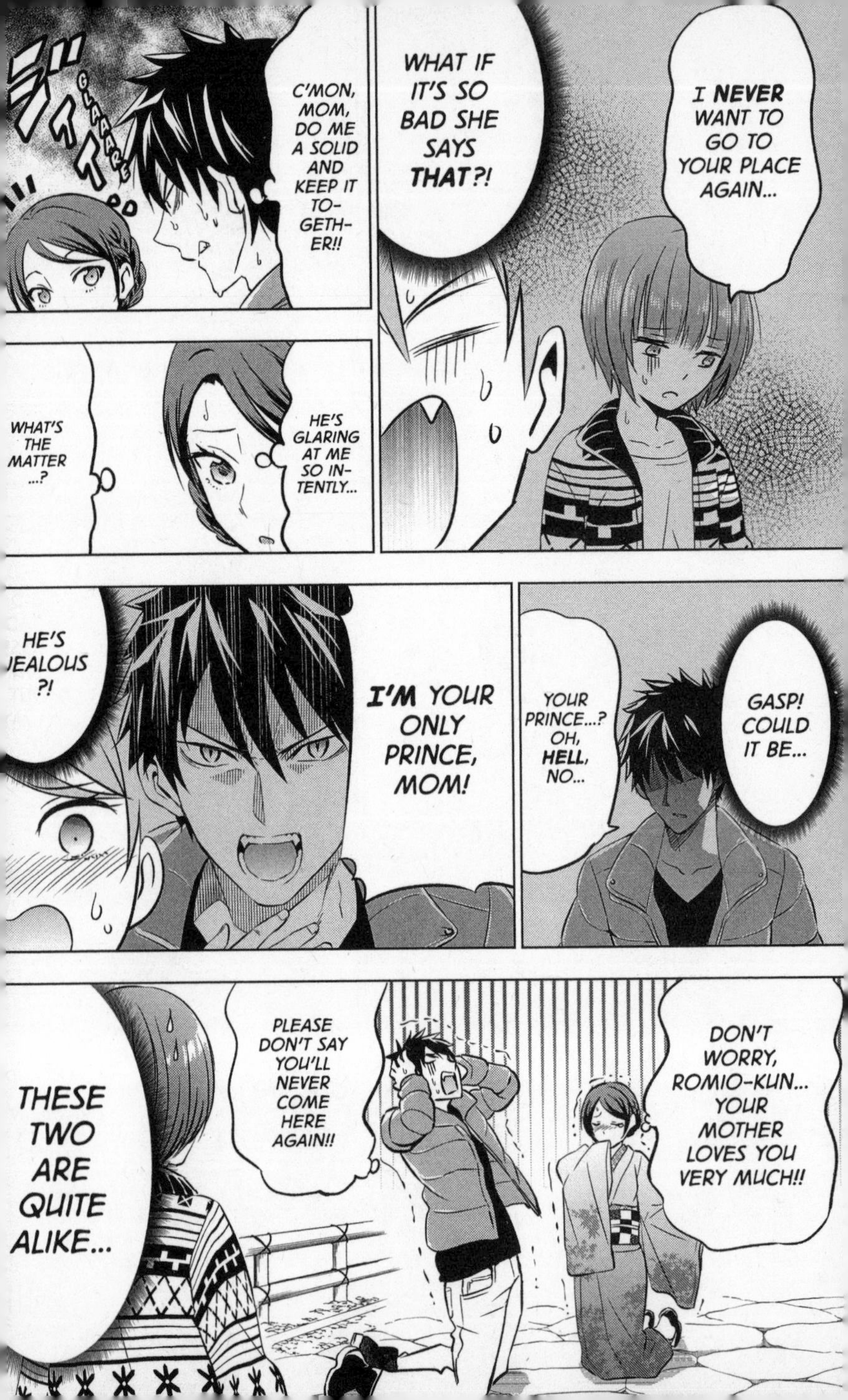
I NEVER WANT TO GO TO YOUR PLACE AGAIN...
WHAT IF IT'S SO BAD SHE SAYS THAT?!
C'MON, MOM, DO ME A SOLID AND KEEP IT TO-GETH-ER!!
GLAAARE
HE'S GLARING AT ME SO IN-TENTLY...
WHAT'S THE MATTER ...?
GASP! COULD IT BE...
YOUR PRINCE...? OH, HELL, NO...
I'M YOUR ONLY PRINCE, MOM!
HE'S JEALOUS ?!
DON'T WORRY, ROMIO-KUN... YOUR MOTHER LOVES YOU VERY MUCH!!
PLEASE DON'T SAY YOU'LL NEVER COME HERE AGAIN!!
THESE TWO ARE QUITE ALIKE...

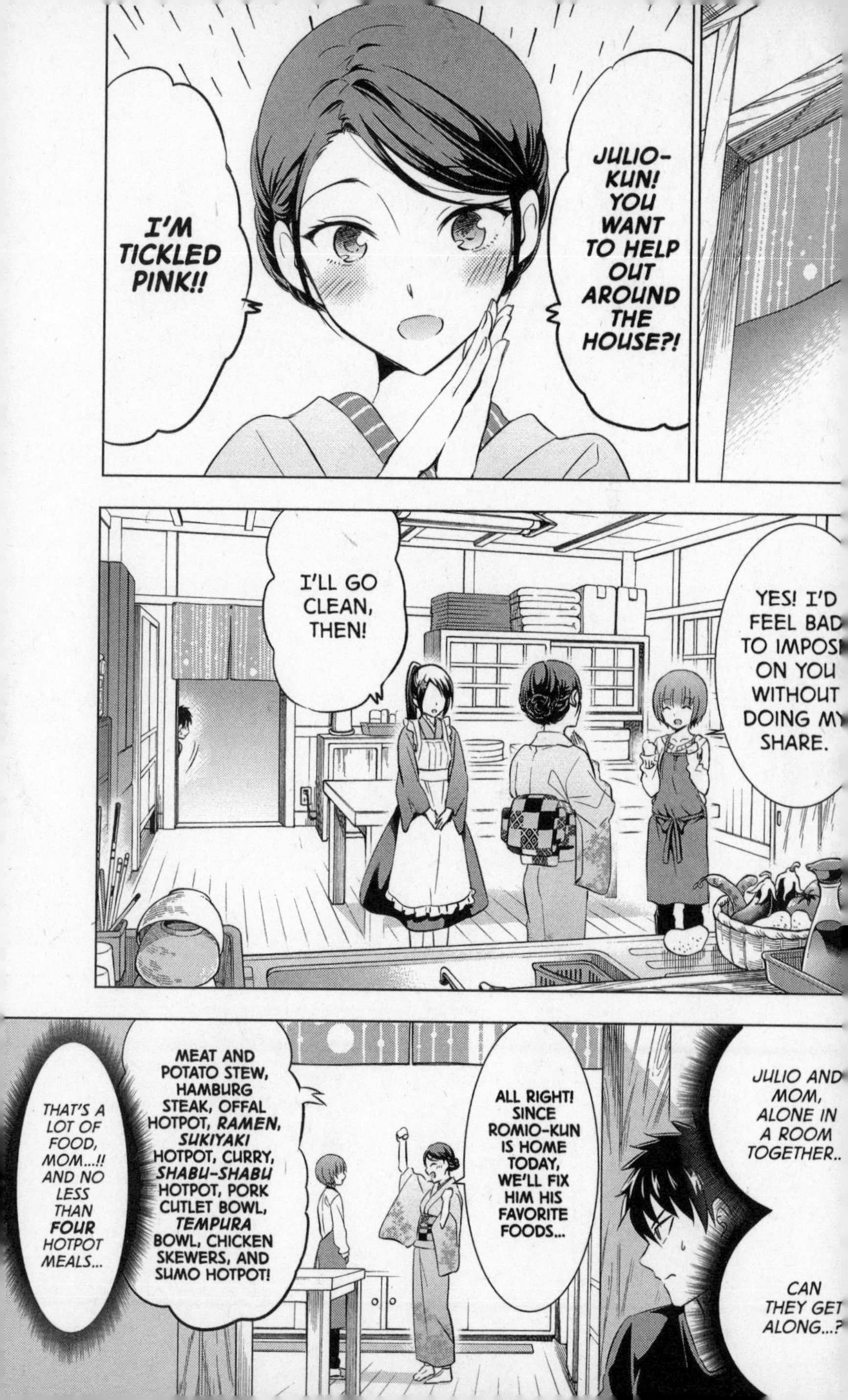

JULIO-KUN! YOU WANT TO HELP OUT AROUND THE HOUSE?!
I'M TICKLED PINK!!
YES! I'D FEEL BAD TO IMPOS ON YOU WITHOUT DOING MY SHARE.
I'LL GO CLEAN, THEN!
JULIO AND MOM, ALONE IN A ROOM TOGETHER..
CAN THEY GET ALONG...?
ALL RIGHT! SINCE ROMIO-KUN IS HOME TODAY, WE'LL FIX HIM HIS FAVORITE FOODS...
MEAT AND POTATO STEW, HAMBURG STEAK, OFFAL HOTPOT, *RAMEN*, *SUKIYAKI* HOTPOT, CURRY, *SHABU-SHABU* HOTPOT, PORK CUTLET BOWL, *TEMPURA* BOWL, CHICKEN SKEWERS, AND SUMO HOTPOT!
THAT'S A LOT OF FOOD, MOM...!! AND NO LESS THAN **FOUR** HOTPOT MEALS...

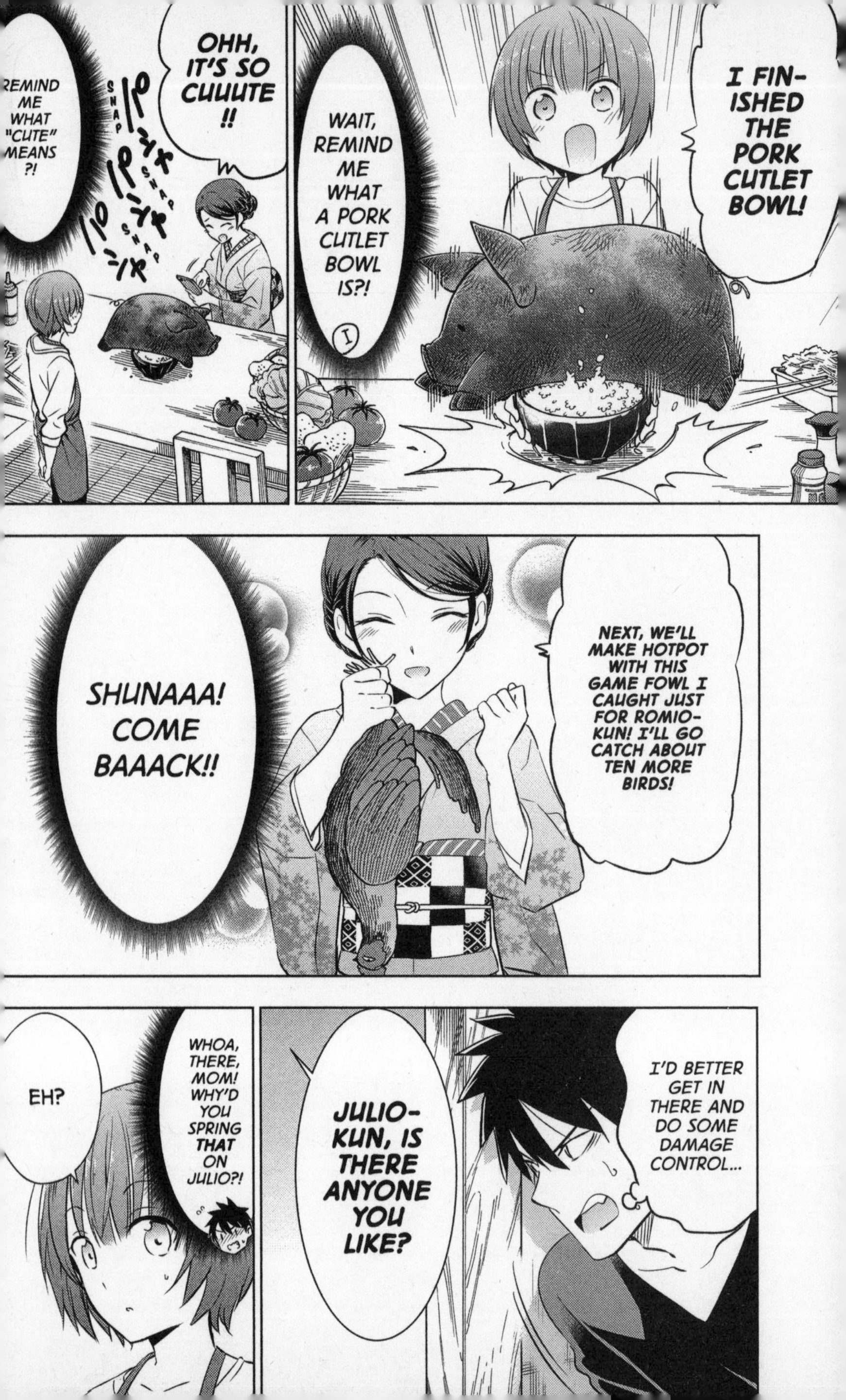

I FIN-ISHED THE PORK CUTLET BOWL!
WAIT, REMIND ME WHAT A PORK CUTLET BOWL IS?!
OHH, IT'S SO CUUUTE!!
SNAP
SNAP
SNAP
REMIND ME WHAT "CUTE" MEANS?!
NEXT, WE'LL MAKE HOTPOT WITH THIS GAME FOWL I CAUGHT JUST FOR ROMIO-KUN! I'LL GO CATCH ABOUT TEN MORE BIRDS!
SHUNAAA! COME BAAACK!!
I'D BETTER GET IN THERE AND DO SOME DAMAGE CONTROL...
JULIO-KUN, IS THERE ANYONE YOU LIKE?
WHOA, THERE, MOM! WHY'D YOU SPRING THAT ON JULIO?!
EH?

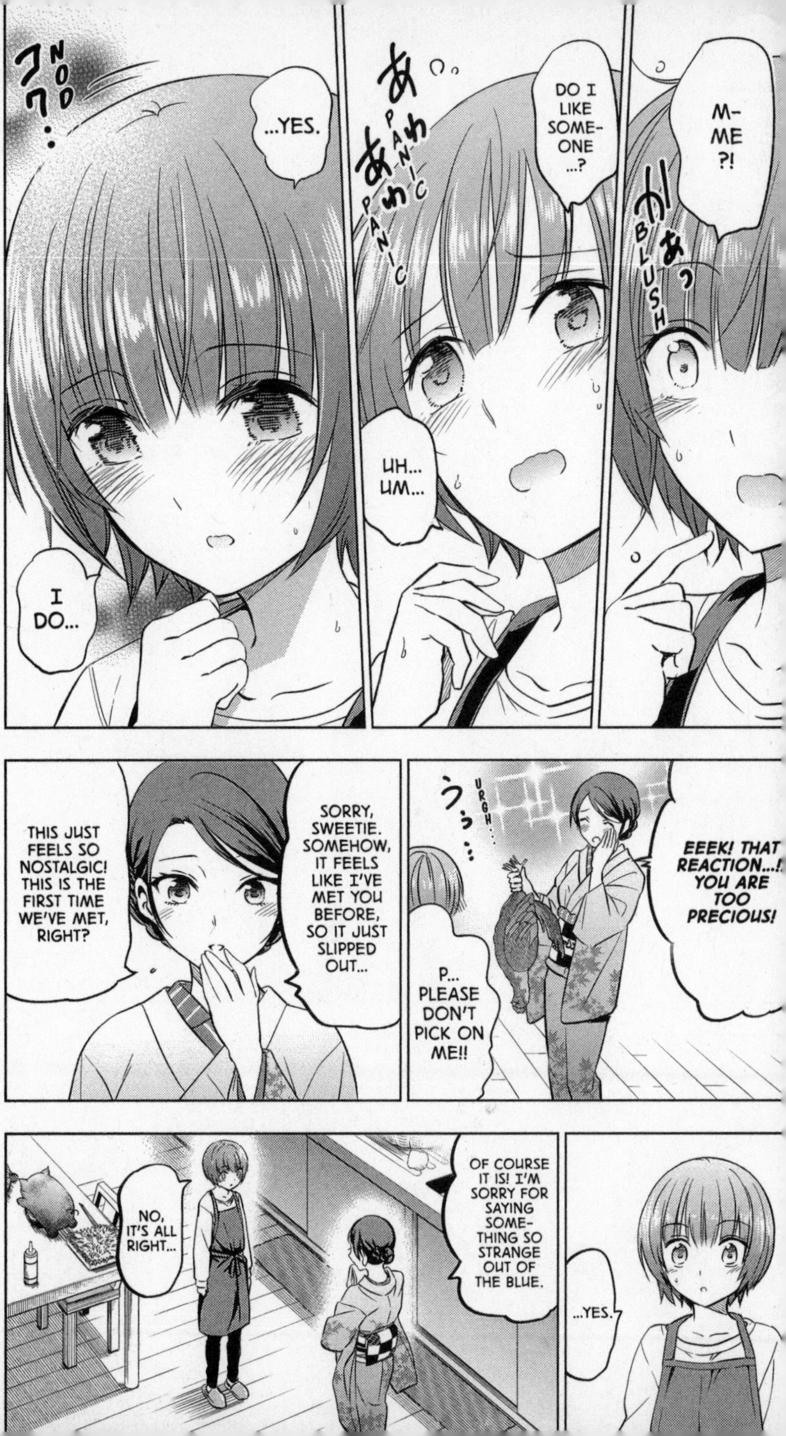
M-ME?!
わぁっ
BLUSH
DO I LIKE SOME-ONE ...?
あわあわ
PANIC PANIC
UH... UM...
...YES.
コクッ
NOD
I DO...
EEEK! THAT REACTION...! YOU ARE TOO PRECIOUS!
うぅ...
URGH...
P... PLEASE DON'T PICK ON ME!!
SORRY, SWEETIE. SOMEHOW, IT FEELS LIKE I'VE MET YOU BEFORE, SO IT JUST SLIPPED OUT...
THIS JUST FEELS SO NOSTALGIC! THIS IS THE FIRST TIME WE'VE MET, RIGHT?
...YES.
OF COURSE IT IS! I'M SORRY FOR SAYING SOME-THING SO STRANGE OUT OF THE BLUE.
NO, IT'S ALL RIGHT...

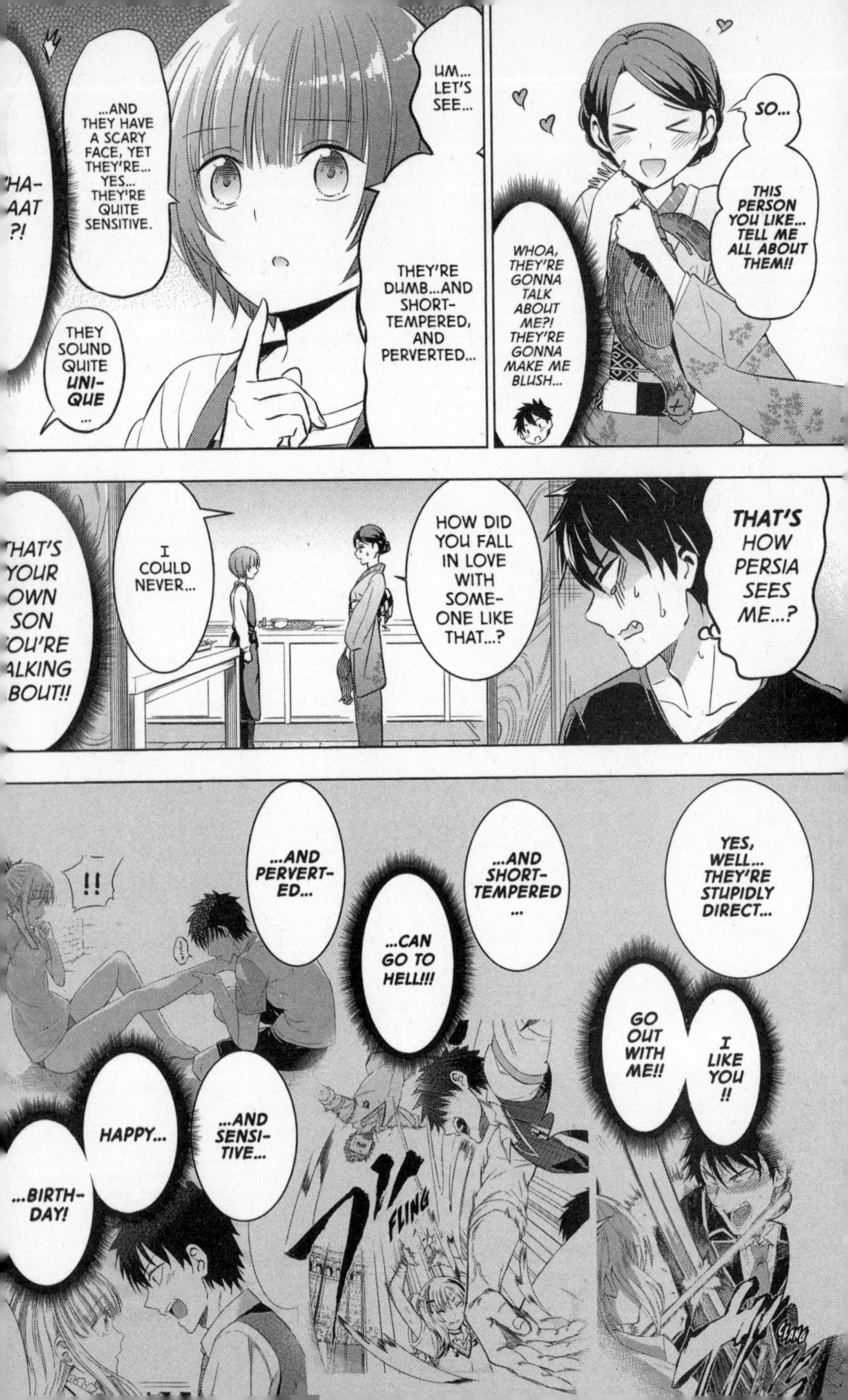
SO...
THIS PERSON YOU LIKE... TELL ME ALL ABOUT THEM!!
WHOA, THEY'RE GONNA TALK ABOUT ME?! THEY'RE GONNA MAKE ME BLUSH...
UM... LET'S SEE...
THEY'RE DUMB...AND SHORT-TEMPERED, AND PERVERTED...
...AND THEY HAVE A SCARY FACE, YET THEY'RE... YES... THEY'RE QUITE SENSITIVE.
THEY SOUND QUITE UNIQUE ...
HA-AAT ?!
THAT'S HOW PERSIA SEES ME...?
HOW DID YOU FALL IN LOVE WITH SOME-ONE LIKE THAT...?
I COULD NEVER...
HAT'S YOUR OWN SON OU'RE ALKING BOUT!!
YES, WELL... THEY'RE STUPIDLY DIRECT...
I LIKE YOU!!
GO OUT WITH ME!!
CLANG
...AND SHORT-TEMPERED ...
...CAN GO TO HELL!!!
FLING
...AND PERVERT-ED...
!!
...AND SENSI-TIVE...
HAPPY...
...BIRTH-DAY!

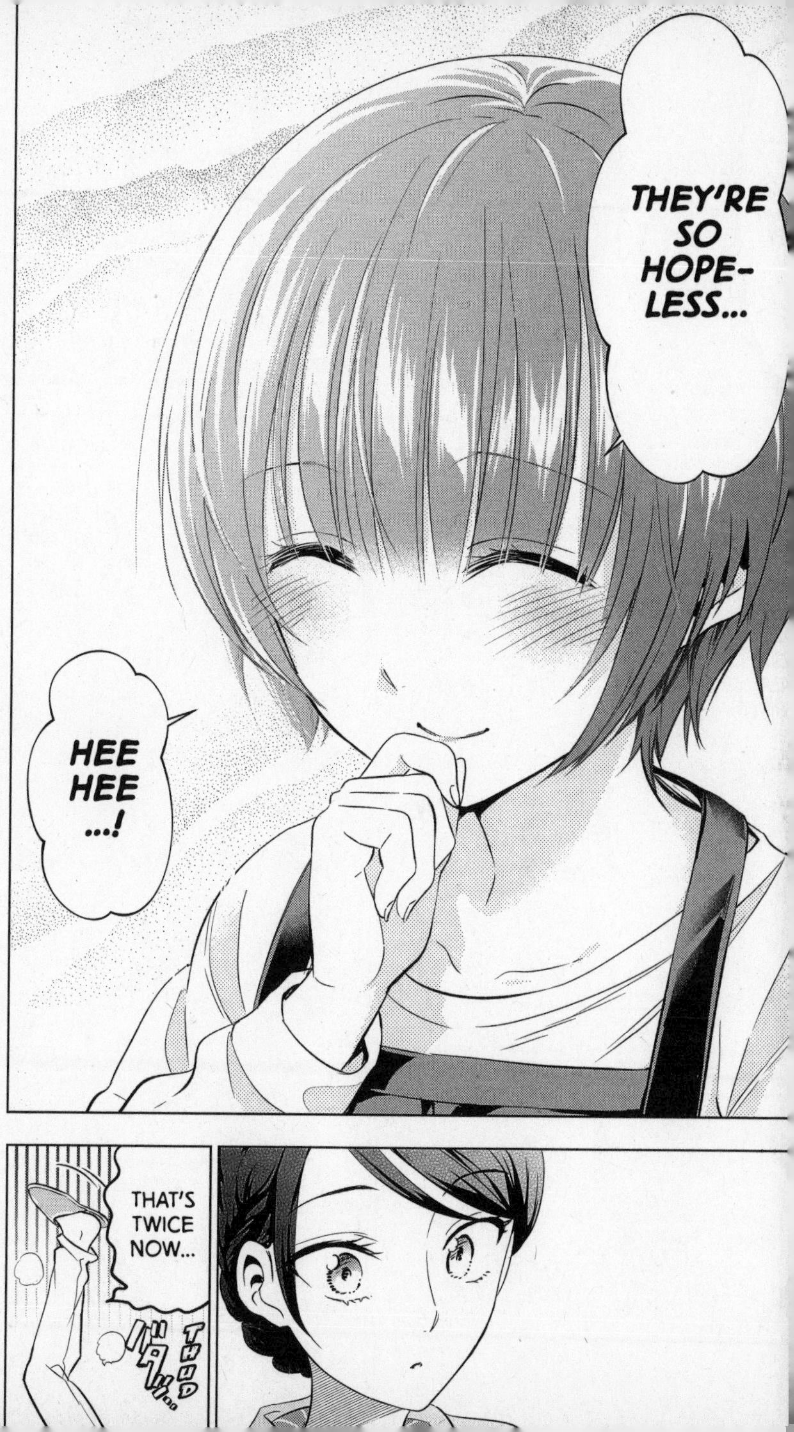
THEY'RE SO HOPE-LESS...
HEE HEE ...!
THAT'S TWICE NOW...
THUD

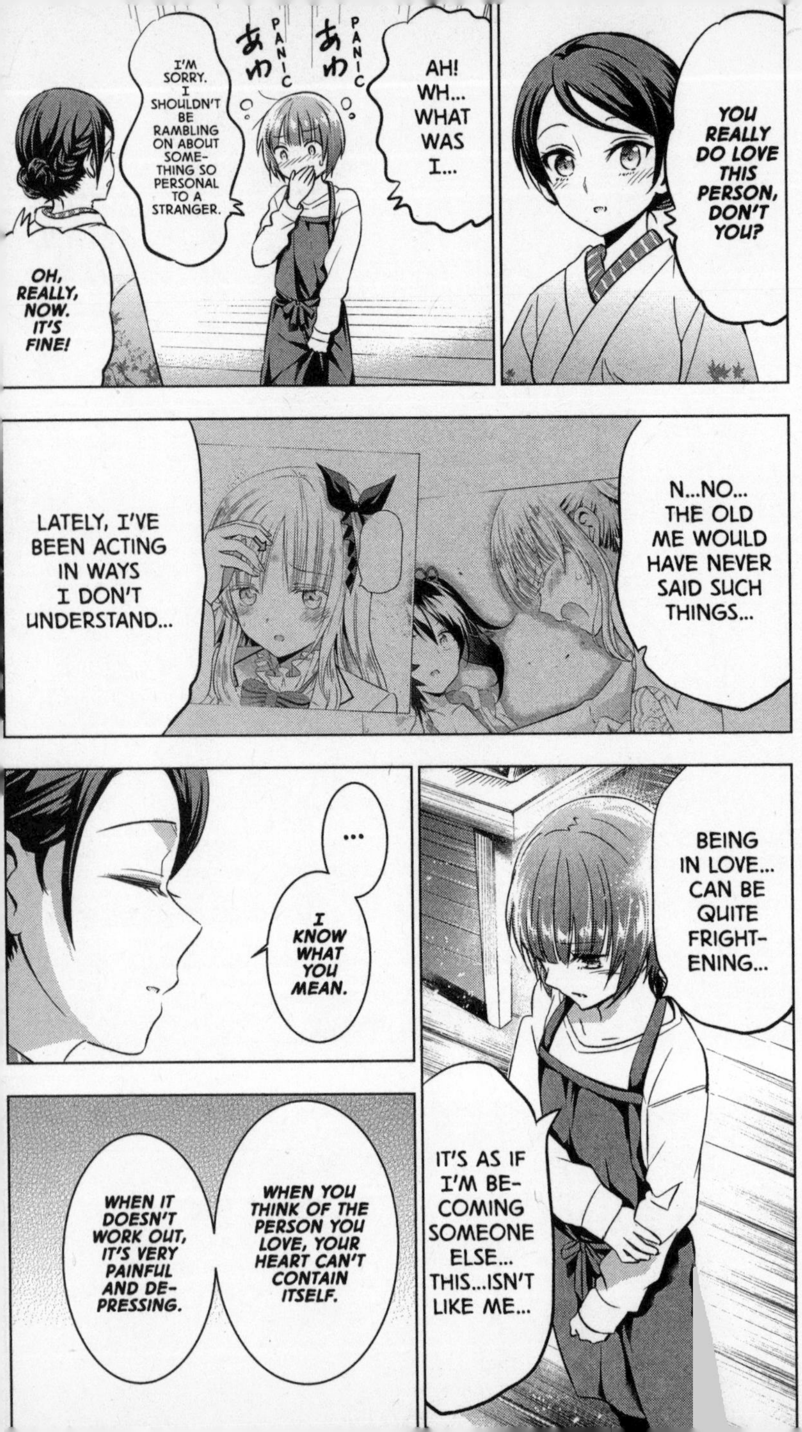
YOU REALLY DO LOVE THIS PERSON, DON'T YOU?
AH! WH... WHAT WAS I...
あわ PANIC
あわ PANIC
I'M SORRY. I SHOULDN'T BE RAMBLING ON ABOUT SOME-THING SO PERSONAL TO A STRANGER.
OH, REALLY, NOW. IT'S FINE!
N...NO... THE OLD ME WOULD HAVE NEVER SAID SUCH THINGS...
LATELY, I'VE BEEN ACTING IN WAYS I DON'T UNDERSTAND...
BEING IN LOVE... CAN BE QUITE FRIGHT-ENING...
IT'S AS IF I'M BE-COMING SOMEONE ELSE... THIS...ISN'T LIKE ME...
...
I KNOW WHAT YOU MEAN.
WHEN YOU THINK OF THE PERSON YOU LOVE, YOUR HEART CAN'T CONTAIN ITSELF.
WHEN IT DOESN'T WORK OUT, IT'S VERY PAINFUL AND DE-PRESSING.

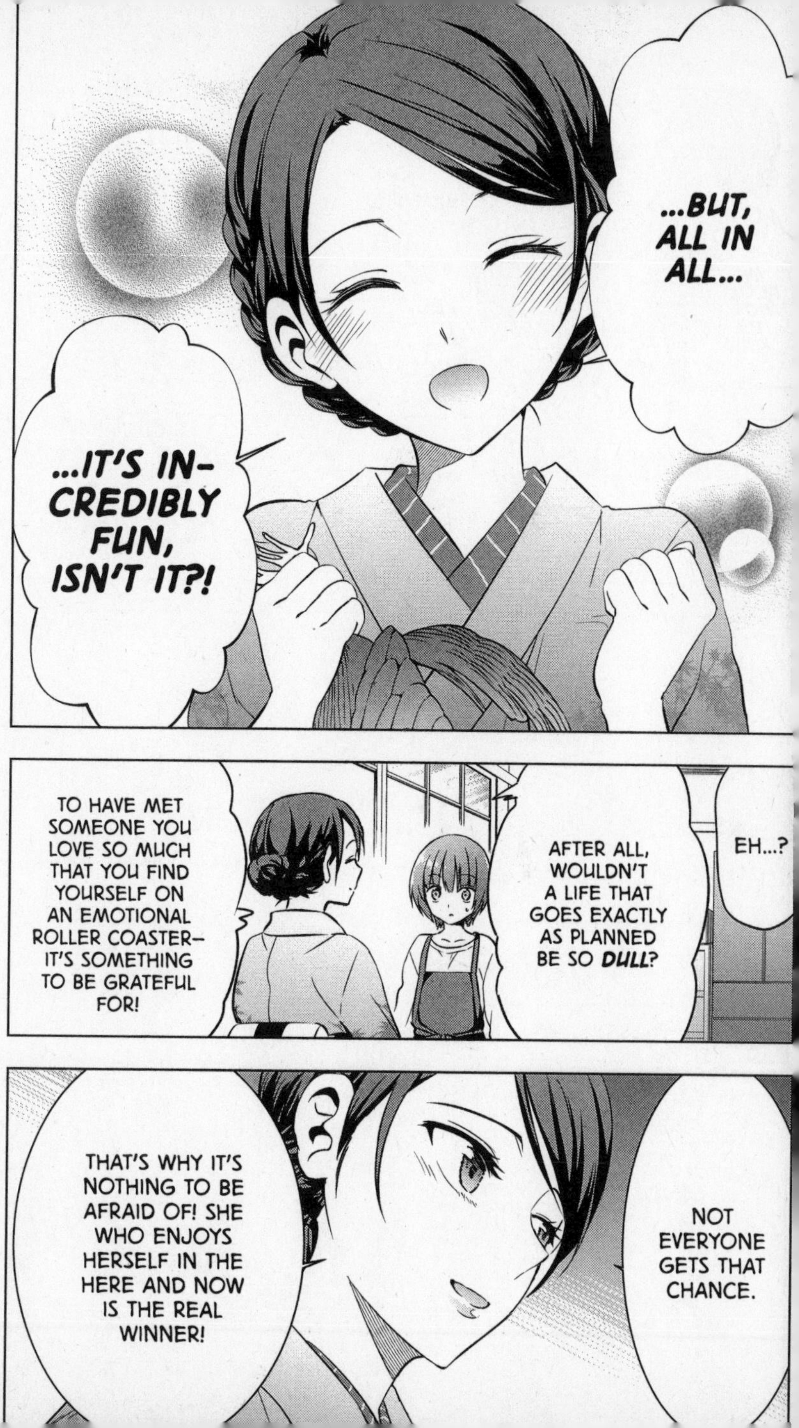
...BUT, ALL IN ALL...
...IT'S IN-CREDIBLY FUN, ISN'T IT?!
EH...?
AFTER ALL, WOULDN'T A LIFE THAT GOES EXACTLY AS PLANNED BE SO *DULL*?
TO HAVE MET SOMEONE YOU LOVE SO MUCH THAT YOU FIND YOURSELF ON AN EMOTIONAL ROLLER COASTER– IT'S SOMETHING TO BE GRATEFUL FOR!
NOT EVERYONE GETS THAT CHANCE.
THAT'S WHY IT'S NOTHING TO BE AFRAID OF! SHE WHO ENJOYS HERSELF IN THE HERE AND NOW IS THE REAL WINNER!

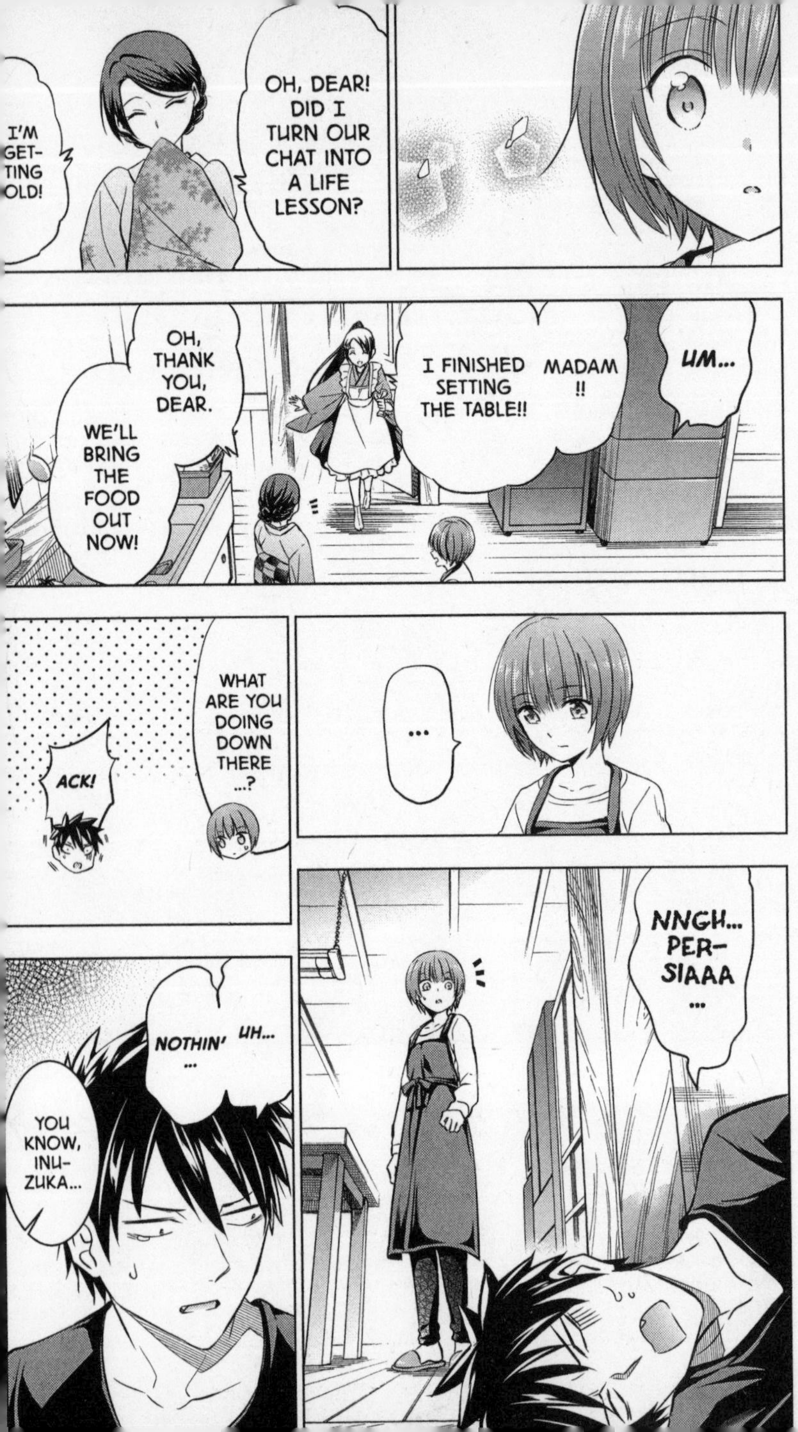
OH, DEAR! DID I TURN OUR CHAT INTO A LIFE LESSON?
I'M GET-TING OLD!
UM...
MADAM !!
I FINISHED SETTING THE TABLE!!
OH, THANK YOU, DEAR.
WE'LL BRING THE FOOD OUT NOW!
...
WHAT ARE YOU DOING DOWN THERE ...?
ACK!
NNGH... PER-SIAAA ...
UH...
NOTHIN' ...
YOU KNOW, INU-ZUKA...

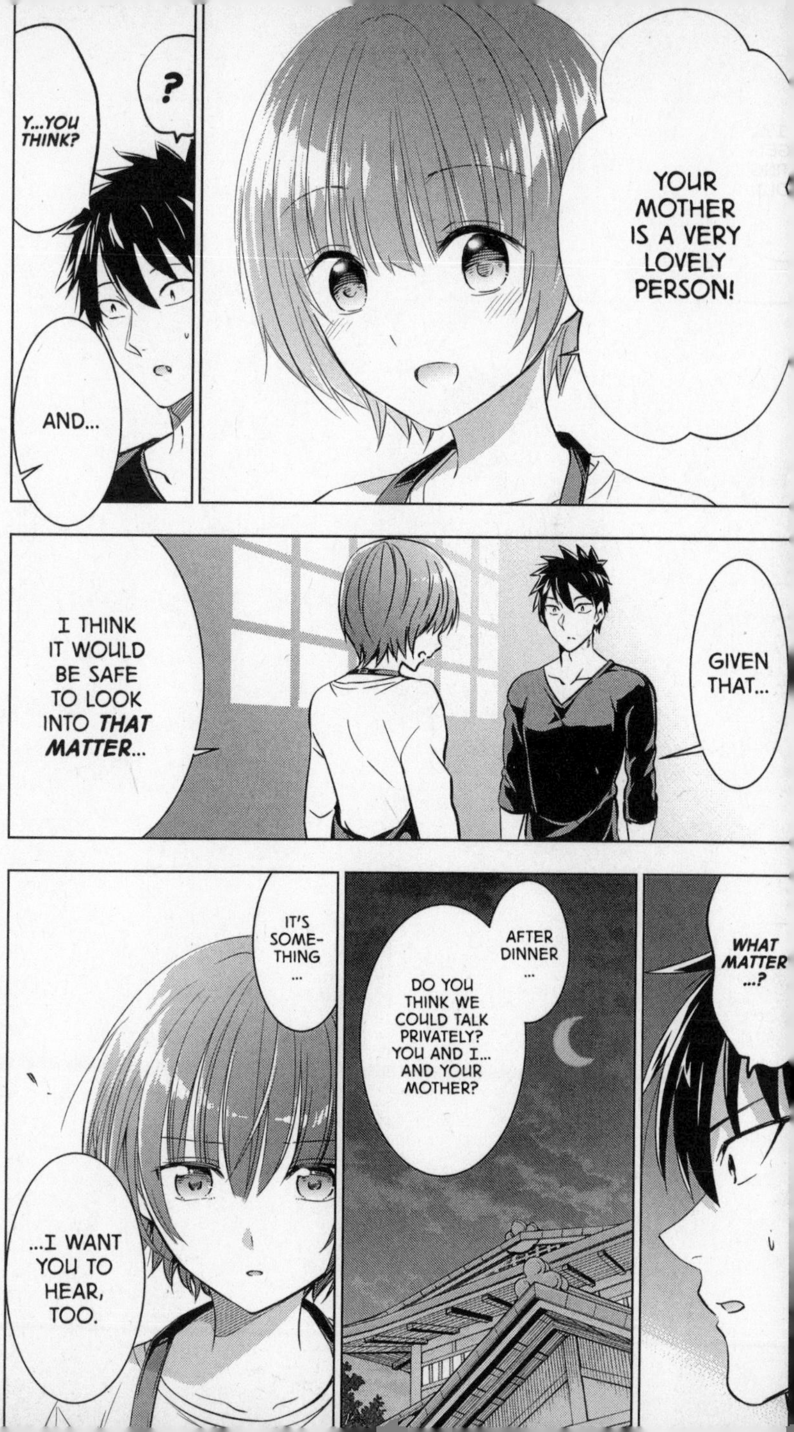
YOUR MOTHER IS A VERY LOVELY PERSON!
?
Y...YOU THINK?
AND...
GIVEN THAT...
I THINK IT WOULD BE SAFE TO LOOK INTO *THAT MATTER*...
WHAT MATTER ...?
AFTER DINNER ...
DO YOU THINK WE COULD TALK PRIVATELY? YOU AND I... AND YOUR MOTHER?
IT'S SOME-THING ...
...I WANT YOU TO HEAR, TOO.

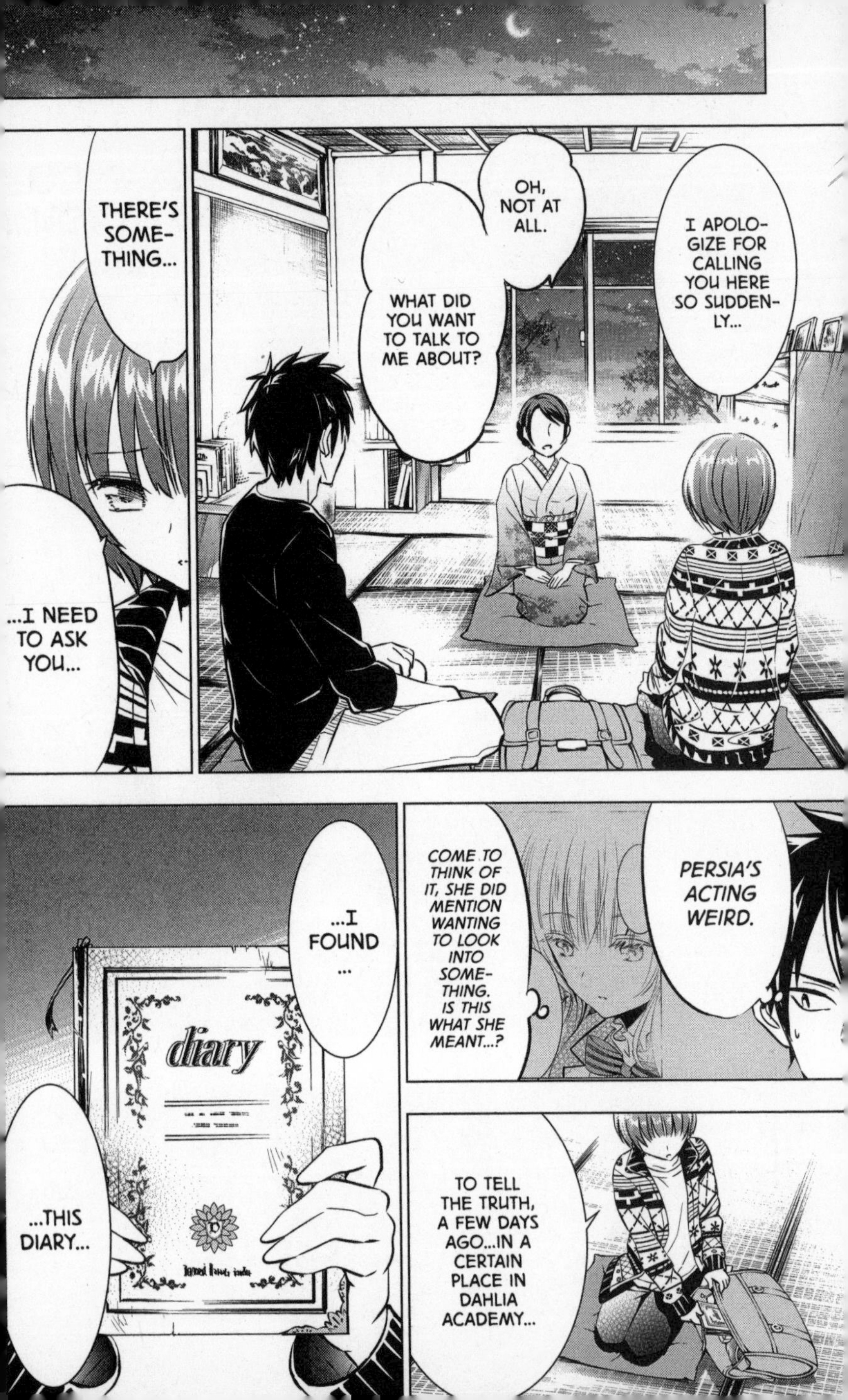
I APOLO-GIZE FOR CALLING YOU HERE SO SUDDEN-LY...
OH, NOT AT ALL.
WHAT DID YOU WANT TO TALK TO ME ABOUT?
THERE'S SOME-THING...
...I NEED TO ASK YOU...
PERSIA'S ACTING WEIRD.
COME TO THINK OF IT, SHE DID MENTION WANTING TO LOOK INTO SOME-THING. IS THIS WHAT SHE MEANT...?
TO TELL THE TRUTH, A FEW DAYS AGO...IN A CERTAIN PLACE IN DAHLIA ACADEMY...
...I FOUND ...
diary
...THIS DIARY...

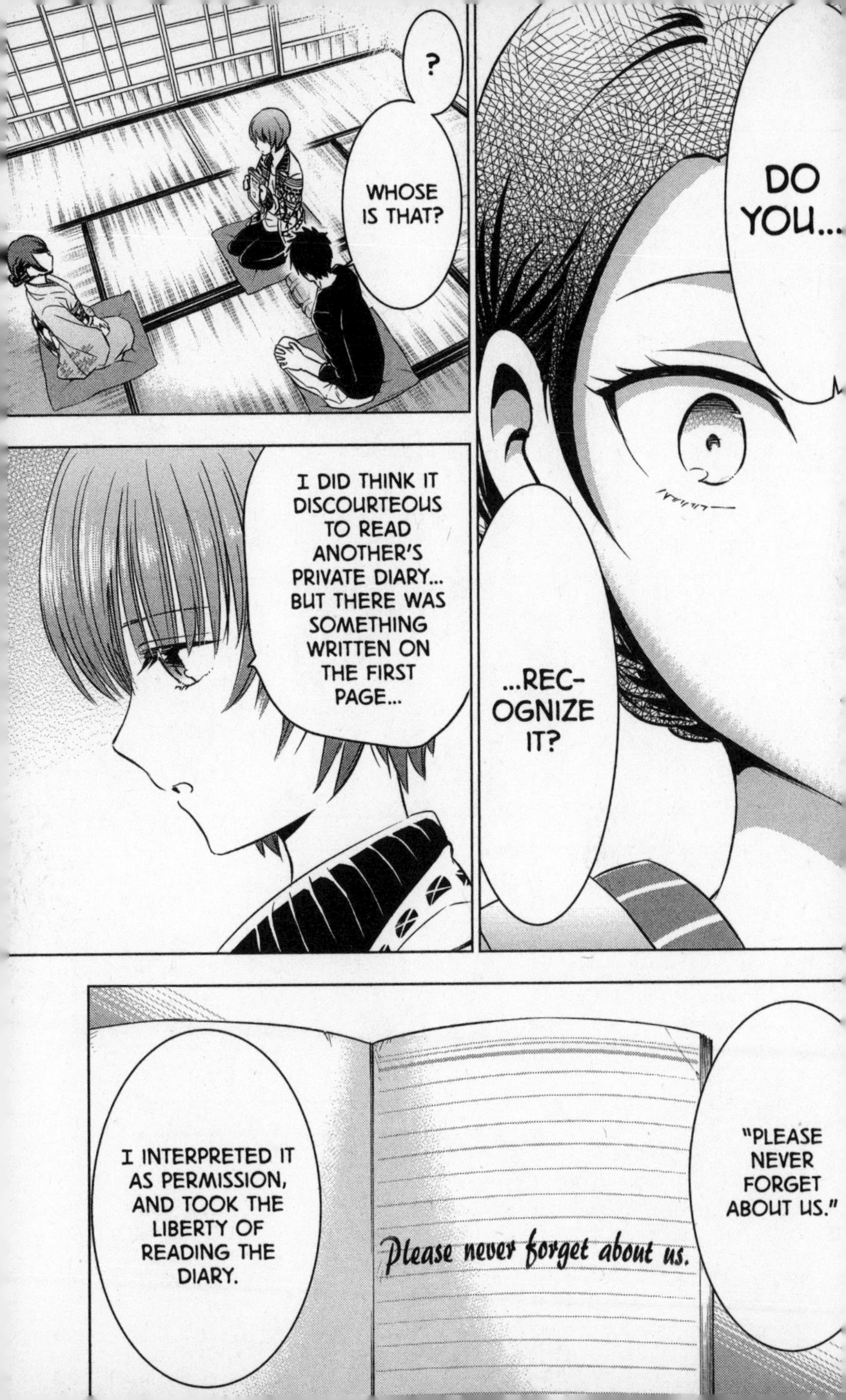
DO YOU...
...REC-OGNIZE IT?
?
WHOSE IS THAT?
I DID THINK IT DISCOURTEOUS TO READ ANOTHER'S PRIVATE DIARY... BUT THERE WAS SOMETHING WRITTEN ON THE FIRST PAGE...
"PLEASE NEVER FORGET ABOUT US."
Please never forget about us.
I INTERPRETED IT AS PERMISSION, AND TOOK THE LIBERTY OF READING THE DIARY.

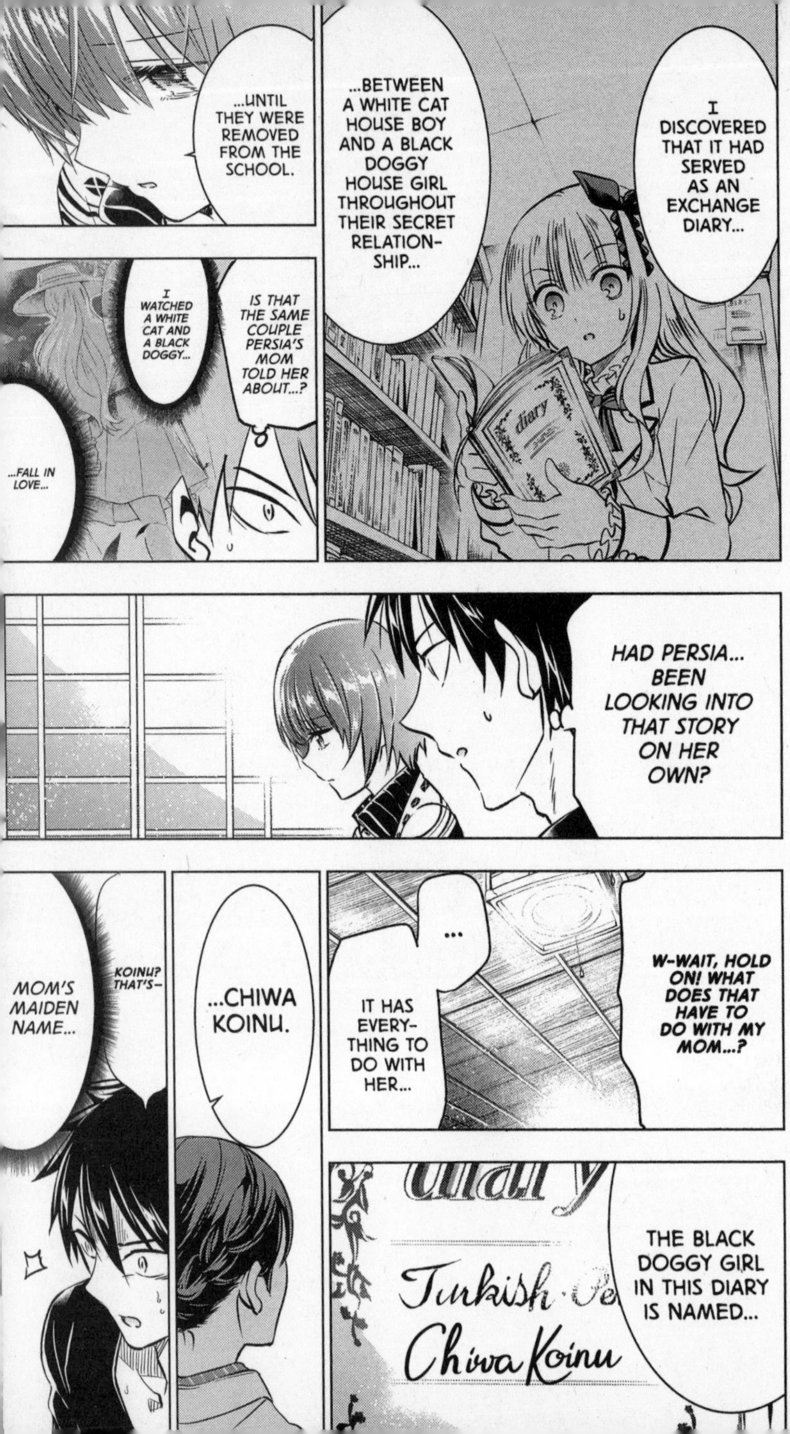
I DISCOVERED THAT IT HAD SERVED AS AN EXCHANGE DIARY...
...BETWEEN A WHITE CAT HOUSE BOY AND A BLACK DOGGY HOUSE GIRL THROUGHOUT THEIR SECRET RELATION-SHIP...
...UNTIL THEY WERE REMOVED FROM THE SCHOOL.
IS THAT THE SAME COUPLE PERSIA'S MOM TOLD HER ABOUT...?
I WATCHED A WHITE CAT AND A BLACK DOGGY...
...FALL IN LOVE...
HAD PERSIA... BEEN LOOKING INTO THAT STORY ON HER OWN?
W-WAIT, HOLD ON! WHAT DOES THAT HAVE TO DO WITH MY MOM...?
...
IT HAS EVERY-THING TO DO WITH HER...
THE BLACK DOGGY GIRL IN THIS DIARY IS NAMED...
Chiwa Koinu
...CHIWA KOINU.
KOINU? THAT'S—
MOM'S MAIDEN NAME...

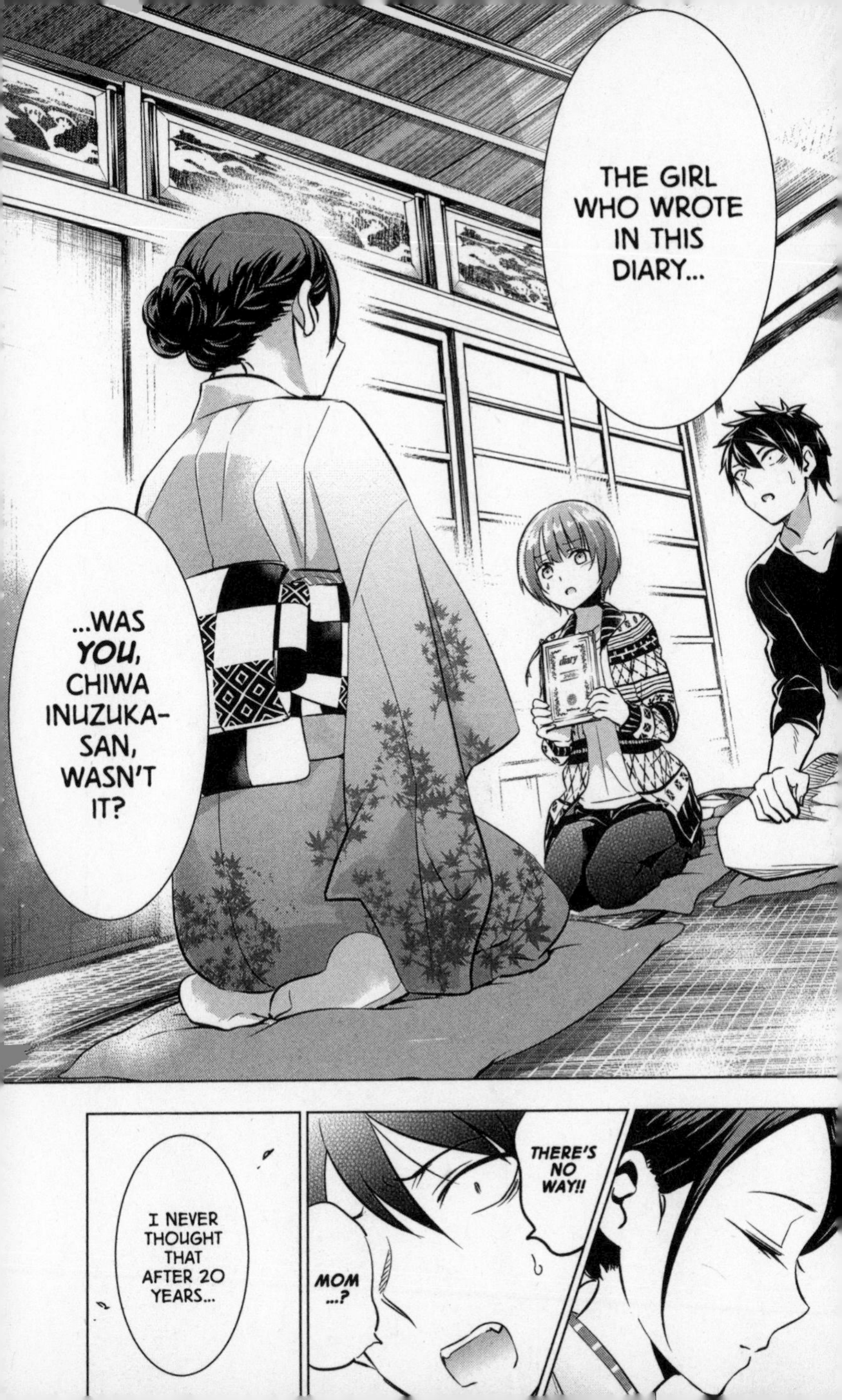
THE GIRL WHO WROTE IN THIS DIARY...
...WAS *YOU*, CHIWA INUZUKA-SAN, WASN'T IT?
THERE'S NO WAY!!
MOM ...?
I NEVER THOUGHT THAT AFTER 20 YEARS...

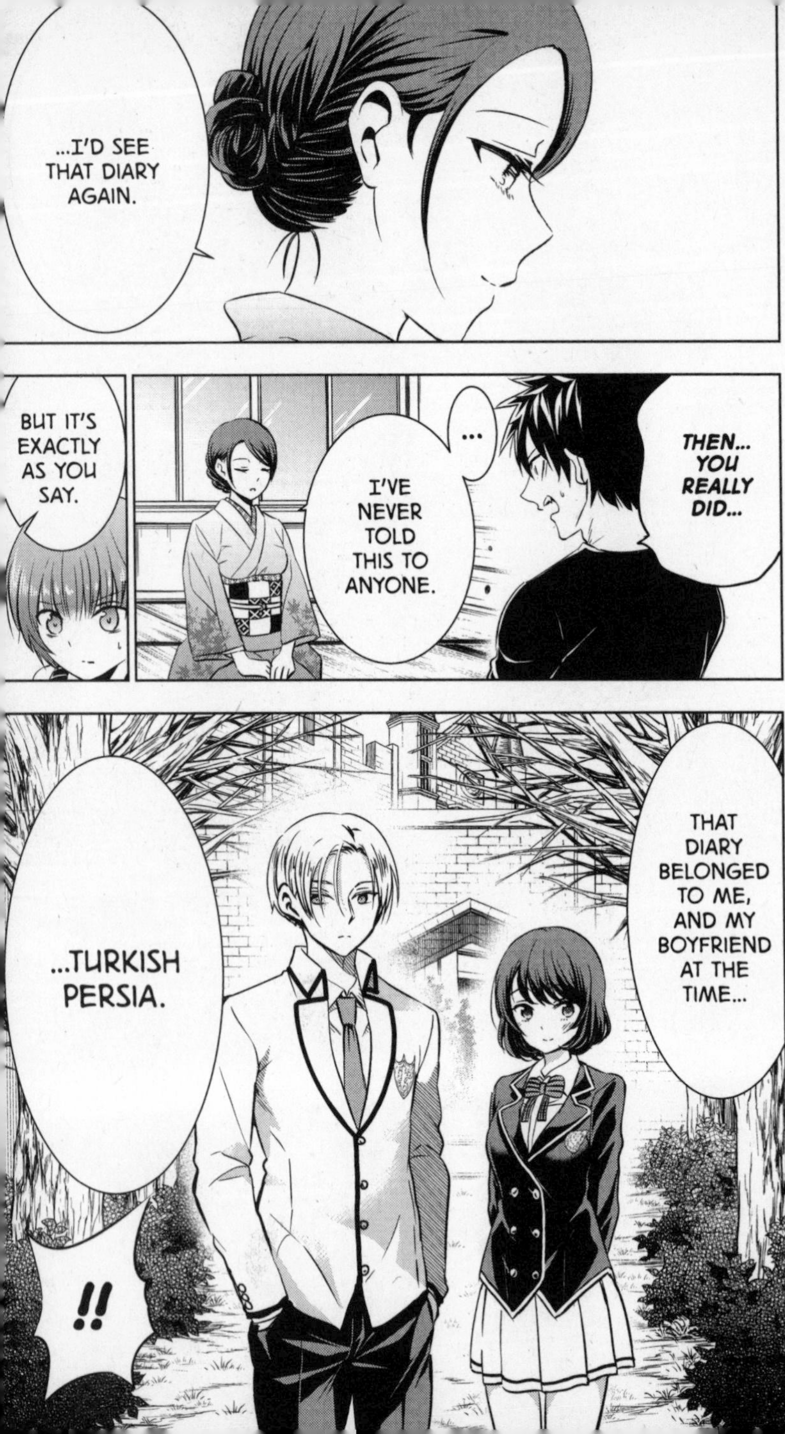
...I'D SEE THAT DIARY AGAIN.
THEN... YOU REALLY DID...
...
I'VE NEVER TOLD THIS TO ANYONE.
BUT IT'S EXACTLY AS YOU SAY.
THAT DIARY BELONGED TO ME, AND MY BOYFRIEND AT THE TIME...
...TURKISH PERSIA.
!!

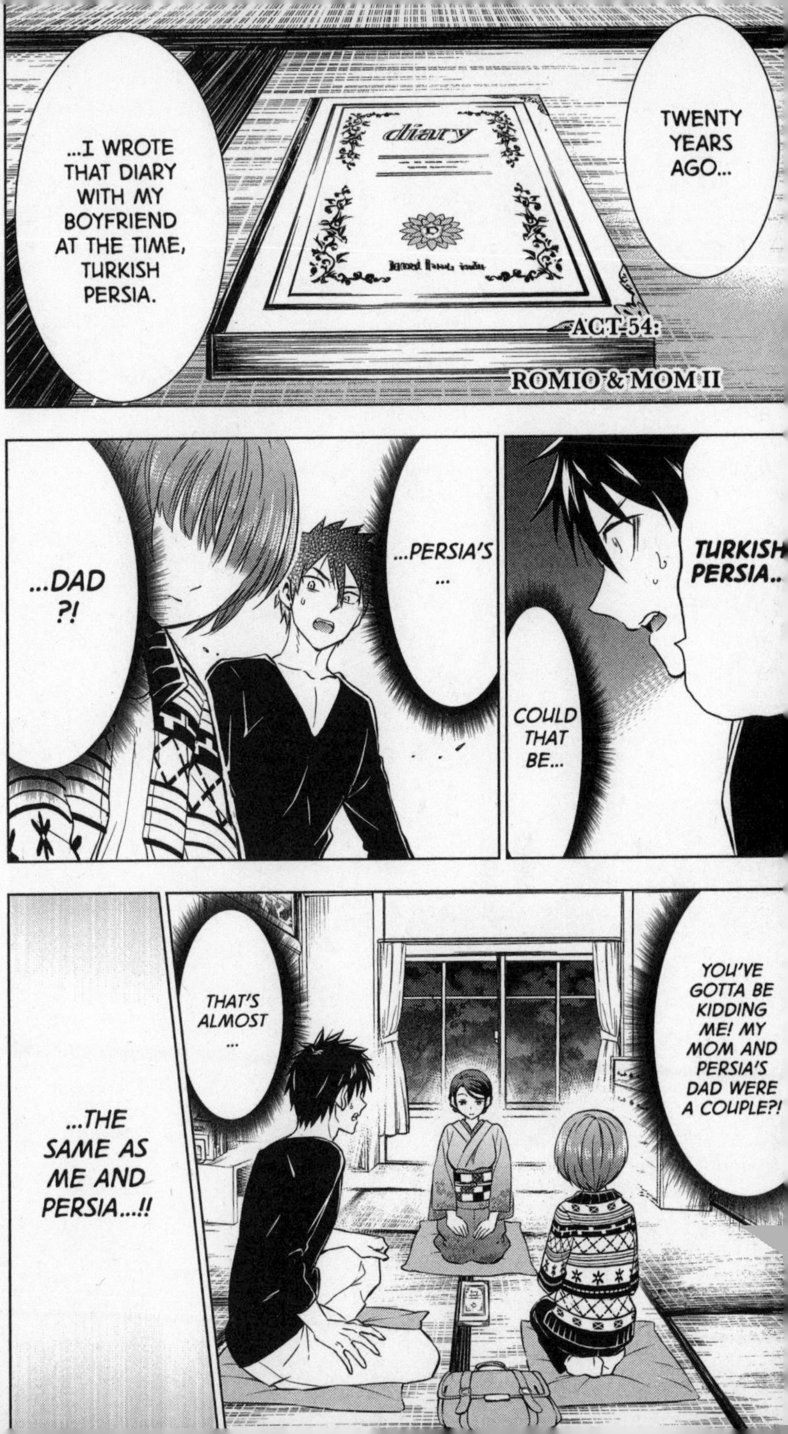
TWENTY YEARS AGO...
...I WROTE THAT DIARY WITH MY BOYFRIEND AT THE TIME, TURKISH PERSIA.
diary
ACT 54:
ROMIO & MOM II
TURKISH PERSIA..
COULD THAT BE...
...PERSIA'S ...
...DAD ?!
YOU'VE GOTTA BE KIDDING ME! MY MOM AND PERSIA'S DAD WERE A COUPLE?!
THAT'S ALMOST ...
...THE SAME AS ME AND PERSIA...!!

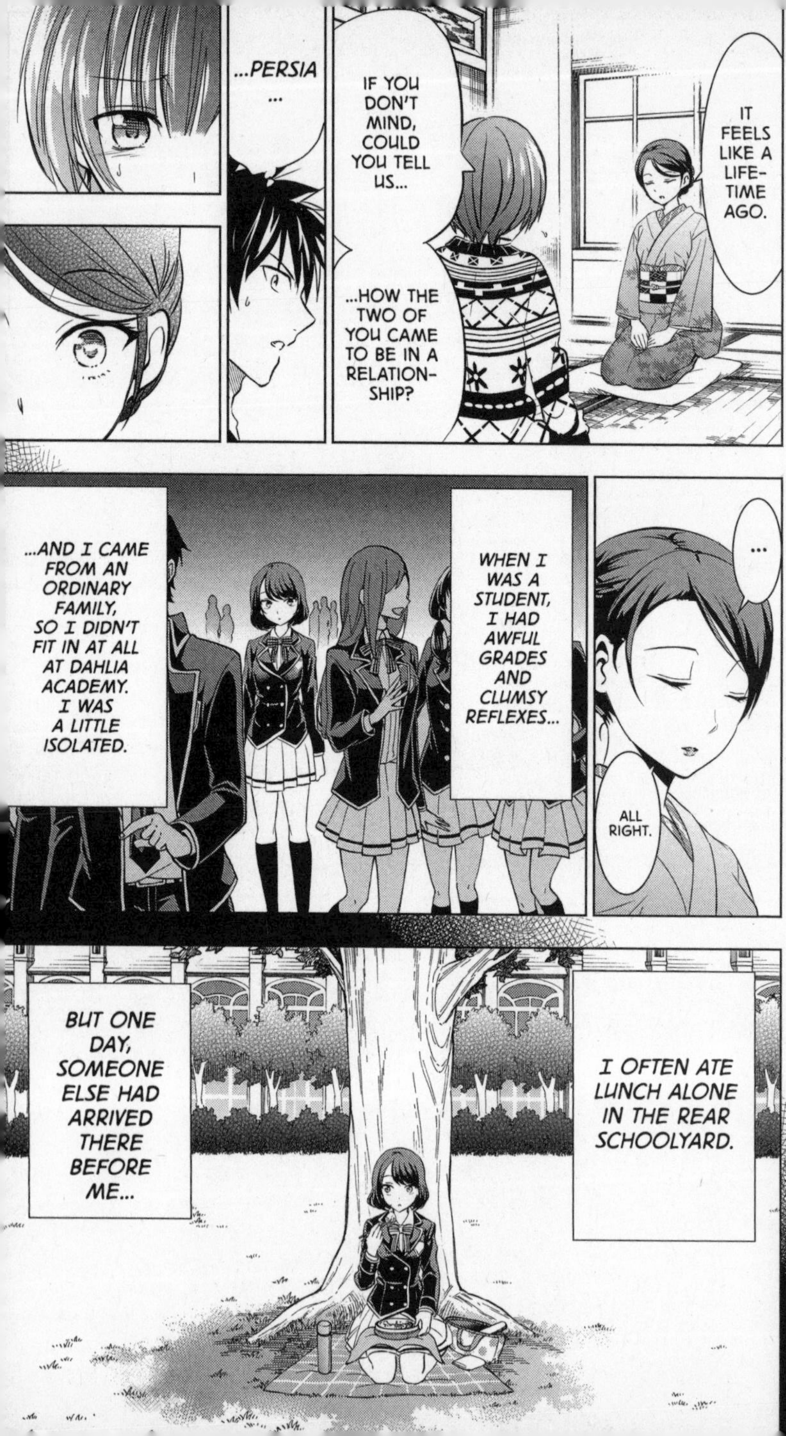
IT FEELS LIKE A LIFE-TIME AGO.
IF YOU DON'T MIND, COULD YOU TELL US...
...HOW THE TWO OF YOU CAME TO BE IN A RELATION-SHIP?
...PERSIA ...
...
ALL RIGHT.
WHEN I WAS A STUDENT, I HAD AWFUL GRADES AND CLUMSY REFLEXES...
...AND I CAME FROM AN ORDINARY FAMILY, SO I DIDN'T FIT IN AT ALL AT DAHLIA ACADEMY. I WAS A LITTLE ISOLATED.
I OFTEN ATE LUNCH ALONE IN THE REAR SCHOOLYARD.
BUT ONE DAY, SOMEONE ELSE HAD ARRIVED THERE BEFORE ME...

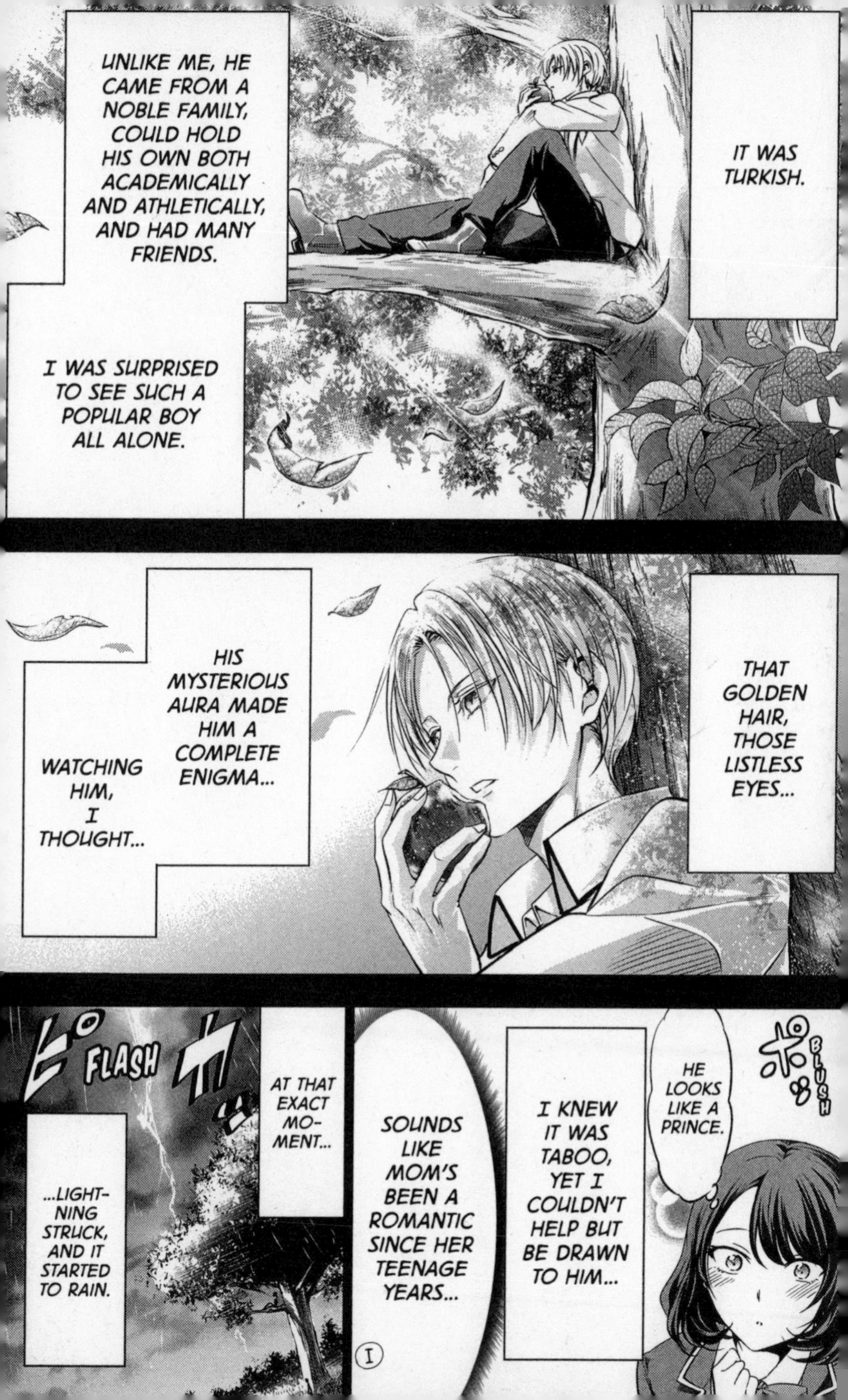
IT WAS TURKISH.
UNLIKE ME, HE CAME FROM A NOBLE FAMILY, COULD HOLD HIS OWN BOTH ACADEMICALLY AND ATHLETICALLY, AND HAD MANY FRIENDS.
I WAS SURPRISED TO SEE SUCH A POPULAR BOY ALL ALONE.
THAT GOLDEN HAIR, THOSE LISTLESS EYES...
HIS MYSTERIOUS AURA MADE HIM A COMPLETE ENIGMA...
WATCHING HIM, I THOUGHT...
BLUSH
HE LOOKS LIKE A PRINCE.
I KNEW IT WAS TABOO, YET I COULDN'T HELP BUT BE DRAWN TO HIM...
SOUNDS LIKE MOM'S BEEN A ROMANTIC SINCE HER TEENAGE YEARS...
AT THAT EXACT MO-MENT...
FLASH
...LIGHT-NING STRUCK, AND IT STARTED TO RAIN.

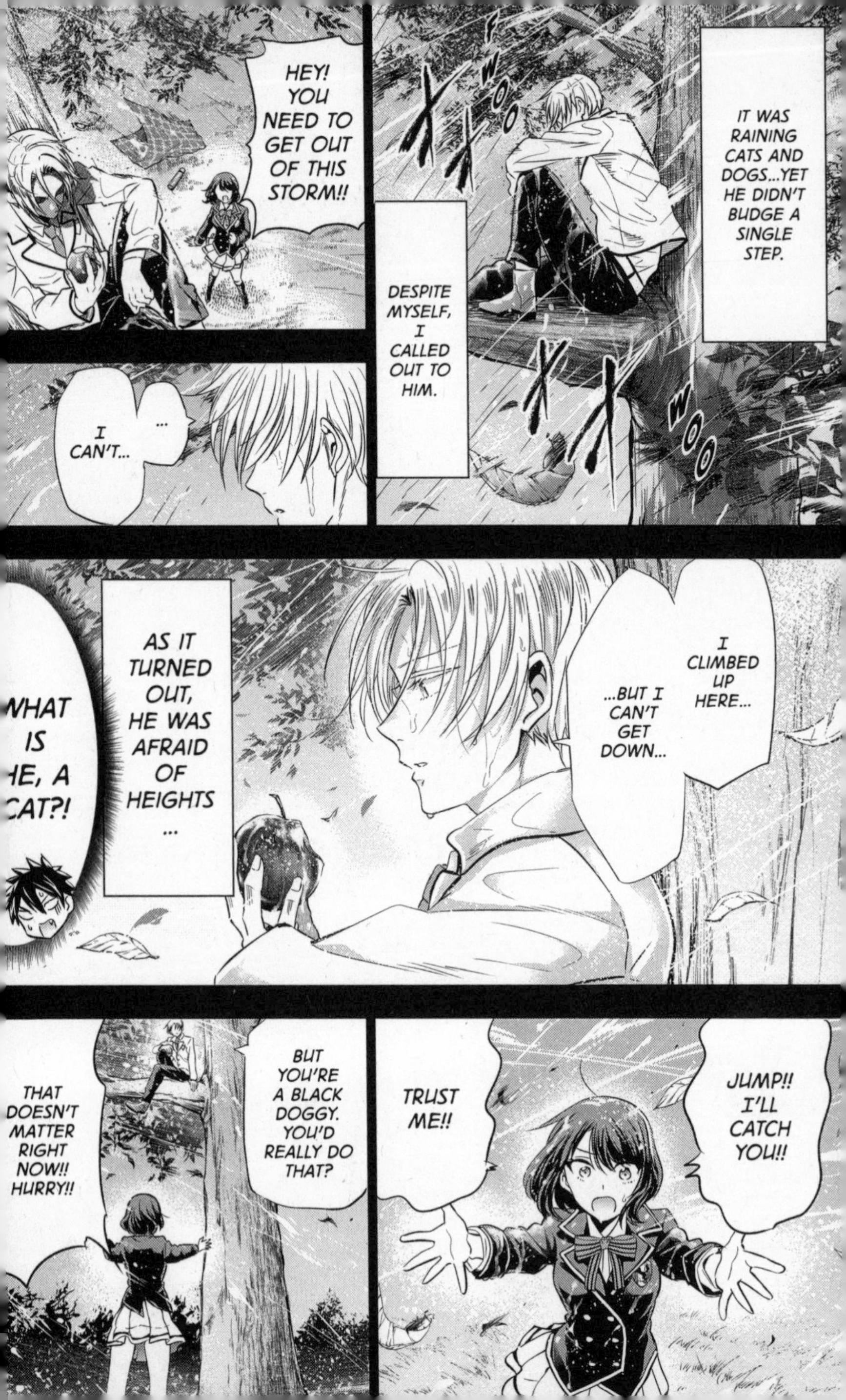
IT WAS RAINING CATS AND DOGS...YET HE DIDN'T BUDGE A SINGLE STEP.
FWOO
DESPITE MYSELF, I CALLED OUT TO HIM.
WOO
HEY! YOU NEED TO GET OUT OF THIS STORM!!
...
I CAN'T...
I CLIMBED UP HERE...
...BUT I CAN'T GET DOWN...
AS IT TURNED OUT, HE WAS AFRAID OF HEIGHTS...
WHAT IS HE, A CAT?!
JUMP!! I'LL CATCH YOU!!
TRUST ME!!
BUT YOU'RE A BLACK DOGGY. YOU'D REALLY DO THAT?
THAT DOESN'T MATTER RIGHT NOW!! HURRY!!

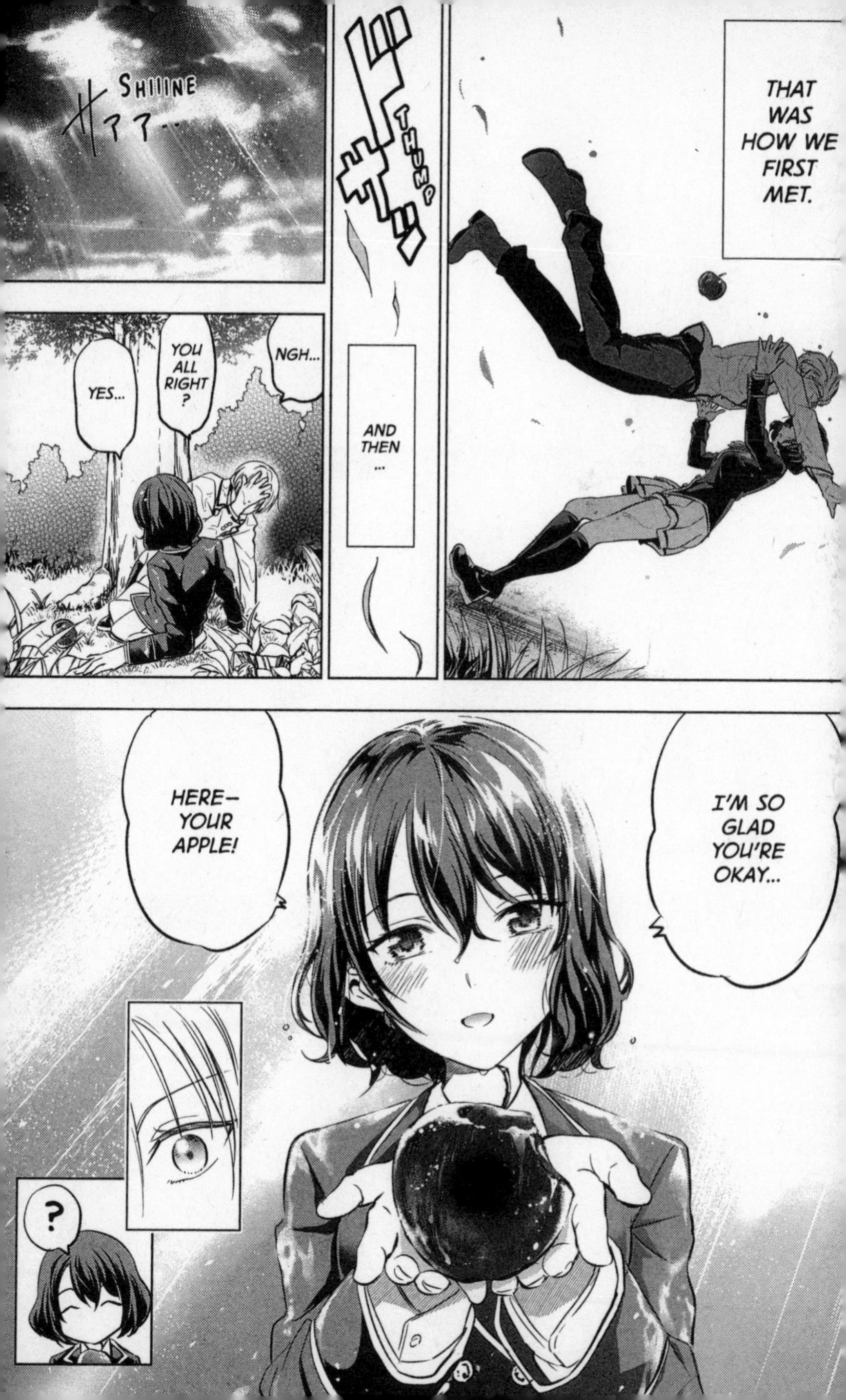
THAT WAS HOW WE FIRST MET.
THUMP
AND THEN ...
SHIIINE
サァァ…
NGH...
YOU ALL RIGHT?
YES...
I'M SO GLAD YOU'RE OKAY...
HERE— YOUR APPLE!
?

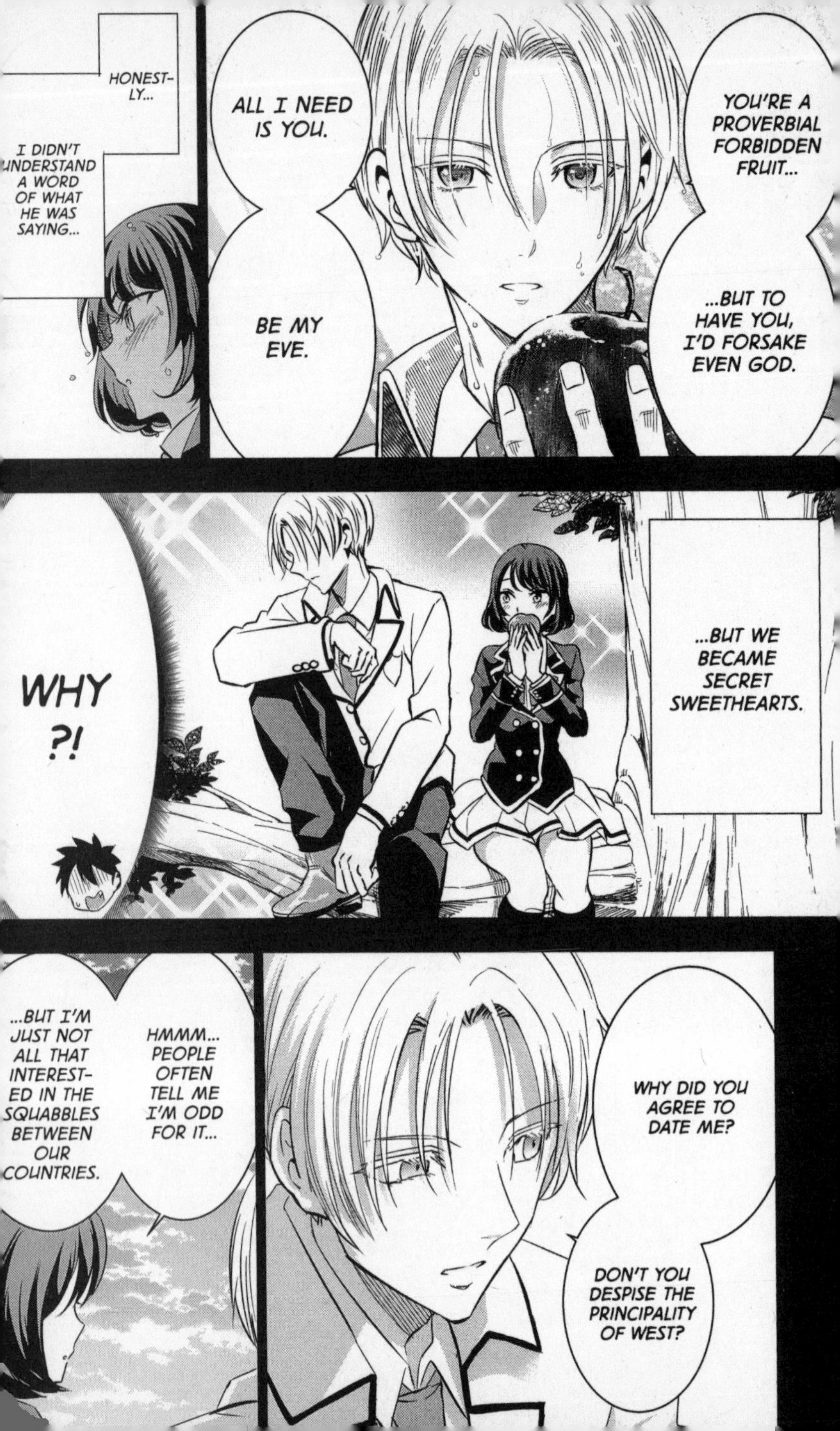
YOU'RE A PROVERBIAL FORBIDDEN FRUIT...
...BUT TO HAVE YOU, I'D FORSAKE EVEN GOD.
ALL I NEED IS YOU.
BE MY EVE.
HONESTLY...
I DIDN'T UNDERSTAND A WORD OF WHAT HE WAS SAYING...
...BUT WE BECAME SECRET SWEETHEARTS.
WHY?!
WHY DID YOU AGREE TO DATE ME?
DON'T YOU DESPISE THE PRINCIPALITY OF WEST?
HMMM... PEOPLE OFTEN TELL ME I'M ODD FOR IT...
...BUT I'M JUST NOT ALL THAT INTERESTED IN THE SQUABBLES BETWEEN OUR COUNTRIES.

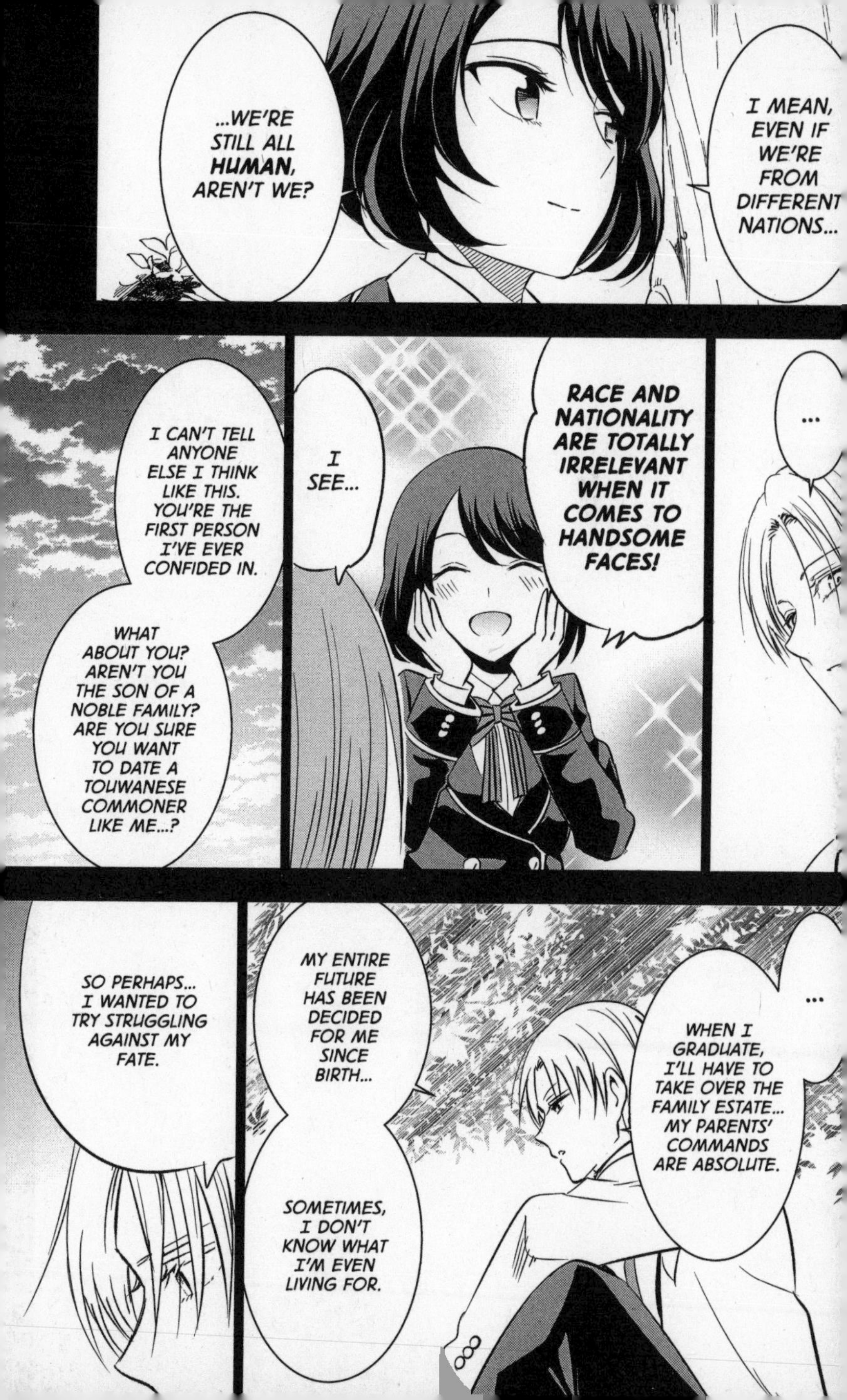
I MEAN, EVEN IF WE'RE FROM DIFFERENT NATIONS...
...WE'RE STILL ALL **HUMAN**, AREN'T WE?
...
RACE AND NATIONALITY ARE TOTALLY IRRELEVANT WHEN IT COMES TO HANDSOME FACES!
I SEE...
I CAN'T TELL ANYONE ELSE I THINK LIKE THIS. YOU'RE THE FIRST PERSON I'VE EVER CONFIDED IN.
WHAT ABOUT YOU? AREN'T YOU THE SON OF A NOBLE FAMILY? ARE YOU SURE YOU WANT TO DATE A TOUWANESE COMMONER LIKE ME...?
...
WHEN I GRADUATE, I'LL HAVE TO TAKE OVER THE FAMILY ESTATE... MY PARENTS' COMMANDS ARE ABSOLUTE.
MY ENTIRE FUTURE HAS BEEN DECIDED FOR ME SINCE BIRTH...
SOMETIMES, I DON'T KNOW WHAT I'M EVEN LIVING FOR.
SO PERHAPS... I WANTED TO TRY STRUGGLING AGAINST MY FATE.

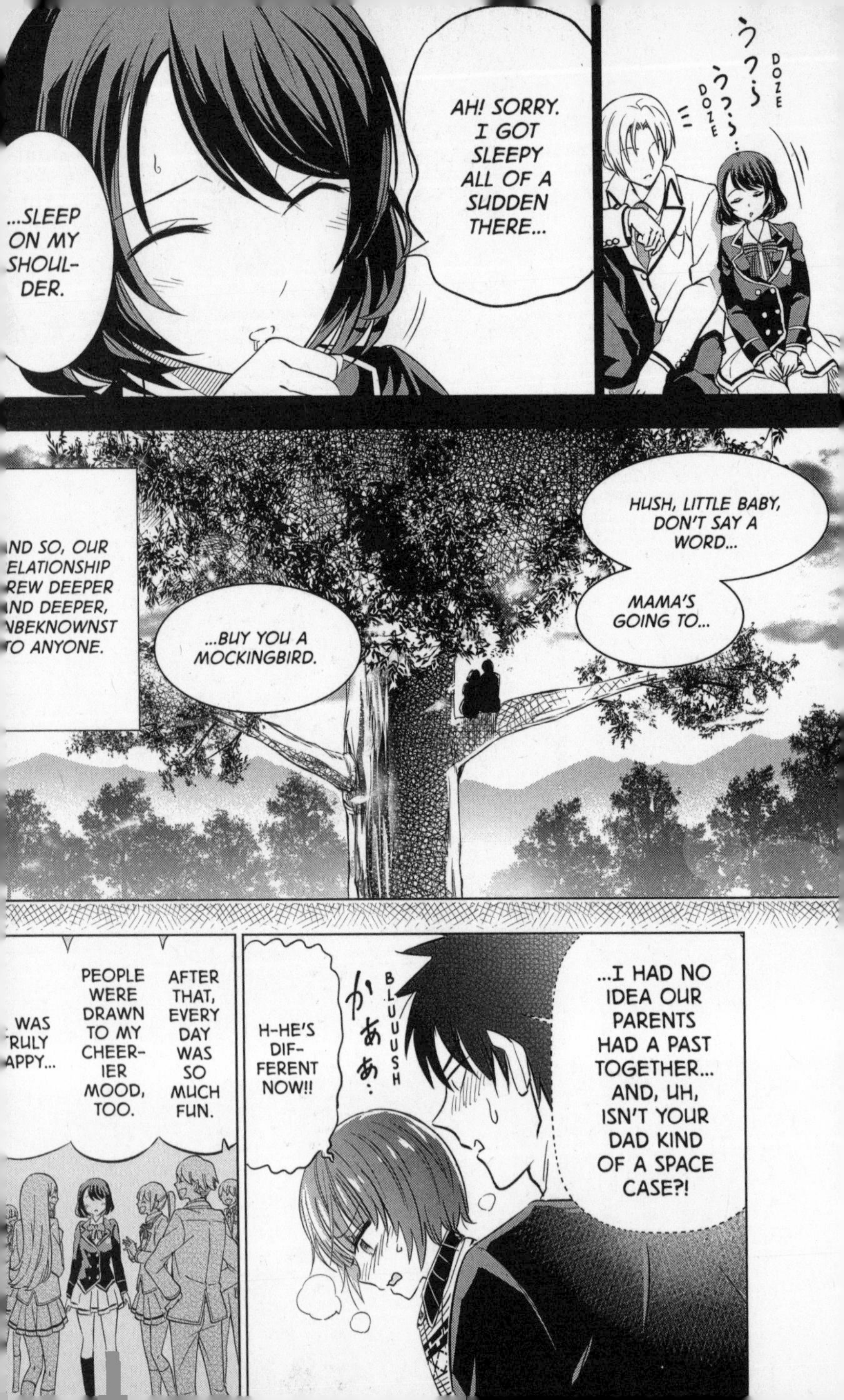
うつらうつら…
DOZE DOZE
AH! SORRY. I GOT SLEEPY ALL OF A SUDDEN THERE...
...SLEEP ON MY SHOUL-DER.
HUSH, LITTLE BABY, DON'T SAY A WORD...
MAMA'S GOING TO...
...BUY YOU A MOCKINGBIRD.
ND SO, OUR ELATIONSHIP REW DEEPER ND DEEPER, NBEKNOWNST TO ANYONE.
...I HAD NO IDEA OUR PARENTS HAD A PAST TOGETHER... AND, UH, ISN'T YOUR DAD KIND OF A SPACE CASE?!
かあぁ… BLUUUSH
H-HE'S DIF-FERENT NOW!!
AFTER THAT, EVERY DAY WAS SO MUCH FUN.
PEOPLE WERE DRAWN TO MY CHEER-IER MOOD, TOO.
WAS RULY APPY...

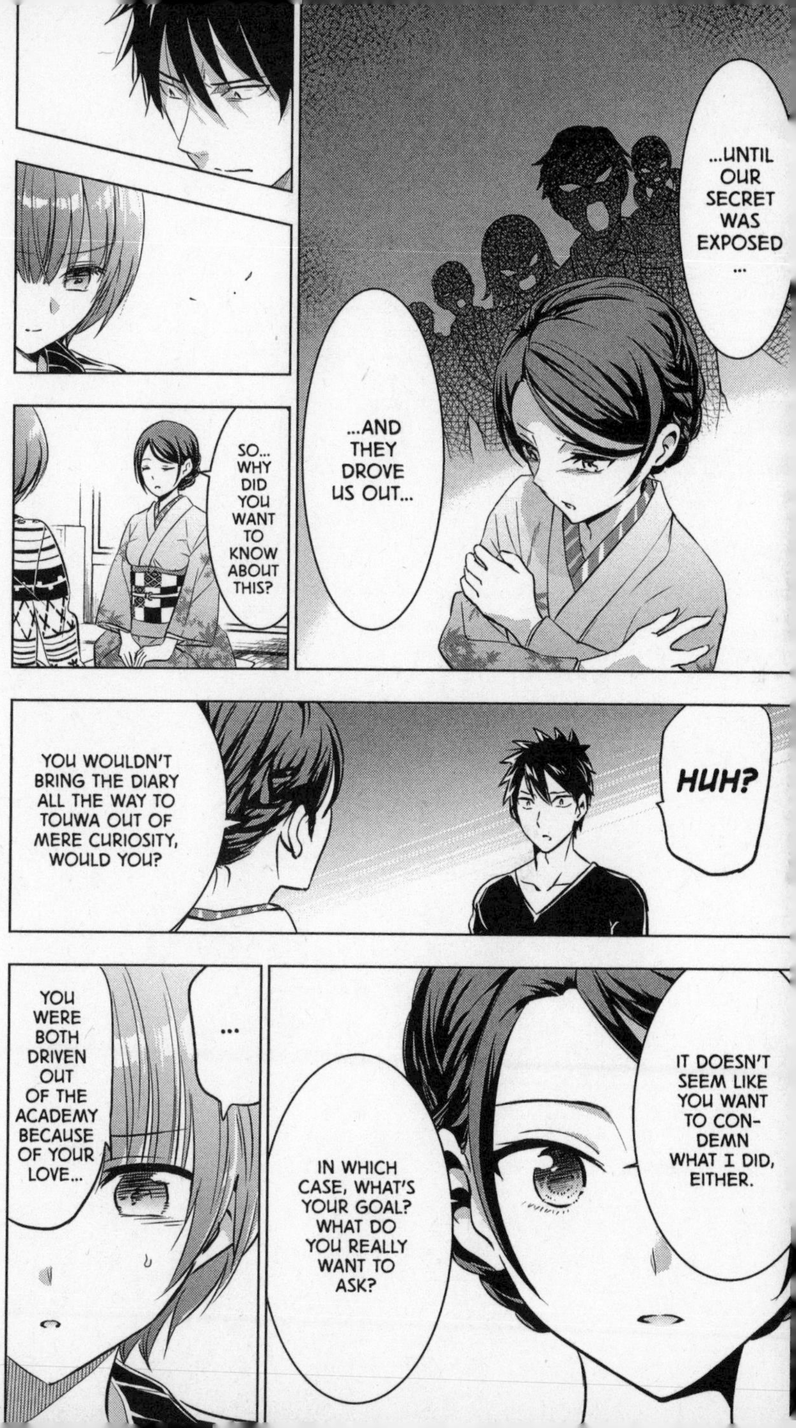
...UNTIL OUR SECRET WAS EXPOSED...
...AND THEY DROVE US OUT...
SO... WHY DID YOU WANT TO KNOW ABOUT THIS?
HUH?
YOU WOULDN'T BRING THE DIARY ALL THE WAY TO TOUWA OUT OF MERE CURIOSITY, WOULD YOU?
IT DOESN'T SEEM LIKE YOU WANT TO CON-DEMN WHAT I DID, EITHER.
IN WHICH CASE, WHAT'S YOUR GOAL? WHAT DO YOU REALLY WANT TO ASK?
...
YOU WERE BOTH DRIVEN OUT OF THE ACADEMY BECAUSE OF YOUR LOVE...

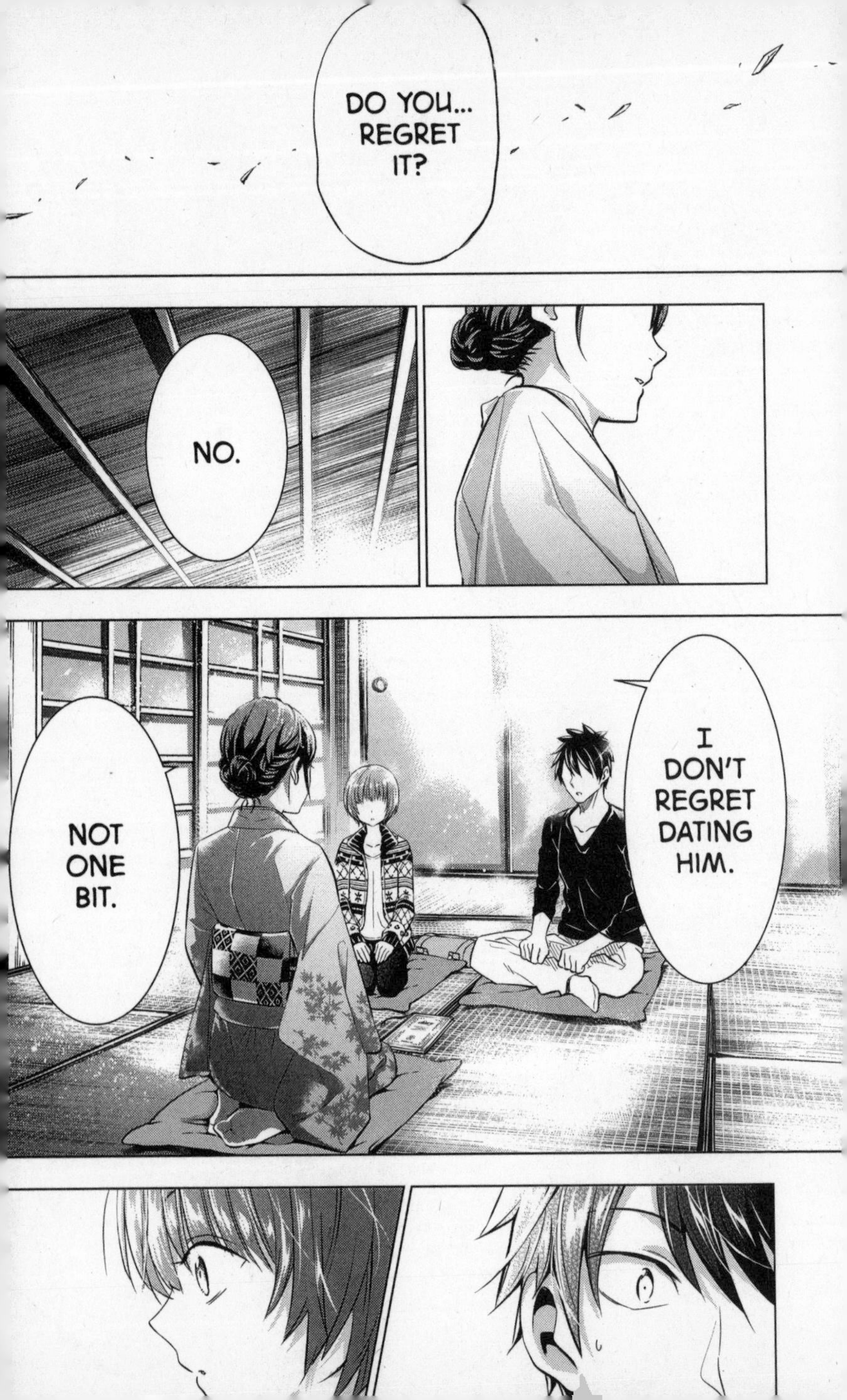
DO YOU... REGRET IT?
NO.
I DON'T REGRET DATING HIM.
NOT ONE BIT.

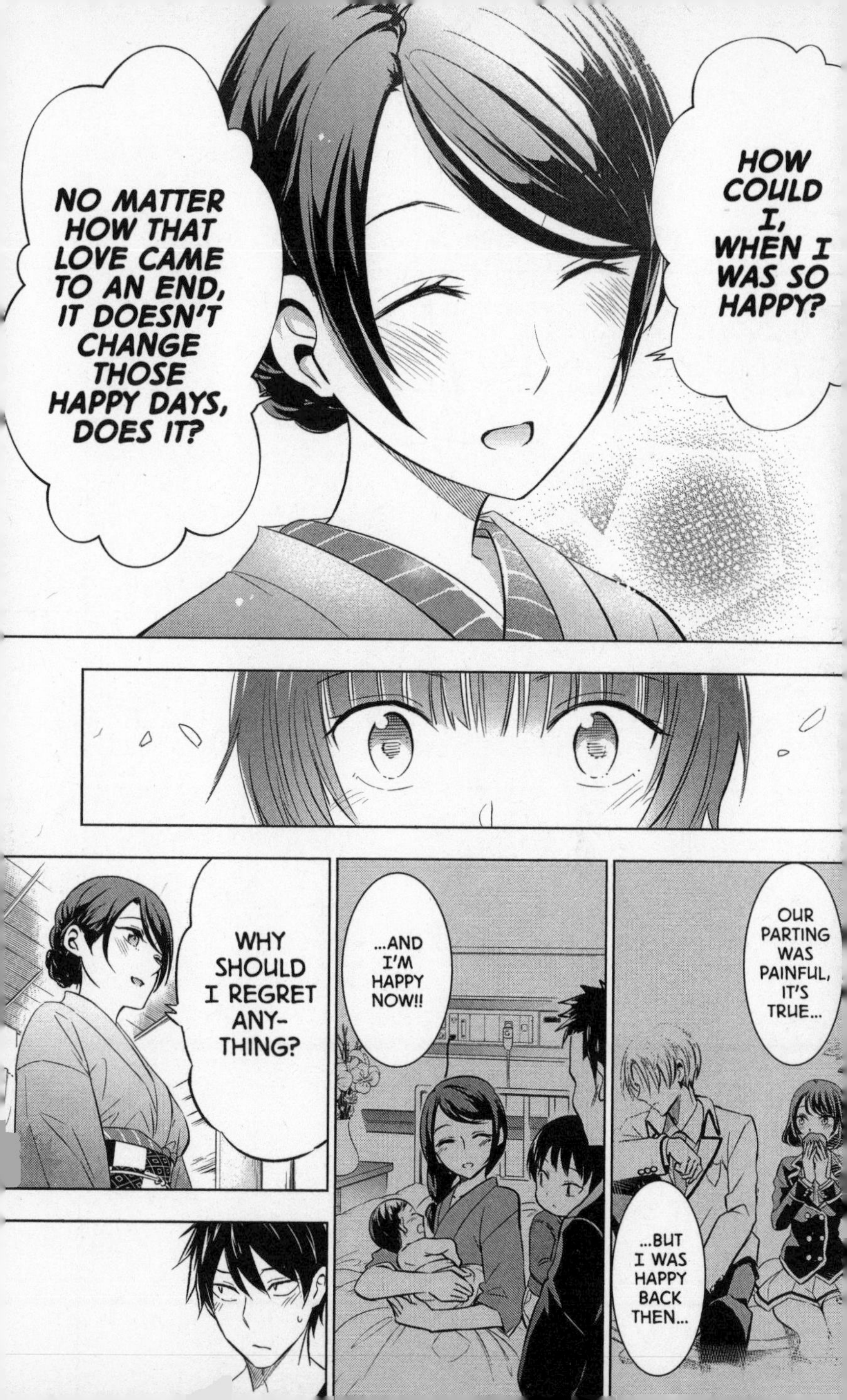
HOW COULD I, WHEN I WAS SO HAPPY?
NO MATTER HOW THAT LOVE CAME TO AN END, IT DOESN'T CHANGE THOSE HAPPY DAYS, DOES IT?
OUR PARTING WAS PAINFUL, IT'S TRUE...
...BUT I WAS HAPPY BACK THEN...
...AND I'M HAPPY NOW!!
WHY SHOULD I REGRET ANY-THING?

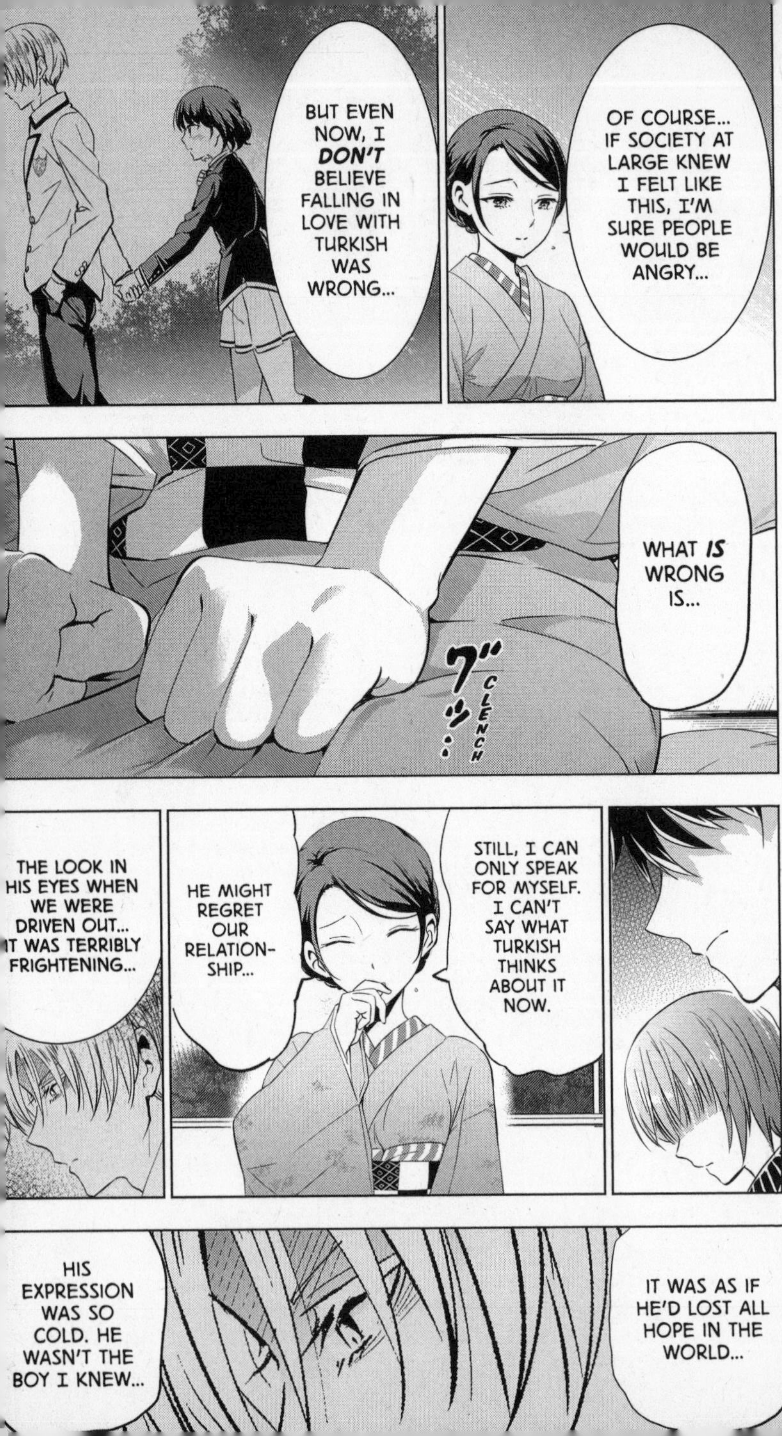
OF COURSE... IF SOCIETY AT LARGE KNEW I FELT LIKE THIS, I'M SURE PEOPLE WOULD BE ANGRY...
BUT EVEN NOW, I **DON'T** BELIEVE FALLING IN LOVE WITH TURKISH WAS WRONG...
WHAT *IS* WRONG IS...
CLENCH
STILL, I CAN ONLY SPEAK FOR MYSELF. I CAN'T SAY WHAT TURKISH THINKS ABOUT IT NOW.
HE MIGHT REGRET OUR RELATION-SHIP...
THE LOOK IN HIS EYES WHEN WE WERE DRIVEN OUT... IT WAS TERRIBLY FRIGHTENING...
IT WAS AS IF HE'D LOST ALL HOPE IN THE WORLD...
HIS EXPRESSION WAS SO COLD. HE WASN'T THE BOY I KNEW...

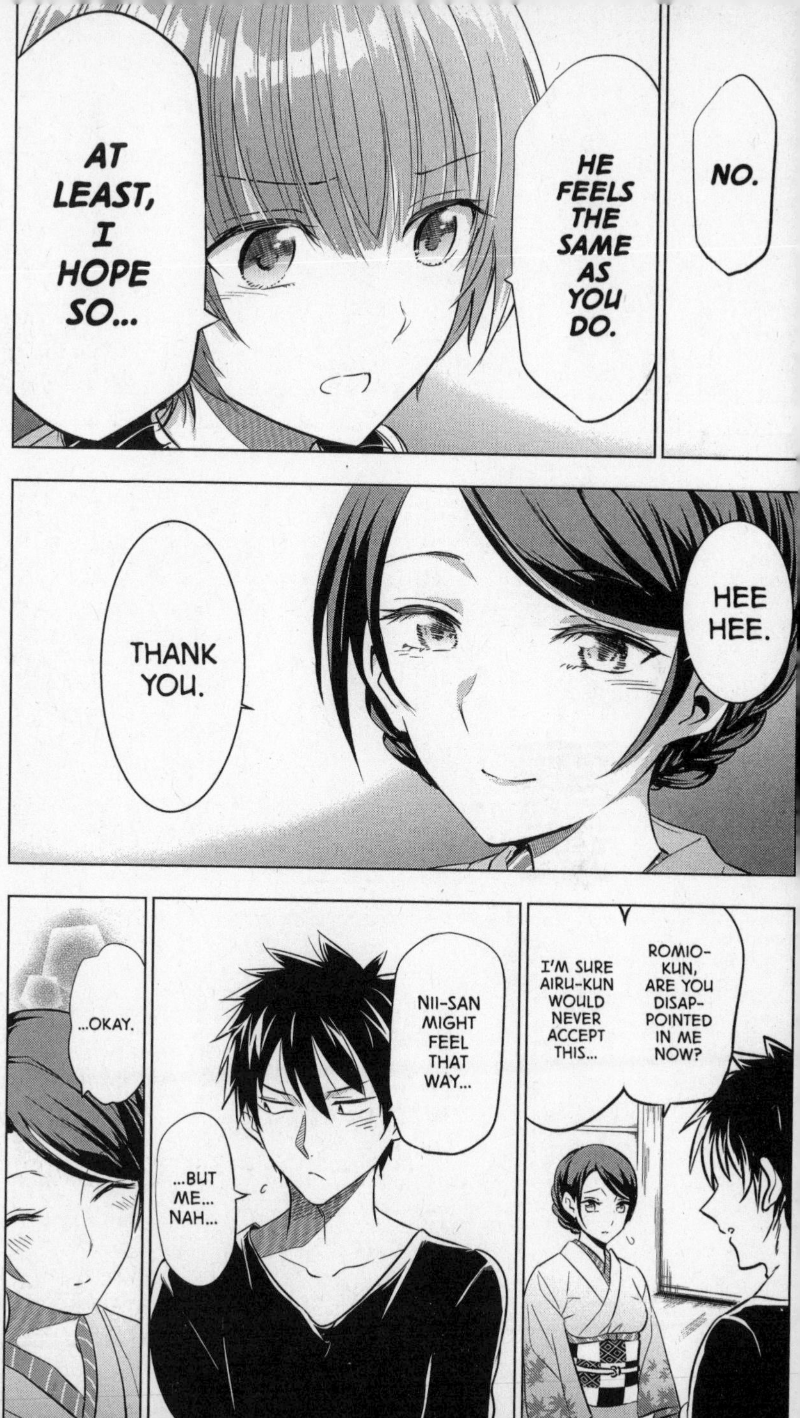
NO.
HE FEELS THE SAME AS YOU DO.
AT LEAST, I HOPE SO...
HEE HEE.
THANK YOU.
ROMIO-KUN, ARE YOU DISAP-POINTED IN ME NOW?
I'M SURE AIRU-KUN WOULD NEVER ACCEPT THIS...
NII-SAN MIGHT FEEL THAT WAY...
...BUT ME... NAH...
...OKAY.

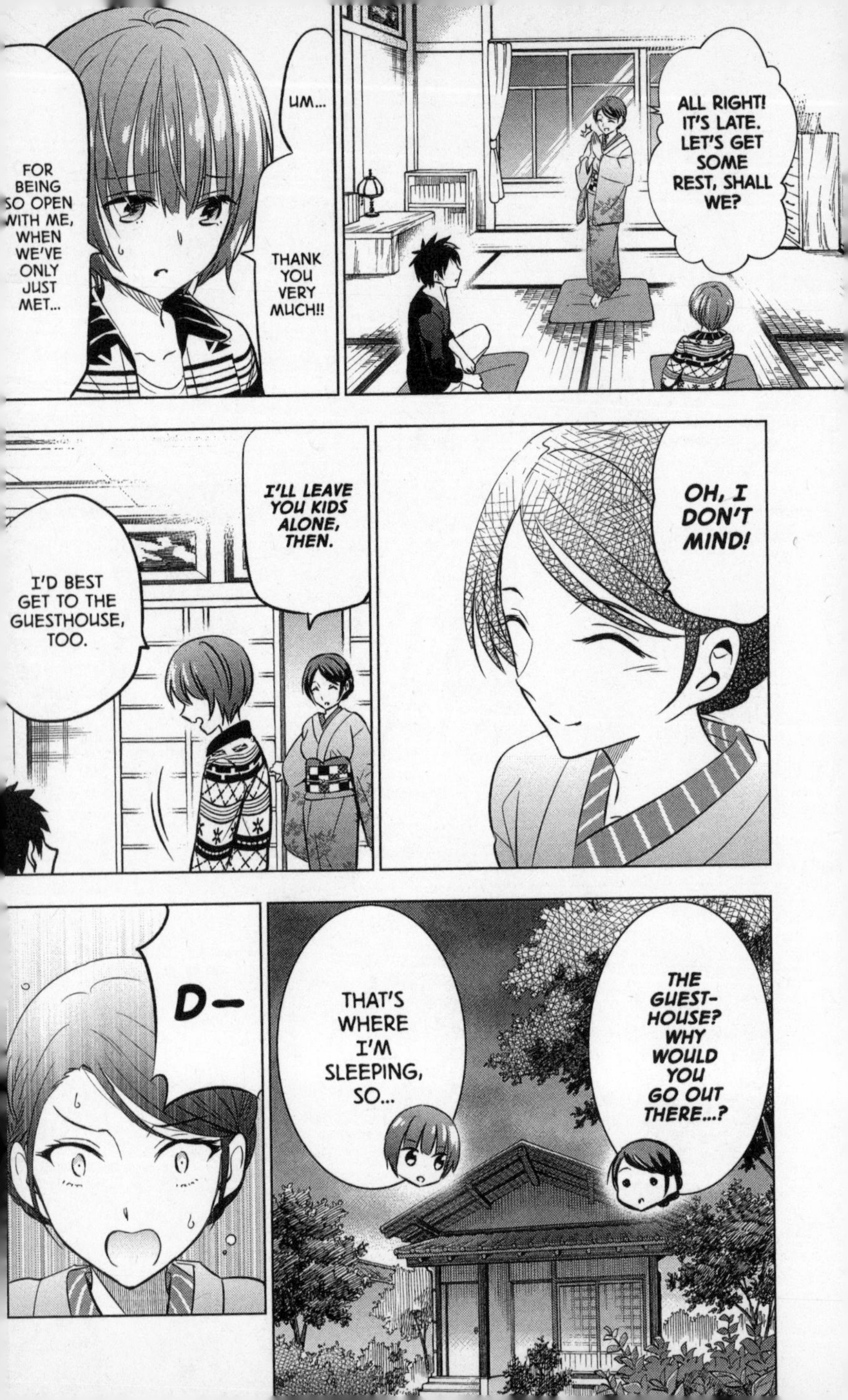
ALL RIGHT! IT'S LATE. LET'S GET SOME REST, SHALL WE?
UM...
THANK YOU VERY MUCH!!
FOR BEING SO OPEN WITH ME, WHEN WE'VE ONLY JUST MET...
OH, I DON'T MIND!
I'LL LEAVE YOU KIDS ALONE, THEN.
I'D BEST GET TO THE GUESTHOUSE, TOO.
THE GUEST-HOUSE? WHY WOULD YOU GO OUT THERE...?
THAT'S WHERE I'M SLEEPING, SO...
D—

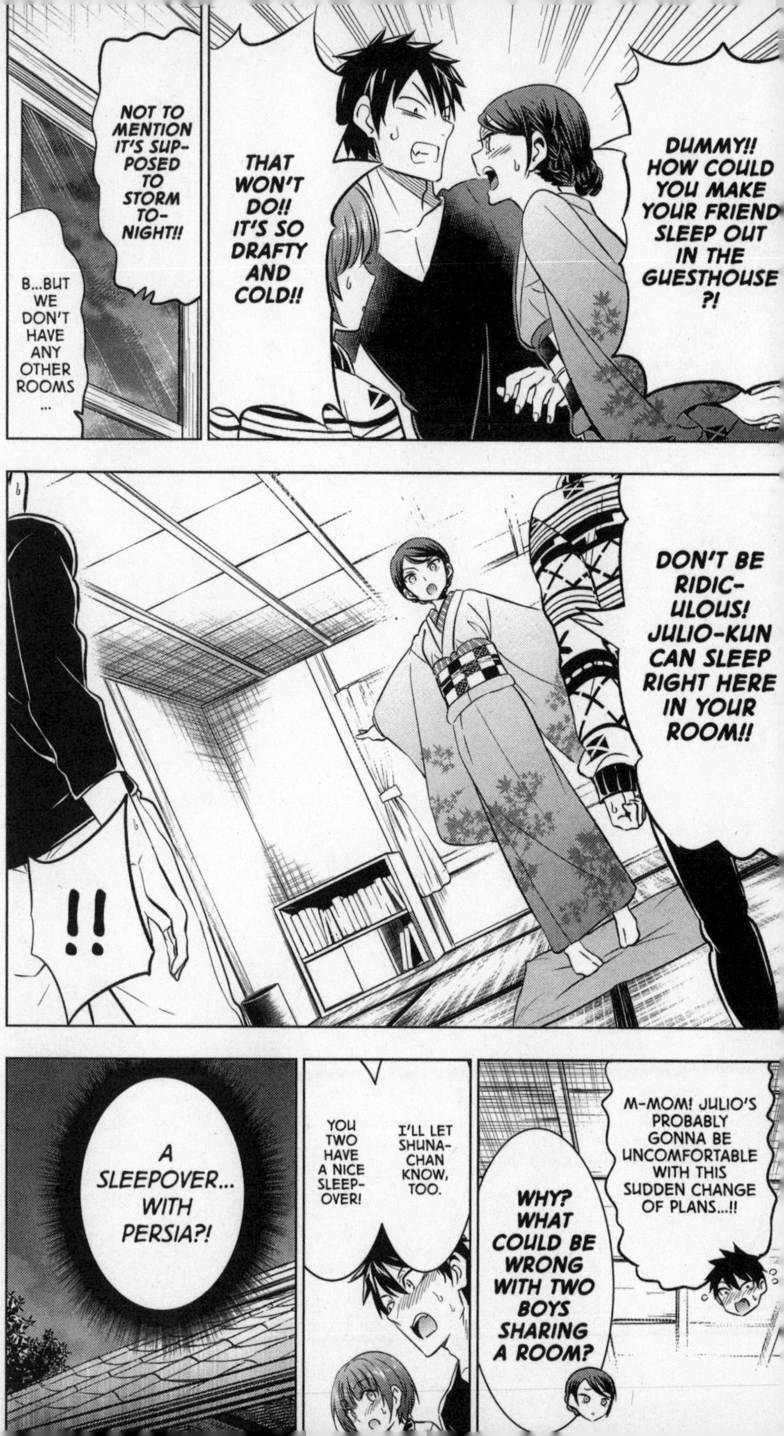
DUMMY!! HOW COULD YOU MAKE YOUR FRIEND SLEEP OUT IN THE GUESTHOUSE ?!
THAT WON'T DO!! IT'S SO DRAFTY AND COLD!!
NOT TO MENTION IT'S SUP-POSED TO STORM TO-NIGHT!!
B...BUT WE DON'T HAVE ANY OTHER ROOMS ...
DON'T BE RIDIC-ULOUS! JULIO-KUN CAN SLEEP RIGHT HERE IN YOUR ROOM!!
!!
M-MOM! JULIO'S PROBABLY GONNA BE UNCOMFORTABLE WITH THIS SUDDEN CHANGE OF PLANS...!!
WHY? WHAT COULD BE WRONG WITH TWO BOYS SHARING A ROOM?
I'LL LET SHUNA-CHAN KNOW, TOO.
YOU TWO HAVE A NICE SLEEP-OVER!
A SLEEPOVER... WITH PERSIA?!

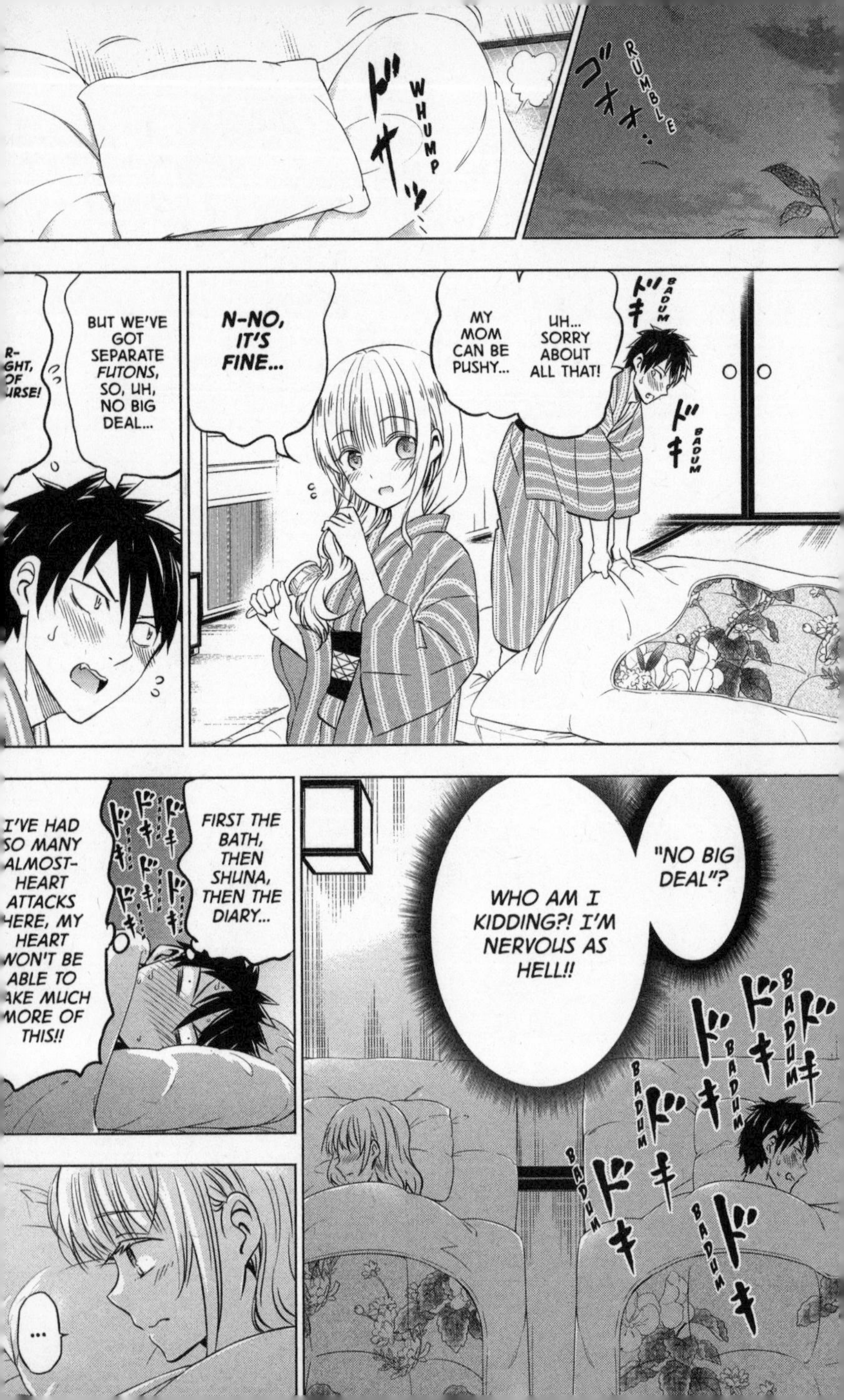
RUMBLE
ゴォォ…
ドサッ
WHUMP
ドキ
BADUM
UH... SORRY ABOUT ALL THAT!
MY MOM CAN BE PUSHY...
ドキ
BADUM
N-NO, IT'S FINE...
BUT WE'VE GOT SEPARATE FUTONS, SO, UH, NO BIG DEAL...
R- GHT, OF URSE!
"NO BIG DEAL"?
WHO AM I KIDDING?! I'M NERVOUS AS HELL!!
ドキ BADUM
ドキ BADUM
ドキ BADUM
ドキ BADUM
ドキ BADUM
FIRST THE BATH, THEN SHUNA, THEN THE DIARY...
ドキドキドキドキドキドキ
I'VE HAD SO MANY ALMOST-HEART ATTACKS HERE, MY HEART WON'T BE ABLE TO TAKE MUCH MORE OF THIS!!
...

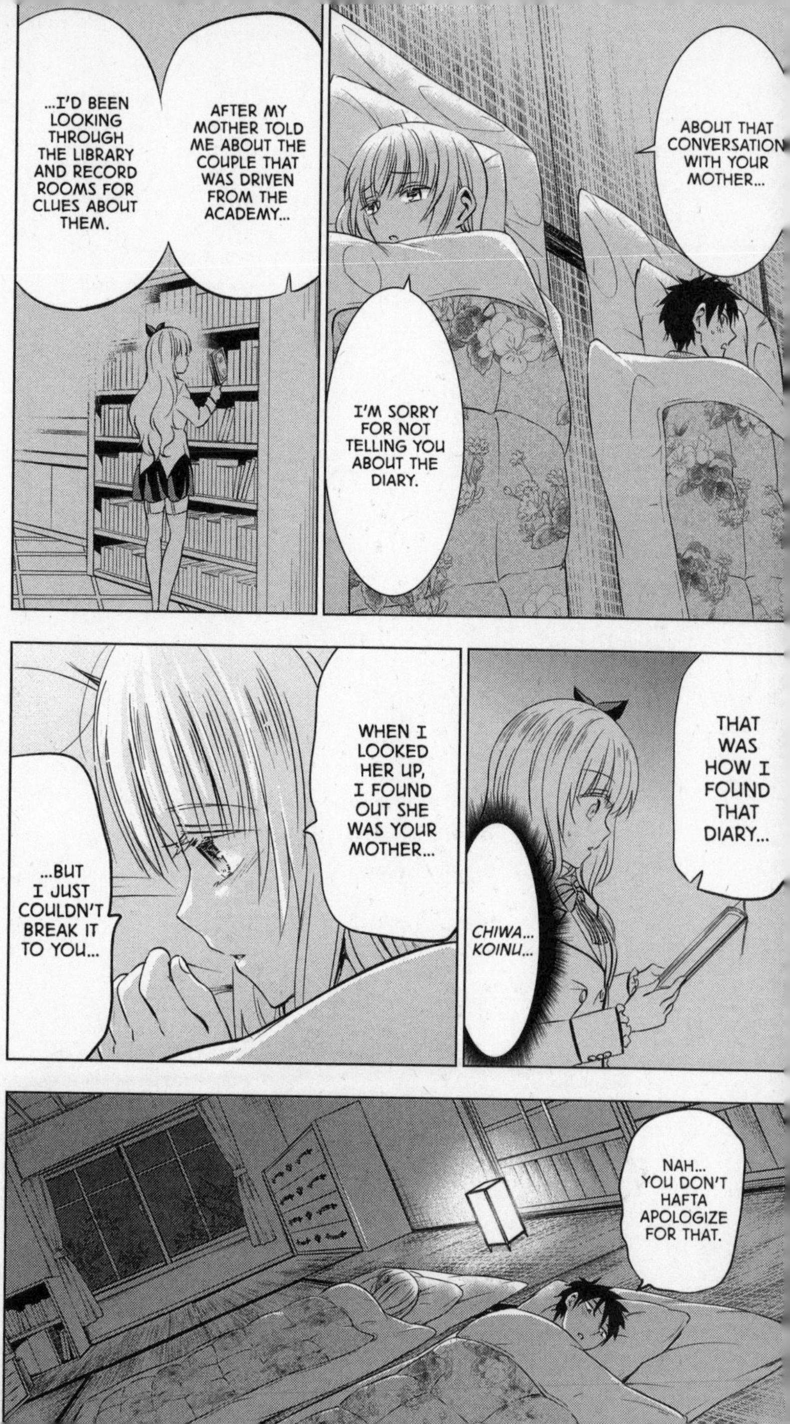
ABOUT THAT CONVERSATION WITH YOUR MOTHER...
I'M SORRY FOR NOT TELLING YOU ABOUT THE DIARY.
AFTER MY MOTHER TOLD ME ABOUT THE COUPLE THAT WAS DRIVEN FROM THE ACADEMY...
...I'D BEEN LOOKING THROUGH THE LIBRARY AND RECORD ROOMS FOR CLUES ABOUT THEM.
THAT WAS HOW I FOUND THAT DIARY...
CHIWA... KOINU...
WHEN I LOOKED HER UP, I FOUND OUT SHE WAS YOUR MOTHER...
...BUT I JUST COULDN'T BREAK IT TO YOU...
NAH... YOU DON'T HAFTA APOLOGIZE FOR THAT.

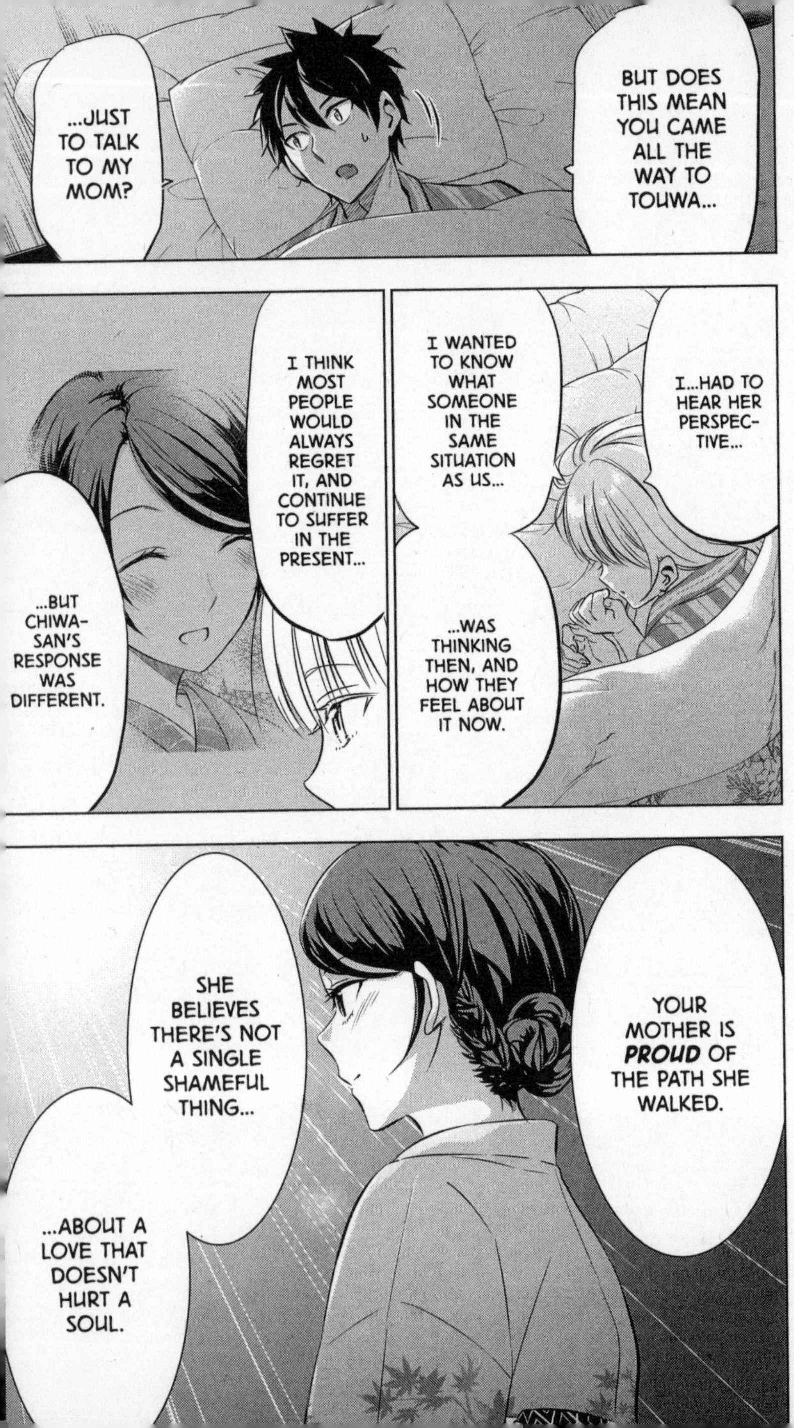
BUT DOES THIS MEAN YOU CAME ALL THE WAY TO TOUWA...
...JUST TO TALK TO MY MOM?
I...HAD TO HEAR HER PERSPEC-TIVE...
I WANTED TO KNOW WHAT SOMEONE IN THE SAME SITUATION AS US...
...WAS THINKING THEN, AND HOW THEY FEEL ABOUT IT NOW.
I THINK MOST PEOPLE WOULD ALWAYS REGRET IT, AND CONTINUE TO SUFFER IN THE PRESENT...
...BUT CHIWA-SAN'S RESPONSE WAS DIFFERENT.
YOUR MOTHER IS ***PROUD*** OF THE PATH SHE WALKED.
SHE BELIEVES THERE'S NOT A SINGLE SHAMEFUL THING...
...ABOUT A LOVE THAT DOESN'T HURT A SOUL.

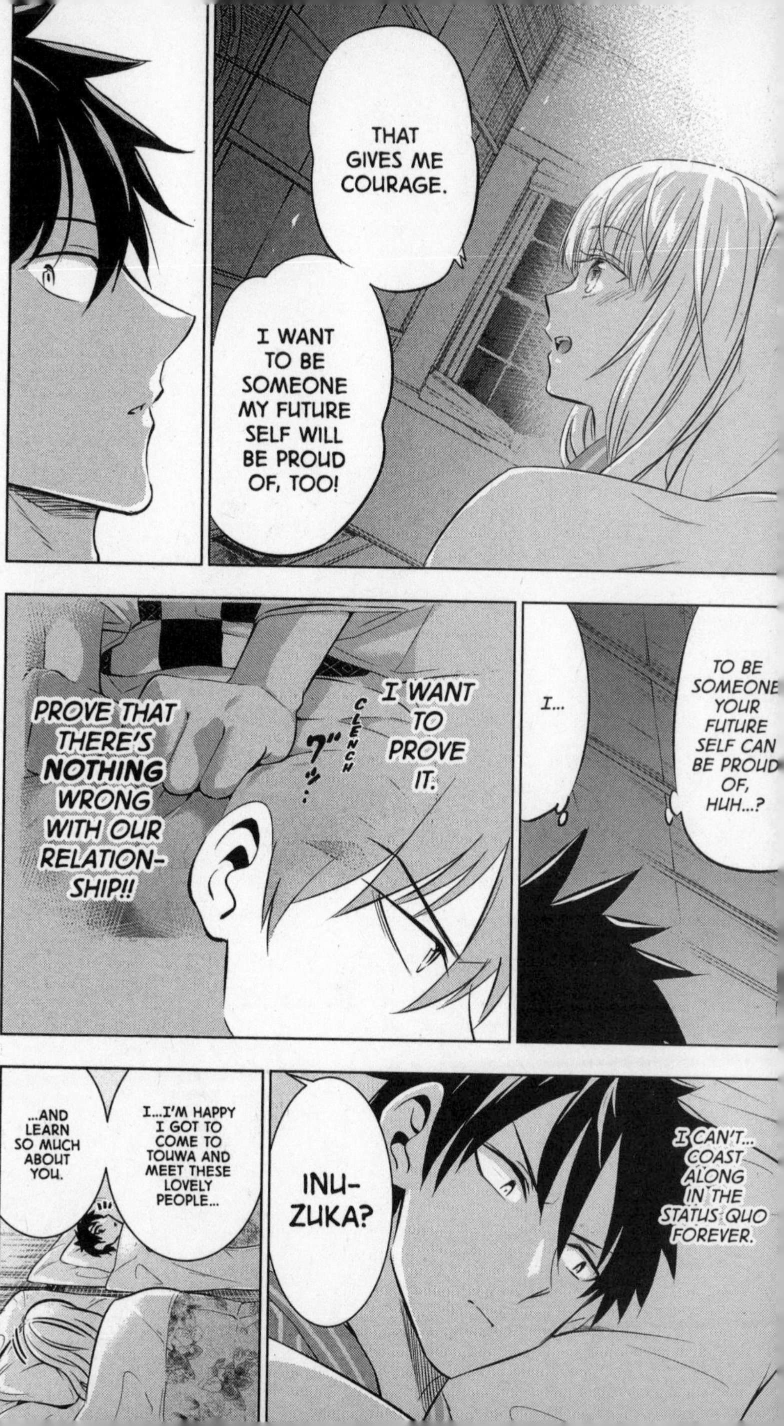
THAT GIVES ME COURAGE.
I WANT TO BE SOMEONE MY FUTURE SELF WILL BE PROUD OF, TOO!
TO BE SOMEONE YOUR FUTURE SELF CAN BE PROUD OF, HUH...?
I...
I WANT TO PROVE IT.
CLENCH
PROVE THAT THERE'S NOTHING WRONG WITH OUR RELATION-SHIP!!
I CAN'T... COAST ALONG IN THE STATUS QUO FOREVER.
INU-ZUKA?
I...I'M HAPPY I GOT TO COME TO TOUWA AND MEET THESE LOVELY PEOPLE...
...AND LEARN SO MUCH ABOUT YOU.

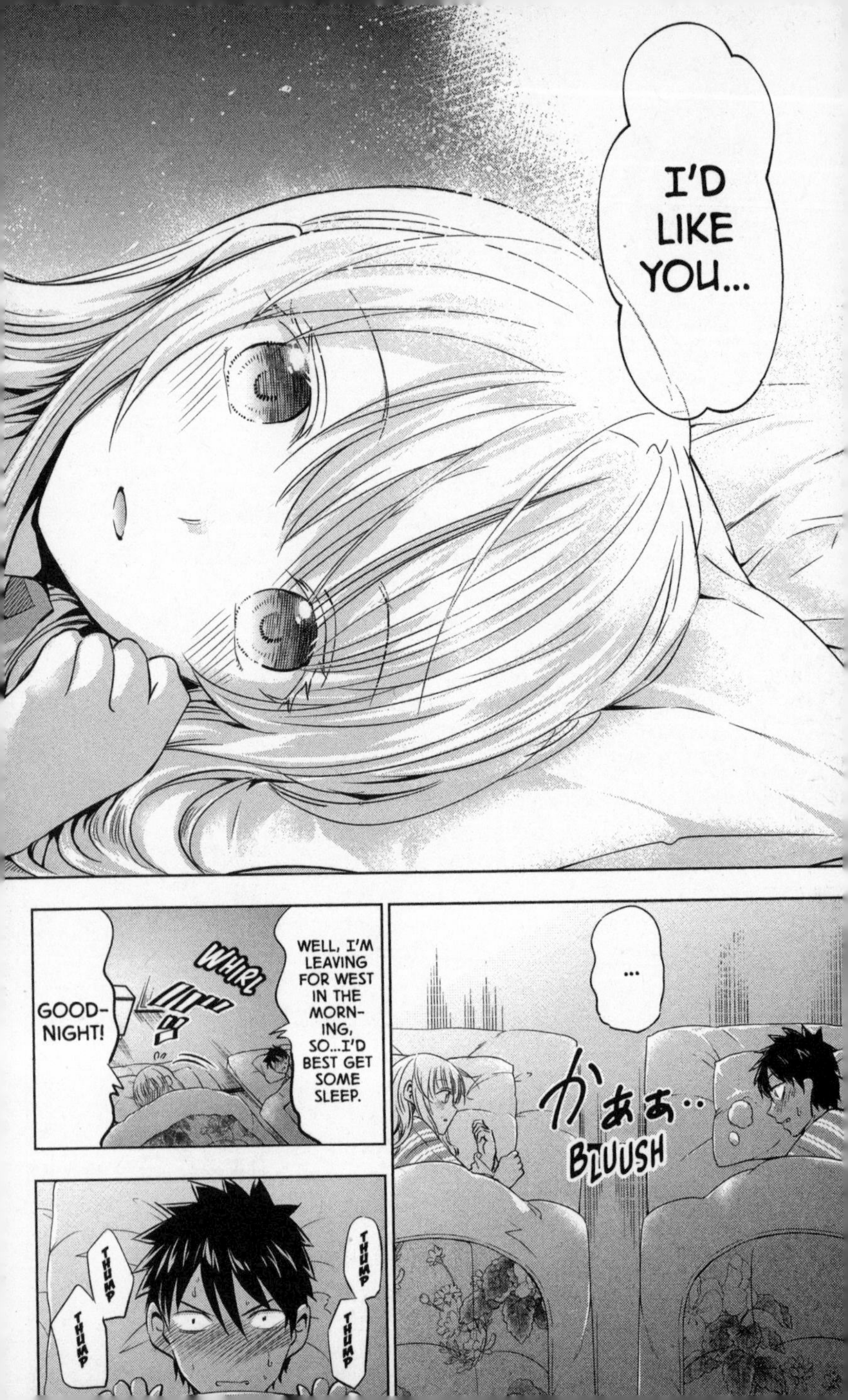
I'D LIKE YOU...
...
かぁぁ..
BLUUSH
WELL, I'M LEAVING FOR WEST IN THE MORN-ING, SO...I'D BEST GET SOME SLEEP.
WHIRL
GOOD-NIGHT!
THUMP
THUMP
THUMP
THUMP

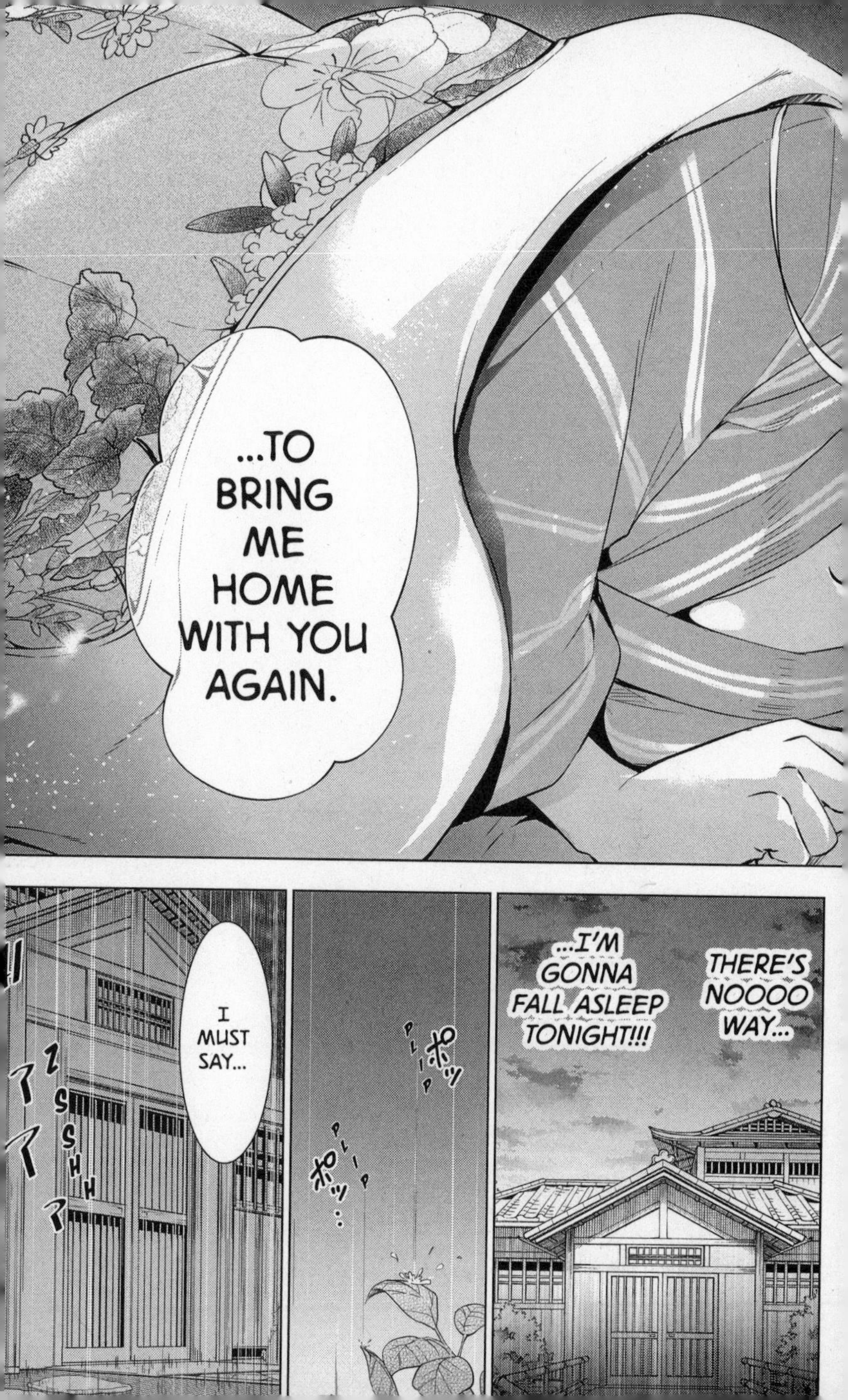
...TO BRING ME HOME WITH YOU AGAIN.
THERE'S NOOOO WAY...
...I'M GONNA FALL ASLEEP TONIGHT!!!
ポッ PLIP
ポッ... PLIP
I MUST SAY...
ザァァァ ZSHHH

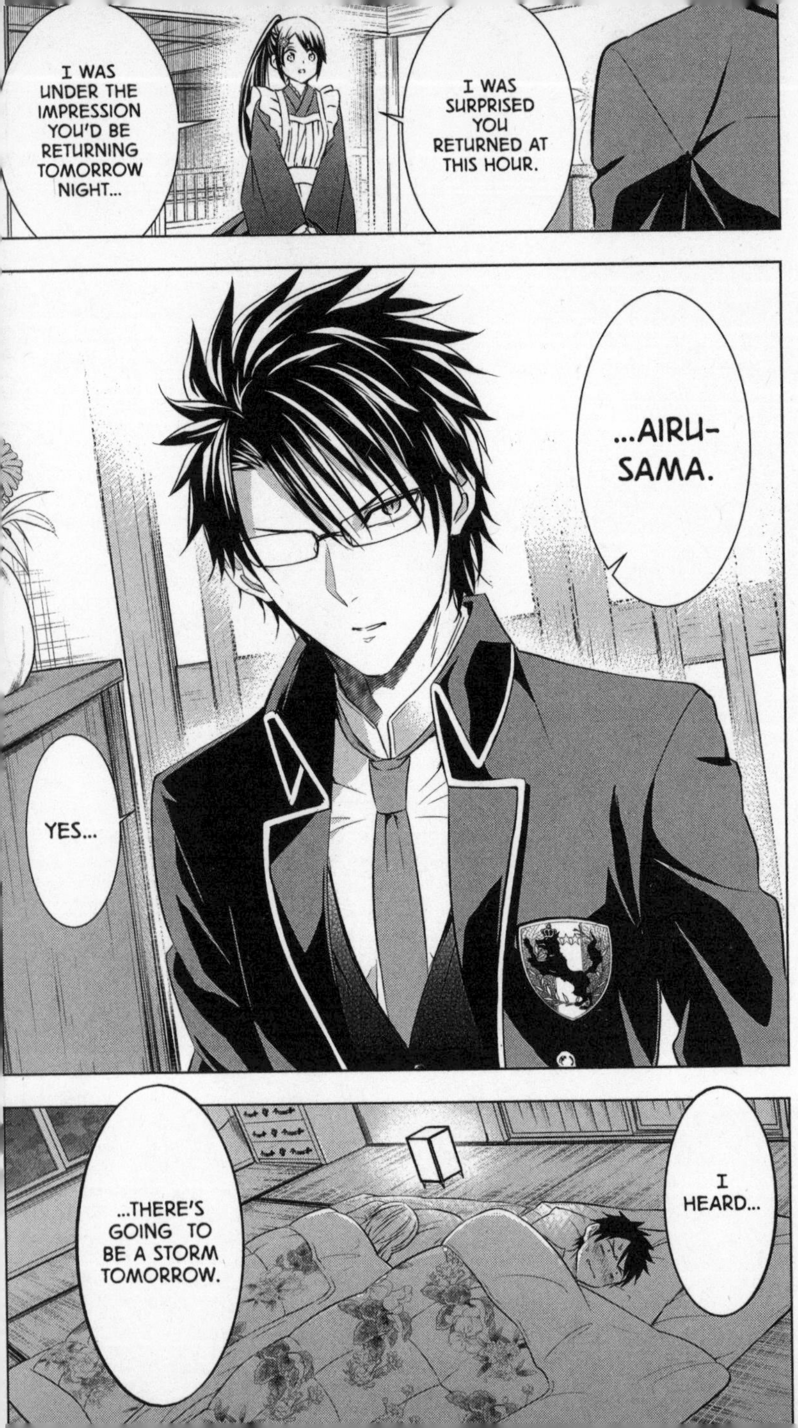
I WAS SURPRISED YOU RETURNED AT THIS HOUR.
I WAS UNDER THE IMPRESSION YOU'D BE RETURNING TOMORROW NIGHT...
...AIRU-SAMA.
YES...
I HEARD...
...THERE'S GOING TO BE A STORM TOMORROW.

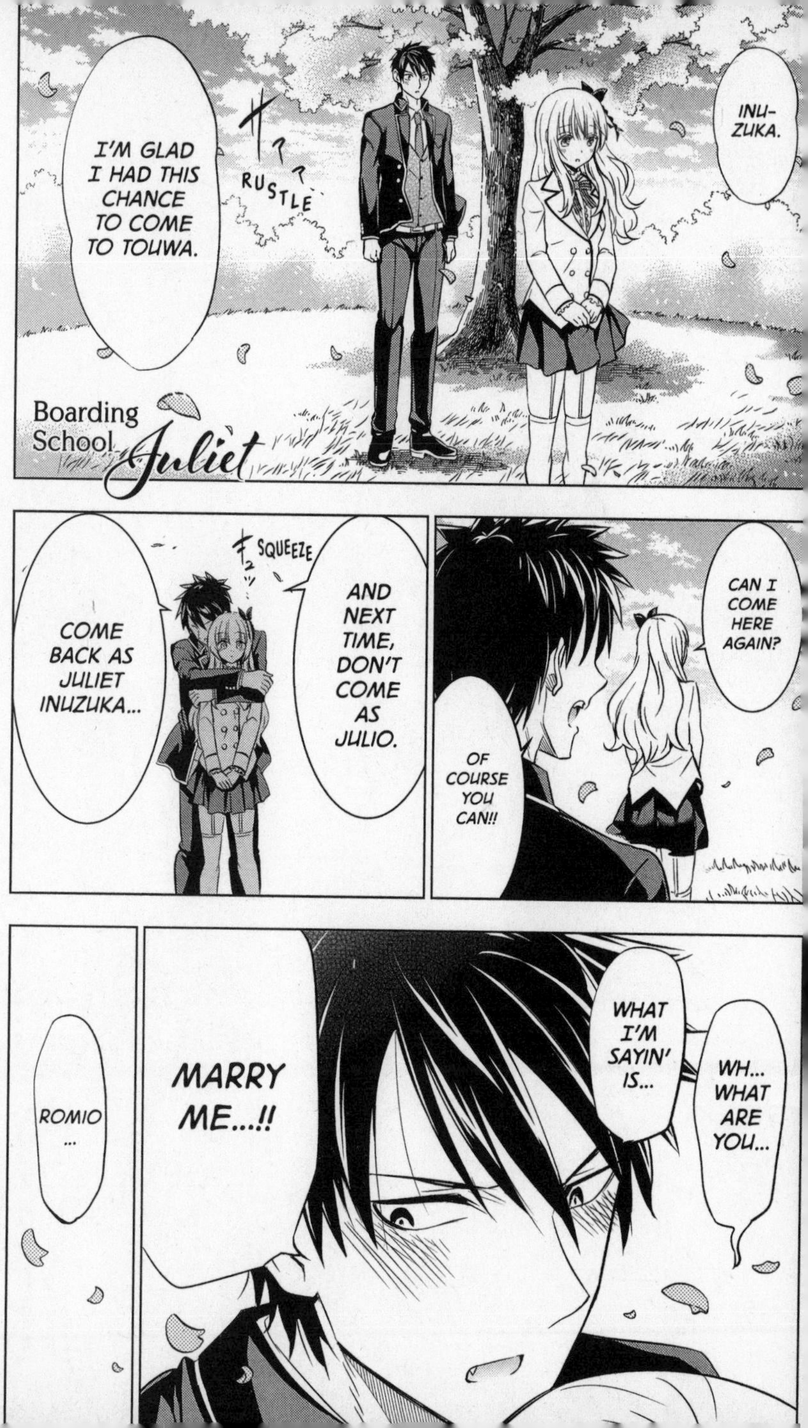
INU-ZUKA.
RUSTLE
I'M GLAD I HAD THIS CHANCE TO COME TO TOUWA.
Boarding School Juliet
CAN I COME HERE AGAIN?
OF COURSE YOU CAN!!
AND NEXT TIME, DON'T COME AS JULIO.
SQUEEZE
COME BACK AS JULIET INUZUKA...
WH... WHAT ARE YOU...
WHAT I'M SAYIN' IS...
MARRY ME...!!
ROMIO ...

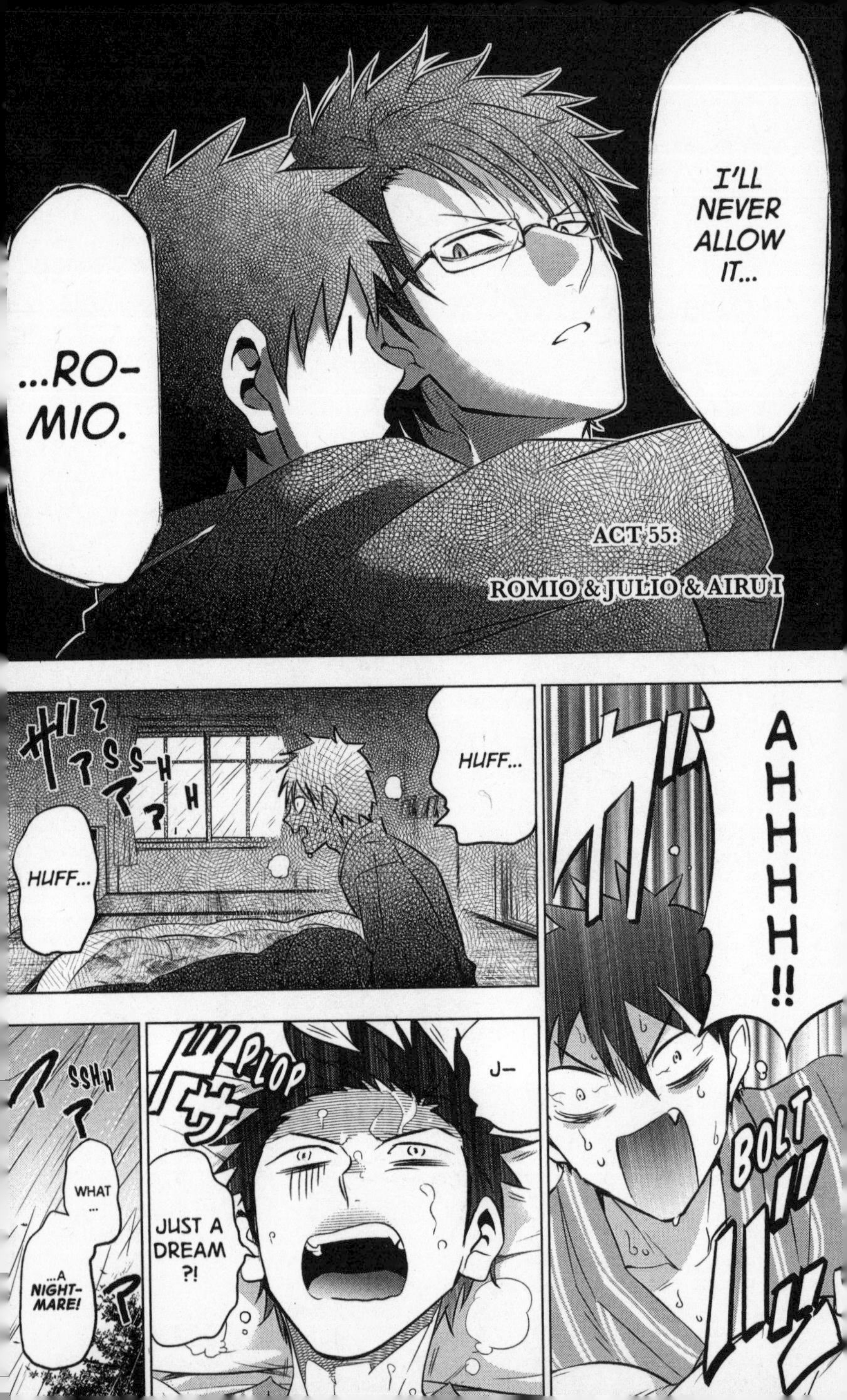
I'LL NEVER ALLOW IT...
...RO-MIO.
ACT 55:
ROMIO & JULIO & AIRU I
AHHHH!!
BOLT
SSHH
HUFF...
HUFF...
PLOP
J—
JUST A DREAM ?!
SSHH
WHAT ...
...A NIGHT-MARE!

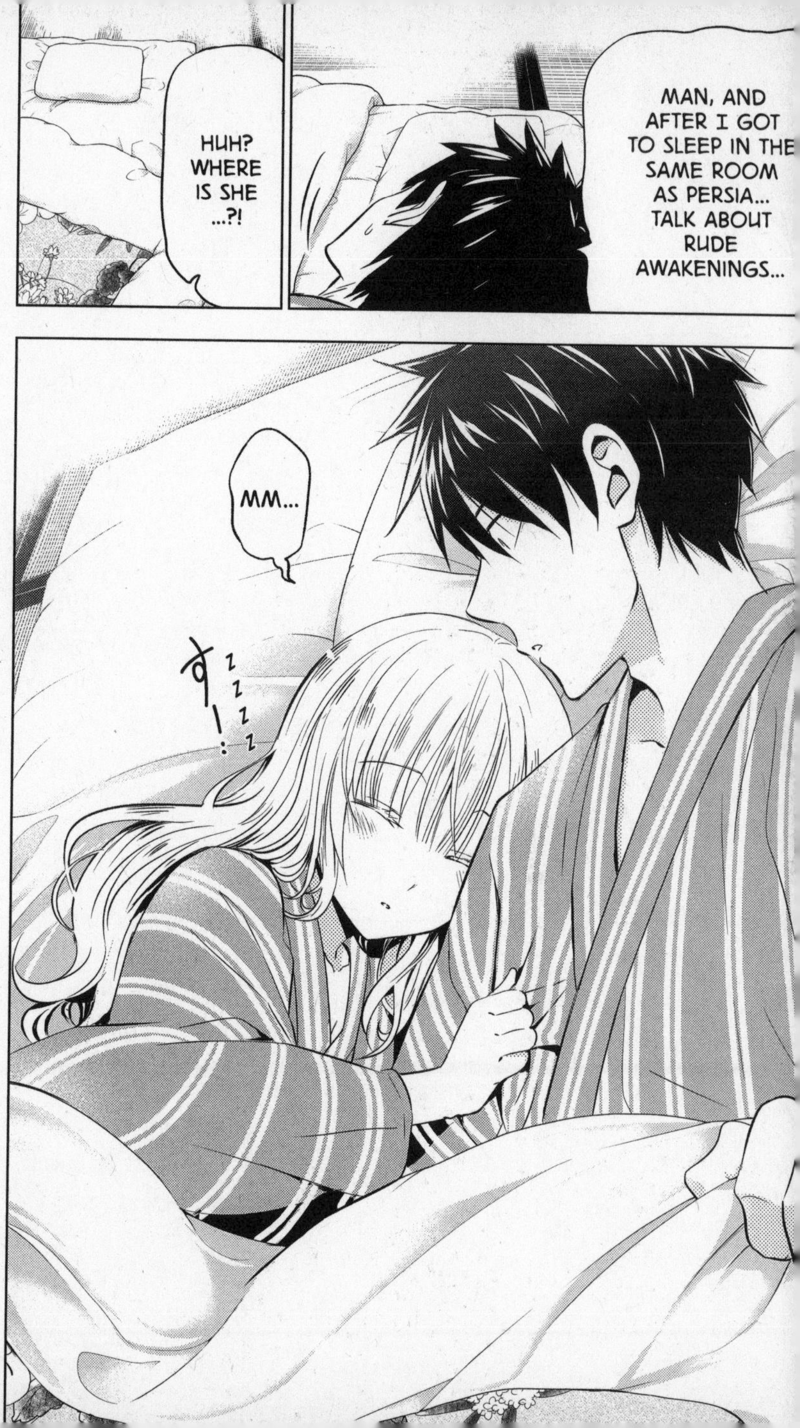
MAN, AND AFTER I GOT TO SLEEP IN THE SAME ROOM AS PERSIA... TALK ABOUT RUDE AWAKENINGS...
HUH? WHERE IS SHE ...?!
MM...
すー
ZZZZ

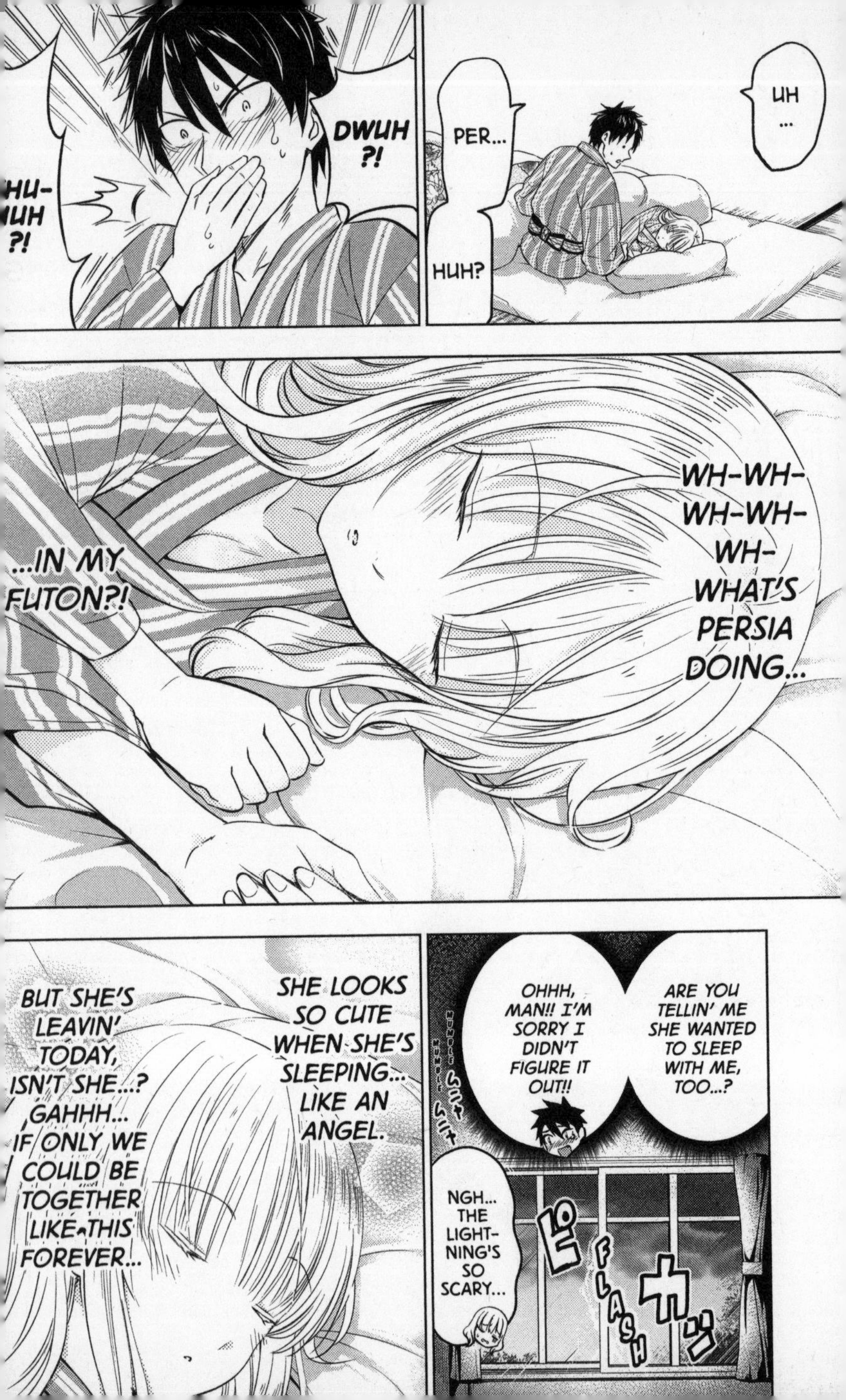
UH ...
PER...
HUH?
DWUH ?!
HU-UH ?!
WH-WH-WH-WH-WH-WHAT'S PERSIA DOING...
...IN MY FUTON?!
ARE YOU TELLIN' ME SHE WANTED TO SLEEP WITH ME, TOO...?
OHHH, MAN!! I'M SORRY I DIDN'T FIGURE IT OUT!!
MUMBLE MUMBLE
NGH... THE LIGHT-NING'S SO SCARY...
FLASH
SHE LOOKS SO CUTE WHEN SHE'S SLEEPING... LIKE AN ANGEL.
BUT SHE'S LEAVIN' TODAY, ISN'T SHE...? GAHHH... IF ONLY WE COULD BE TOGETHER LIKE THIS FOREVER...

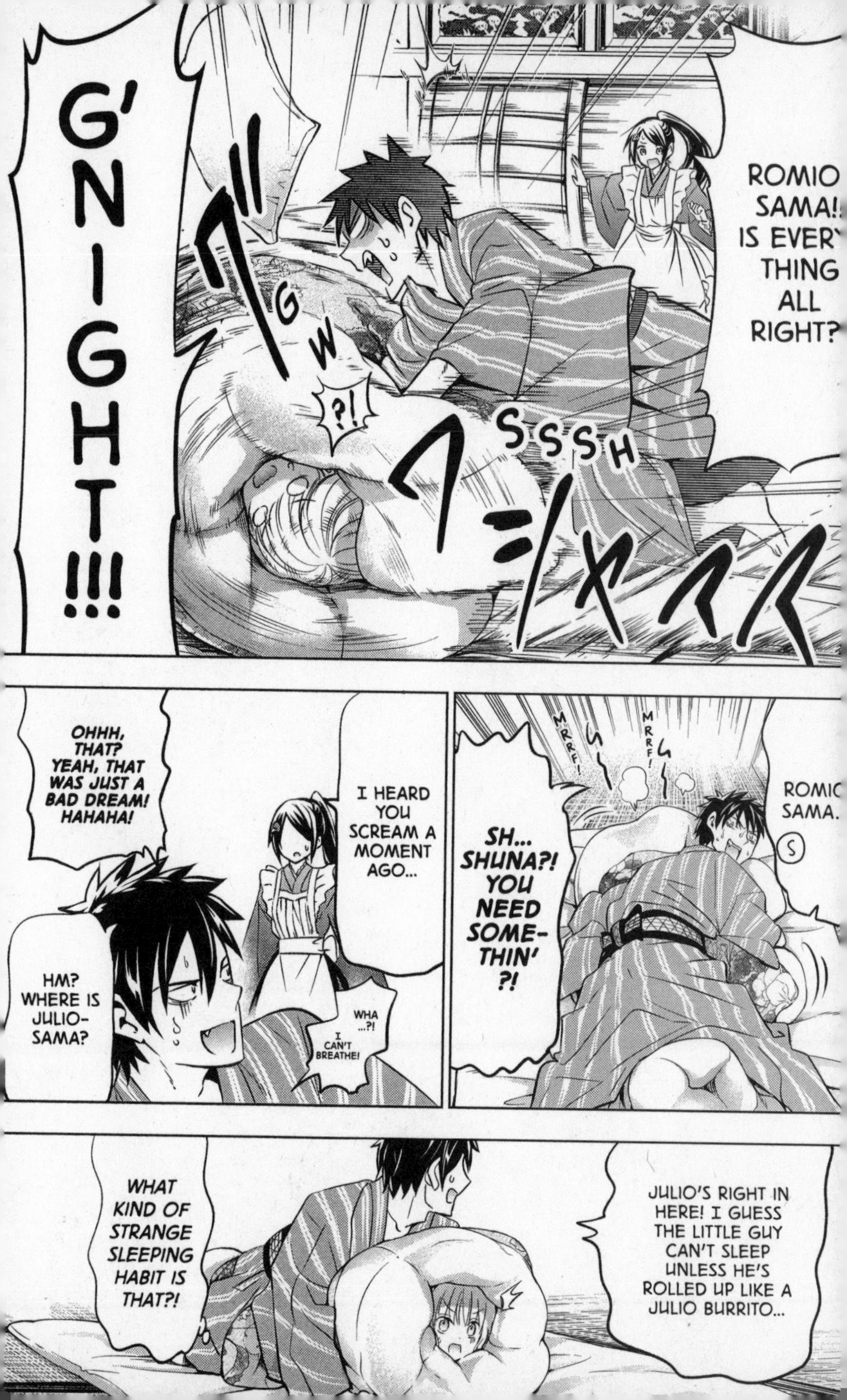
ROMIO SAMA!! IS EVERYTHING ALL RIGHT?
SSSH
?!
GW
G'NIGHT!!!
ROMIO SAMA.
S
MRRF!
MRRF!
SH... SHUNA?! YOU NEED SOME-THIN'?!
I HEARD YOU SCREAM A MOMENT AGO...
OHHH, THAT? YEAH, THAT WAS JUST A BAD DREAM! HAHAHA!
WHA ...?!
I CAN'T BREATHE!
HM? WHERE IS JULIO-SAMA?
JULIO'S RIGHT IN HERE! I GUESS THE LITTLE GUY CAN'T SLEEP UNLESS HE'S ROLLED UP LIKE A JULIO BURRITO...
WHAT KIND OF STRANGE SLEEPING HABIT IS THAT?!

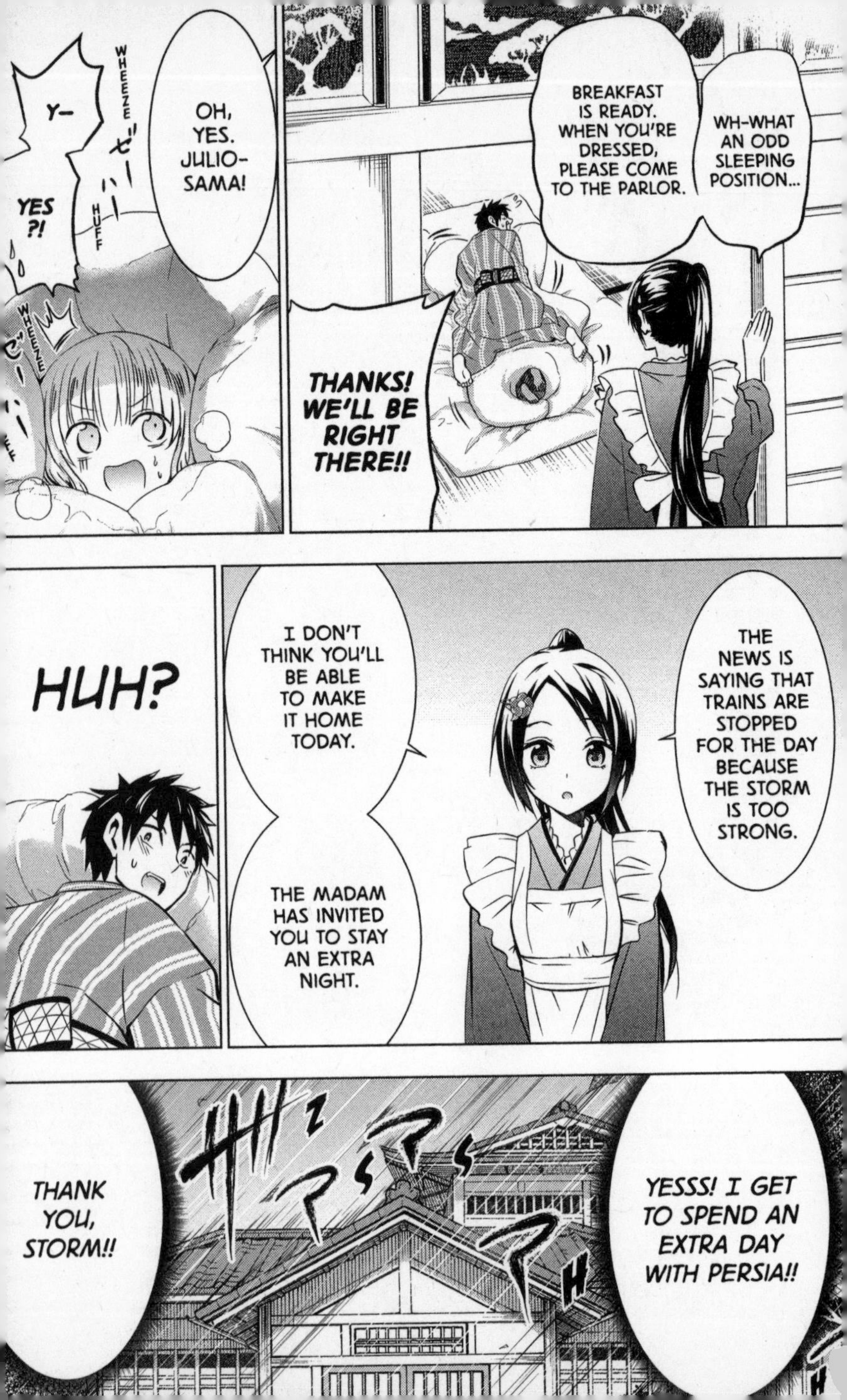
WH-WHAT AN ODD SLEEPING POSITION...
BREAKFAST IS READY. WHEN YOU'RE DRESSED, PLEASE COME TO THE PARLOR.
THANKS! WE'LL BE RIGHT THERE!!
OH, YES. JULIO-SAMA!
WHEEZE
HUFF
Y-
YES?!
WHEEZE
THE NEWS IS SAYING THAT TRAINS ARE STOPPED FOR THE DAY BECAUSE THE STORM IS TOO STRONG.
I DON'T THINK YOU'LL BE ABLE TO MAKE IT HOME TODAY.
THE MADAM HAS INVITED YOU TO STAY AN EXTRA NIGHT.
HUH?
YESSS! I GET TO SPEND AN EXTRA DAY WITH PERSIA!!
THANK YOU, STORM!!

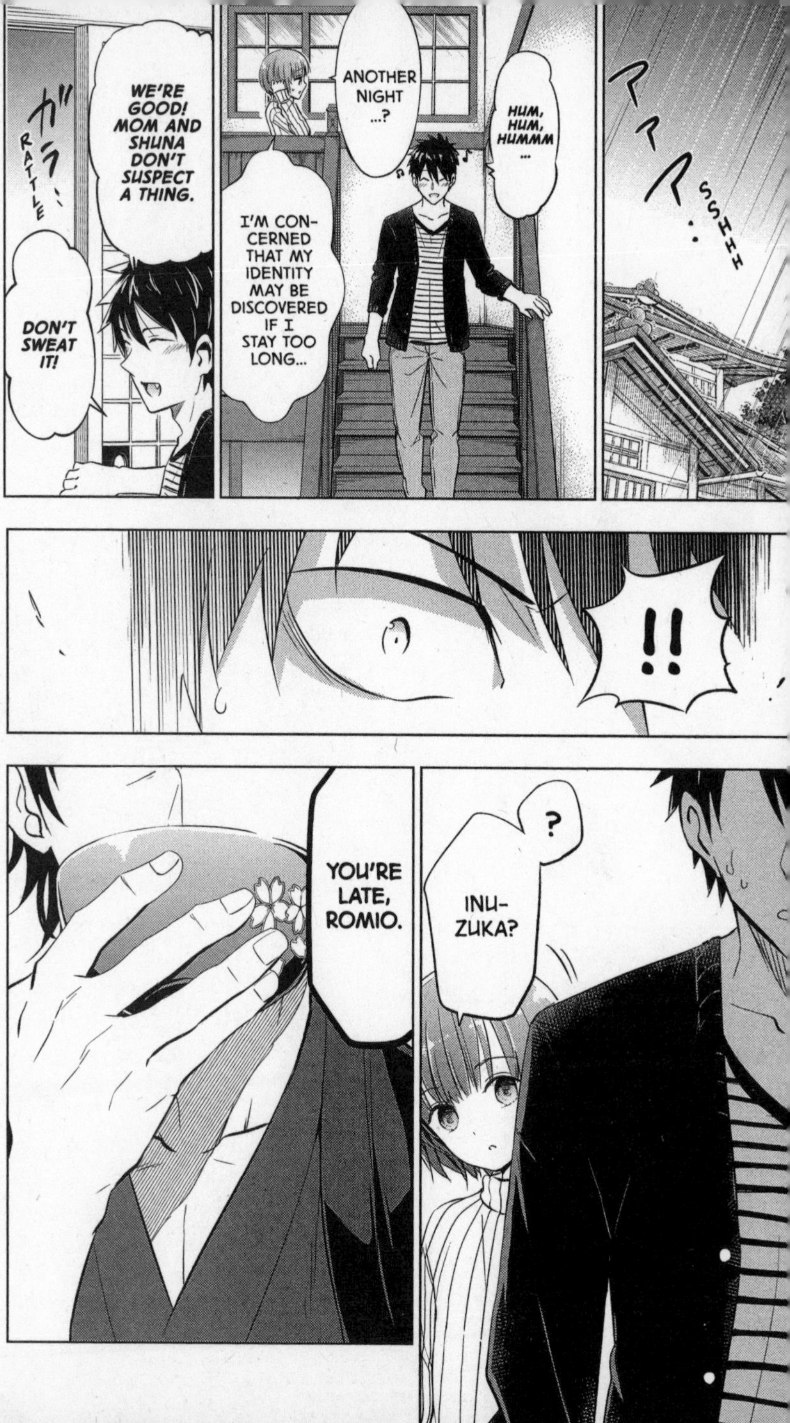
アァァ
SSHHH
HUM, HUM, HUMMM...
ANOTHER NIGHT ...?
I'M CONCERNED THAT MY IDENTITY MAY BE DISCOVERED IF I STAY TOO LONG...
WE'RE GOOD! MOM AND SHUNA DON'T SUSPECT A THING.
ガラ
RATTLE
DON'T SWEAT IT!
!!
?
INU-ZUKA?
YOU'RE LATE, ROMIO.

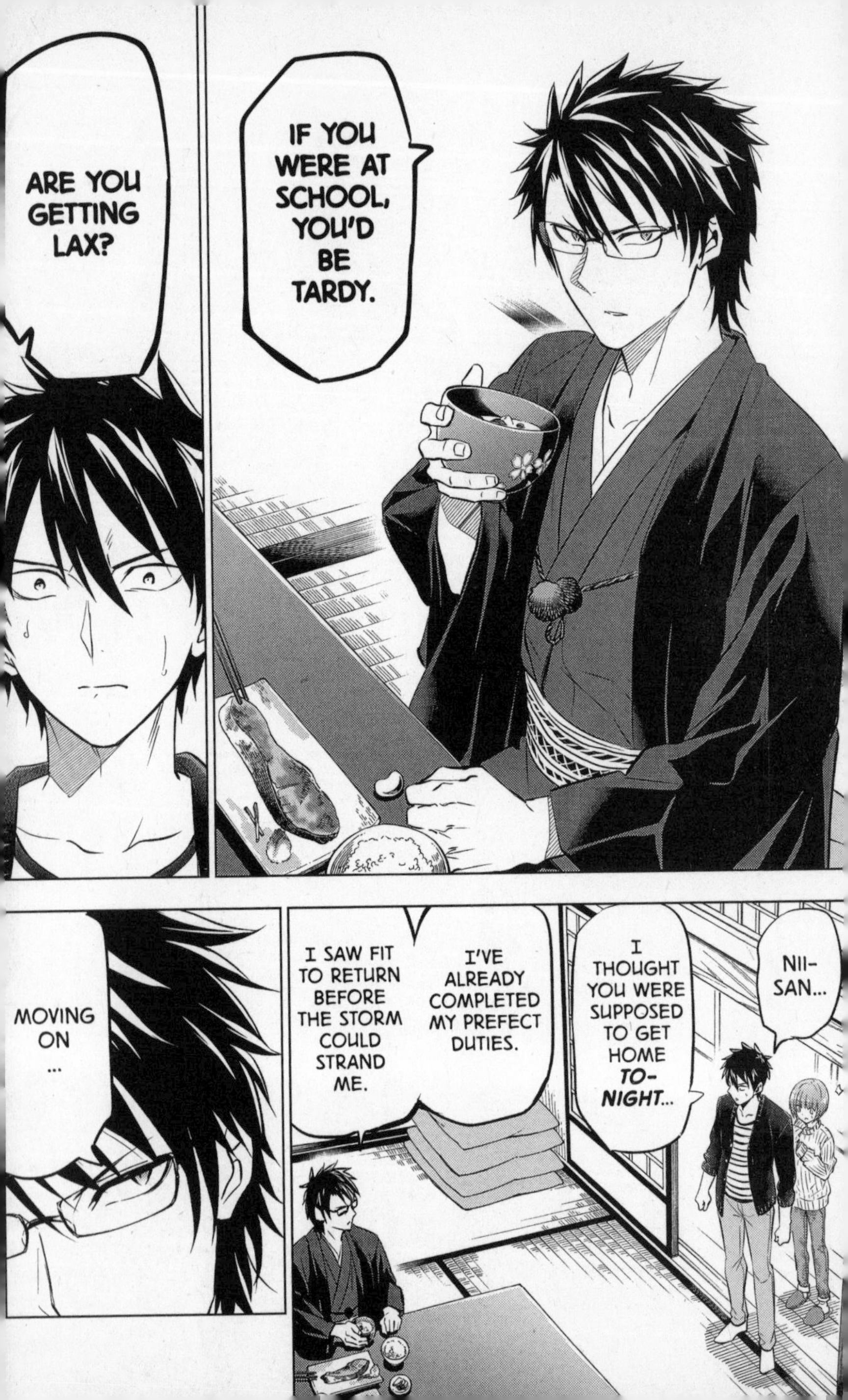
IF YOU WERE AT SCHOOL, YOU'D BE TARDY.
ARE YOU GETTING LAX?
NII-SAN...
I THOUGHT YOU WERE SUPPOSED TO GET HOME ***TO-NIGHT***...
I'VE ALREADY COMPLETED MY PREFECT DUTIES.
I SAW FIT TO RETURN BEFORE THE STORM COULD STRAND ME.
MOVING ON ...

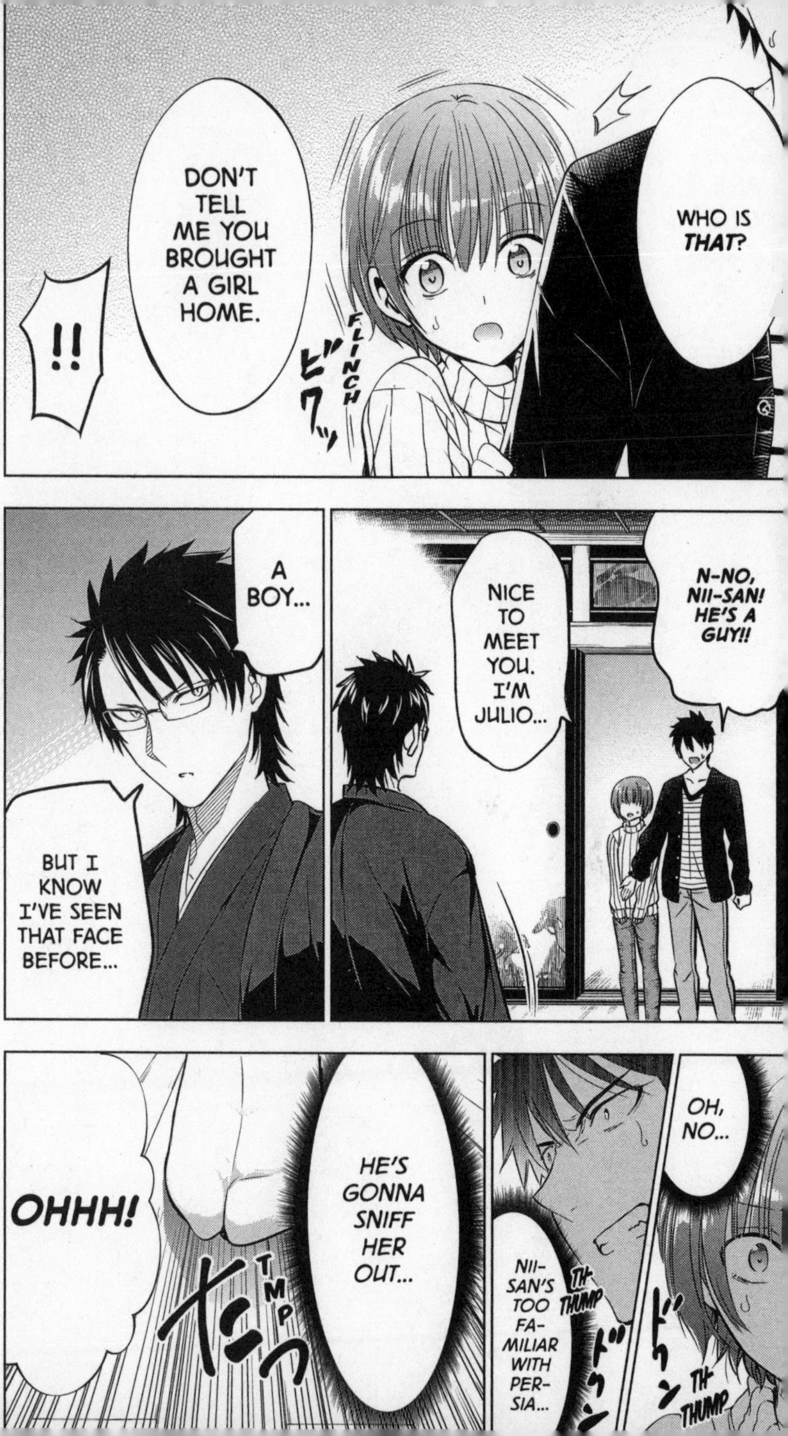
WHO IS *THAT?*
FLINCH
DON'T TELL ME YOU BROUGHT A GIRL HOME.
!!
N-NO, NII-SAN! HE'S A GUY!!
NICE TO MEET YOU. I'M JULIO...
A BOY...
BUT I KNOW I'VE SEEN THAT FACE BEFORE...
OH, NO...
TH-THUMP
NII-SAN'S TOO FA-MILIAR WITH PER-SIA...
TH-THUMP
HE'S GONNA SNIFF HER OUT...
OHHH!
TMP

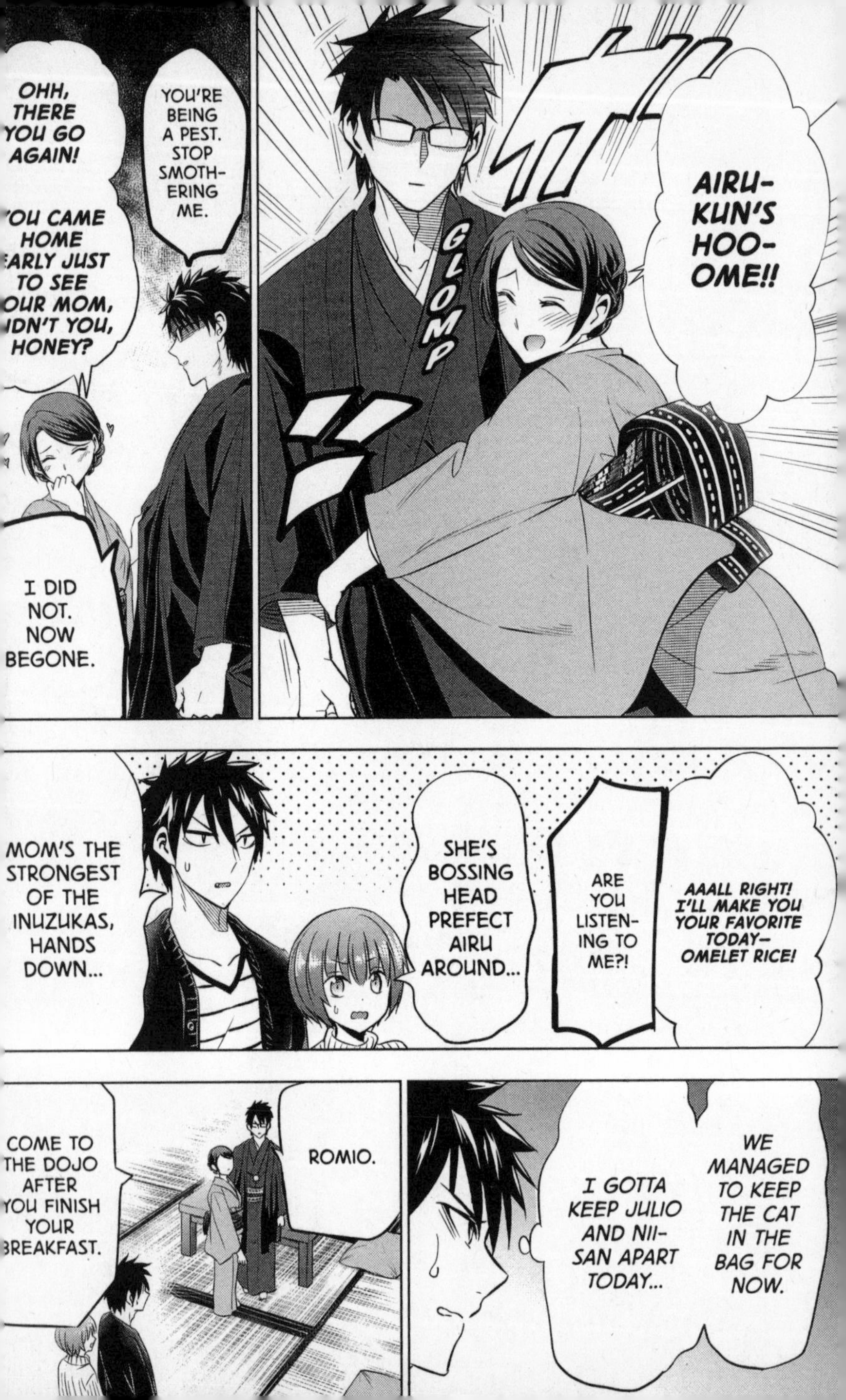
AIRU-KUN'S HOO-OME!!
GLOMP
YOU'RE BEING A PEST. STOP SMOTH-ERING ME.
OHH, THERE YOU GO AGAIN!
OU CAME HOME ARLY JUST TO SEE OUR MOM, IDN'T YOU, HONEY?
I DID NOT. NOW BEGONE.
AAALL RIGHT! I'LL MAKE YOU YOUR FAVORITE TODAY—OMELET RICE!
ARE YOU LISTEN-ING TO ME?!
SHE'S BOSSING HEAD PREFECT AIRU AROUND...
MOM'S THE STRONGEST OF THE INUZUKAS, HANDS DOWN...
WE MANAGED TO KEEP THE CAT IN THE BAG FOR NOW.
I GOTTA KEEP JULIO AND NII-SAN APART TODAY...
ROMIO.
COME TO THE DOJO AFTER OU FINISH YOUR REAKFAST.

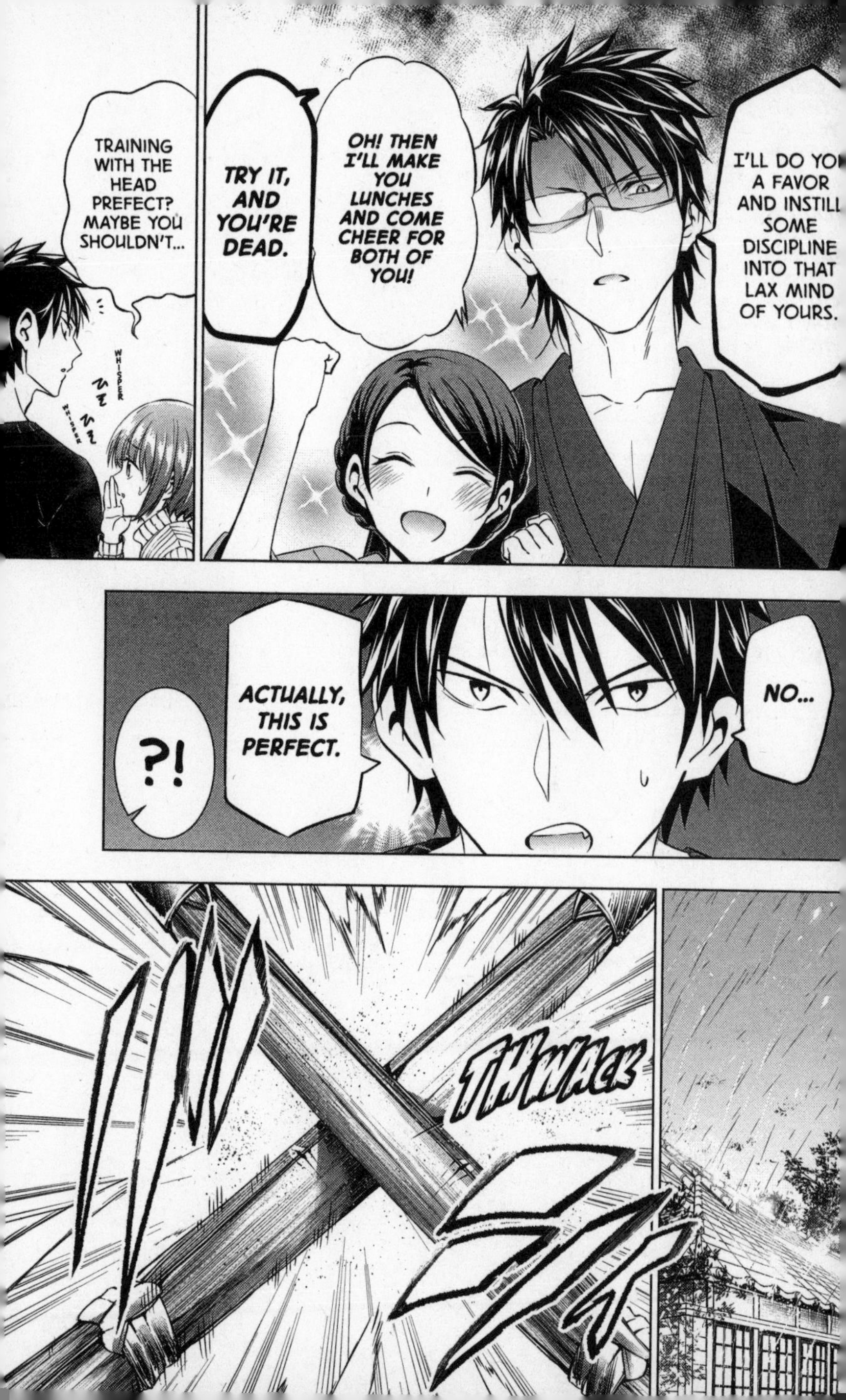
I'LL DO YO A FAVOR AND INSTILL SOME DISCIPLINE INTO THAT LAX MIND OF YOURS.
OH! THEN I'LL MAKE YOU LUNCHES AND COME CHEER FOR BOTH OF YOU!
TRY IT, AND YOU'RE DEAD.
WHISPER
WHISPER
TRAINING WITH THE HEAD PREFECT? MAYBE YOU SHOULDN'T...
NO...
ACTUALLY, THIS IS PERFECT.
?!
THWACK

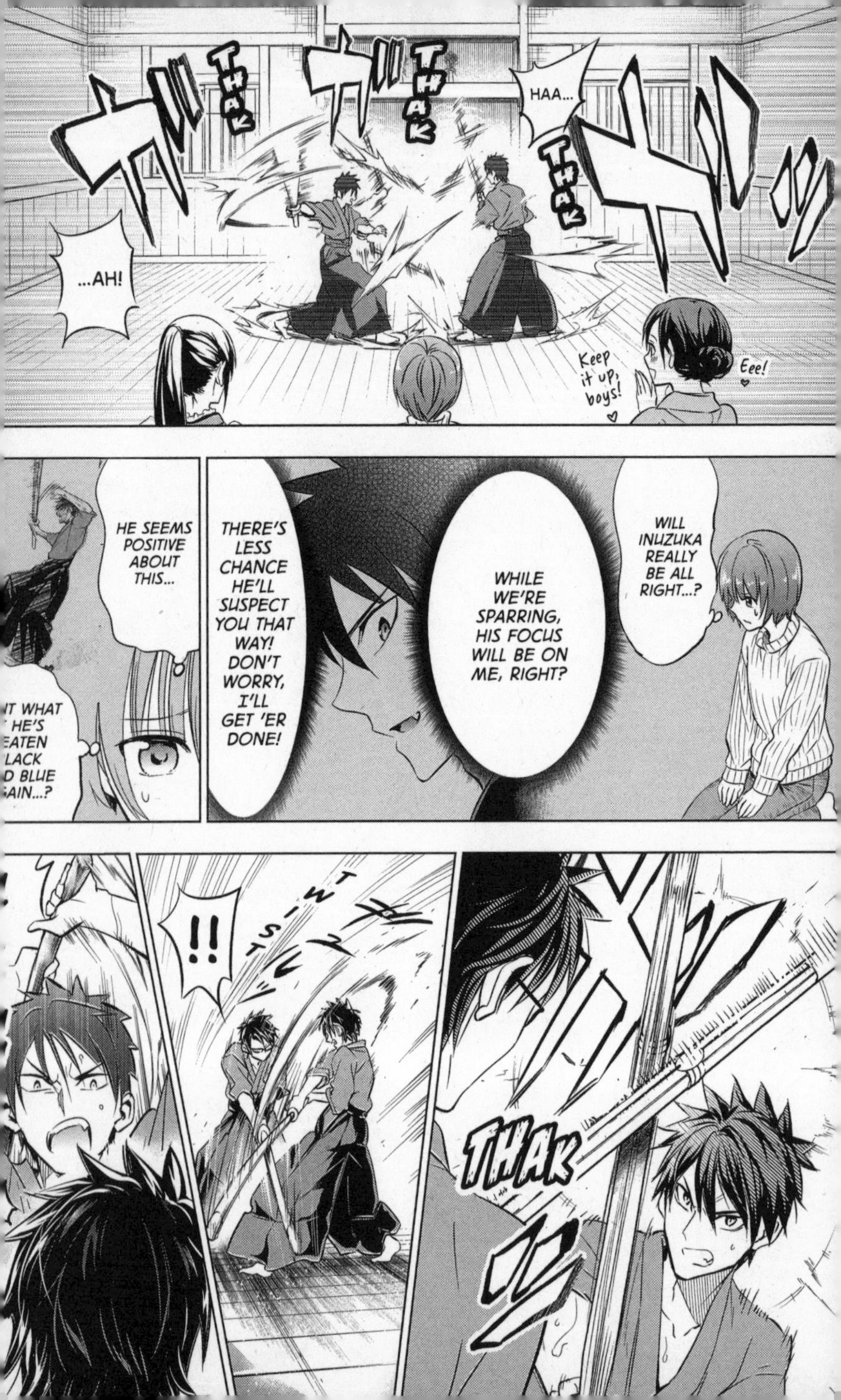
HAA...
THAK
Eee!
Keep it up, boys!
THAK
THAK
...AH!
WILL INUZUKA REALLY BE ALL RIGHT...?
WHILE WE'RE SPARRING, HIS FOCUS WILL BE ON ME, RIGHT?
THERE'S LESS CHANCE HE'LL SUSPECT YOU THAT WAY! DON'T WORRY, I'LL GET 'ER DONE!
HE SEEMS POSITIVE ABOUT THIS...
T WHAT HE'S EATEN LACK D BLUE AIN...?
THAK
TWIST
!!

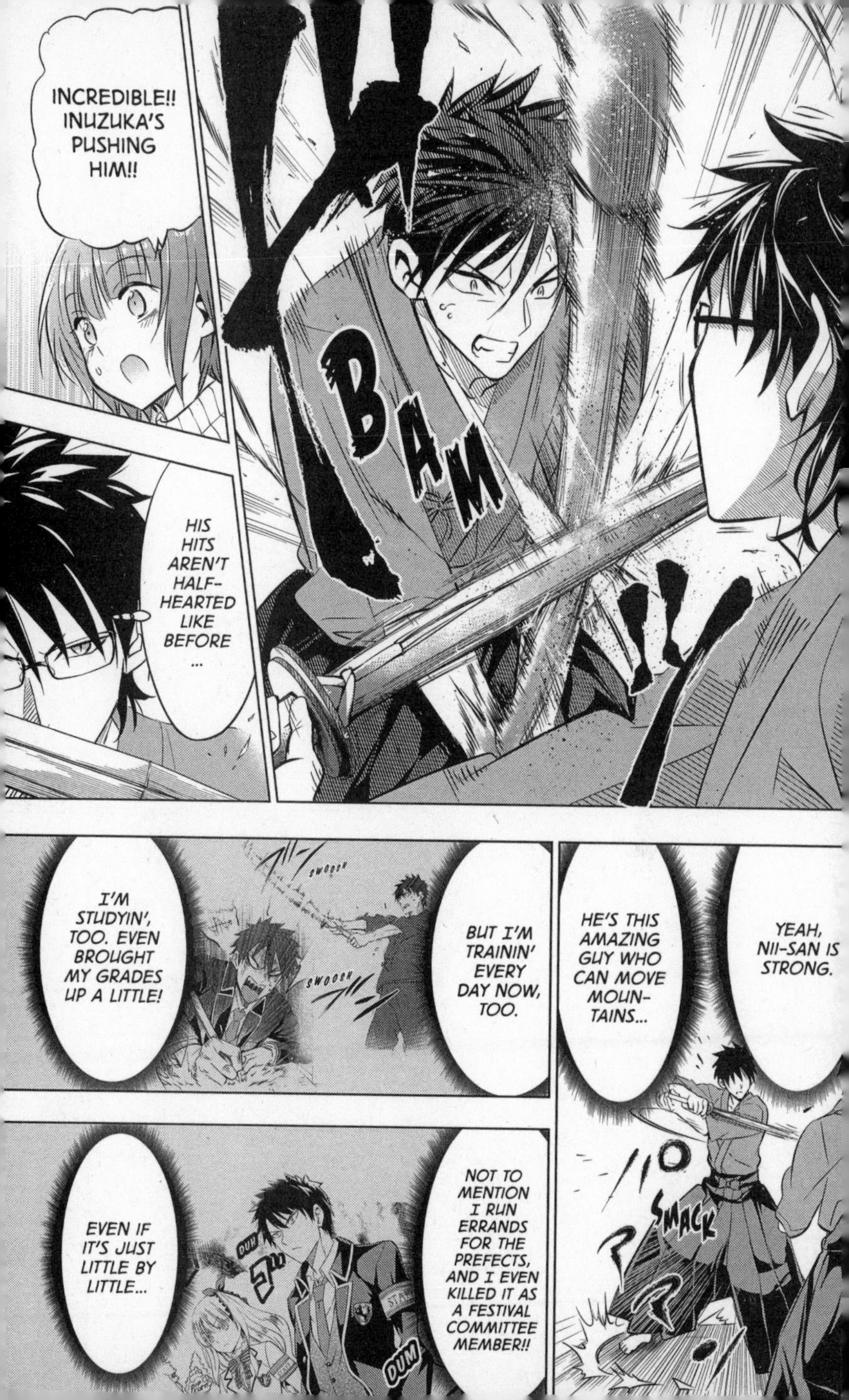
BAM
INCREDIBLE!! INUZUKA'S PUSHING HIM!!
HIS HITS AREN'T HALF-HEARTED LIKE BEFORE ...
YEAH, NII-SAN IS STRONG.
HE'S THIS AMAZING GUY WHO CAN MOVE MOUN-TAINS...
SMACK
BUT I'M TRAININ' EVERY DAY NOW, TOO.
SWOOSH
SWOOSH
I'M STUDYIN', TOO. EVEN BROUGHT MY GRADES UP A LITTLE!
NOT TO MENTION I RUN ERRANDS FOR THE PREFECTS, AND I EVEN KILLED IT AS A FESTIVAL COMMITTEE MEMBER!!
DUM
DUM
EVEN IF IT'S JUST LITTLE BY LITTLE...

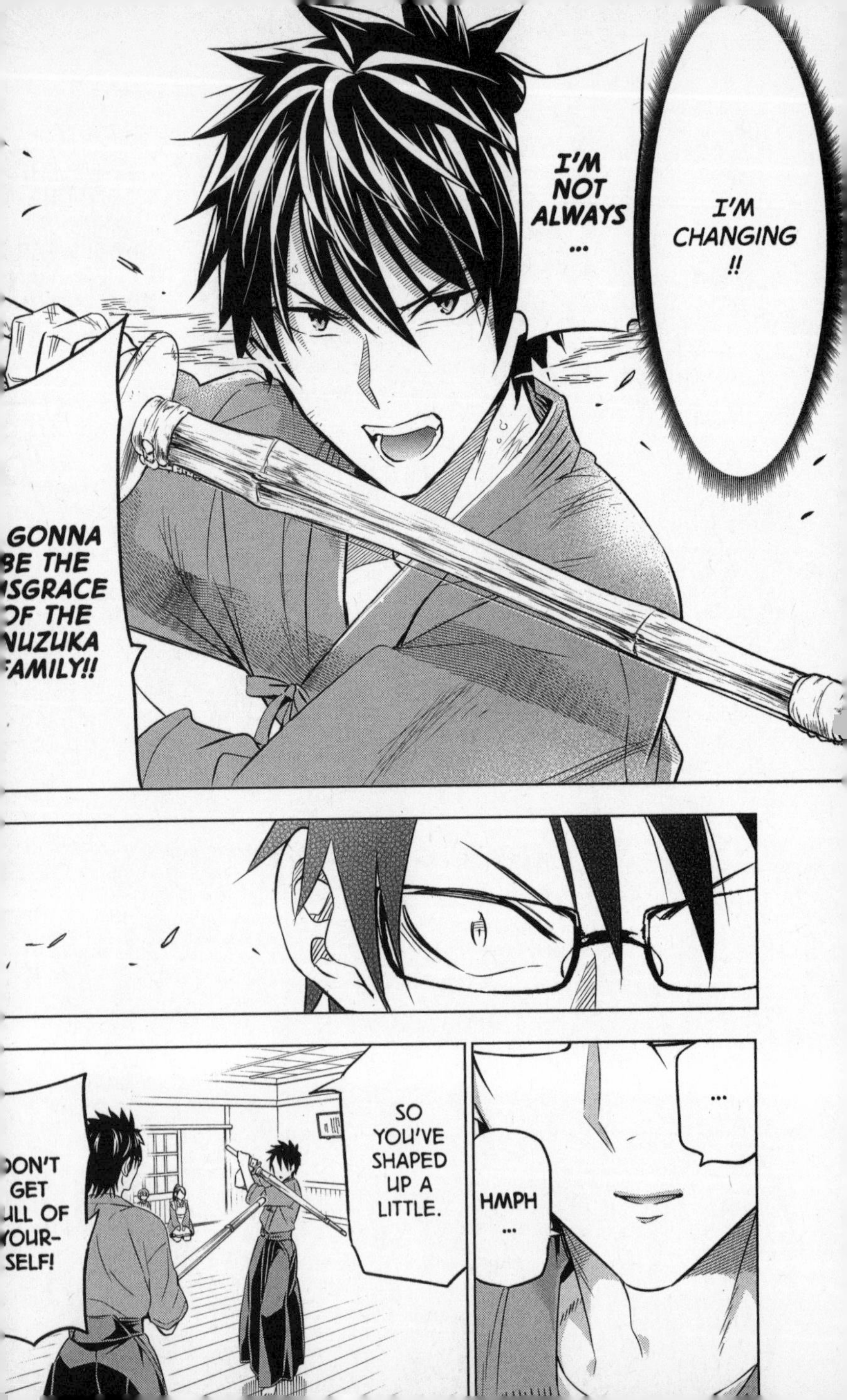
I'M CHANGING !!
I'M NOT ALWAYS ...
GONNA BE THE ISGRACE OF THE NUZUKA AMILY!!
...
HMPH ...
SO YOU'VE SHAPED UP A LITTLE.
ON'T GET ULL OF OUR- SELF!

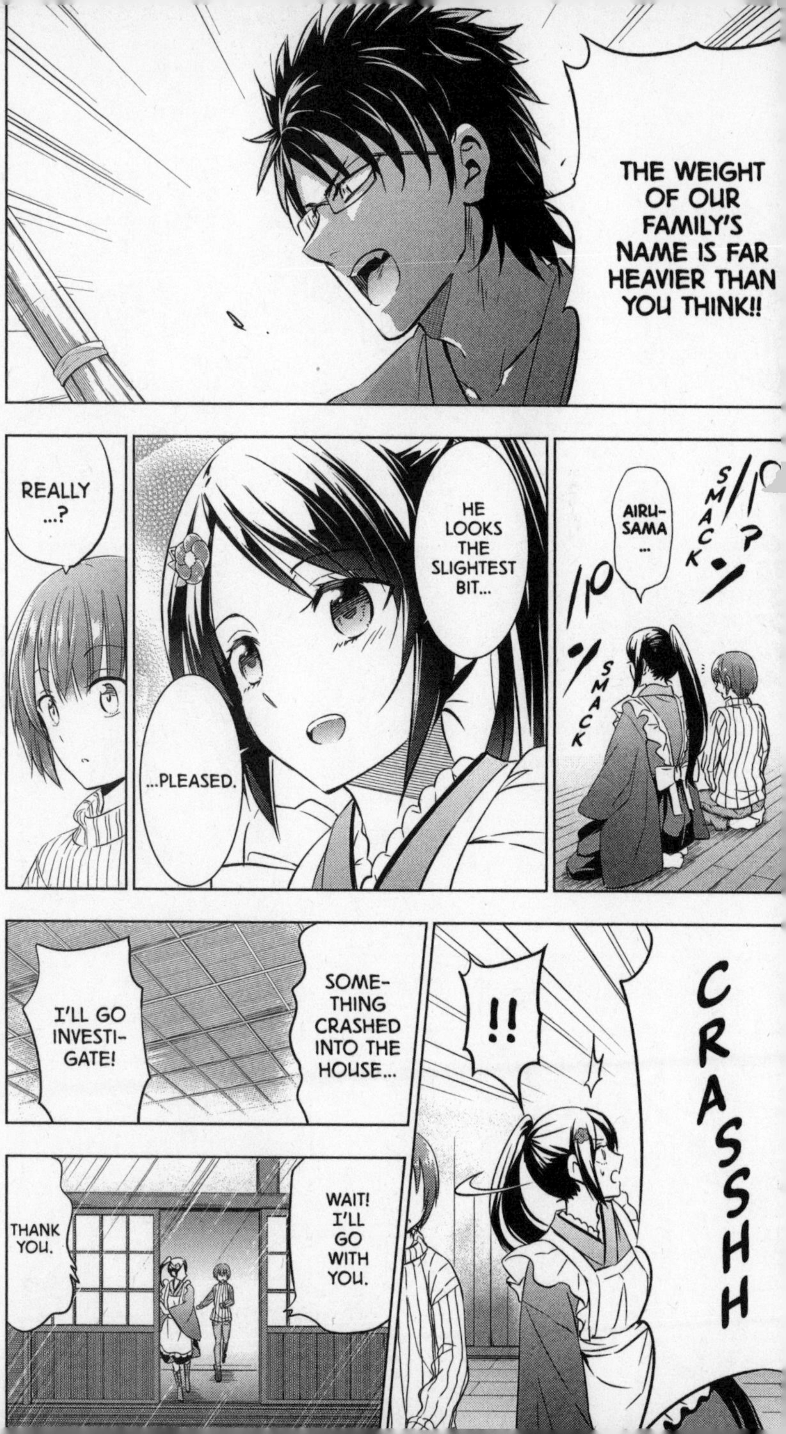
THE WEIGHT OF OUR FAMILY'S NAME IS FAR HEAVIER THAN YOU THINK!!
SMACK
AIRU-SAMA ...
SMACK
?
HE LOOKS THE SLIGHTEST BIT...
...PLEASED.
REALLY ...?
CRASSHH
!!
SOME-THING CRASHED INTO THE HOUSE...
I'LL GO INVESTI-GATE!
WAIT! I'LL GO WITH YOU.
THANK YOU.

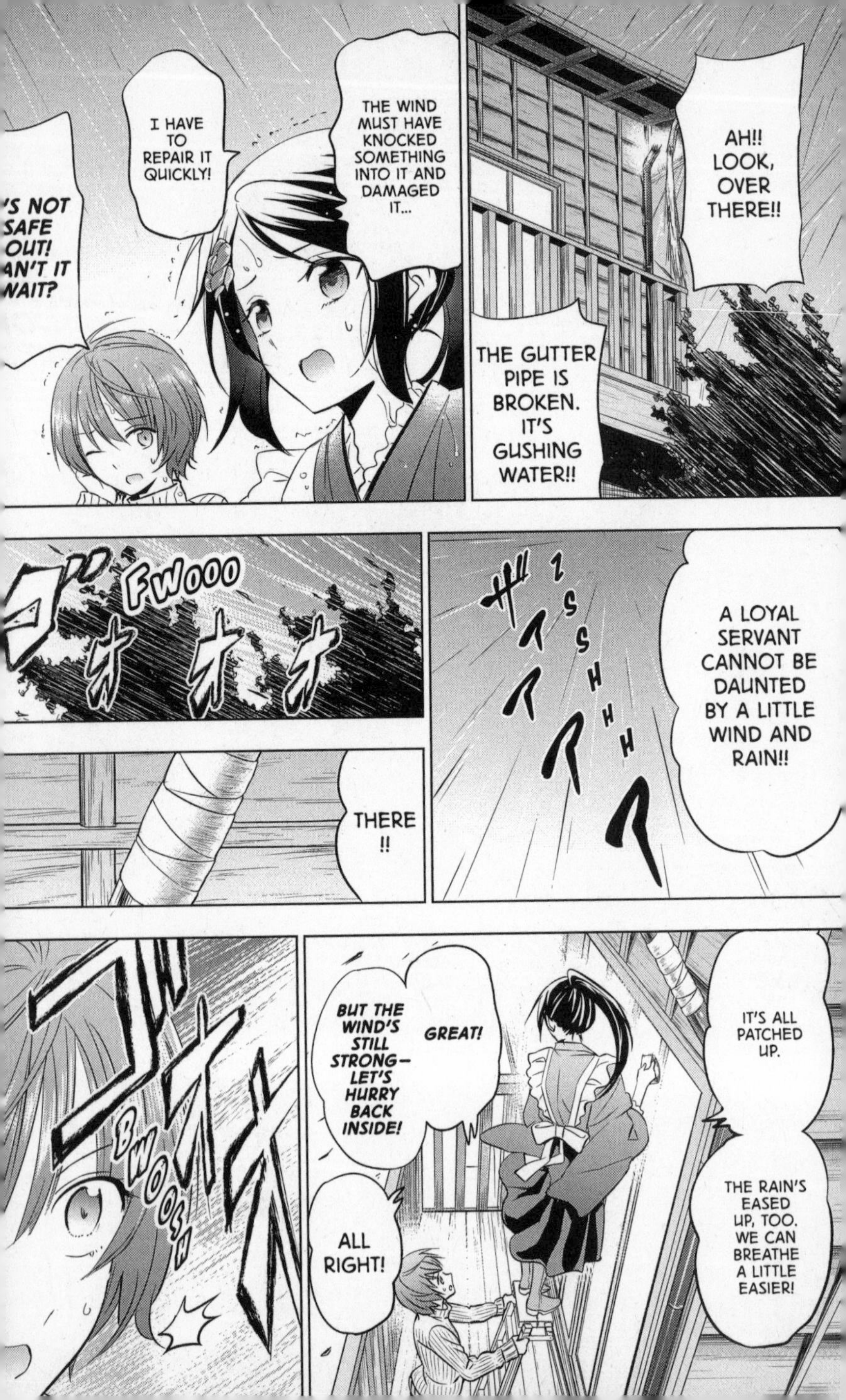
AH!! LOOK, OVER THERE!!
THE GUTTER PIPE IS BROKEN. IT'S GUSHING WATER!!
THE WIND MUST HAVE KNOCKED SOMETHING INTO IT AND DAMAGED IT...
I HAVE TO REPAIR IT QUICKLY!
'S NOT SAFE OUT! AN'T IT WAIT?
A LOYAL SERVANT CANNOT BE DAUNTED BY A LITTLE WIND AND RAIN!!
ZSSHHH
FWOOO
THERE !!
IT'S ALL PATCHED UP.
THE RAIN'S EASED UP, TOO. WE CAN BREATHE A LITTLE EASIER!
GREAT!
BUT THE WIND'S STILL STRONG— LET'S HURRY BACK INSIDE!
ALL RIGHT!
BWOOSH

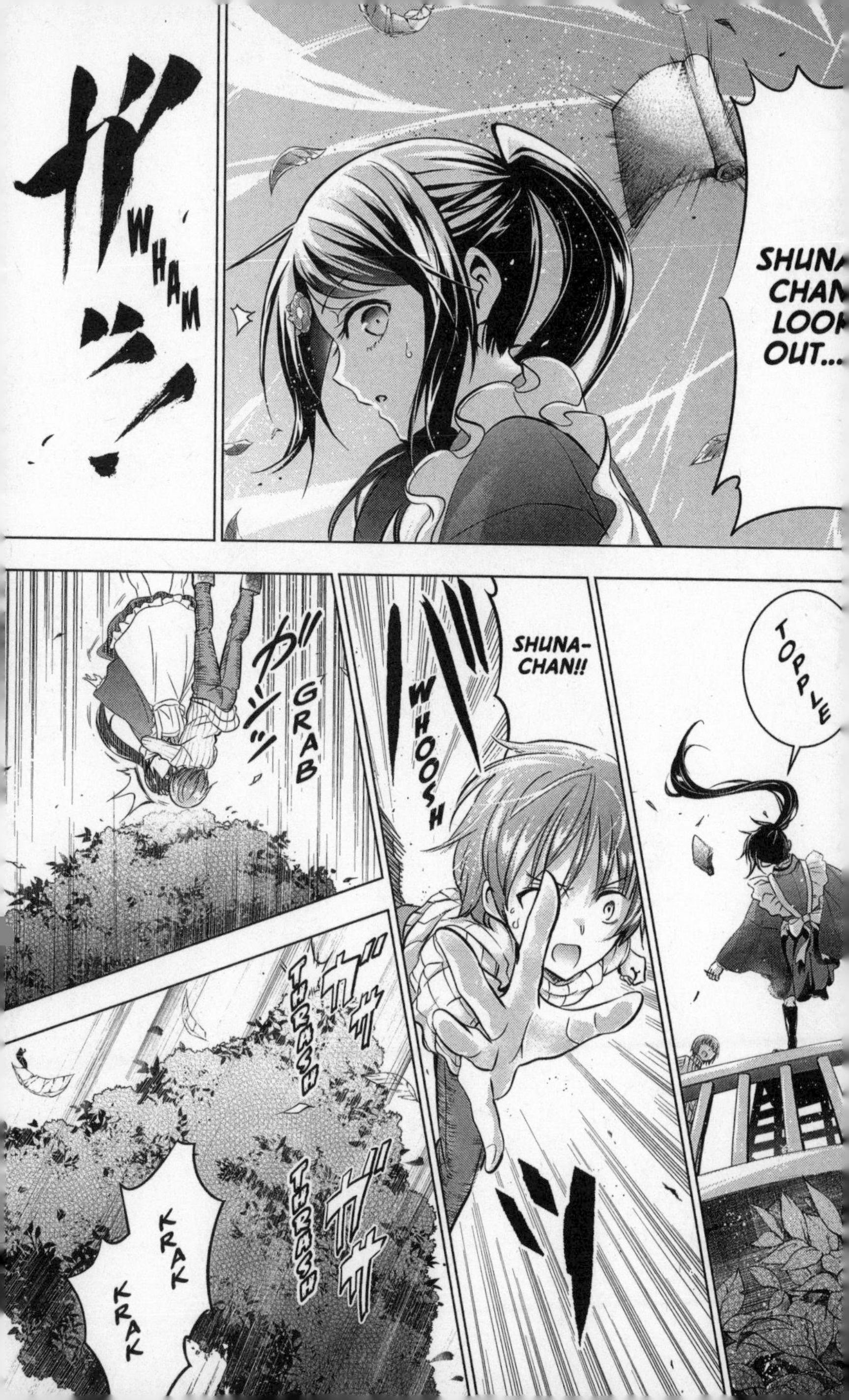
SHUNA CHAN LOOK OUT...
WHAM
TOPPLE
SHUNA-CHAN!!
WHOOSH
GRAB
THRASH
THRASH
KRAK
KRAK

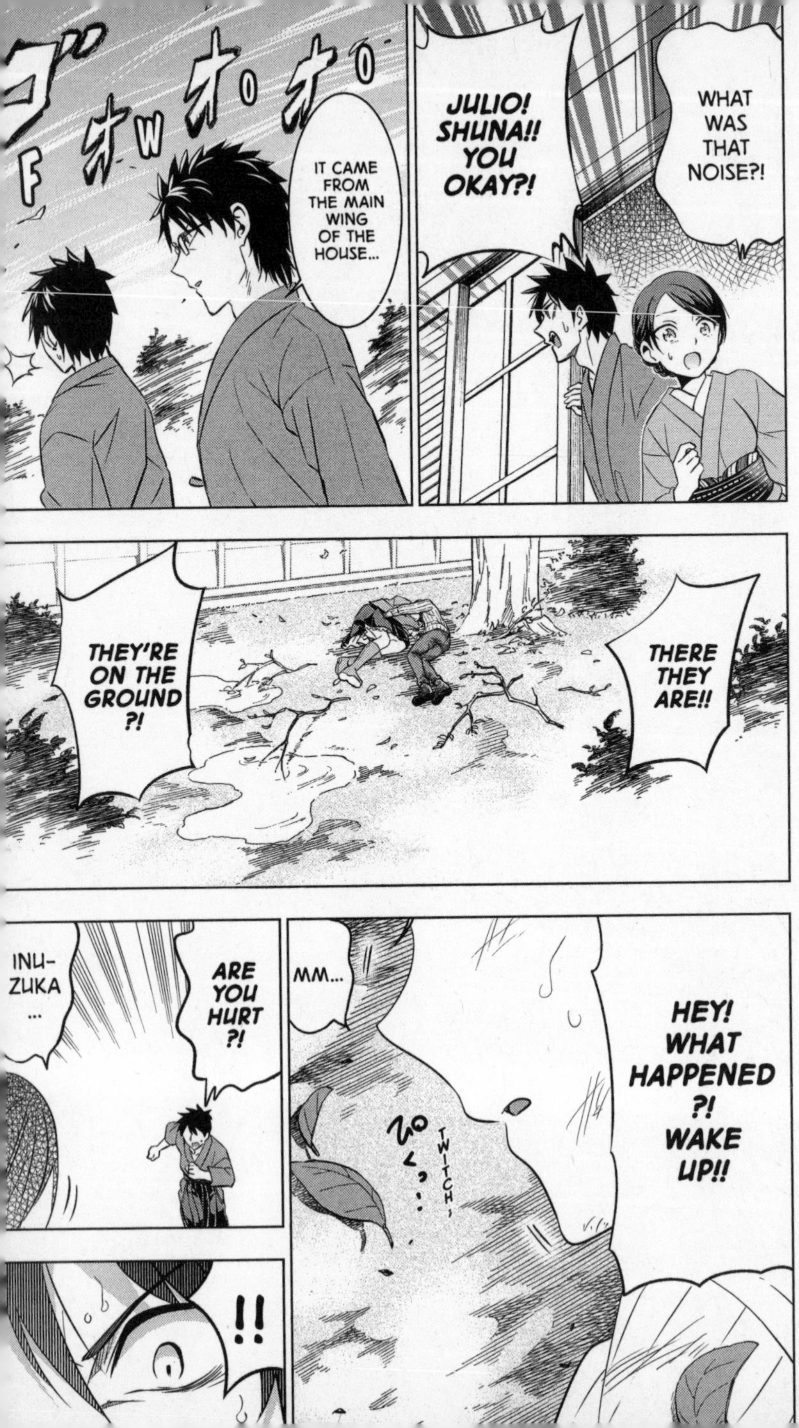
WHAT WAS THAT NOISE?!
JULIO! SHUNA!! YOU OKAY?!
FWOO
IT CAME FROM THE MAIN WING OF THE HOUSE...
THERE THEY ARE!!
THEY'RE ON THE GROUND?!
HEY! WHAT HAPPENED?! WAKE UP!!
MM...
TWITCH
ARE YOU HURT?!
INU-ZUKA...
!!

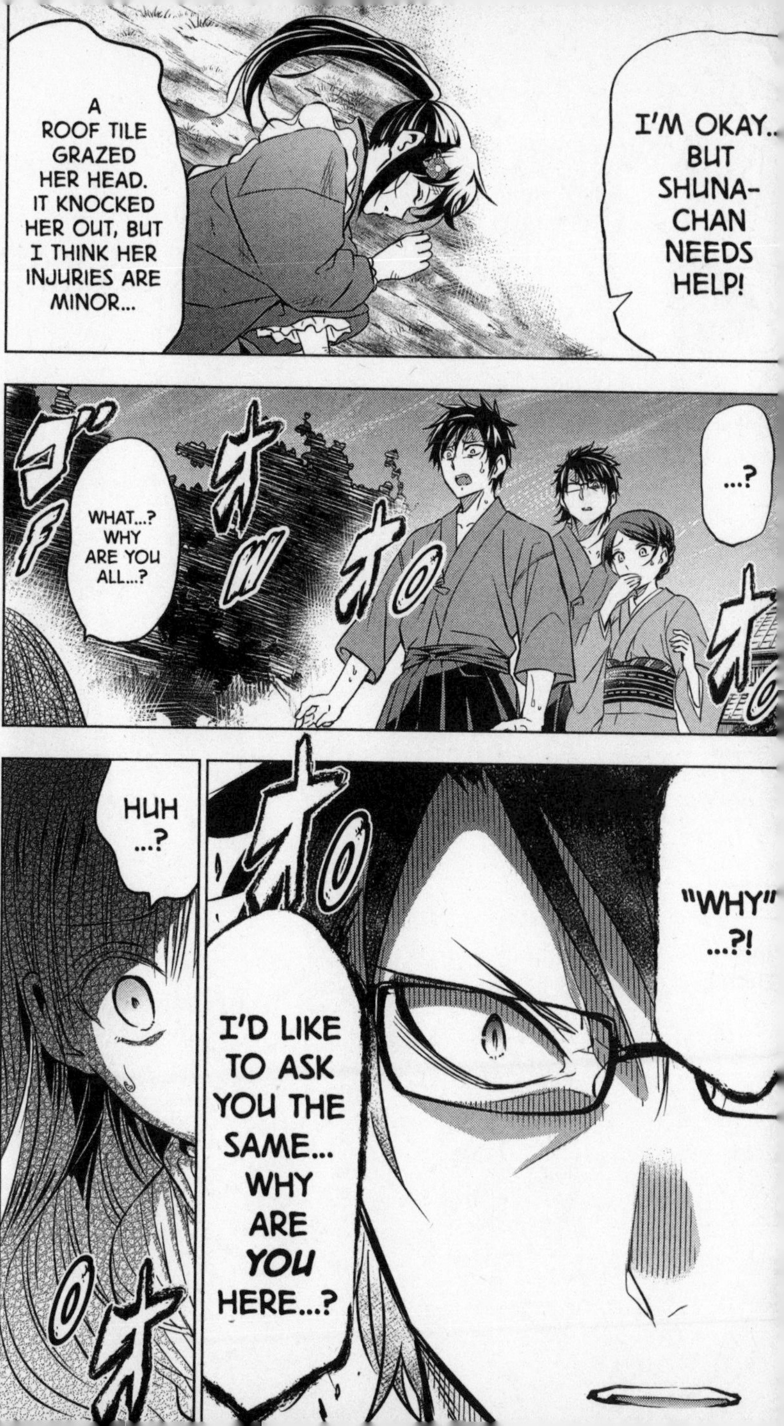
I'M OKAY... BUT SHUNA-CHAN NEEDS HELP!
A ROOF TILE GRAZED HER HEAD. IT KNOCKED HER OUT, BUT I THINK HER INJURIES ARE MINOR...
...?
WHAT...? WHY ARE YOU ALL...?
"WHY" ...?!
I'D LIKE TO ASK YOU THE SAME... WHY ARE *YOU* HERE...?
HUH ...?

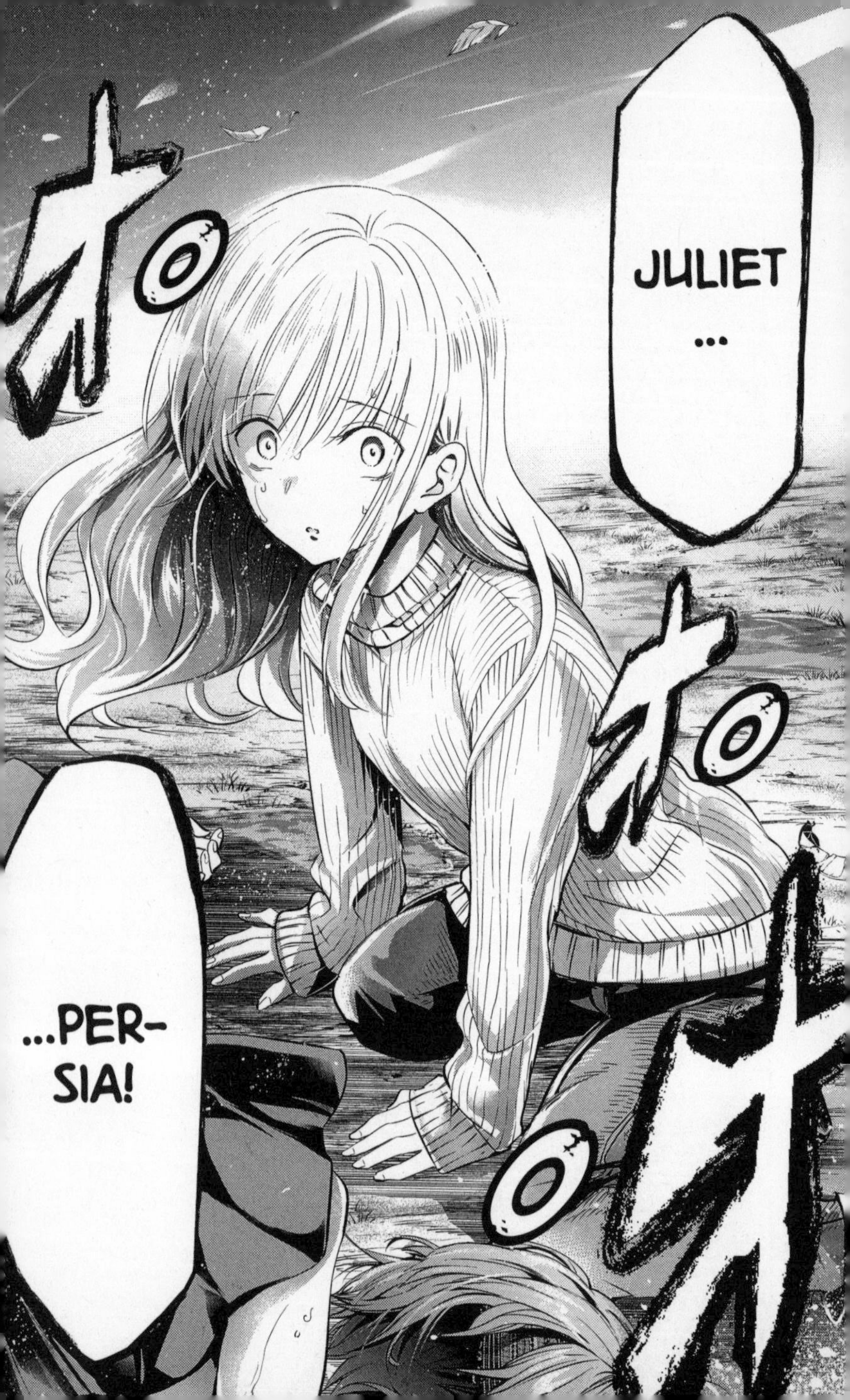
JULIET ...
...PER-SIA!

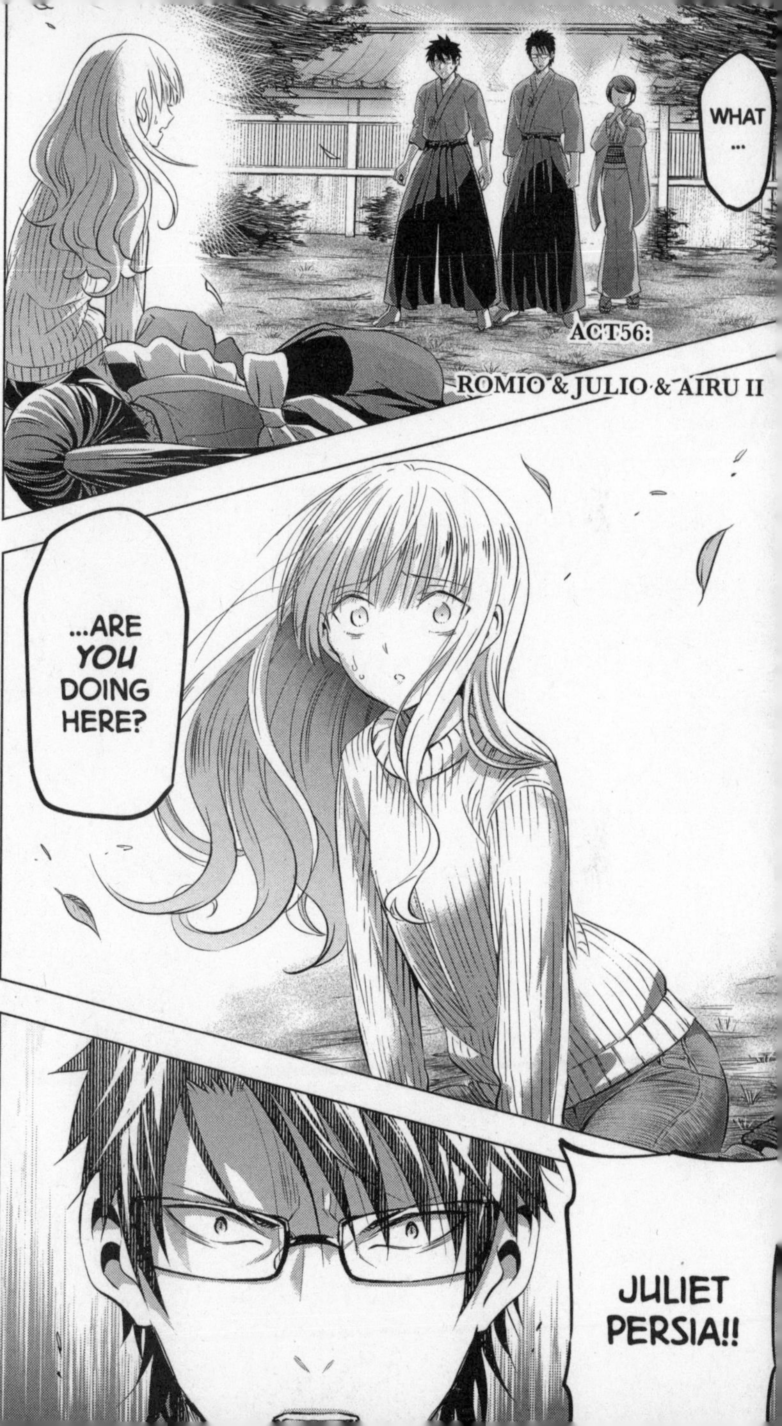
WHAT ...
ACT 56:
ROMIO & JULIO & AIRU II
...ARE *YOU* DOING HERE?
JULIET PERSIA!!

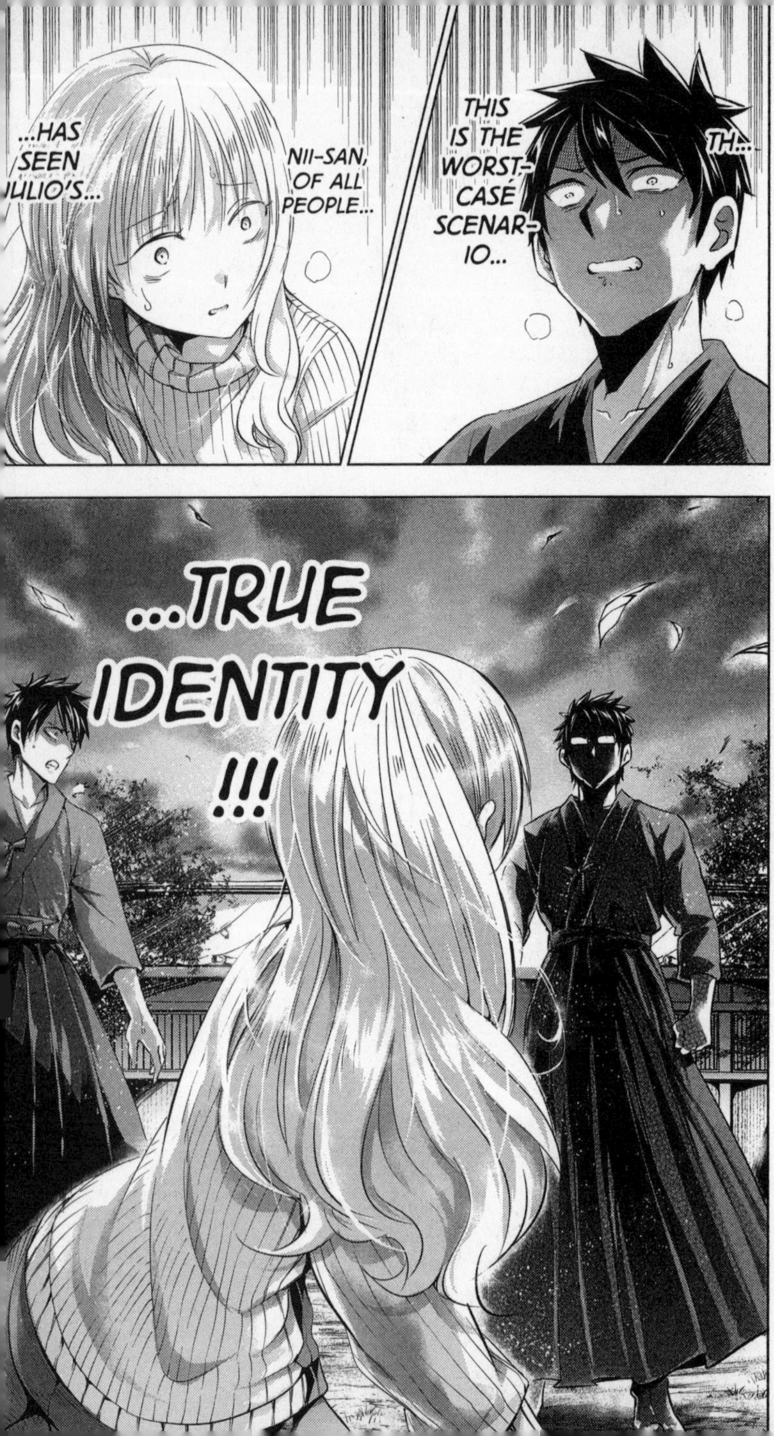
TH...
THIS IS THE WORST-CASE SCENARIO...
NII-SAN, OF ALL PEOPLE...
...HAS SEEN ULIO'S...
...TRUE IDENTITY !!!

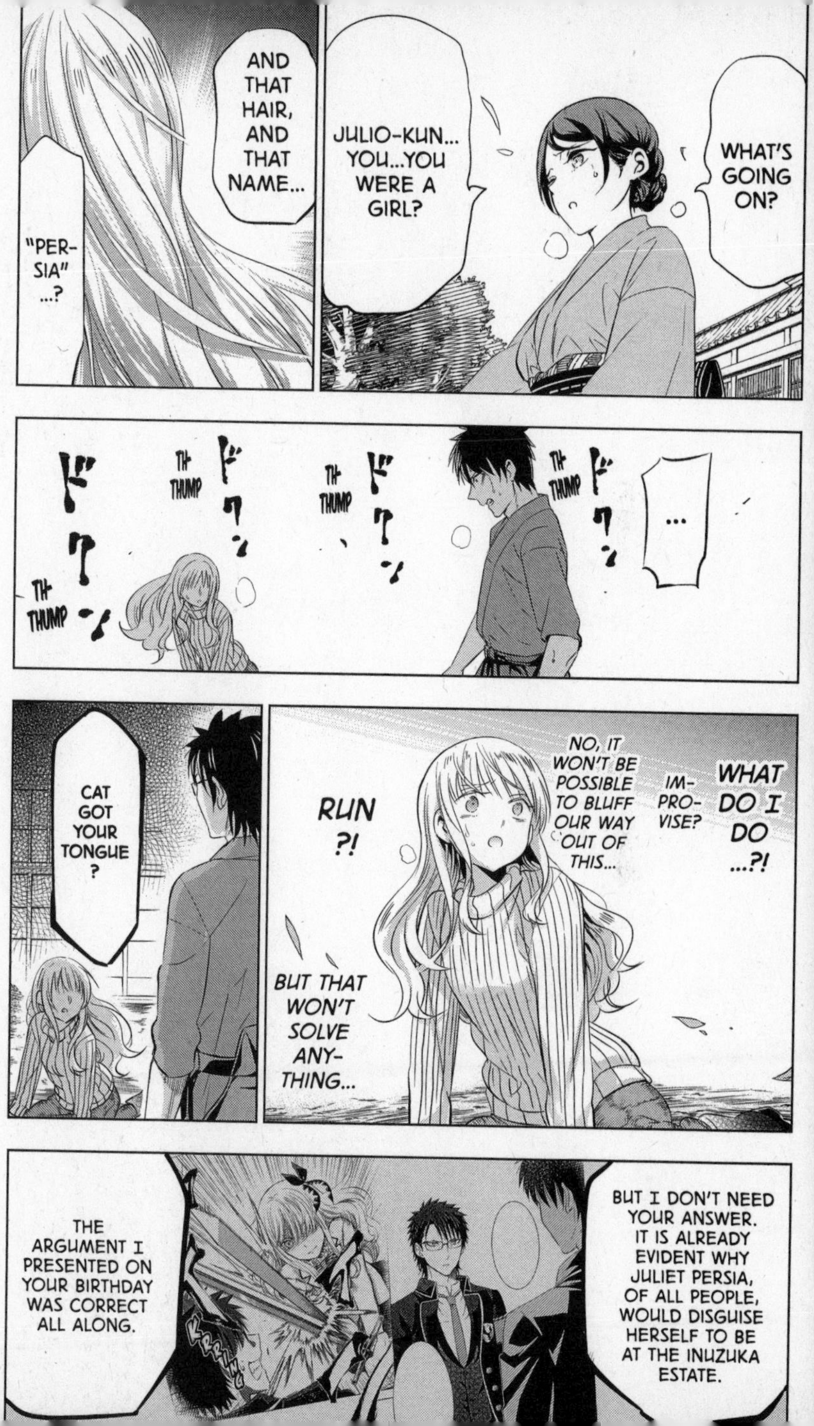
WHAT'S GOING ON?
JULIO-KUN... YOU...YOU WERE A GIRL?
AND THAT HAIR, AND THAT NAME...
"PER-SIA" ...?
...
TH-THUMP
ドクン
TH-THUMP
ドクン
TH-THUMP
ドクン
TH-THUMP
ドクン
WHAT DO I DO ...?!
IM-PRO-VISE?
NO, IT WON'T BE POSSIBLE TO BLUFF OUR WAY OUT OF THIS...
RUN ?!
BUT THAT WON'T SOLVE ANYTHING...
CAT GOT YOUR TONGUE ?
BUT I DON'T NEED YOUR ANSWER. IT IS ALREADY EVIDENT WHY JULIET PERSIA, OF ALL PEOPLE, WOULD DISGUISE HERSELF TO BE AT THE INUZUKA ESTATE.
THE ARGUMENT I PRESENTED ON YOUR BIRTHDAY WAS CORRECT ALL ALONG.
KRRING

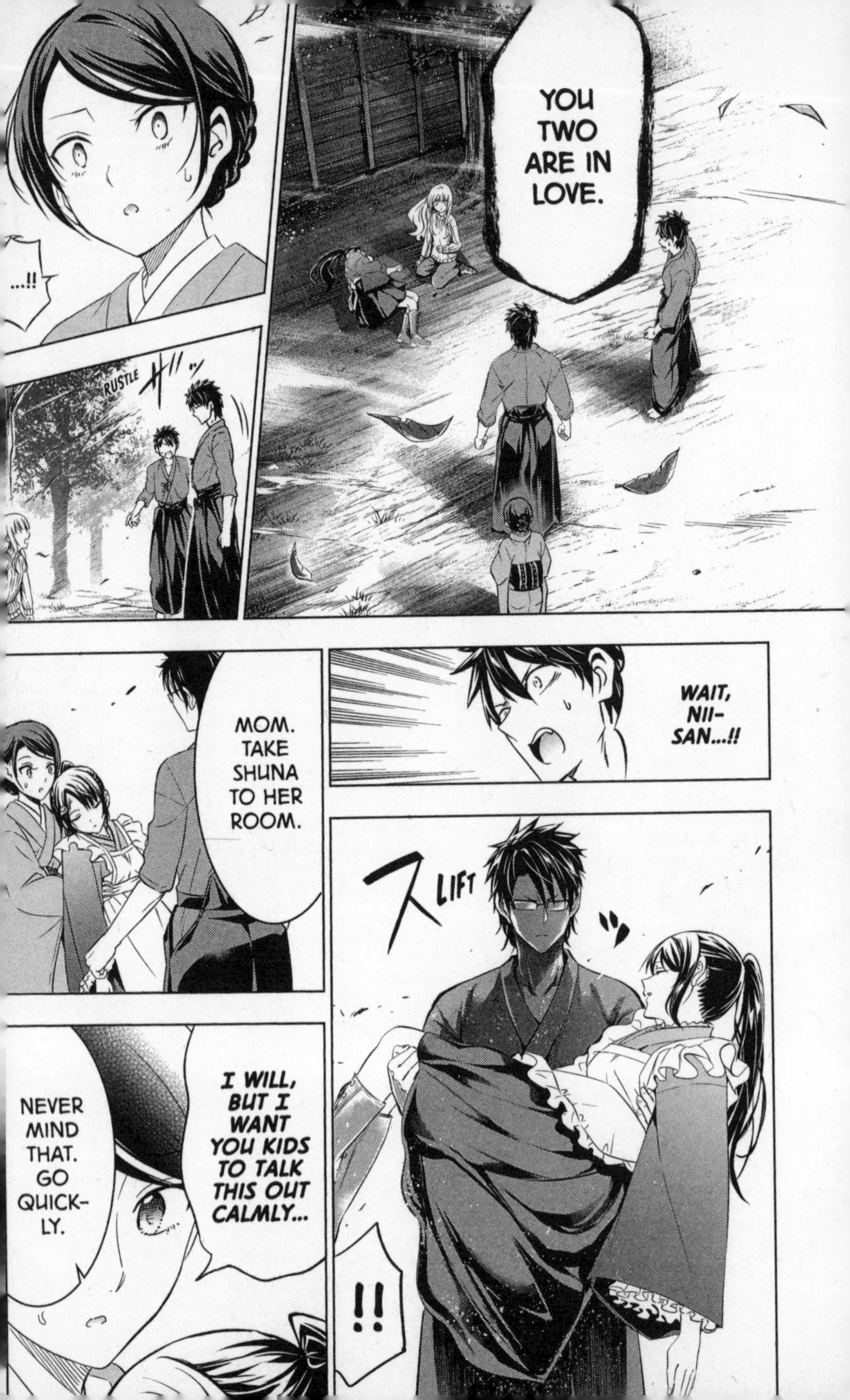
YOU TWO ARE IN LOVE.
...!!
RUSTLE
WAIT, NII-SAN...!!
MOM. TAKE SHUNA TO HER ROOM.
LIFT
!!
I WILL, BUT I WANT YOU KIDS TO TALK THIS OUT CALMLY...
NEVER MIND THAT. GO QUICKLY.

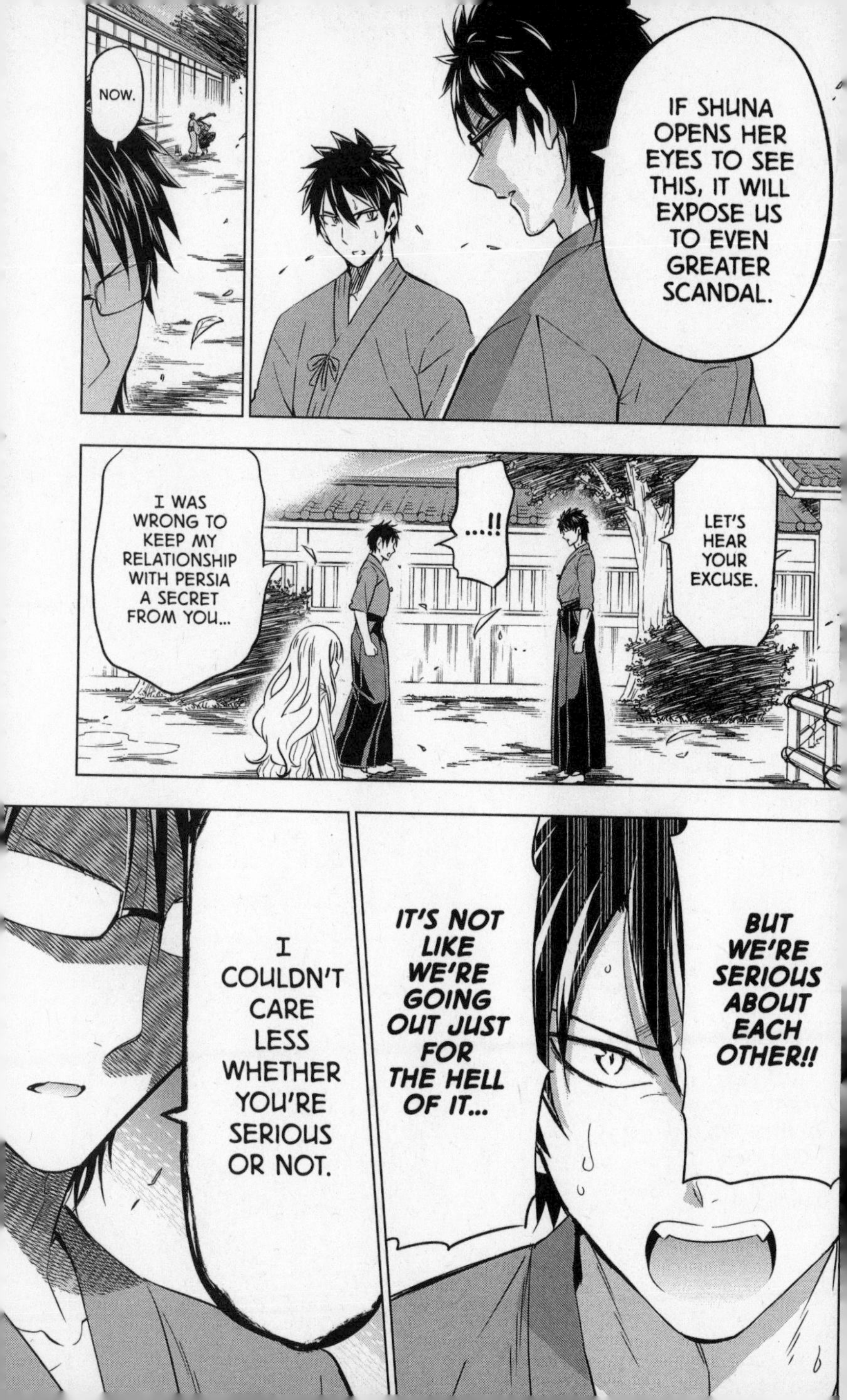
IF SHUNA OPENS HER EYES TO SEE THIS, IT WILL EXPOSE US TO EVEN GREATER SCANDAL.
NOW.
LET'S HEAR YOUR EXCUSE.
...!!
I WAS WRONG TO KEEP MY RELATIONSHIP WITH PERSIA A SECRET FROM YOU...
IT'S NOT LIKE WE'RE GOING OUT JUST FOR THE HELL OF IT...
BUT WE'RE SERIOUS ABOUT EACH OTHER!!
I COULDN'T CARE LESS WHETHER YOU'RE SERIOUS OR NOT.

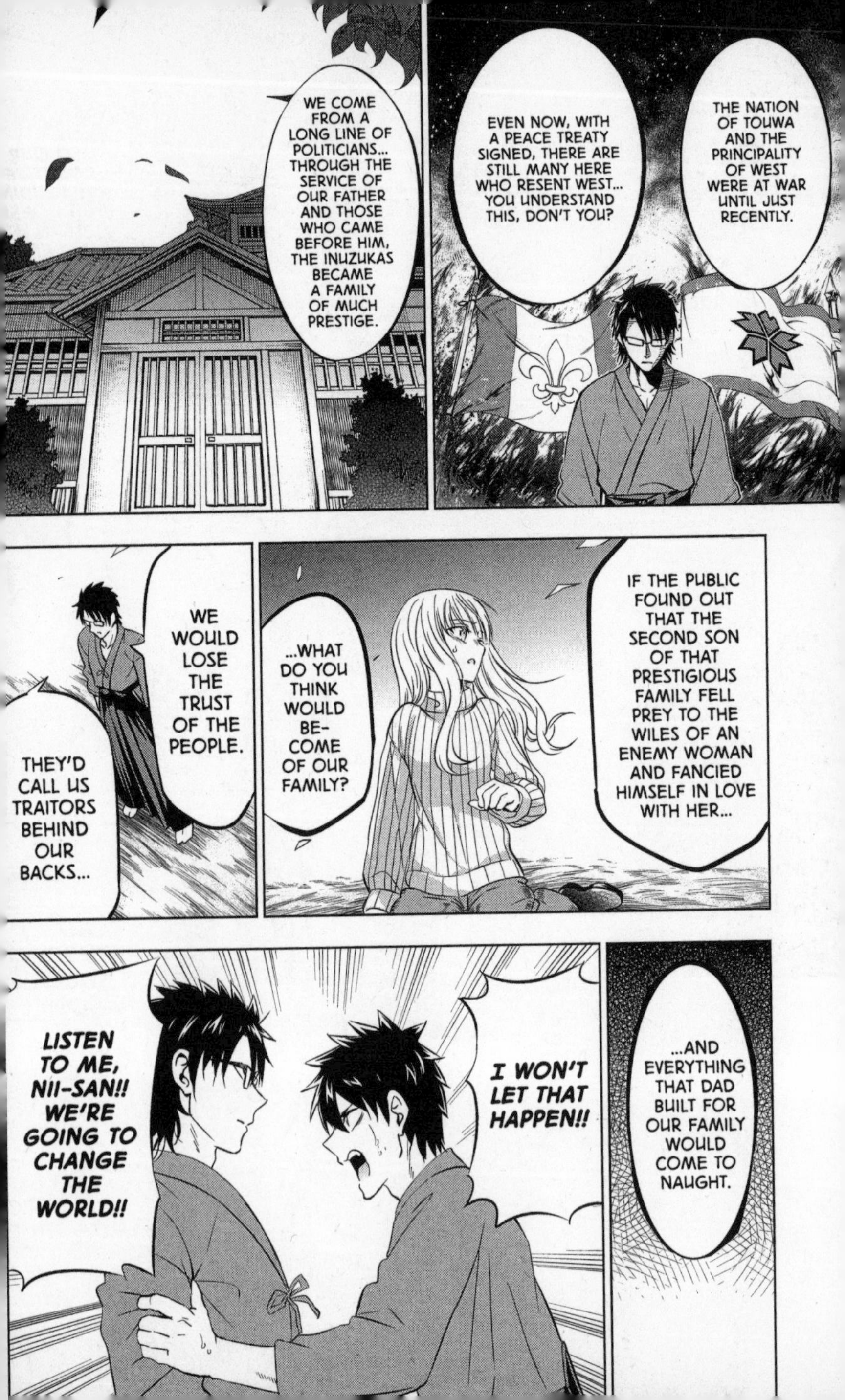

THE NATION OF TOUWA AND THE PRINCIPALITY OF WEST WERE AT WAR UNTIL JUST RECENTLY.
EVEN NOW, WITH A PEACE TREATY SIGNED, THERE ARE STILL MANY HERE WHO RESENT WEST... YOU UNDERSTAND THIS, DON'T YOU?
WE COME FROM A LONG LINE OF POLITICIANS... THROUGH THE SERVICE OF OUR FATHER AND THOSE WHO CAME BEFORE HIM, THE INUZUKAS BECAME A FAMILY OF MUCH PRESTIGE.
IF THE PUBLIC FOUND OUT THAT THE SECOND SON OF THAT PRESTIGIOUS FAMILY FELL PREY TO THE WILES OF AN ENEMY WOMAN AND FANCIED HIMSELF IN LOVE WITH HER...
...WHAT DO YOU THINK WOULD BE-COME OF OUR FAMILY?
WE WOULD LOSE THE TRUST OF THE PEOPLE.
THEY'D CALL US TRAITORS BEHIND OUR BACKS...
...AND EVERYTHING THAT DAD BUILT FOR OUR FAMILY WOULD COME TO NAUGHT.
I WON'T LET THAT HAPPEN!!
LISTEN TO ME, NII-SAN!! WE'RE GOING TO CHANGE THE WORLD!!

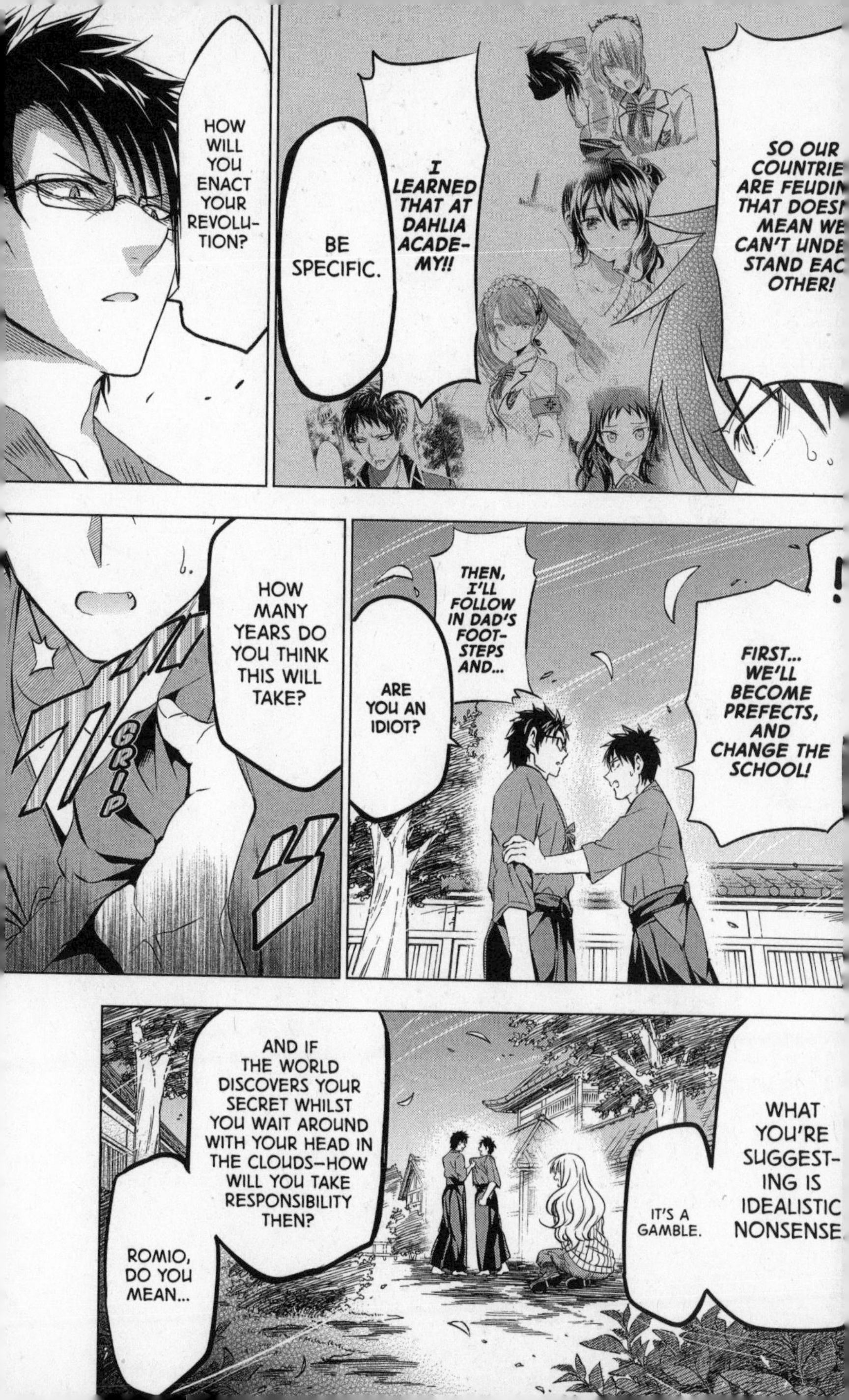
SO OUR COUNTRIE ARE FEUDIN THAT DOESI MEAN WE CAN'T UNDE STAND EAC OTHER!
I LEARNED THAT AT DAHLIA ACADE-MY!!
BE SPECIFIC.
HOW WILL YOU ENACT YOUR REVOLU-TION?
!
FIRST... WE'LL BECOME PREFECTS, AND CHANGE THE SCHOOL!
THEN, I'LL FOLLOW IN DAD'S FOOT-STEPS AND...
ARE YOU AN IDIOT?
HOW MANY YEARS DO YOU THINK THIS WILL TAKE?
GRIP
WHAT YOU'RE SUGGEST-ING IS IDEALISTIC NONSENSE
IT'S A GAMBLE.
AND IF THE WORLD DISCOVERS YOUR SECRET WHILST YOU WAIT AROUND WITH YOUR HEAD IN THE CLOUDS—HOW WILL YOU TAKE RESPONSIBILITY THEN?
ROMIO, DO YOU MEAN...

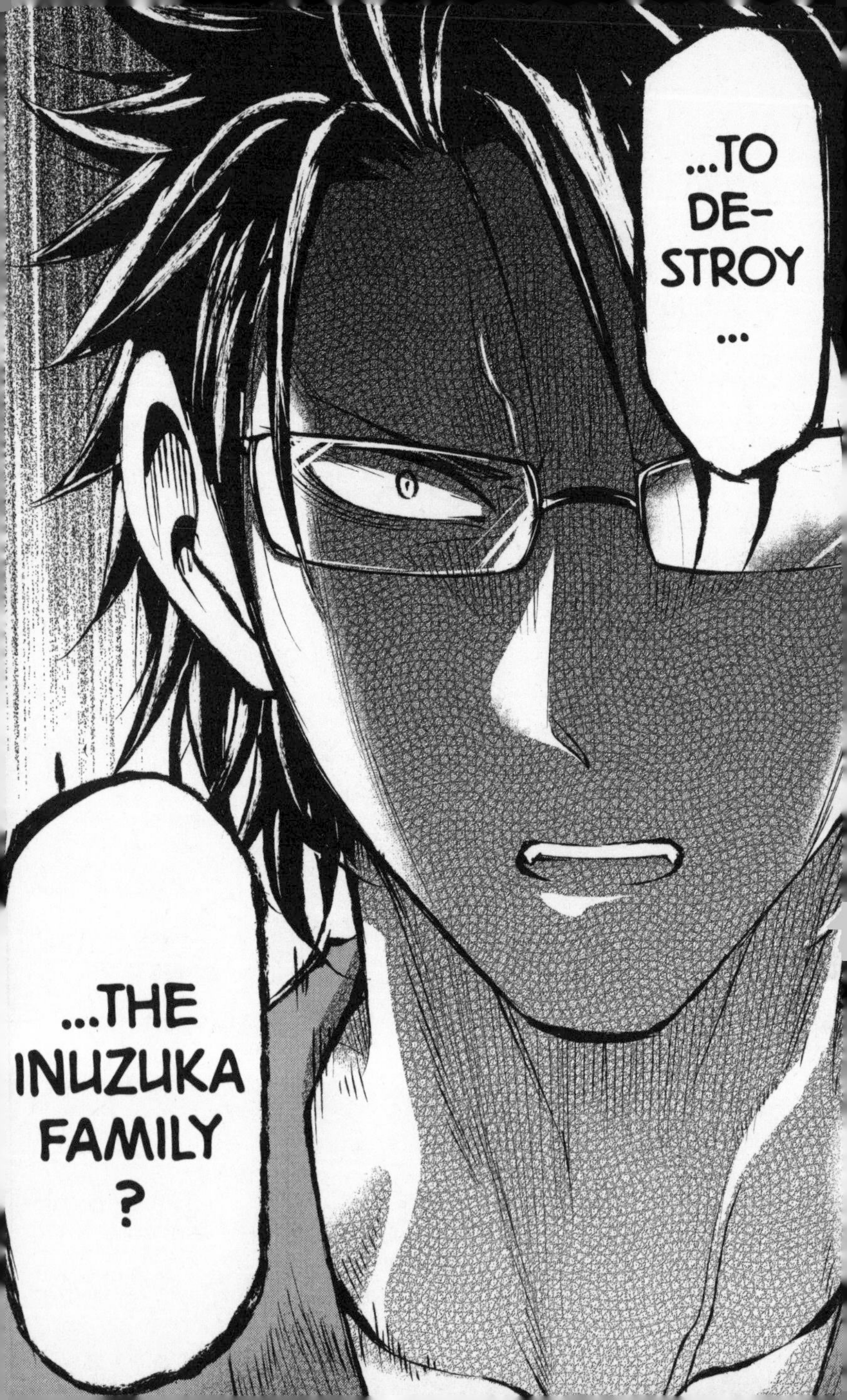
...TO DE-STROY ...
...THE INUZUKA FAMILY ?

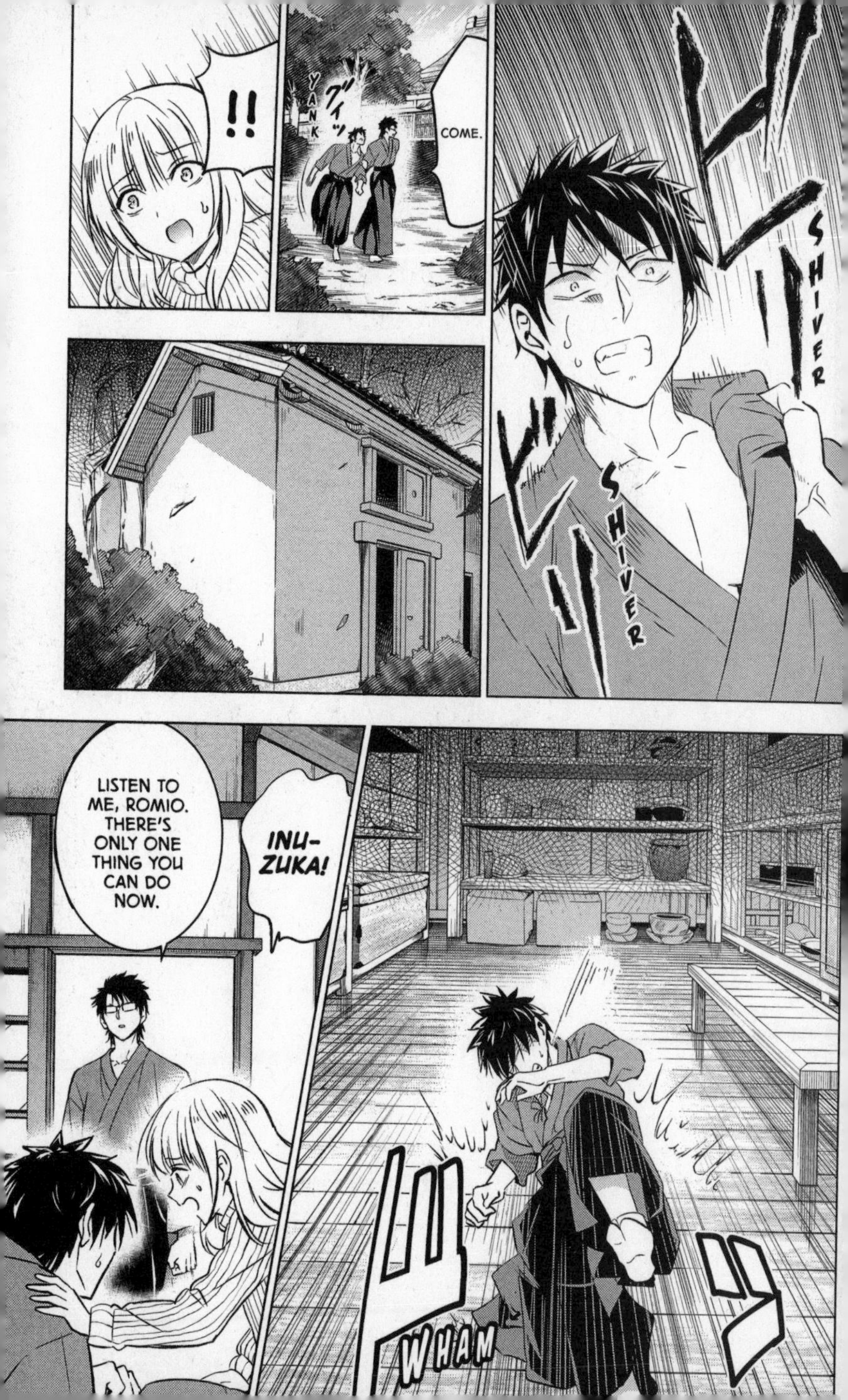

SHIVER
SHIVER
COME.
YANK
グイッ
!!
WHAM
INU-ZUKA!
LISTEN TO ME, ROMIO. THERE'S ONLY ONE THING YOU CAN DO NOW.

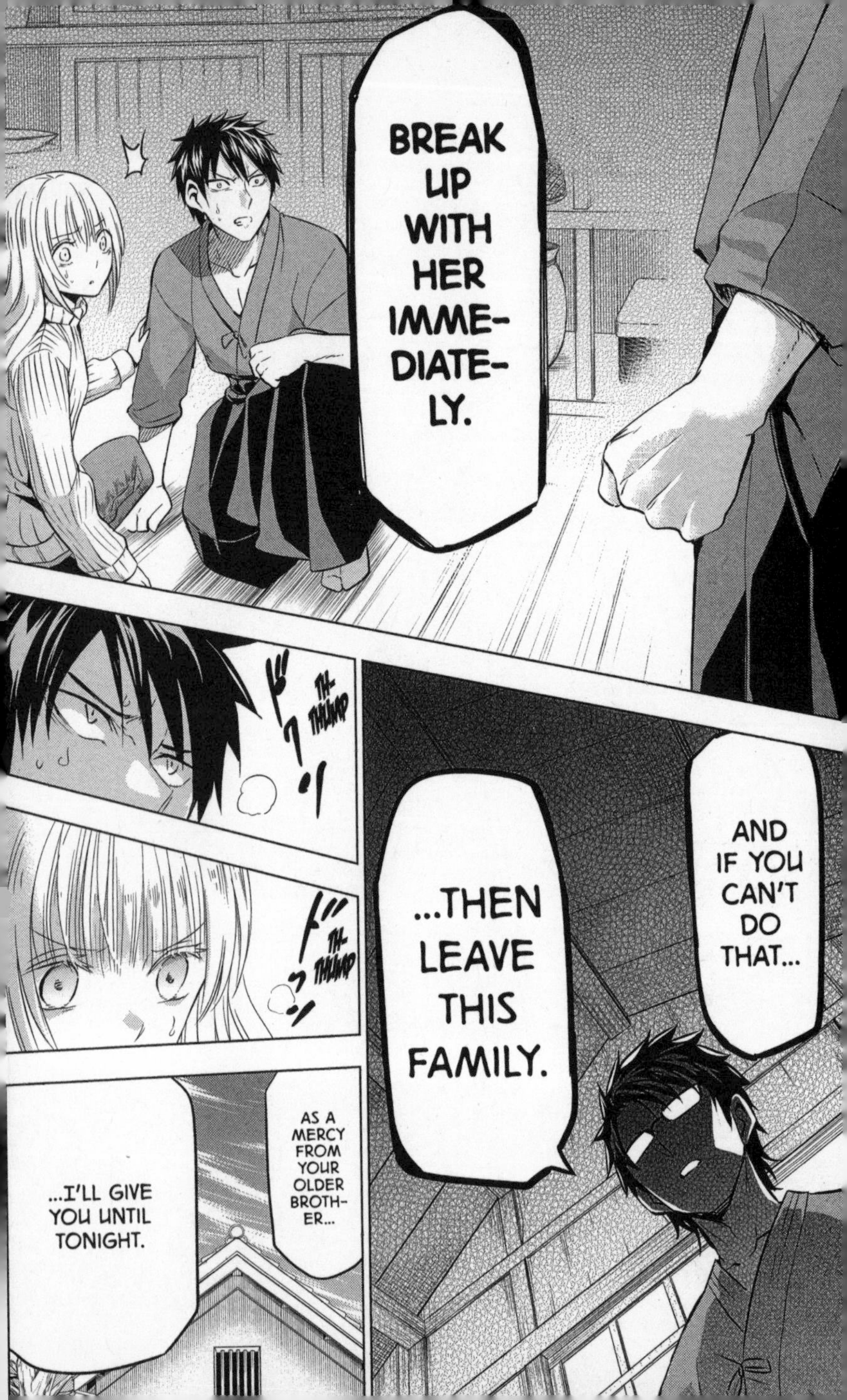
BREAK UP WITH HER IMMEDIATELY.
AND IF YOU CAN'T DO THAT...
...THEN LEAVE THIS FAMILY.
TH-THUMP
TH-THUMP
AS A MERCY FROM YOUR OLDER BROTHER...
...I'LL GIVE YOU UNTIL TONIGHT.

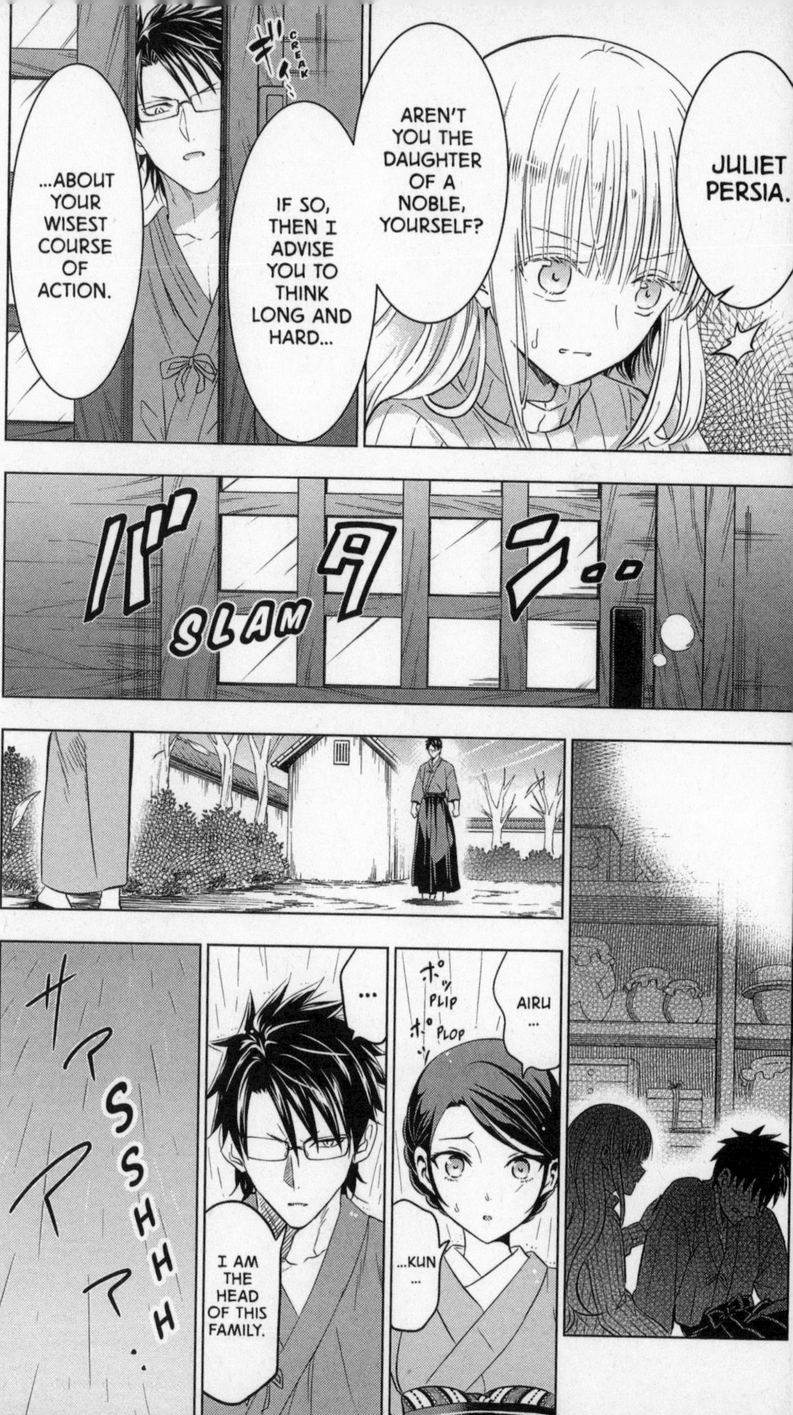
JULIET PERSIA.
AREN'T YOU THE DAUGHTER OF A NOBLE, YOURSELF?
CREAK
IF SO, THEN I ADVISE YOU TO THINK LONG AND HARD...
...ABOUT YOUR WISEST COURSE OF ACTION.
SLAM
PLIP
PLOP
AIRU ...
...KUN ...
...
I AM THE HEAD OF THIS FAMILY.
SSHHH

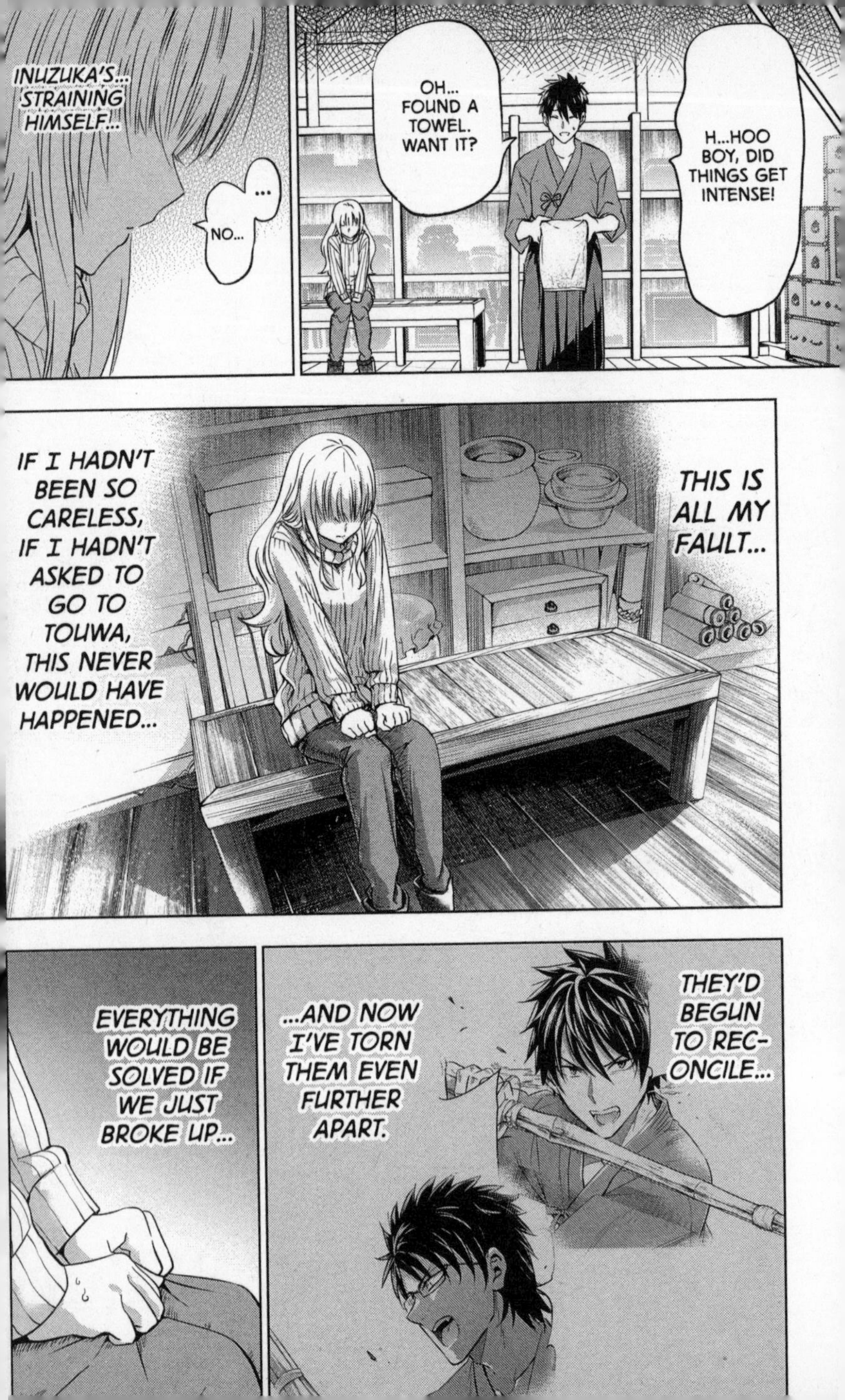
H...HOO BOY, DID THINGS GET INTENSE!
OH... FOUND A TOWEL. WANT IT?
... NO...
INUZUKA'S... STRAINING HIMSELF...
THIS IS ALL MY FAULT...
IF I HADN'T BEEN SO CARELESS, IF I HADN'T ASKED TO GO TO TOUWA, THIS NEVER WOULD HAVE HAPPENED...
THEY'D BEGUN TO REC-ONCILE...
...AND NOW I'VE TORN THEM EVEN FURTHER APART.
EVERYTHING WOULD BE SOLVED IF WE JUST BROKE UP...

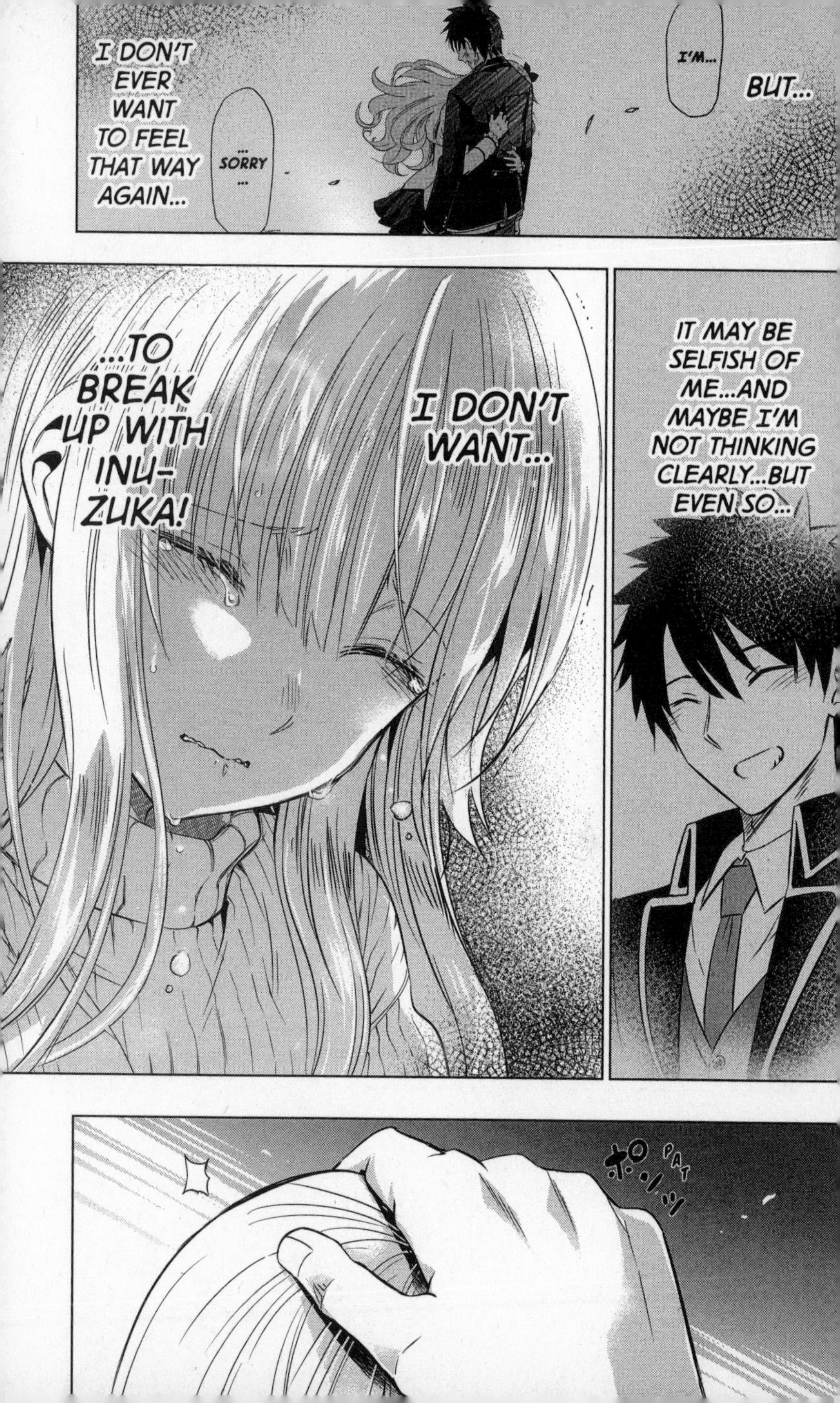
BUT...
I'M...
...SORRY...
I DON'T EVER WANT TO FEEL THAT WAY AGAIN...
IT MAY BE SELFISH OF ME...AND MAYBE I'M NOT THINKING CLEARLY...BUT EVEN SO...
I DON'T WANT...
...TO BREAK UP WITH INU-ZUKA!
PAT

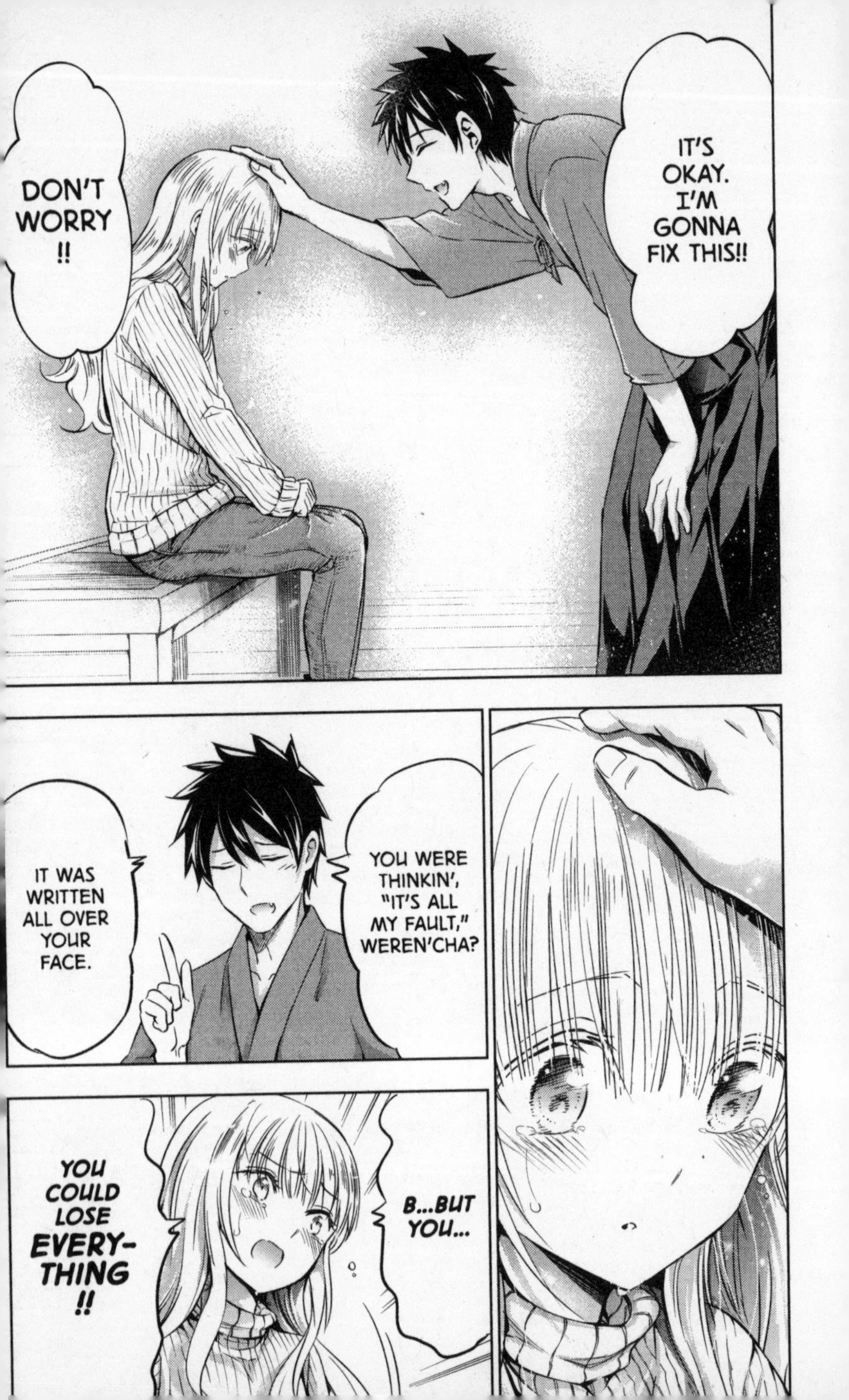
IT'S OKAY. I'M GONNA FIX THIS!!
DON'T WORRY!!
YOU WERE THINKIN', "IT'S ALL MY FAULT," WEREN'CHA?
IT WAS WRITTEN ALL OVER YOUR FACE.
B...BUT YOU...
YOU COULD LOSE EVERYTHING!!

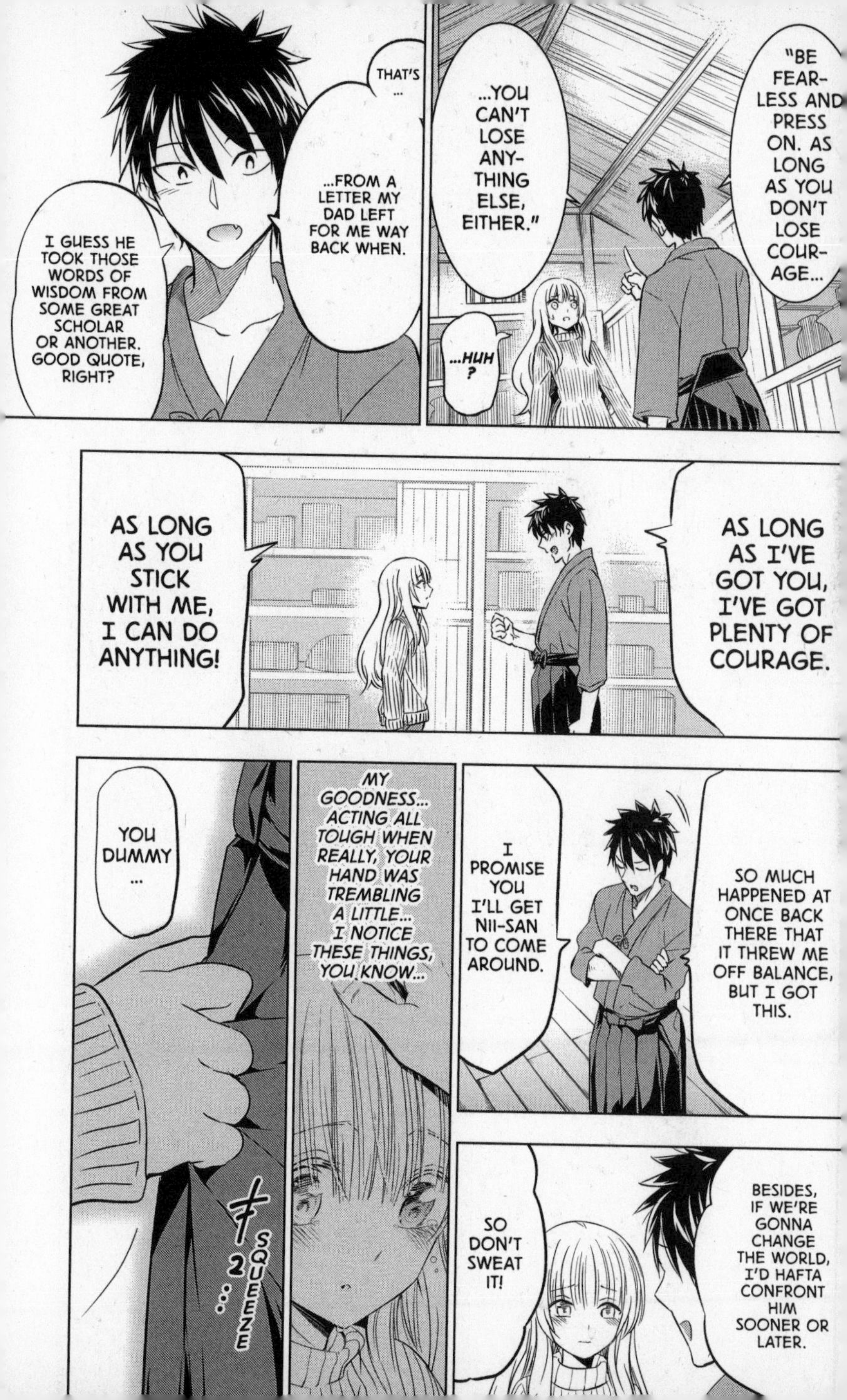
"BE FEARLESS AND PRESS ON. AS LONG AS YOU DON'T LOSE COURAGE...
...YOU CAN'T LOSE ANYTHING ELSE, EITHER."
...HUH?
THAT'S...
...FROM A LETTER MY DAD LEFT FOR ME WAY BACK WHEN.
I GUESS HE TOOK THOSE WORDS OF WISDOM FROM SOME GREAT SCHOLAR OR ANOTHER. GOOD QUOTE, RIGHT?
AS LONG AS I'VE GOT YOU, I'VE GOT PLENTY OF COURAGE.
AS LONG AS YOU STICK WITH ME, I CAN DO ANYTHING!
SO MUCH HAPPENED AT ONCE BACK THERE THAT IT THREW ME OFF BALANCE, BUT I GOT THIS.
I PROMISE YOU I'LL GET NII-SAN TO COME AROUND.
BESIDES, IF WE'RE GONNA CHANGE THE WORLD, I'D HAFTA CONFRONT HIM SOONER OR LATER.
SO DON'T SWEAT IT!
MY GOODNESS... ACTING ALL TOUGH WHEN REALLY, YOUR HAND WAS TREMBLING A LITTLE... I NOTICE THESE THINGS, YOU KNOW...
YOU DUMMY...
SQUEEZE...

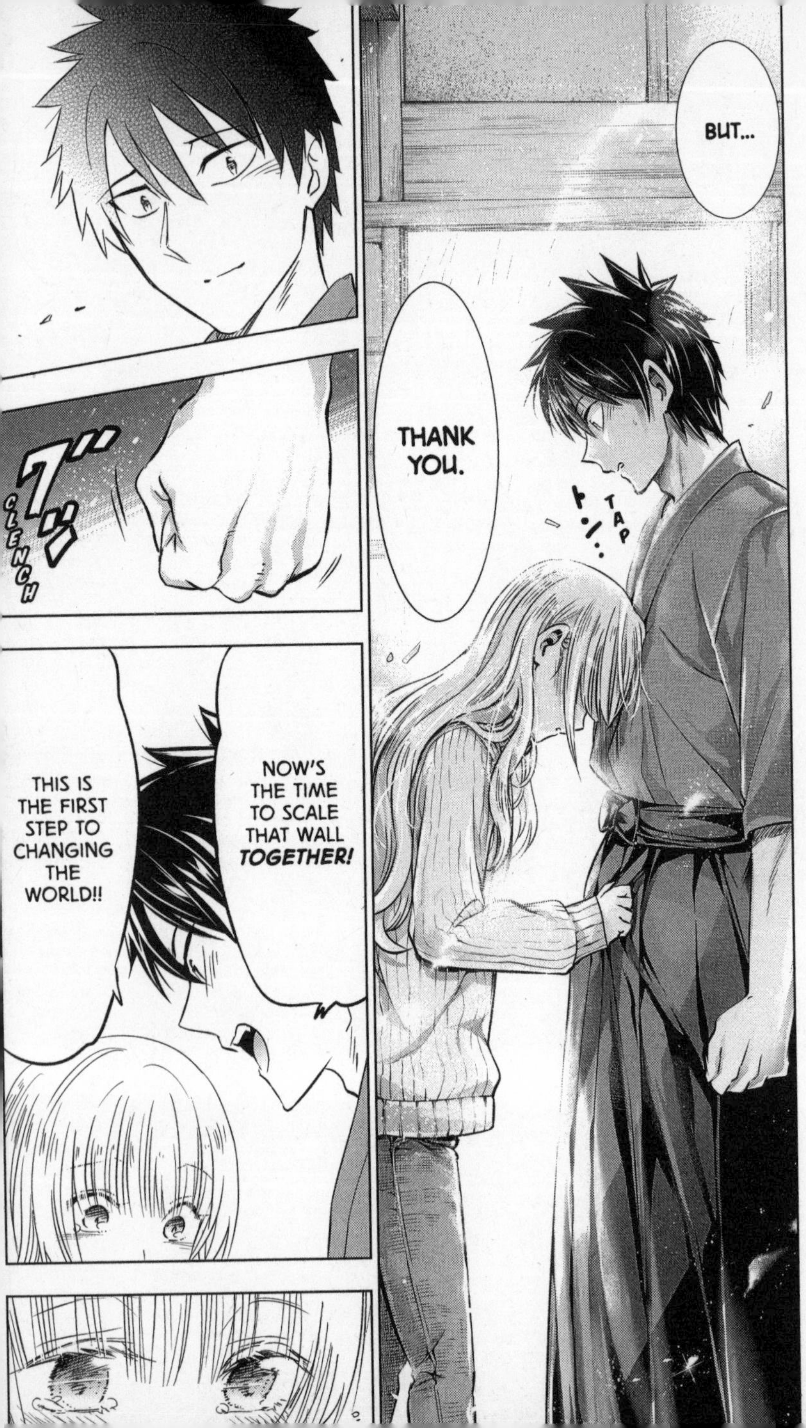
BUT...
THANK YOU.
TAP
CLENCH
NOW'S THE TIME TO SCALE THAT WALL TOGETHER!
THIS IS THE FIRST STEP TO CHANGING THE WORLD!!

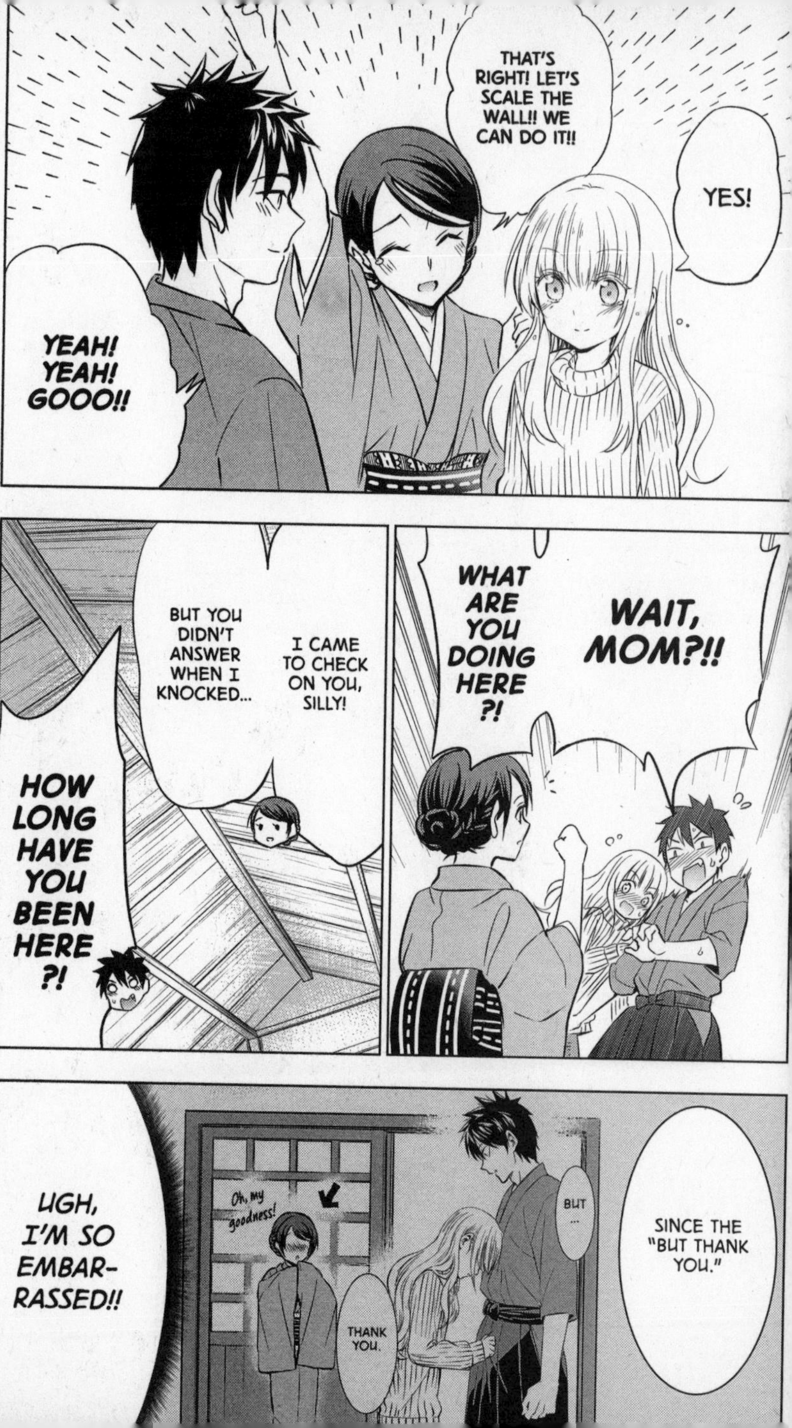
THAT'S RIGHT! LET'S SCALE THE WALL!! WE CAN DO IT!!
YES!
YEAH! YEAH! GOOO!!
WAIT, MOM?!!
WHAT ARE YOU DOING HERE?!
I CAME TO CHECK ON YOU, SILLY!
BUT YOU DIDN'T ANSWER WHEN I KNOCKED...
HOW LONG HAVE YOU BEEN HERE?!
SINCE THE "BUT THANK YOU."
BUT ...
THANK YOU.
Oh, my goodness!
UGH, I'M SO EMBARRASSED!!

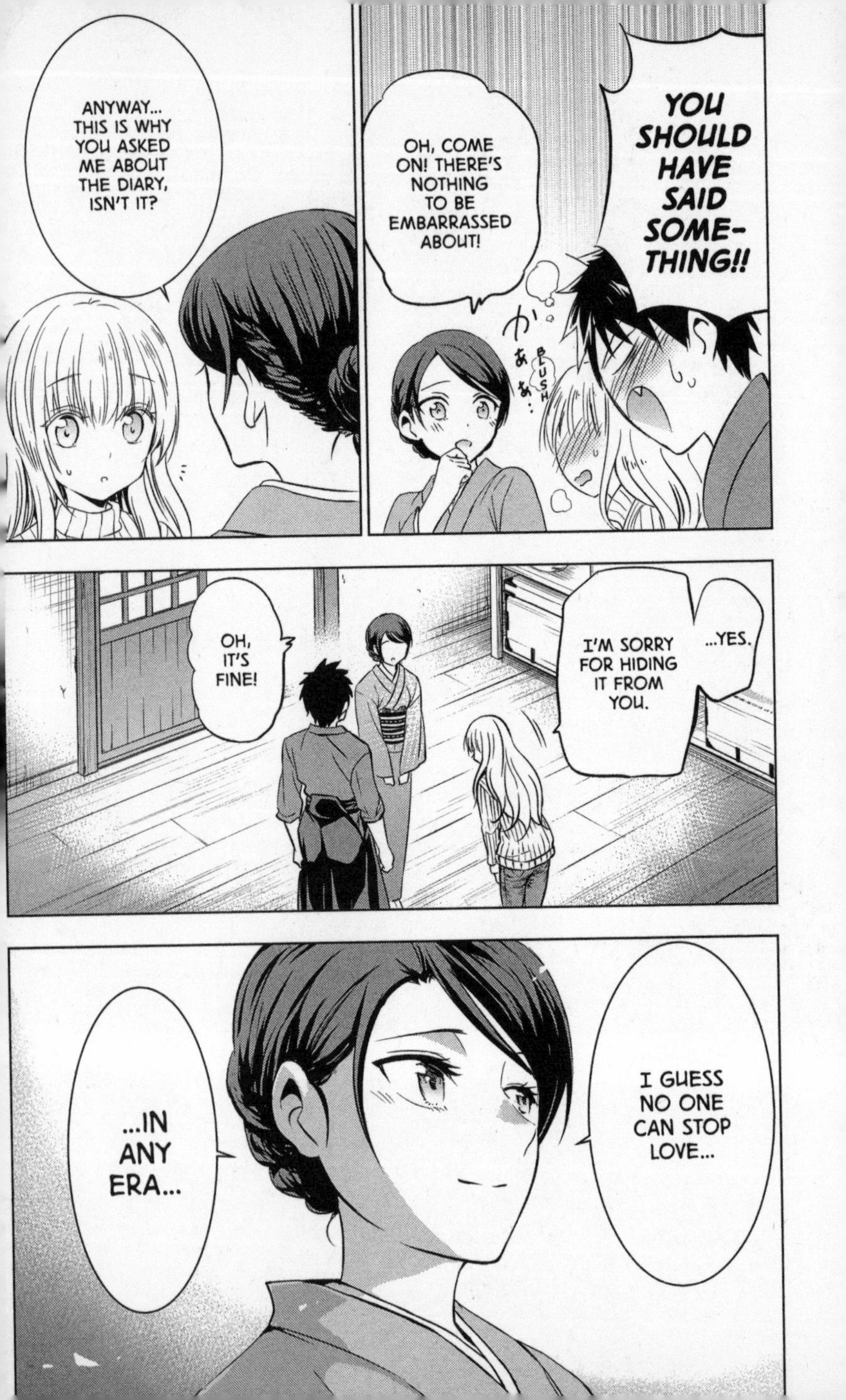

YOU SHOULD HAVE SAID SOME-THING!!
BLUSH
OH, COME ON! THERE'S NOTHING TO BE EMBARRASSED ABOUT!
ANYWAY... THIS IS WHY YOU ASKED ME ABOUT THE DIARY, ISN'T IT?
...YES.
I'M SORRY FOR HIDING IT FROM YOU.
OH, IT'S FINE!
I GUESS NO ONE CAN STOP LOVE...
...IN ANY ERA...

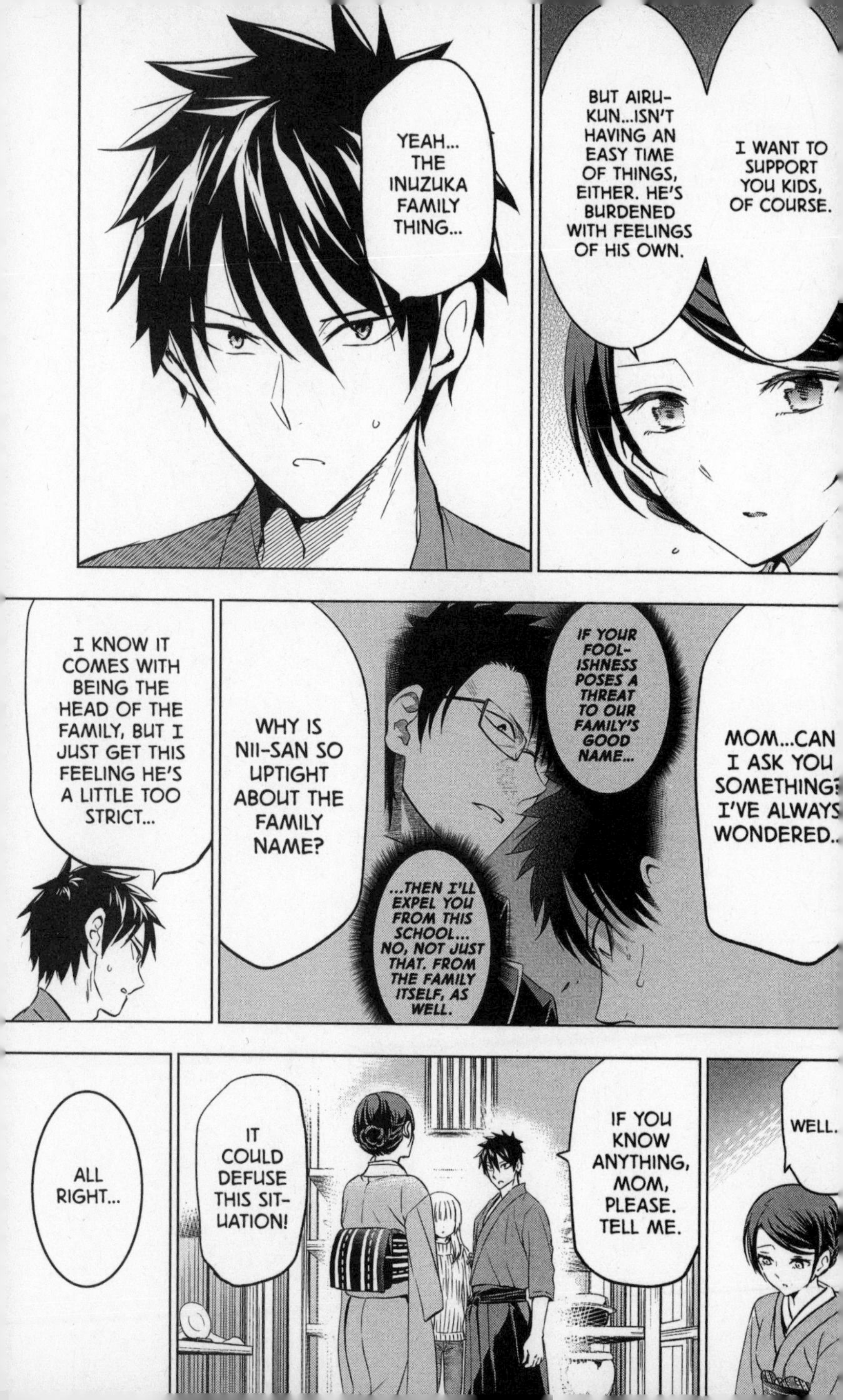
I WANT TO SUPPORT YOU KIDS, OF COURSE.
BUT AIRU-KUN...ISN'T HAVING AN EASY TIME OF THINGS, EITHER. HE'S BURDENED WITH FEELINGS OF HIS OWN.
YEAH... THE INUZUKA FAMILY THING...
MOM...CAN I ASK YOU SOMETHING? I'VE ALWAYS WONDERED...
IF YOUR FOOLISHNESS POSES A THREAT TO OUR FAMILY'S GOOD NAME...
...THEN I'LL EXPEL YOU FROM THIS SCHOOL... NO, NOT JUST THAT. FROM THE FAMILY ITSELF, AS WELL.
WHY IS NII-SAN SO UPTIGHT ABOUT THE FAMILY NAME?
I KNOW IT COMES WITH BEING THE HEAD OF THE FAMILY, BUT I JUST GET THIS FEELING HE'S A LITTLE TOO STRICT...
WELL.
IF YOU KNOW ANYTHING, MOM, PLEASE. TELL ME.
IT COULD DEFUSE THIS SITUATION!
ALL RIGHT...

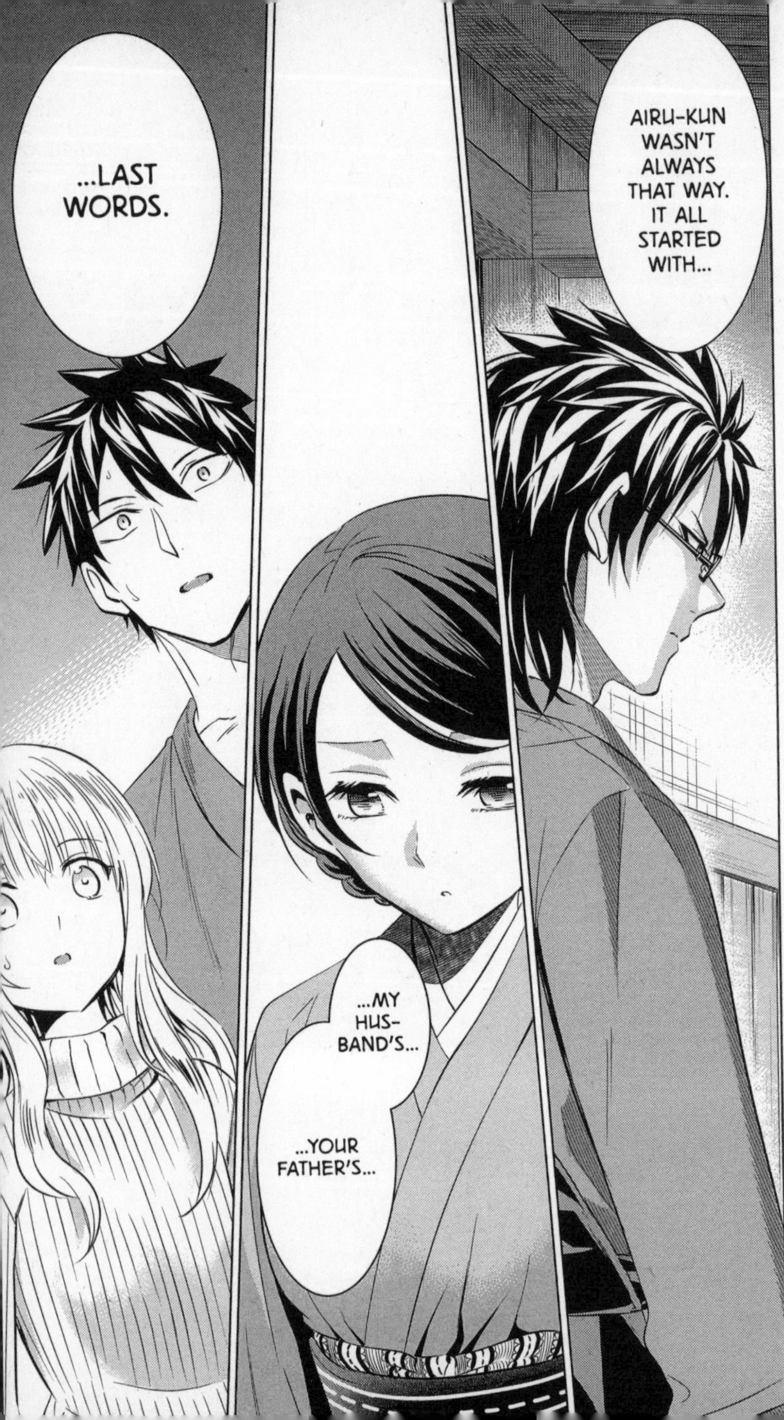
AIRU-KUN WASN'T ALWAYS THAT WAY. IT ALL STARTED WITH...
...MY HUS-BAND'S...
...YOUR FATHER'S...
...LAST WORDS.

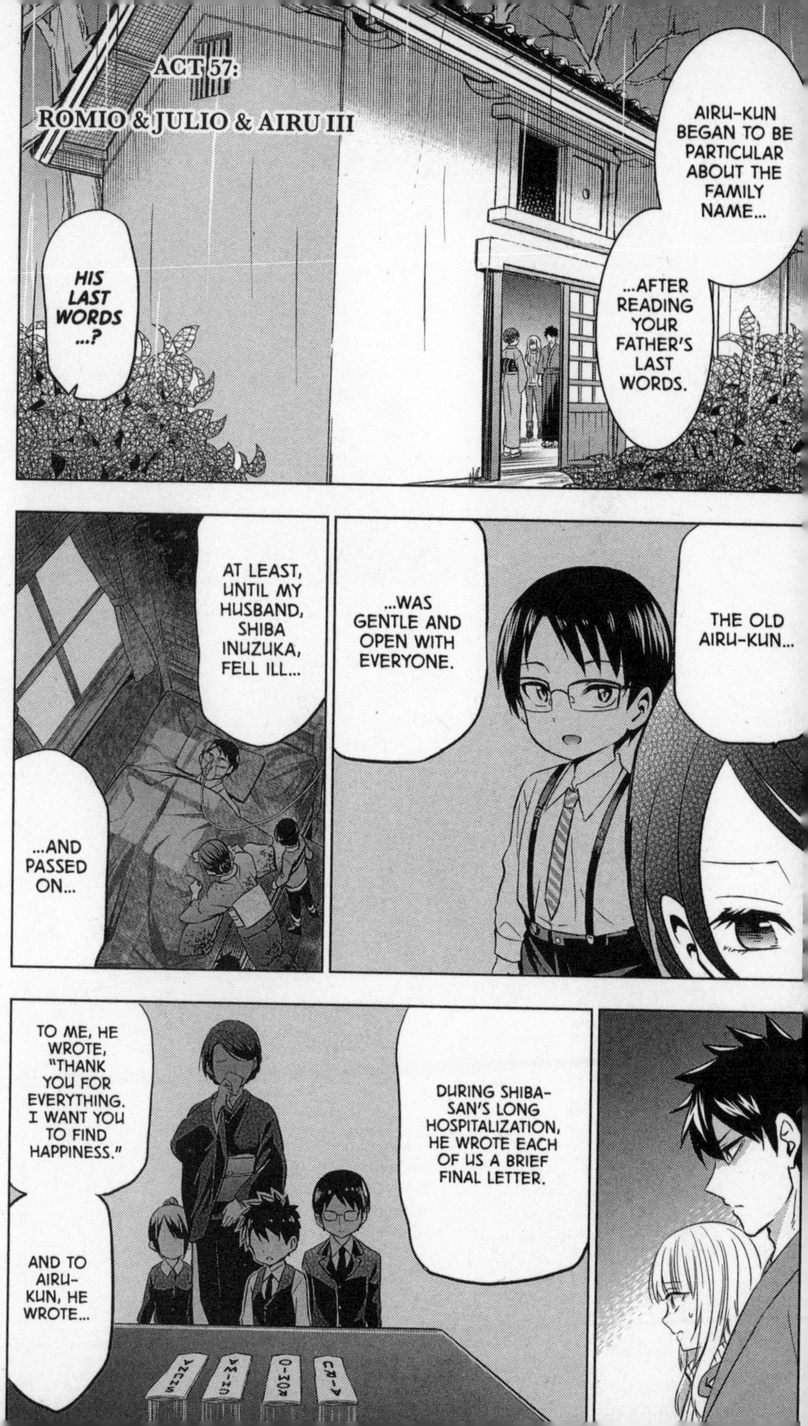
ACT 57:
ROMIO & JULIO & AIRU III
AIRU-KUN BEGAN TO BE PARTICULAR ABOUT THE FAMILY NAME...
...AFTER READING YOUR FATHER'S LAST WORDS.
HIS LAST WORDS ...?
THE OLD AIRU-KUN...
...WAS GENTLE AND OPEN WITH EVERYONE.
AT LEAST, UNTIL MY HUSBAND, SHIBA INUZUKA, FELL ILL...
...AND PASSED ON...
DURING SHIBA-SAN'S LONG HOSPITALIZATION, HE WROTE EACH OF US A BRIEF FINAL LETTER.
TO ME, HE WROTE, "THANK YOU FOR EVERYTHING. I WANT YOU TO FIND HAPPINESS."
AND TO AIRU-KUN, HE WROTE...

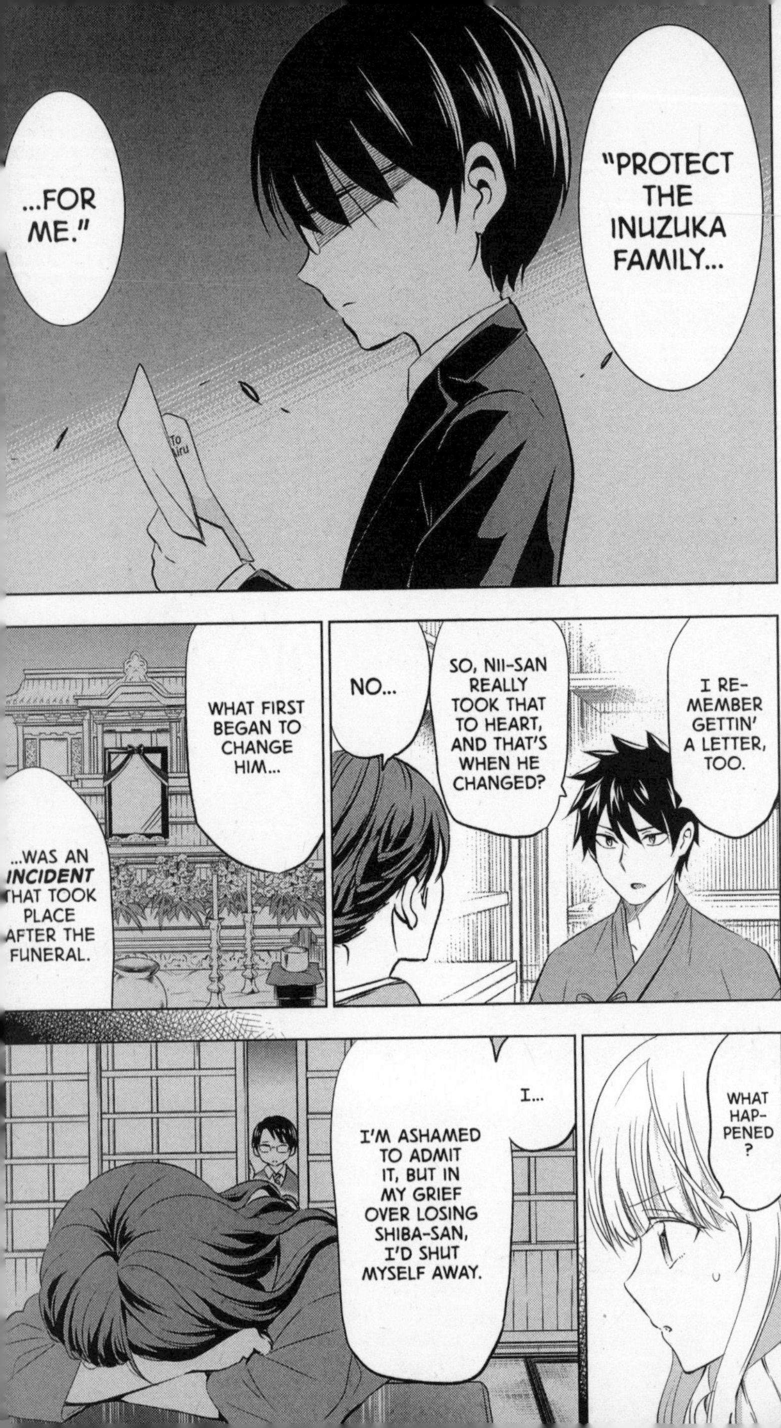
"PROTECT THE INUZUKA FAMILY...
...FOR ME."
I REMEMBER GETTIN' A LETTER, TOO.
SO, NII-SAN REALLY TOOK THAT TO HEART, AND THAT'S WHEN HE CHANGED?
NO...
WHAT FIRST BEGAN TO CHANGE HIM...
...WAS AN *INCIDENT* THAT TOOK PLACE AFTER THE FUNERAL.
WHAT HAPPENED?
I...
I'M ASHAMED TO ADMIT IT, BUT IN MY GRIEF OVER LOSING SHIBA-SAN, I'D SHUT MYSELF AWAY.

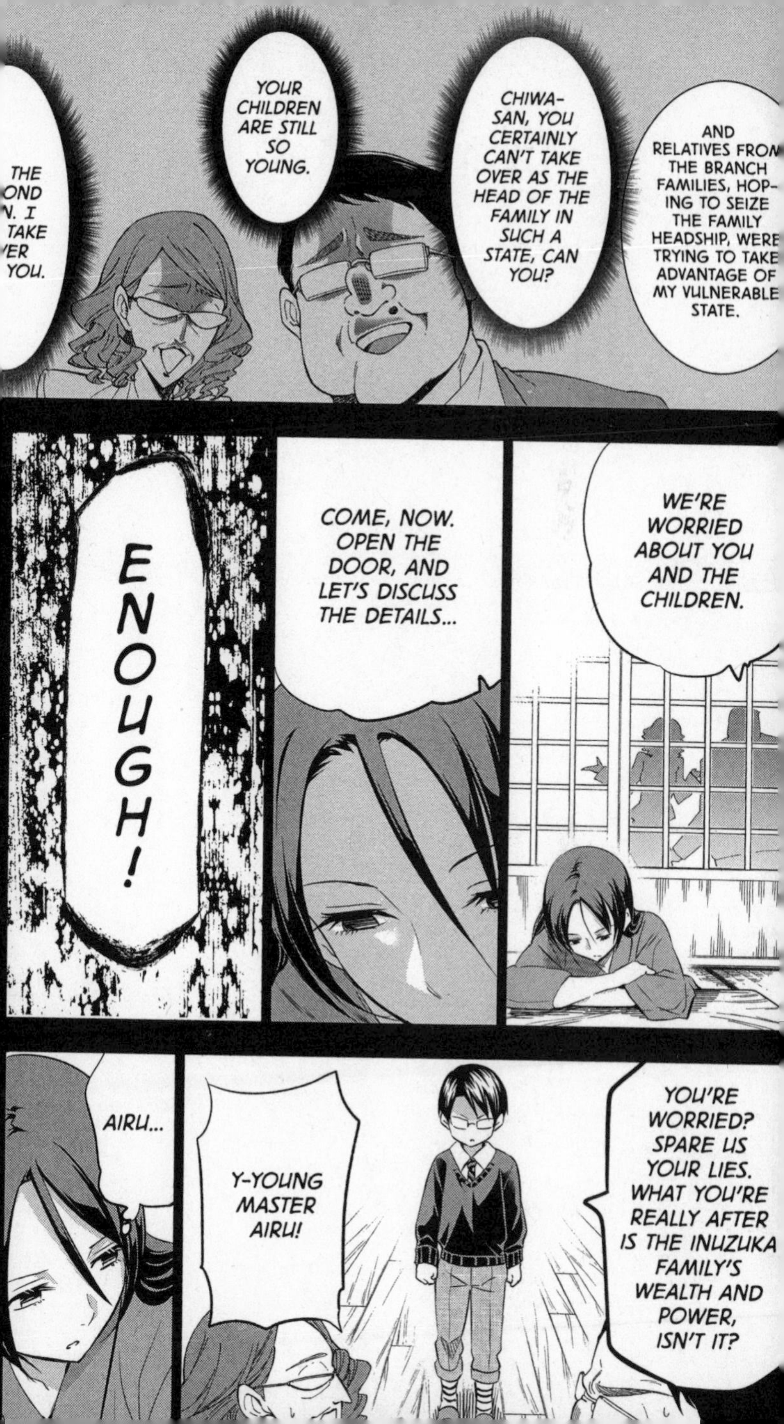
AND RELATIVES FROM THE BRANCH FAMILIES, HOPING TO SEIZE THE FAMILY HEADSHIP, WERE TRYING TO TAKE ADVANTAGE OF MY VULNERABLE STATE.
CHIWA-SAN, YOU CERTAINLY CAN'T TAKE OVER AS THE HEAD OF THE FAMILY IN SUCH A STATE, CAN YOU?
YOUR CHILDREN ARE STILL SO YOUNG.
THE OND N. I TAKE ER YOU.
WE'RE WORRIED ABOUT YOU AND THE CHILDREN.
COME, NOW. OPEN THE DOOR, AND LET'S DISCUSS THE DETAILS...
ENOUGH!
YOU'RE WORRIED? SPARE US YOUR LIES. WHAT YOU'RE REALLY AFTER IS THE INUZUKA FAMILY'S WEALTH AND POWER, ISN'T IT?
Y-YOUNG MASTER AIRU!
AIRU...

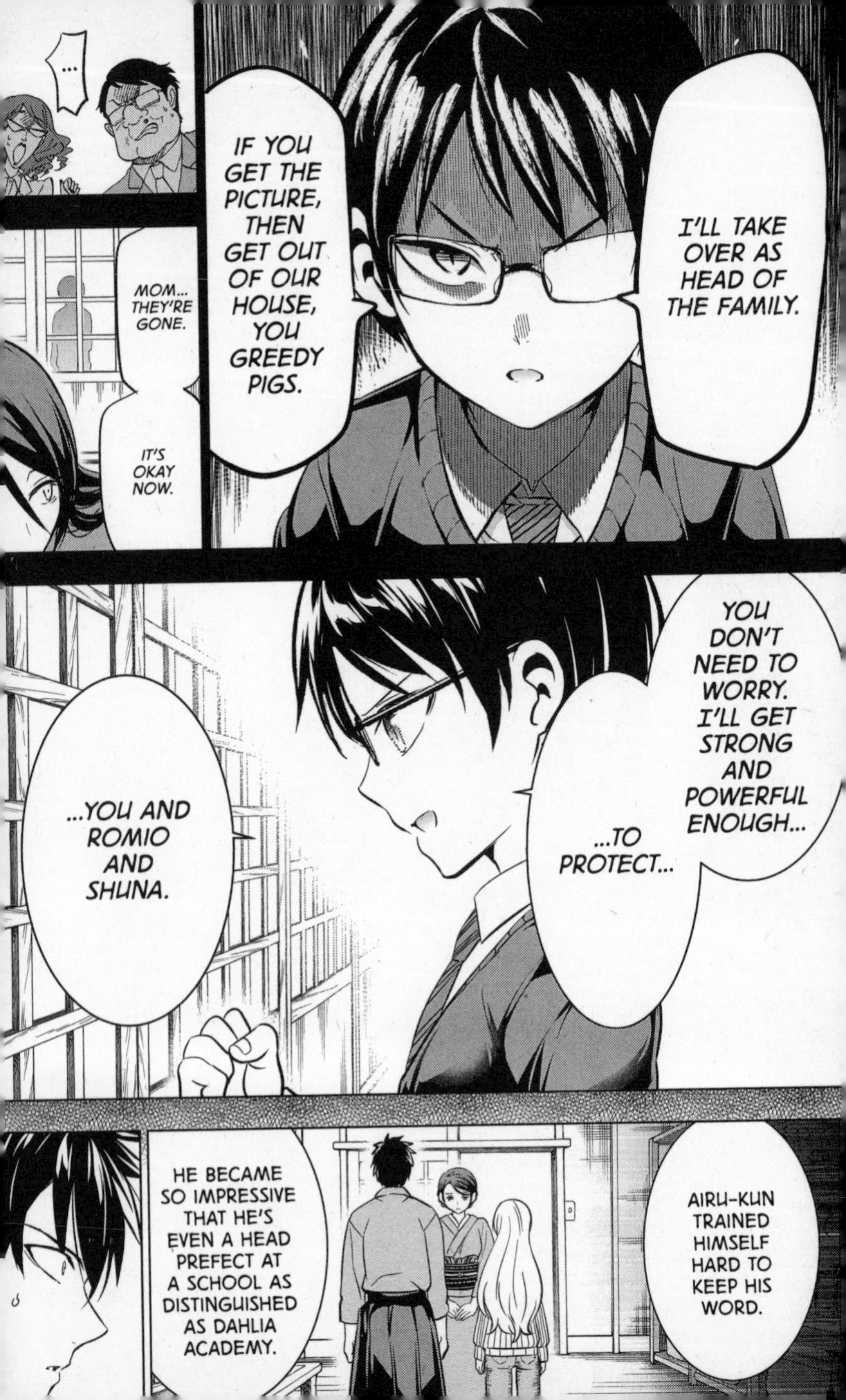
I'LL TAKE OVER AS HEAD OF THE FAMILY.
IF YOU GET THE PICTURE, THEN GET OUT OF OUR HOUSE, YOU GREEDY PIGS.
...
MOM... THEY'RE GONE.
IT'S OKAY NOW.
YOU DON'T NEED TO WORRY. I'LL GET STRONG AND POWERFUL ENOUGH...
...TO PROTECT...
...YOU AND ROMIO AND SHUNA.
AIRU-KUN TRAINED HIMSELF HARD TO KEEP HIS WORD.
HE BECAME SO IMPRESSIVE THAT HE'S EVEN A HEAD PREFECT AT A SCHOOL AS DISTINGUISHED AS DAHLIA ACADEMY.

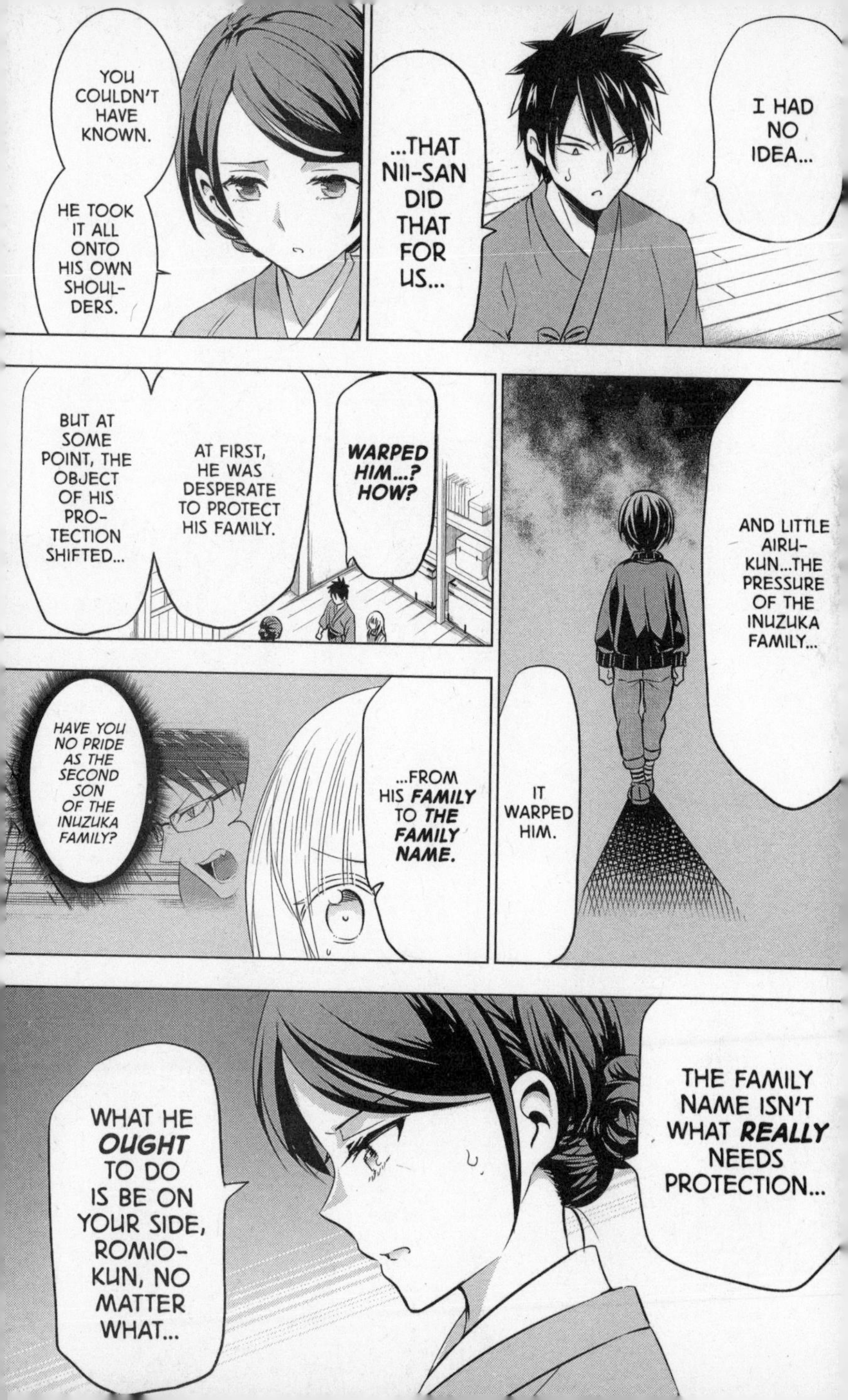

I HAD NO IDEA...
...THAT NII-SAN DID THAT FOR US...
YOU COULDN'T HAVE KNOWN.
HE TOOK IT ALL ONTO HIS OWN SHOULDERS.
AND LITTLE AIRU-KUN...THE PRESSURE OF THE INUZUKA FAMILY...
IT WARPED HIM.
WARPED HIM...? HOW?
AT FIRST, HE WAS DESPERATE TO PROTECT HIS FAMILY.
BUT AT SOME POINT, THE OBJECT OF HIS PROTECTION SHIFTED...
...FROM HIS FAMILY TO THE FAMILY NAME.
HAVE YOU NO PRIDE AS THE SECOND SON OF THE INUZUKA FAMILY?
THE FAMILY NAME ISN'T WHAT REALLY NEEDS PROTECTION...
WHAT HE OUGHT TO DO IS BE ON YOUR SIDE, ROMIO-KUN, NO MATTER WHAT...

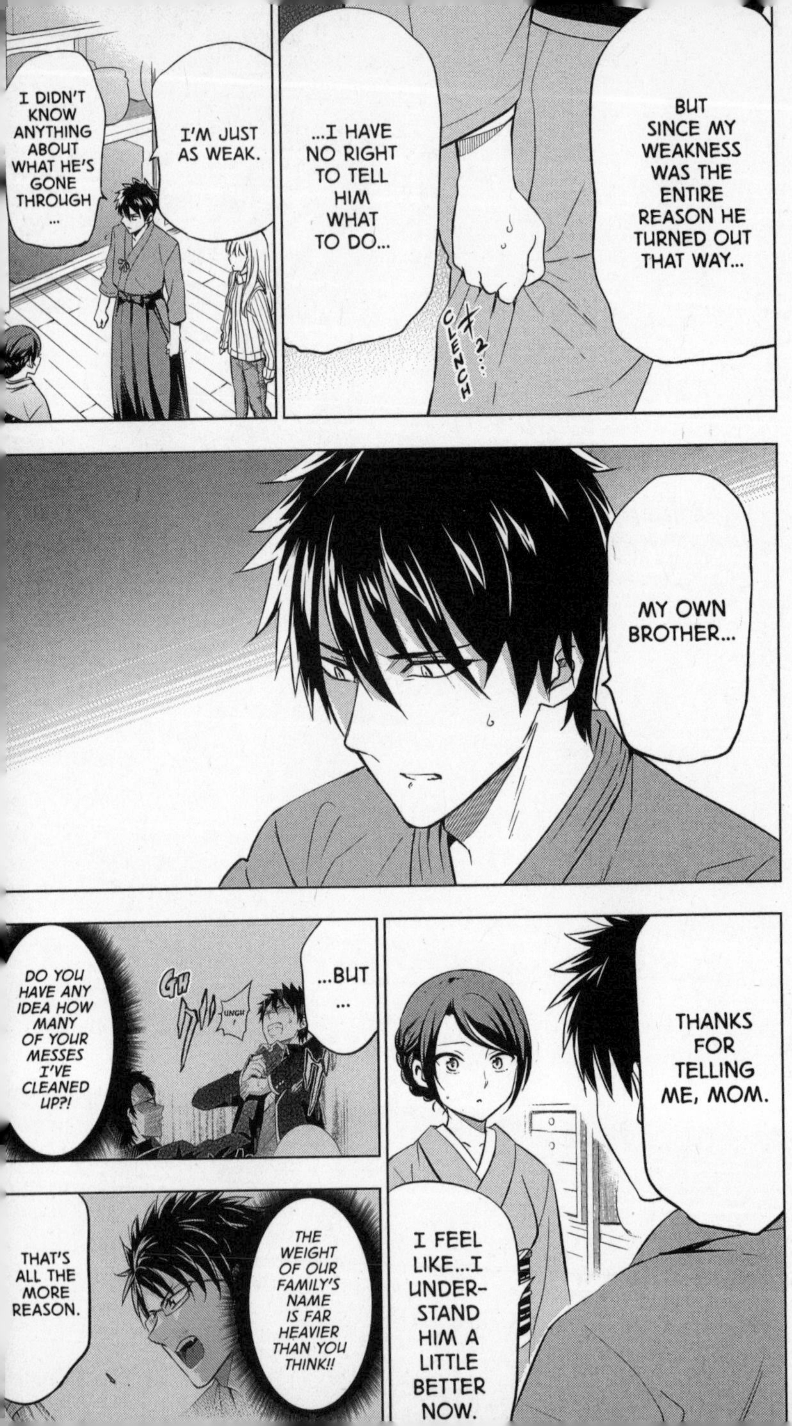
BUT SINCE MY WEAKNESS WAS THE ENTIRE REASON HE TURNED OUT THAT WAY...
...I HAVE NO RIGHT TO TELL HIM WHAT TO DO...
CLENCH
I'M JUST AS WEAK.
I DIDN'T KNOW ANYTHING ABOUT WHAT HE'S GONE THROUGH ...
MY OWN BROTHER...
THANKS FOR TELLING ME, MOM.
I FEEL LIKE...I UNDER-STAND HIM A LITTLE BETTER NOW.
...BUT ...
GH
UNGH!
DO YOU HAVE ANY IDEA HOW MANY OF YOUR MESSES I'VE CLEANED UP?!
THE WEIGHT OF OUR FAMILY'S NAME IS FAR HEAVIER THAN YOU THINK!!
THAT'S ALL THE MORE REASON.

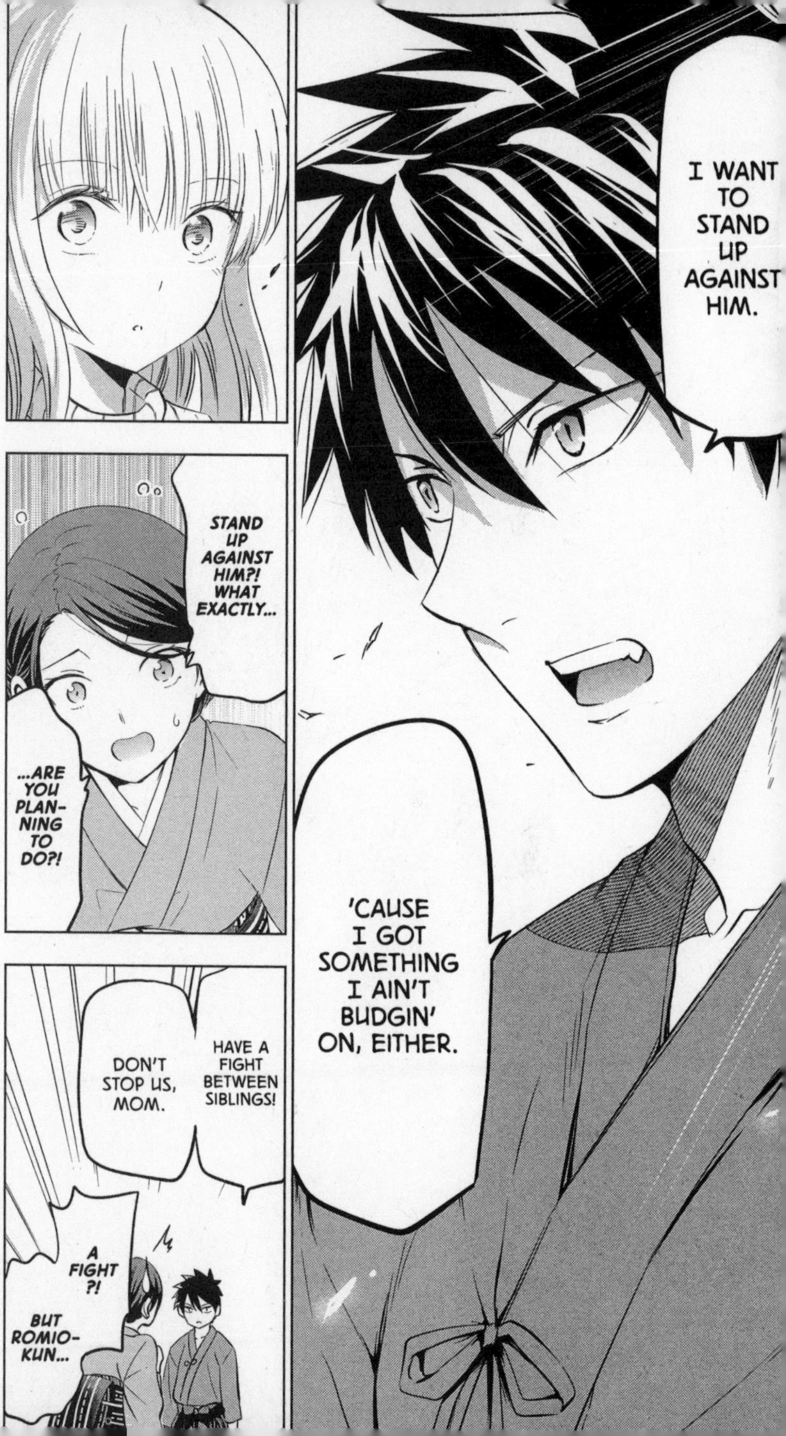

I WANT TO STAND UP AGAINST HIM.
'CAUSE I GOT SOMETHING I AIN'T BUDGIN' ON, EITHER.
STAND UP AGAINST HIM?! WHAT EXACTLY...
...ARE YOU PLANNING TO DO?!
HAVE A FIGHT BETWEEN SIBLINGS!
DON'T STOP US, MOM.
A FIGHT ?!
BUT ROMIO-KUN...

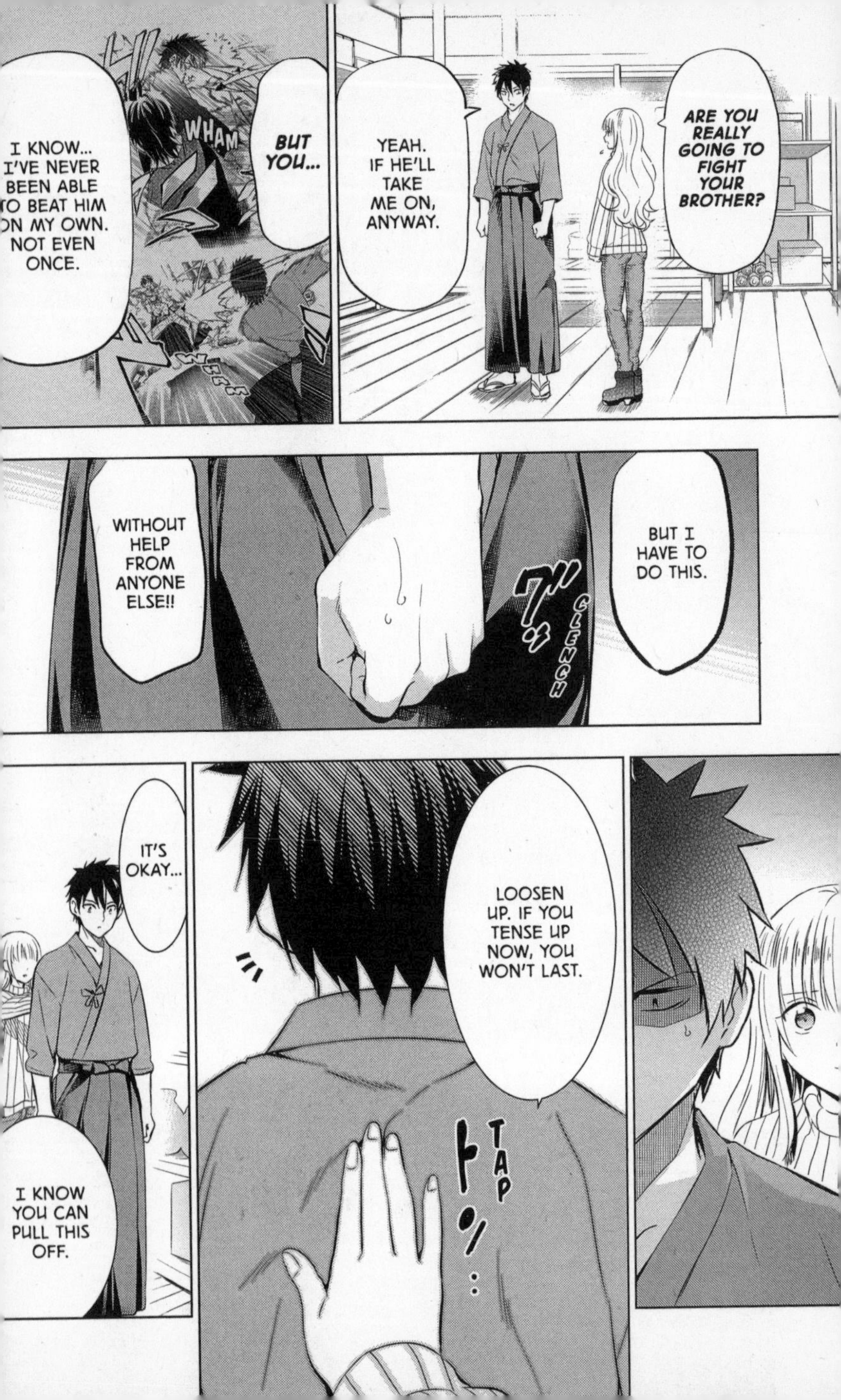
ARE YOU REALLY GOING TO FIGHT YOUR BROTHER?
YEAH. IF HE'LL TAKE ME ON, ANYWAY.
BUT YOU...
WHAM
I KNOW... I'VE NEVER BEEN ABLE TO BEAT HIM ON MY OWN. NOT EVEN ONCE.
WHAP
BUT I HAVE TO DO THIS.
CLENCH
WITHOUT HELP FROM ANYONE ELSE!!
LOOSEN UP. IF YOU TENSE UP NOW, YOU WON'T LAST.
TAP
IT'S OKAY...
I KNOW YOU CAN PULL THIS OFF.

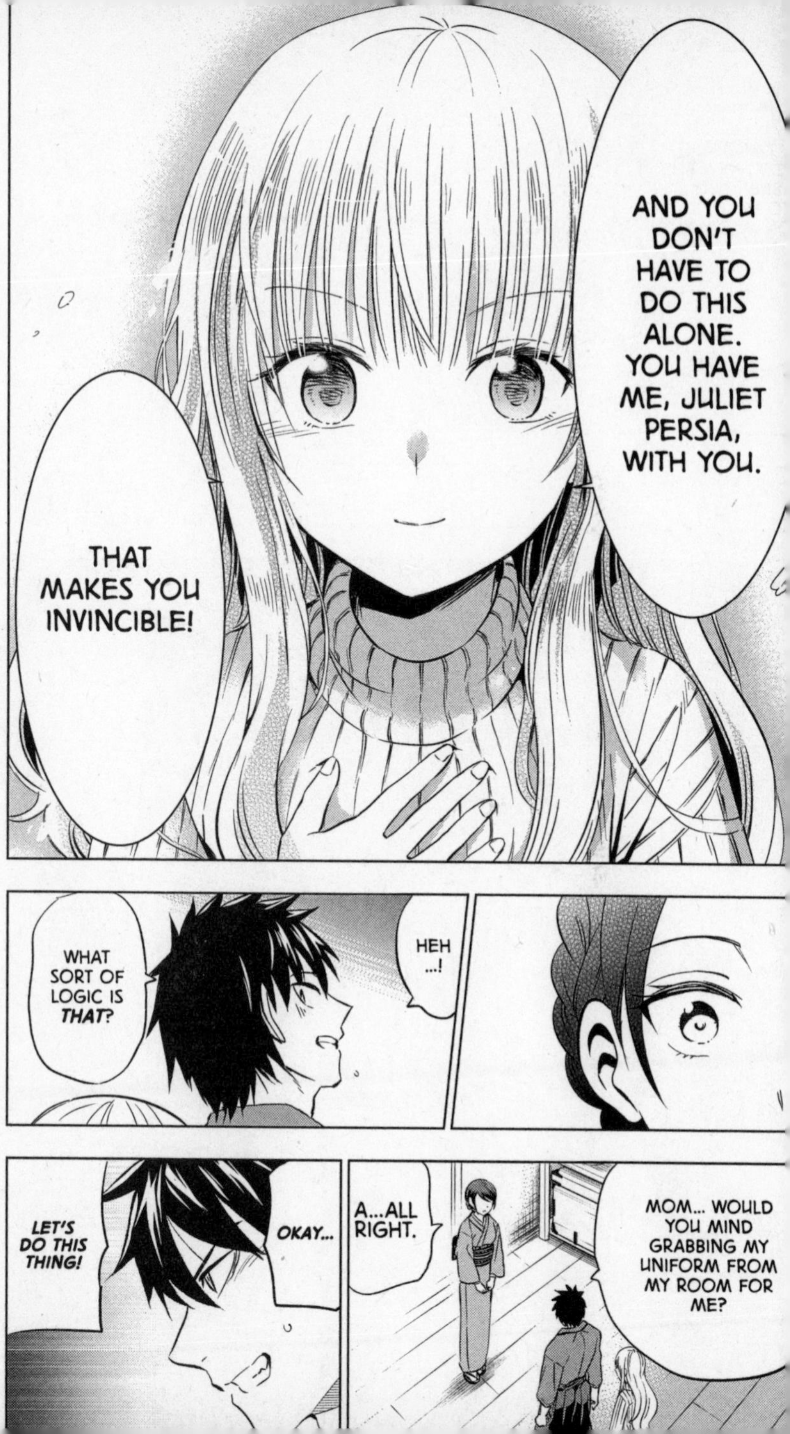
AND YOU DON'T HAVE TO DO THIS ALONE. YOU HAVE ME, JULIET PERSIA, WITH YOU.
THAT MAKES YOU INVINCIBLE!
HEH ...!
WHAT SORT OF LOGIC IS *THAT*?
MOM... WOULD YOU MIND GRABBING MY UNIFORM FROM MY ROOM FOR ME?
A...ALL RIGHT.
OKAY...
LET'S DO THIS THING!

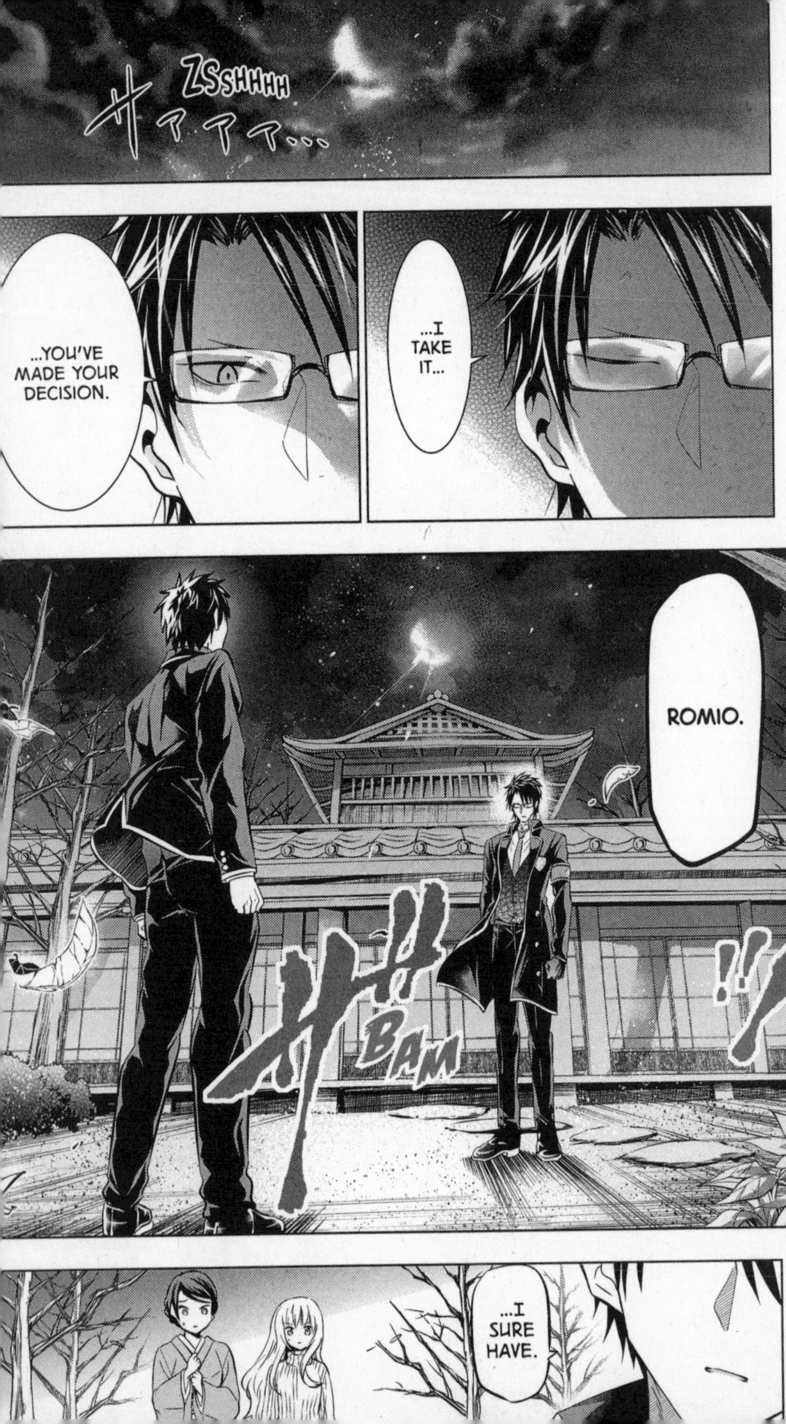
ZSSHHHH
...I TAKE IT...
...YOU'VE MADE YOUR DECISION.
ROMIO.
BAM
!!
...I SURE HAVE.

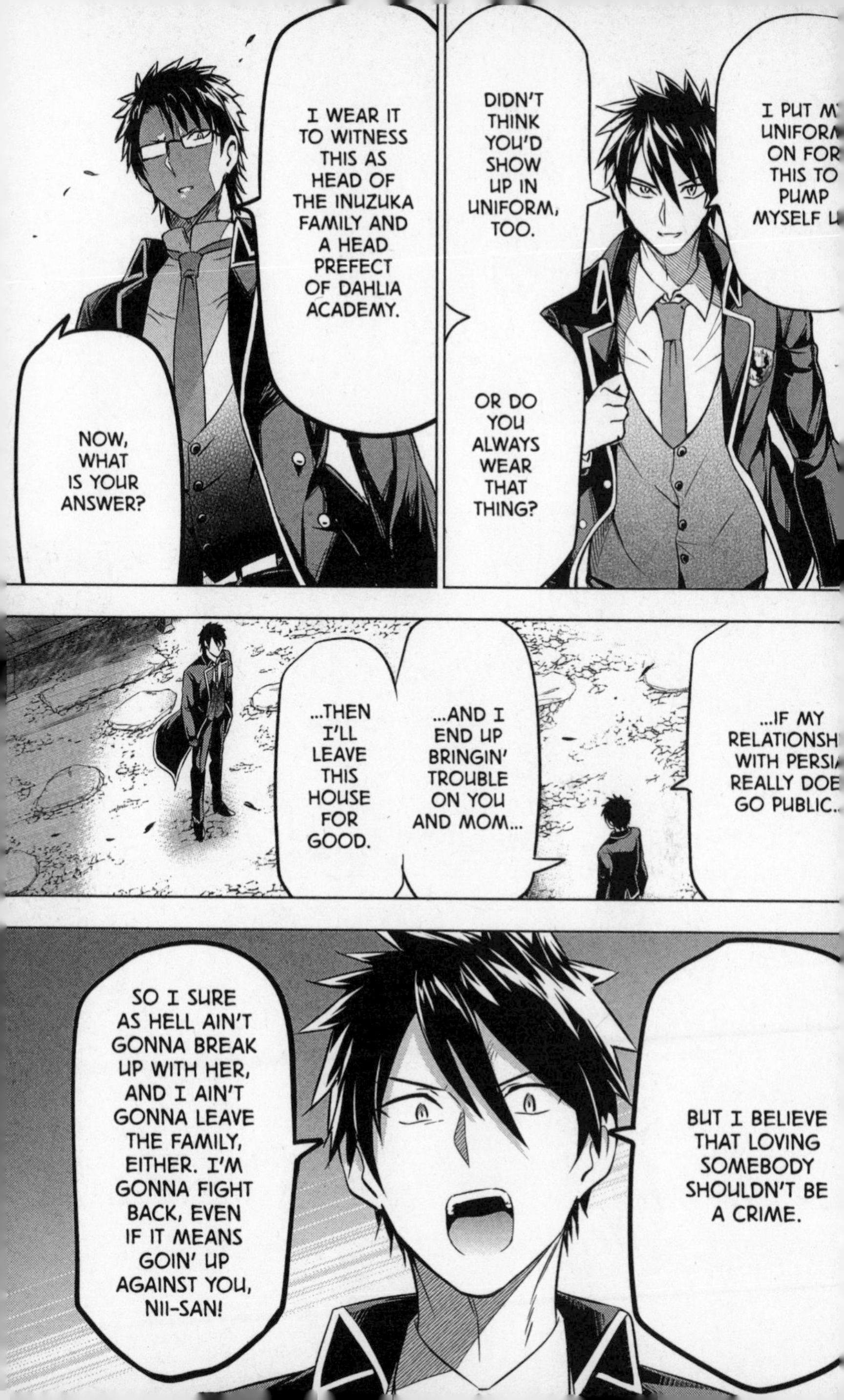
I PUT M UNIFOR ON FOR THIS TO PUMP MYSELF U
DIDN'T THINK YOU'D SHOW UP IN UNIFORM, TOO.
OR DO YOU ALWAYS WEAR THAT THING?
I WEAR IT TO WITNESS THIS AS HEAD OF THE INUZUKA FAMILY AND A HEAD PREFECT OF DAHLIA ACADEMY.
NOW, WHAT IS YOUR ANSWER?
...IF MY RELATIONSH WITH PERSI REALLY DOE GO PUBLIC..
...AND I END UP BRINGIN' TROUBLE ON YOU AND MOM...
...THEN I'LL LEAVE THIS HOUSE FOR GOOD.
BUT I BELIEVE THAT LOVING SOMEBODY SHOULDN'T BE A CRIME.
SO I SURE AS HELL AIN'T GONNA BREAK UP WITH HER, AND I AIN'T GONNA LEAVE THE FAMILY, EITHER. I'M GONNA FIGHT BACK, EVEN IF IT MEANS GOIN' UP AGAINST YOU, NII-SAN!

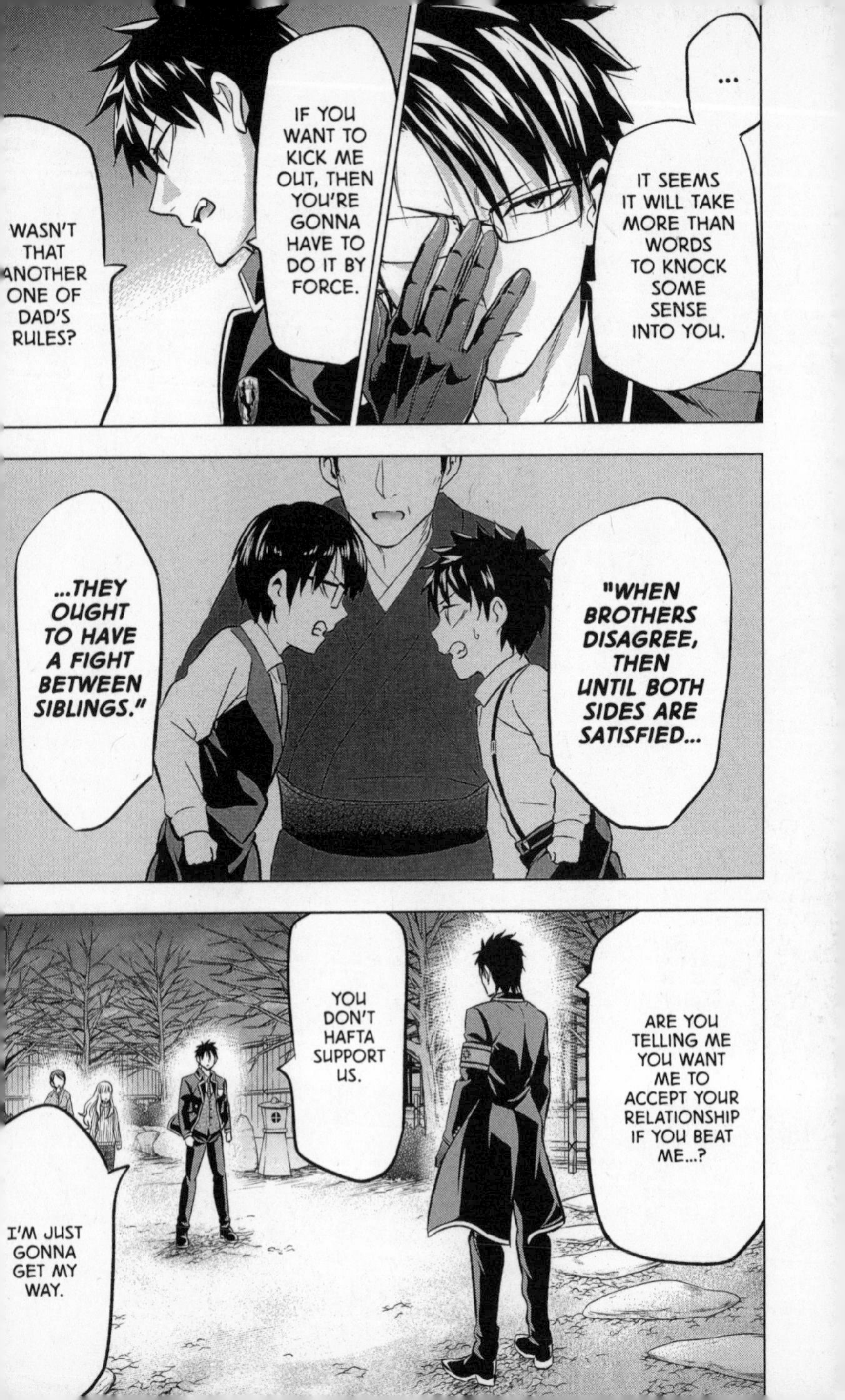
...
IT SEEMS IT WILL TAKE MORE THAN WORDS TO KNOCK SOME SENSE INTO YOU.
IF YOU WANT TO KICK ME OUT, THEN YOU'RE GONNA HAVE TO DO IT BY FORCE.
WASN'T THAT ANOTHER ONE OF DAD'S RULES?
"WHEN BROTHERS DISAGREE, THEN UNTIL BOTH SIDES ARE SATISFIED...
...THEY OUGHT TO HAVE A FIGHT BETWEEN SIBLINGS."
ARE YOU TELLING ME YOU WANT ME TO ACCEPT YOUR RELATIONSHIP IF YOU BEAT ME...?
YOU DON'T HAFTA SUPPORT US.
I'M JUST GONNA GET MY WAY.

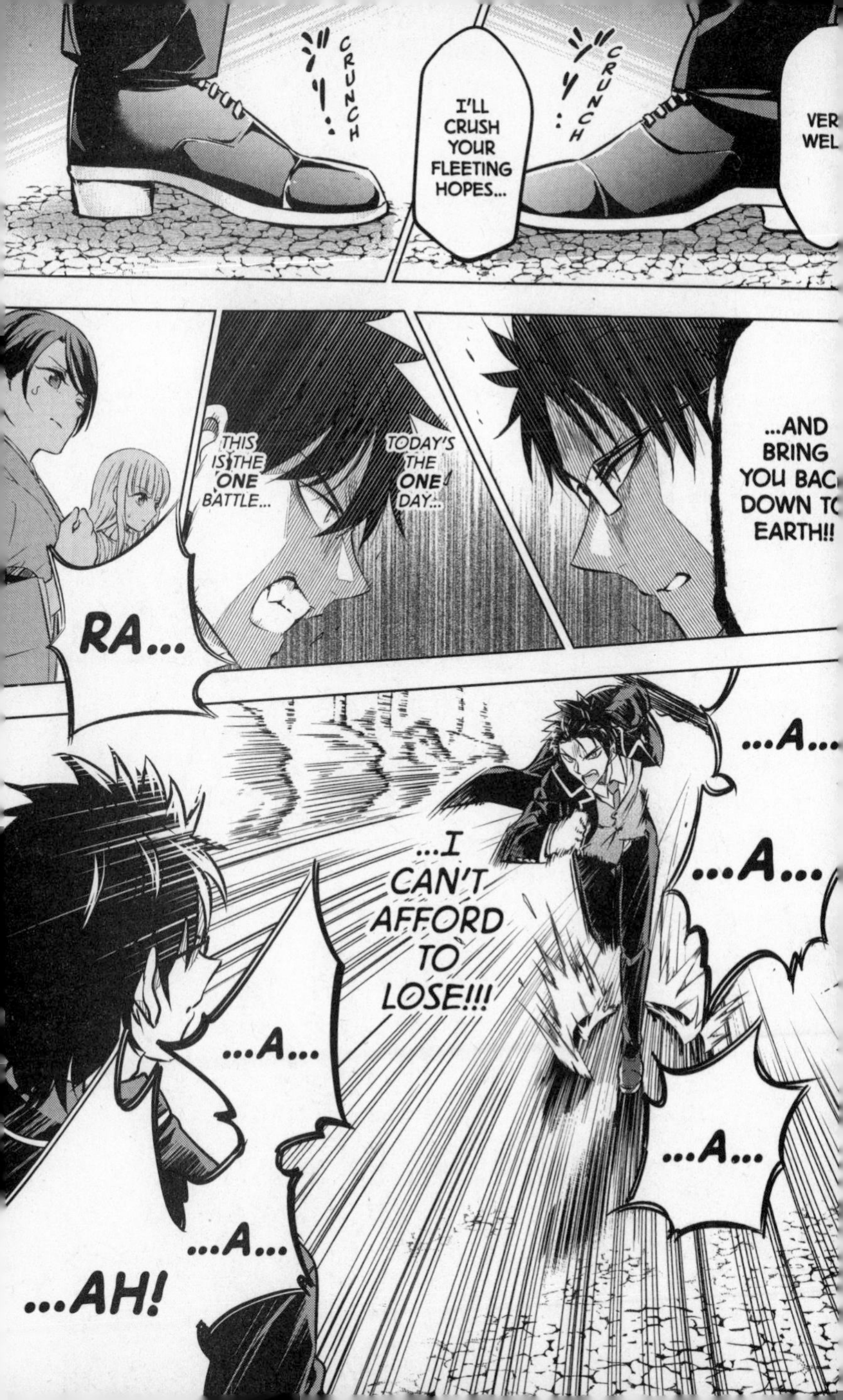
VER
WEL
CRUNCH
I'LL CRUSH YOUR FLEETING HOPES...
CRUNCH
...AND BRING YOU BAC DOWN TC EARTH!!
TODAY'S THE ONE DAY...
THIS IS THE ONE BATTLE...
RA...
...A...
...A...
...I CAN'T AFFORD TO LOSE!!!
...A...
...A...
...A...
...AH!

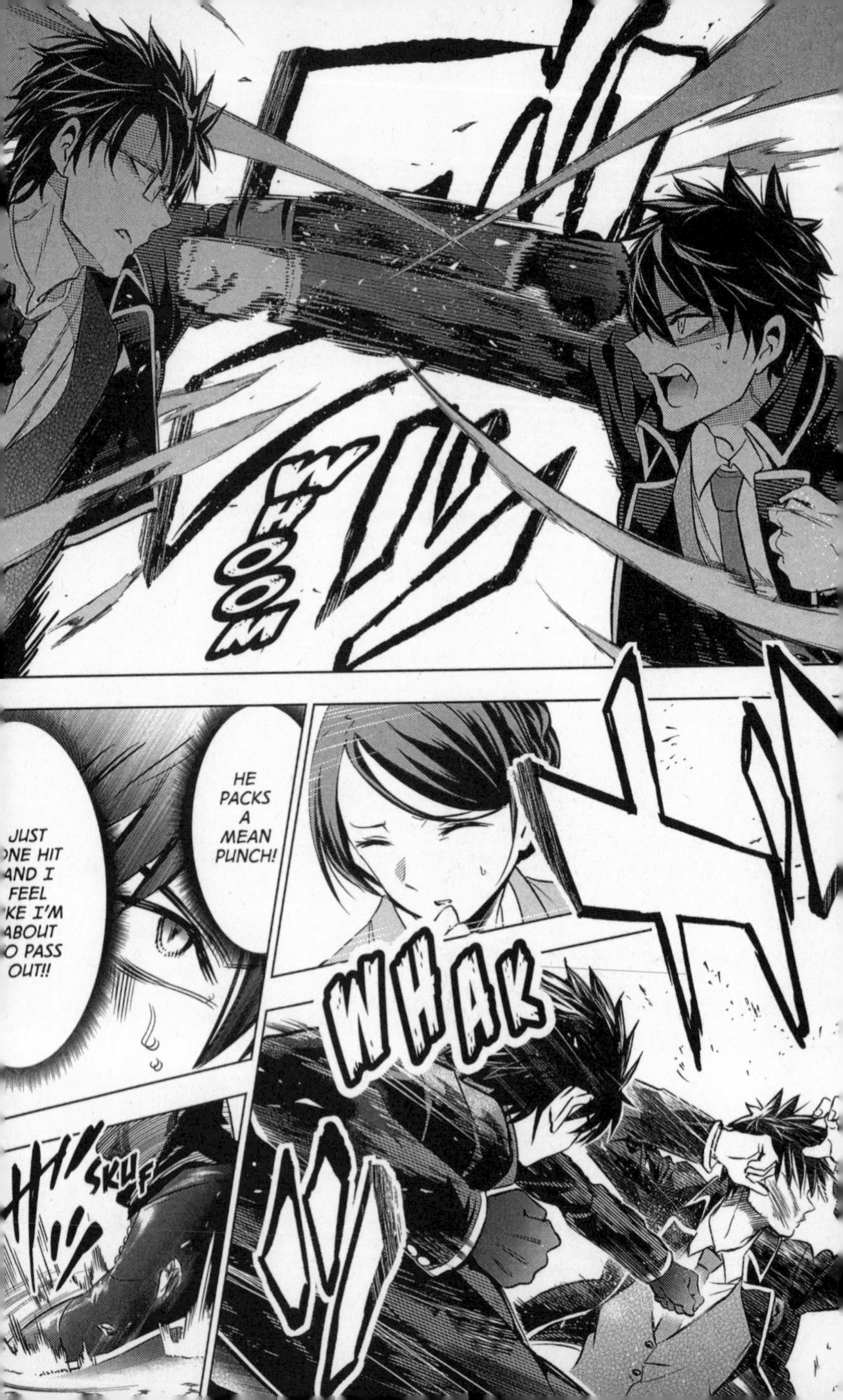
WHOOM
WHAK
HE PACKS A MEAN PUNCH!
JUST ONE HIT AND I FEEL LIKE I'M ABOUT TO PASS OUT!!
SKUF

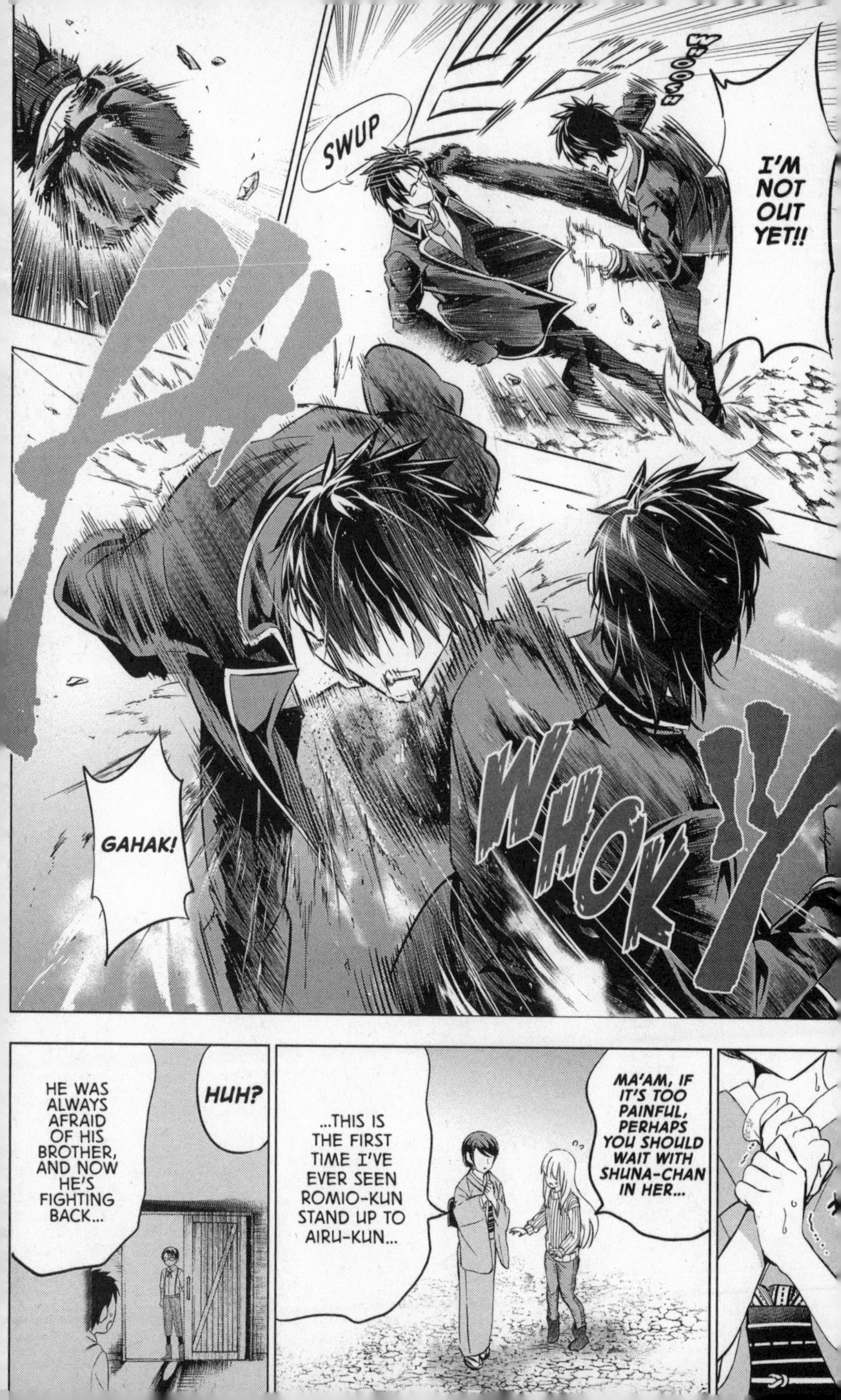
WHOOSH
I'M NOT OUT YET!!
SWUP
GAHAK!
WHOK
MA'AM, IF IT'S TOO PAINFUL, PERHAPS YOU SHOULD WAIT WITH SHUNA-CHAN IN HER...
...THIS IS THE FIRST TIME I'VE EVER SEEN ROMIO-KUN STAND UP TO AIRU-KUN...
HUH?
HE WAS ALWAYS AFRAID OF HIS BROTHER, AND NOW HE'S FIGHTING BACK...

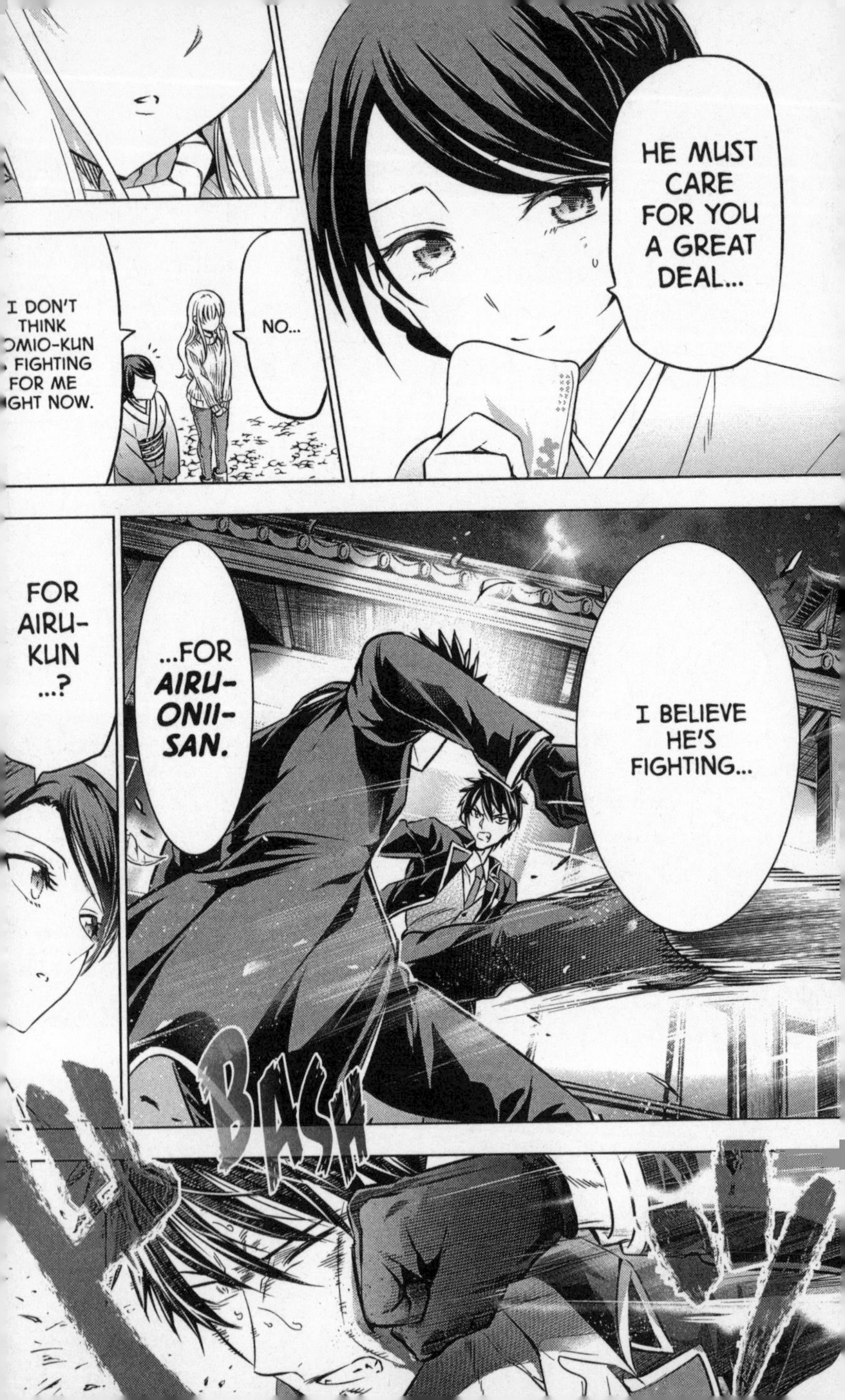
HE MUST CARE FOR YOU A GREAT DEAL...
NO...
I DON'T THINK OMIO-KUN , FIGHTING FOR ME GHT NOW.
I BELIEVE HE'S FIGHTING...
...FOR AIRU-ONII-SAN.
FOR AIRU-KUN ...?
BASH

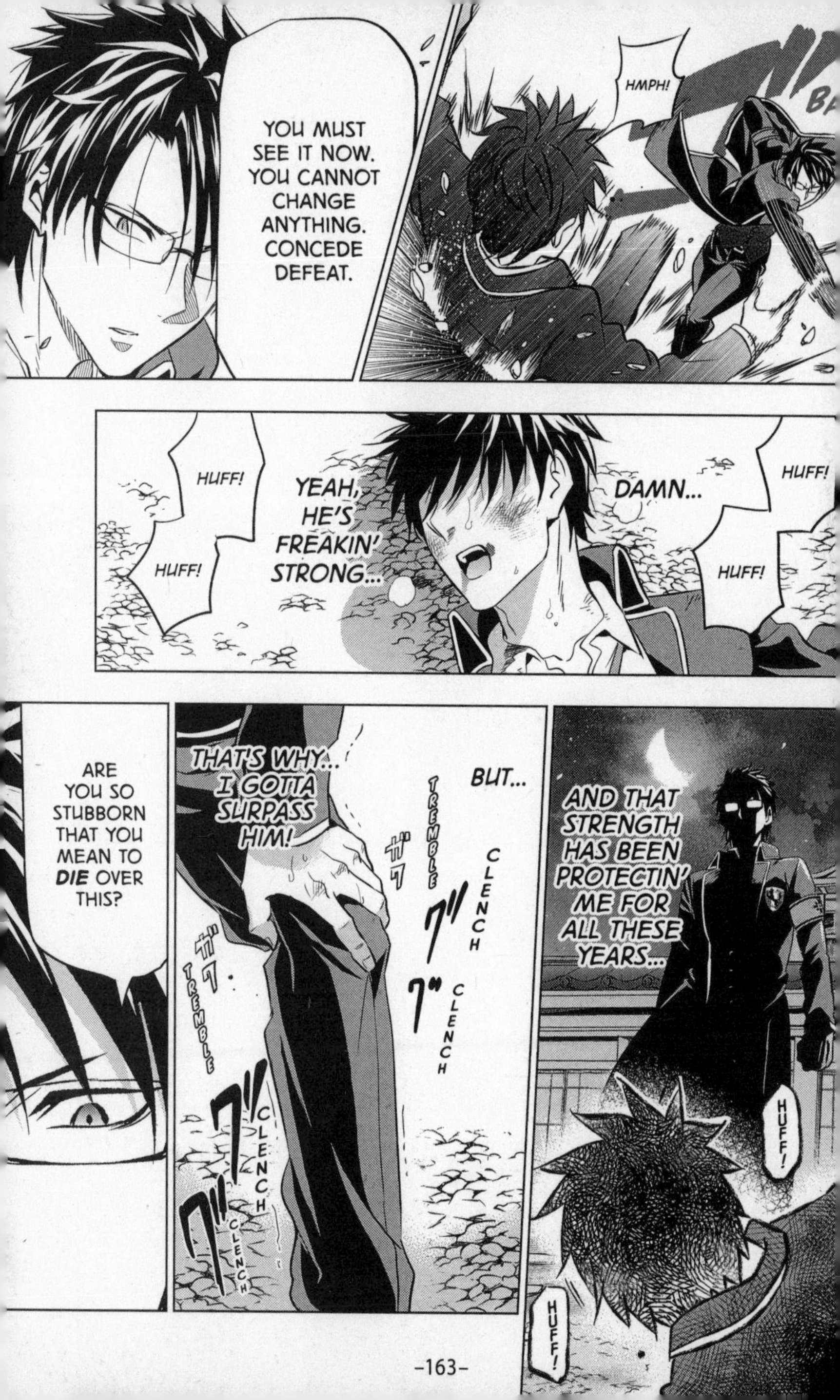
HMPH!
YOU MUST SEE IT NOW. YOU CANNOT CHANGE ANYTHING. CONCEDE DEFEAT.
HUFF!
HUFF!
DAMN...
YEAH, HE'S FREAKIN' STRONG...
HUFF!
HUFF!
AND THAT STRENGTH HAS BEEN PROTECTIN' ME FOR ALL THESE YEARS...
HUFF!
HUFF!
BUT...
TREMBLE
CLENCH
CLENCH
THAT'S WHY... I GOTTA SURPASS HIM!
TREMBLE
CLENCH
CLENCH
ARE YOU SO STUBBORN THAT YOU MEAN TO **DIE** OVER THIS?

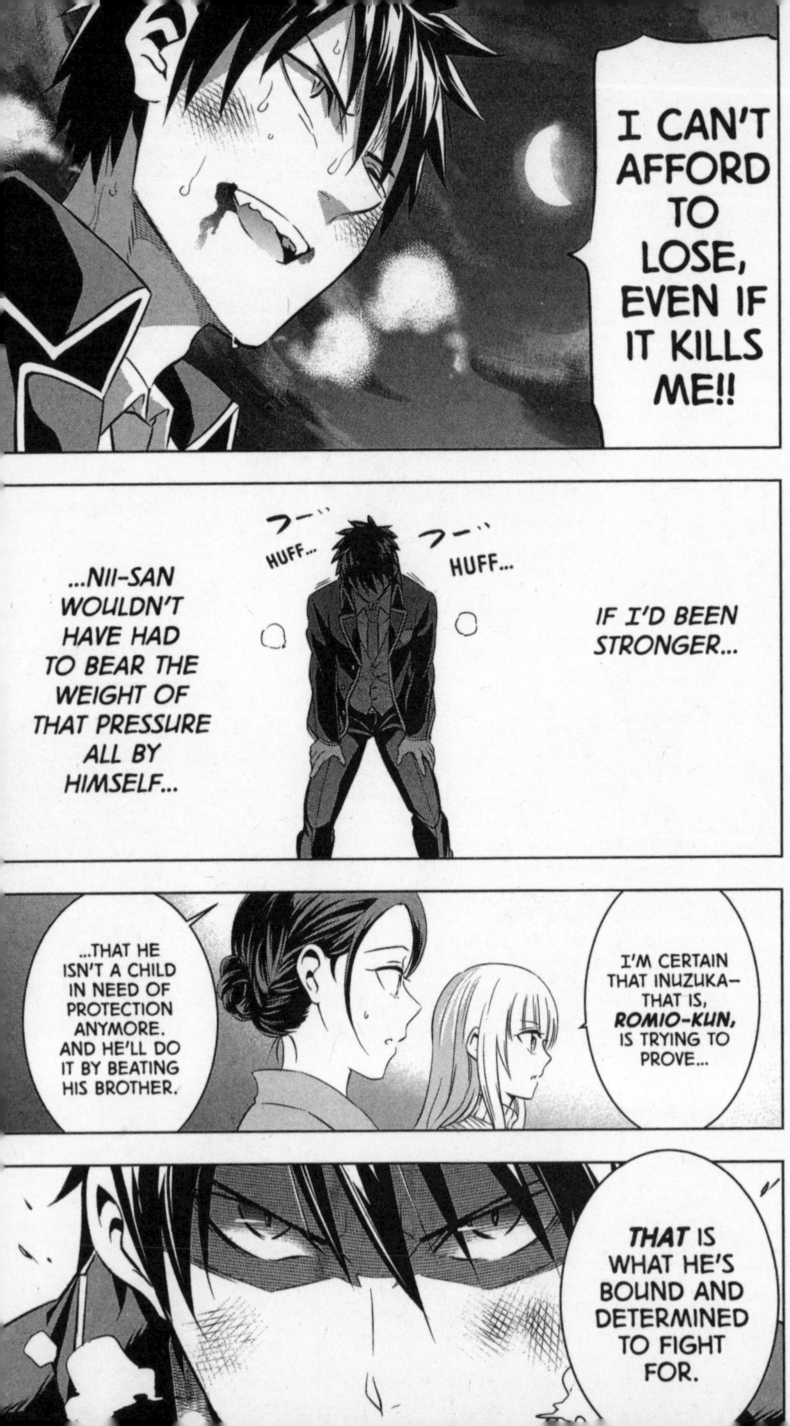
I CAN'T AFFORD TO LOSE, EVEN IF IT KILLS ME!!
IF I'D BEEN STRONGER...
フー HUFF...
フー HUFF...
...NII-SAN WOULDN'T HAVE HAD TO BEAR THE WEIGHT OF THAT PRESSURE ALL BY HIMSELF...
I'M CERTAIN THAT INUZUKA— THAT IS, *ROMIO-KUN,* IS TRYING TO PROVE...
...THAT HE ISN'T A CHILD IN NEED OF PROTECTION ANYMORE. AND HE'LL DO IT BY BEATING HIS BROTHER.
THAT IS WHAT HE'S BOUND AND DETERMINED TO FIGHT FOR.

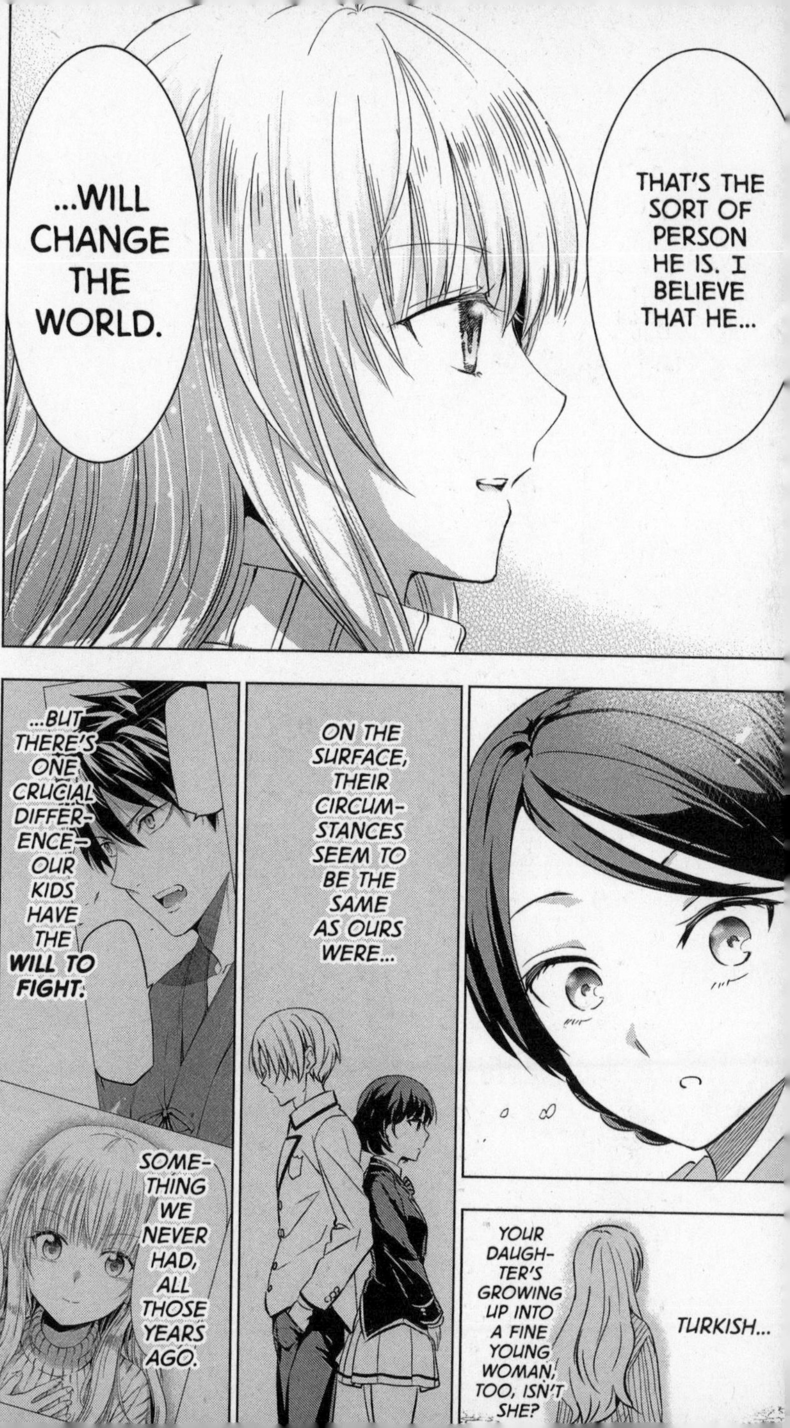
THAT'S THE SORT OF PERSON HE IS. I BELIEVE THAT HE...
...WILL CHANGE THE WORLD.
TURKISH...
YOUR DAUGH-TER'S GROWING UP INTO A FINE YOUNG WOMAN, TOO, ISN'T SHE?
ON THE SURFACE, THEIR CIRCUM-STANCES SEEM TO BE THE SAME AS OURS WERE...
...BUT THERE'S ONE CRUCIAL DIFFER-ENCE—OUR KIDS HAVE THE **WILL TO FIGHT.**
SOME-THING WE NEVER HAD, ALL THOSE YEARS AGO.

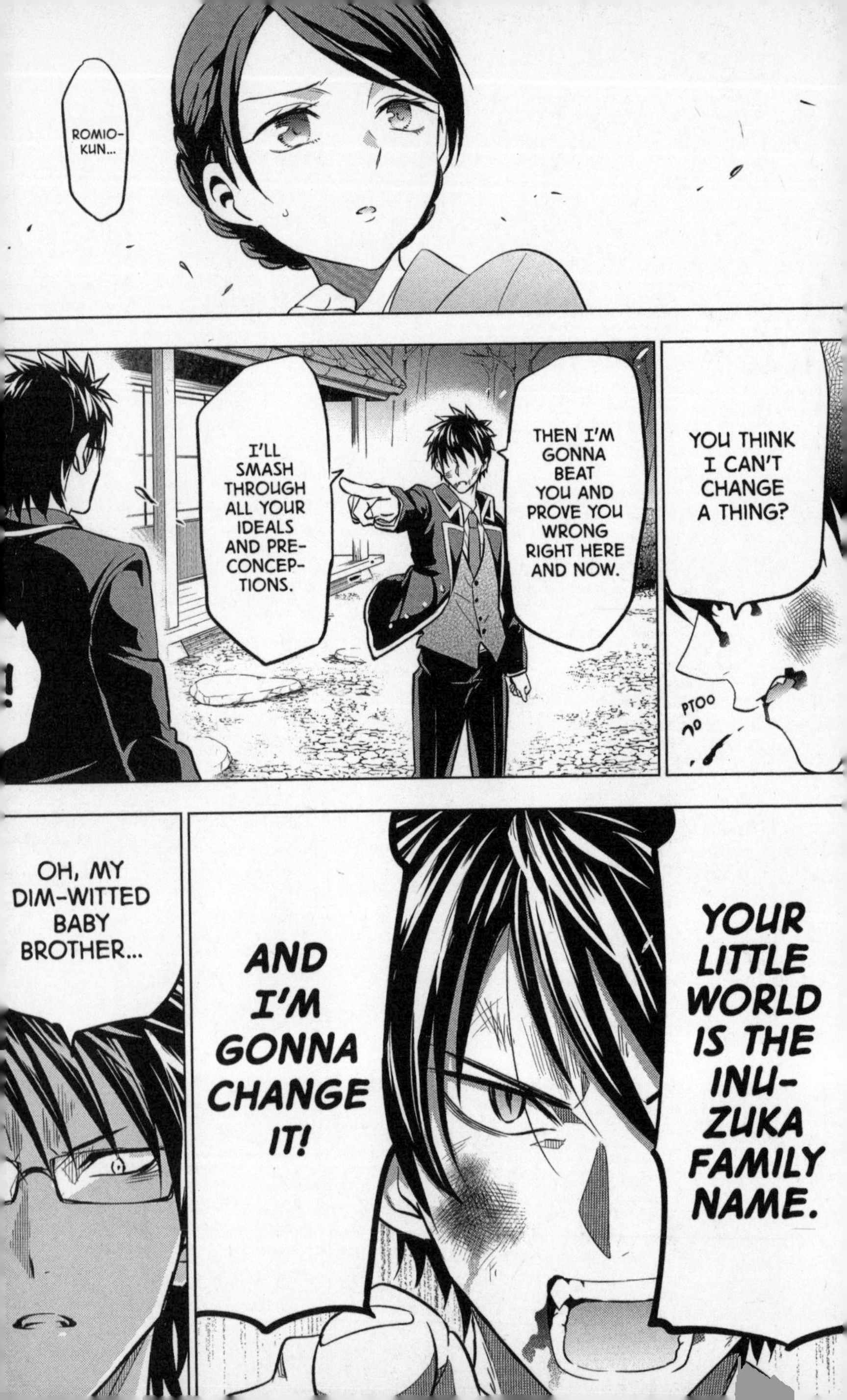
ROMIO-KUN...
YOU THINK I CAN'T CHANGE A THING?
PTOO
THEN I'M GONNA BEAT YOU AND PROVE YOU WRONG RIGHT HERE AND NOW.
I'LL SMASH THROUGH ALL YOUR IDEALS AND PRE-CONCEPTIONS.
!
YOUR LITTLE WORLD IS THE INU-ZUKA FAMILY NAME.
AND I'M GONNA CHANGE IT!
OH, MY DIM-WITTED BABY BROTHER...

ACT 58: ROMIO & JULIO & AIRU IV

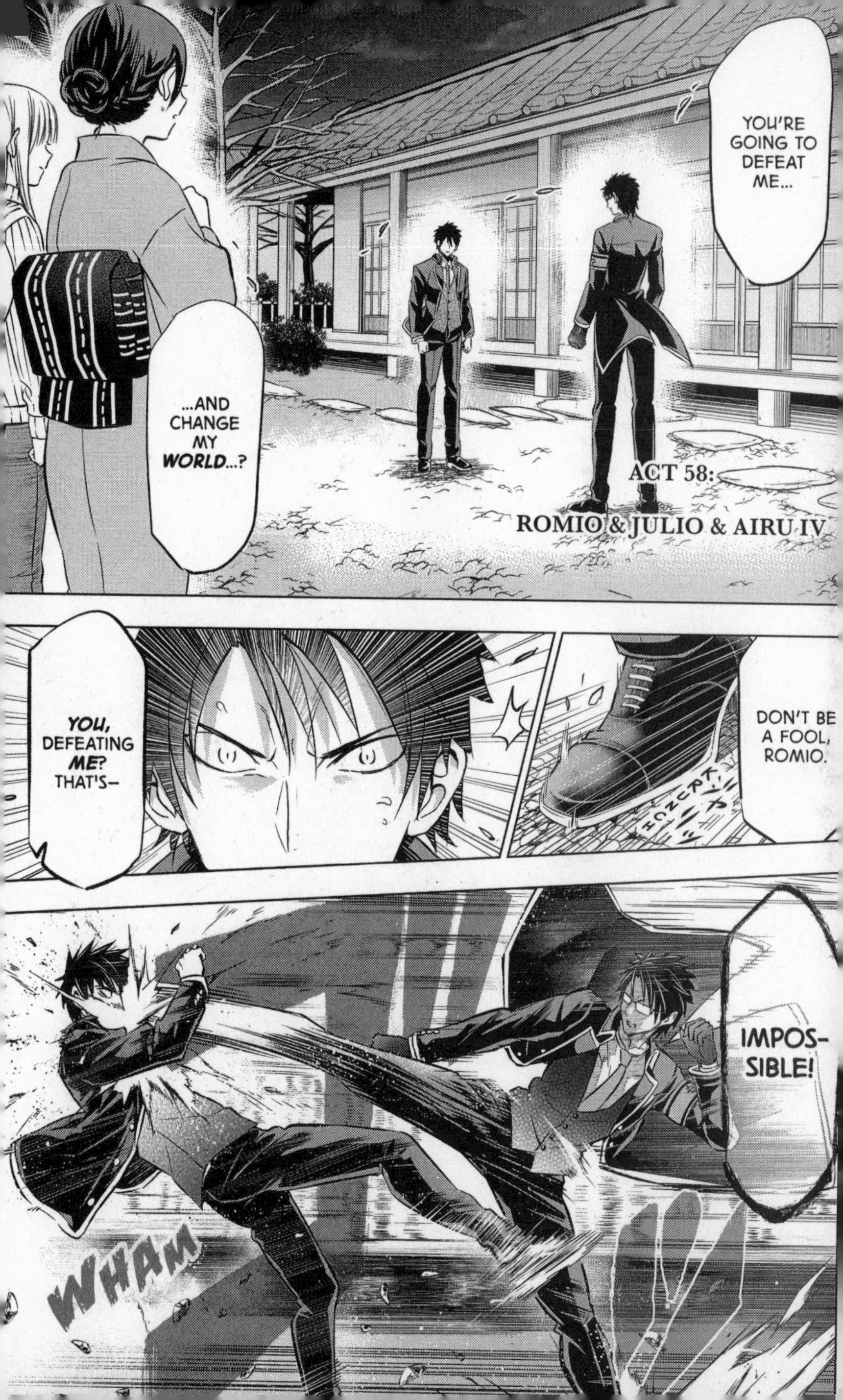
YOU'RE GOING TO DEFEAT ME...
...AND CHANGE MY *WORLD*...?
ACT 58: ROMIO & JULIO & AIRU IV
DON'T BE A FOOL, ROMIO.
YOU, DEFEATING *ME*? THAT'S–
IMPOS-SIBLE!
WHAM

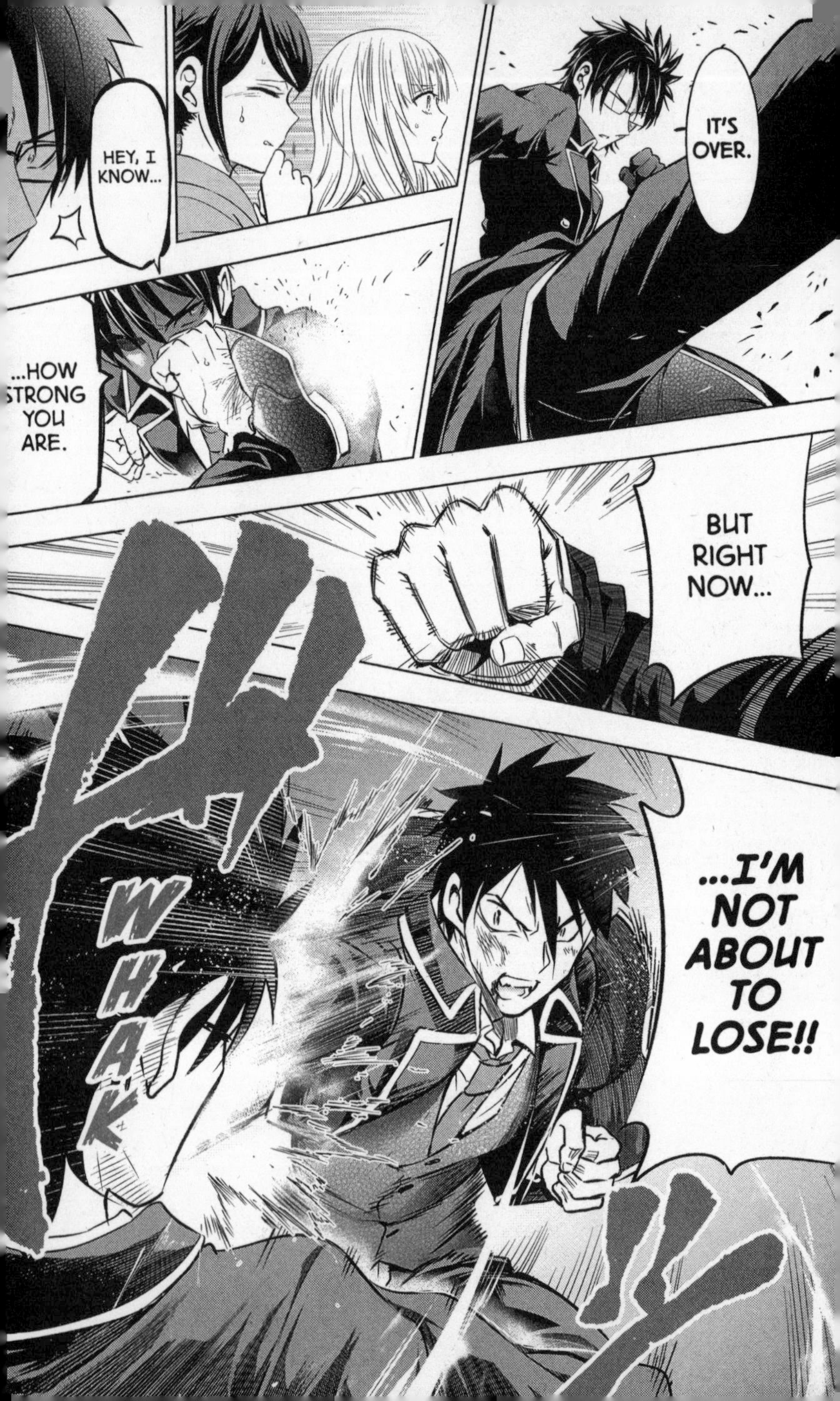
IT'S OVER.
HEY, I KNOW...
...HOW STRONG YOU ARE.
BUT RIGHT NOW...
...I'M NOT ABOUT TO LOSE!!
WHAK

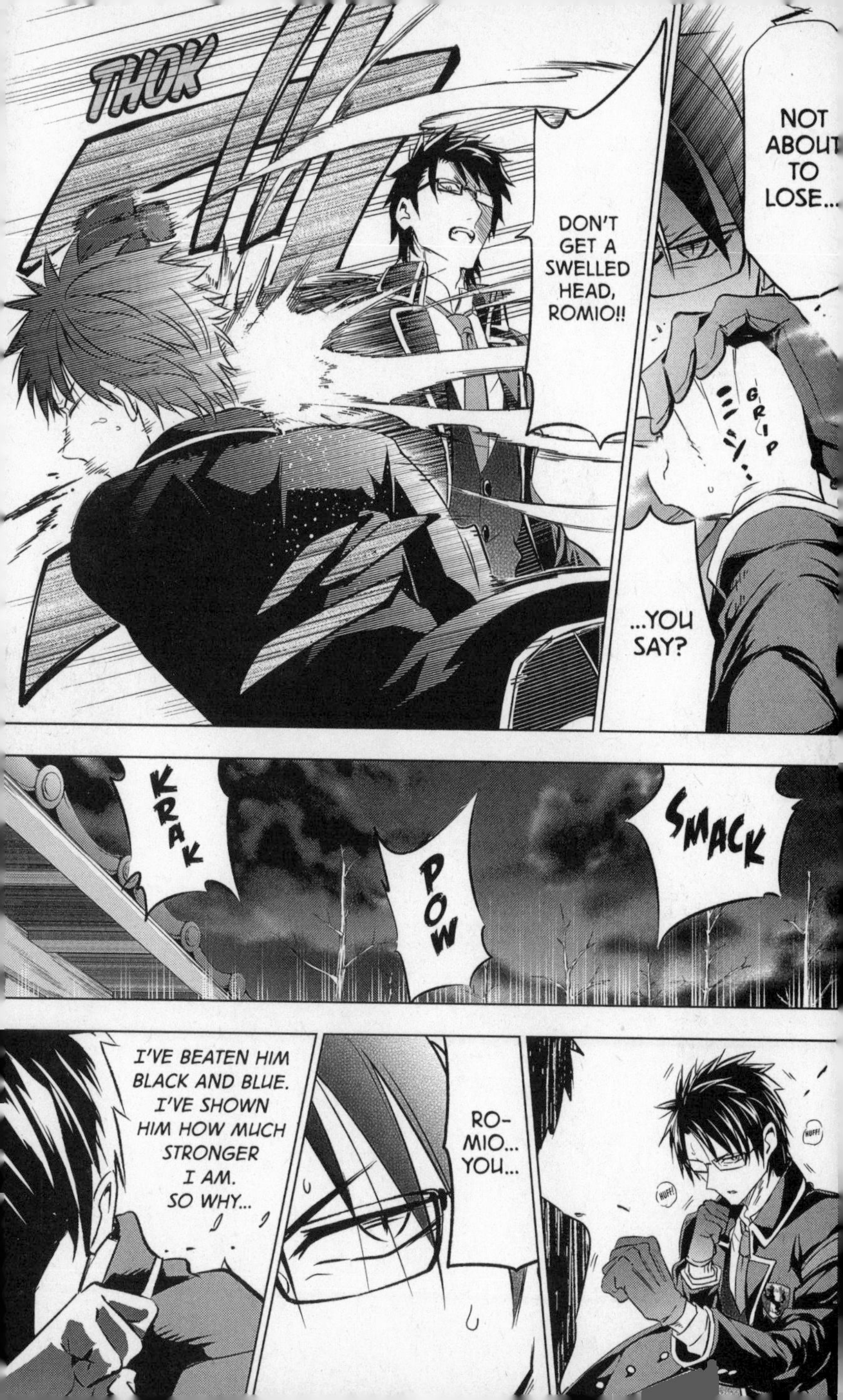
NOT ABOUT TO LOSE...
GRIP
...YOU SAY?
DON'T GET A SWELLED HEAD, ROMIO!!
THOK
SMACK
POW
KRAK
HUFF!
HUFF!
RO-MIO... YOU...
I'VE BEATEN HIM BLACK AND BLUE. I'VE SHOWN HIM HOW MUCH STRONGER I AM. SO WHY...

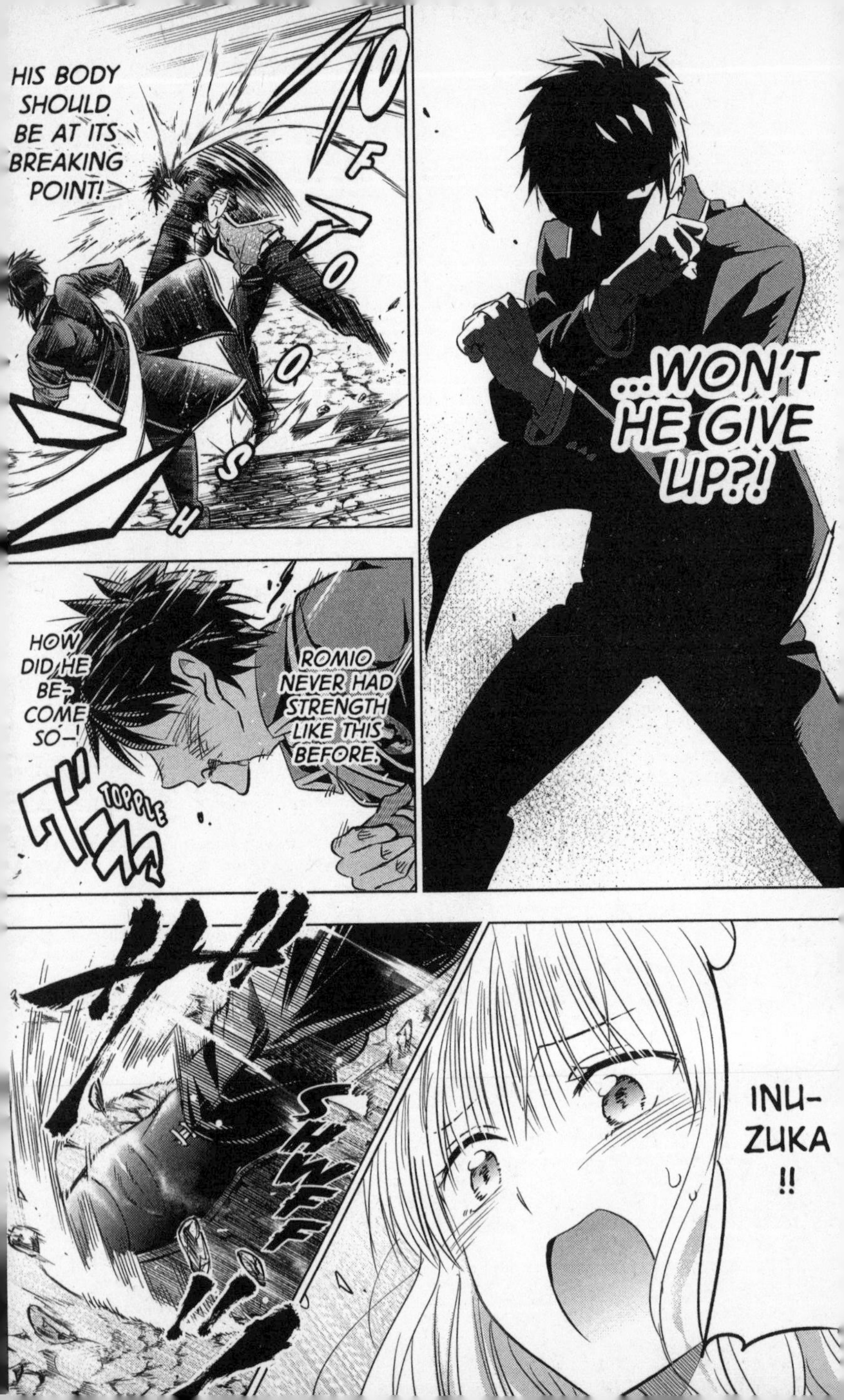
...WON'T HE GIVE UP?!
HIS BODY SHOULD BE AT ITS BREAKING POINT!
FOOSH
ROMIO NEVER HAD STRENGTH LIKE THIS BEFORE.
HOW DID HE BE-COME SO—!
TOPPLE
INU-ZUKA!!
SHWFF

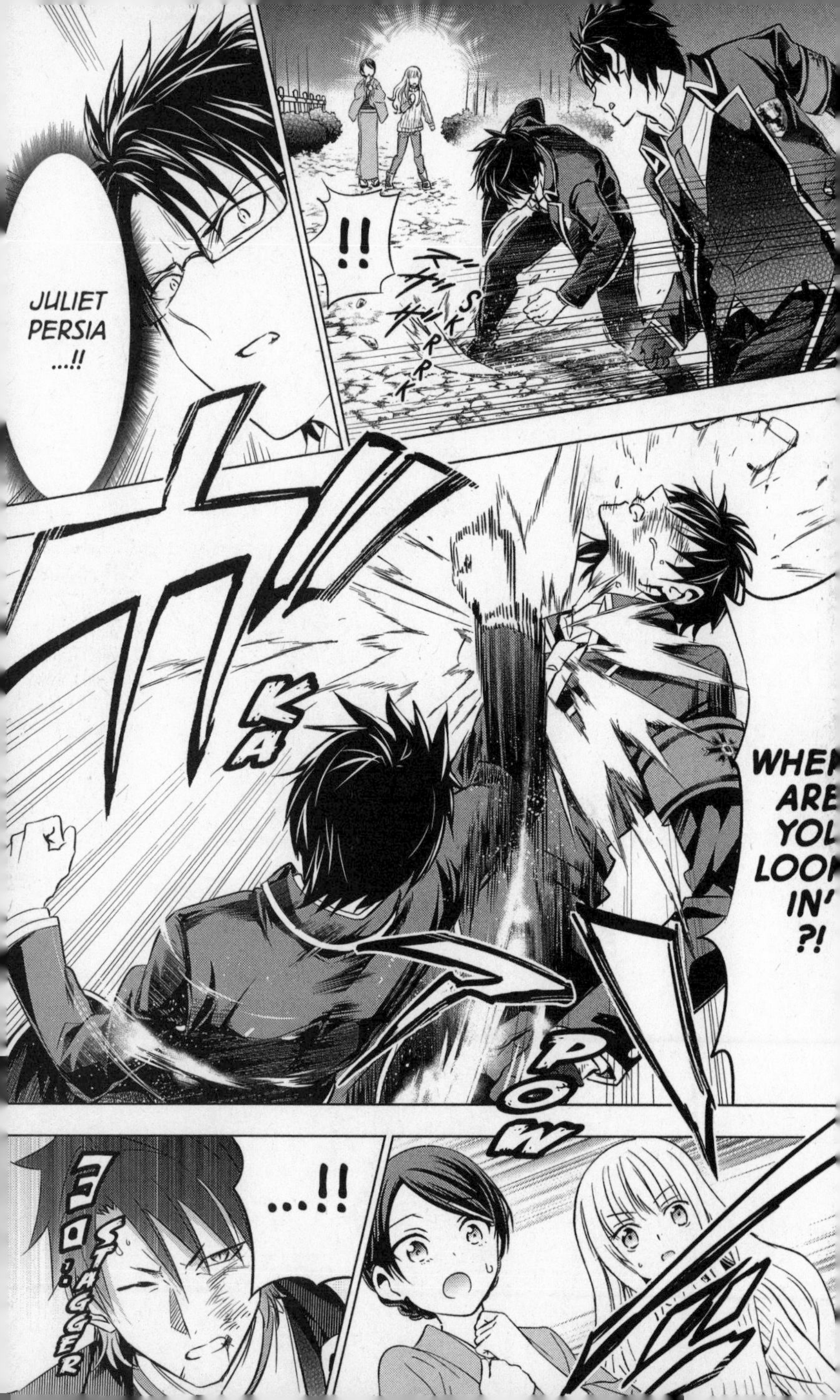

!!
SKRRRK
JULIET PERSIA ...!!
KA
POW
WHE ARE YO LOO IN' ?!
...!!
STAGGER

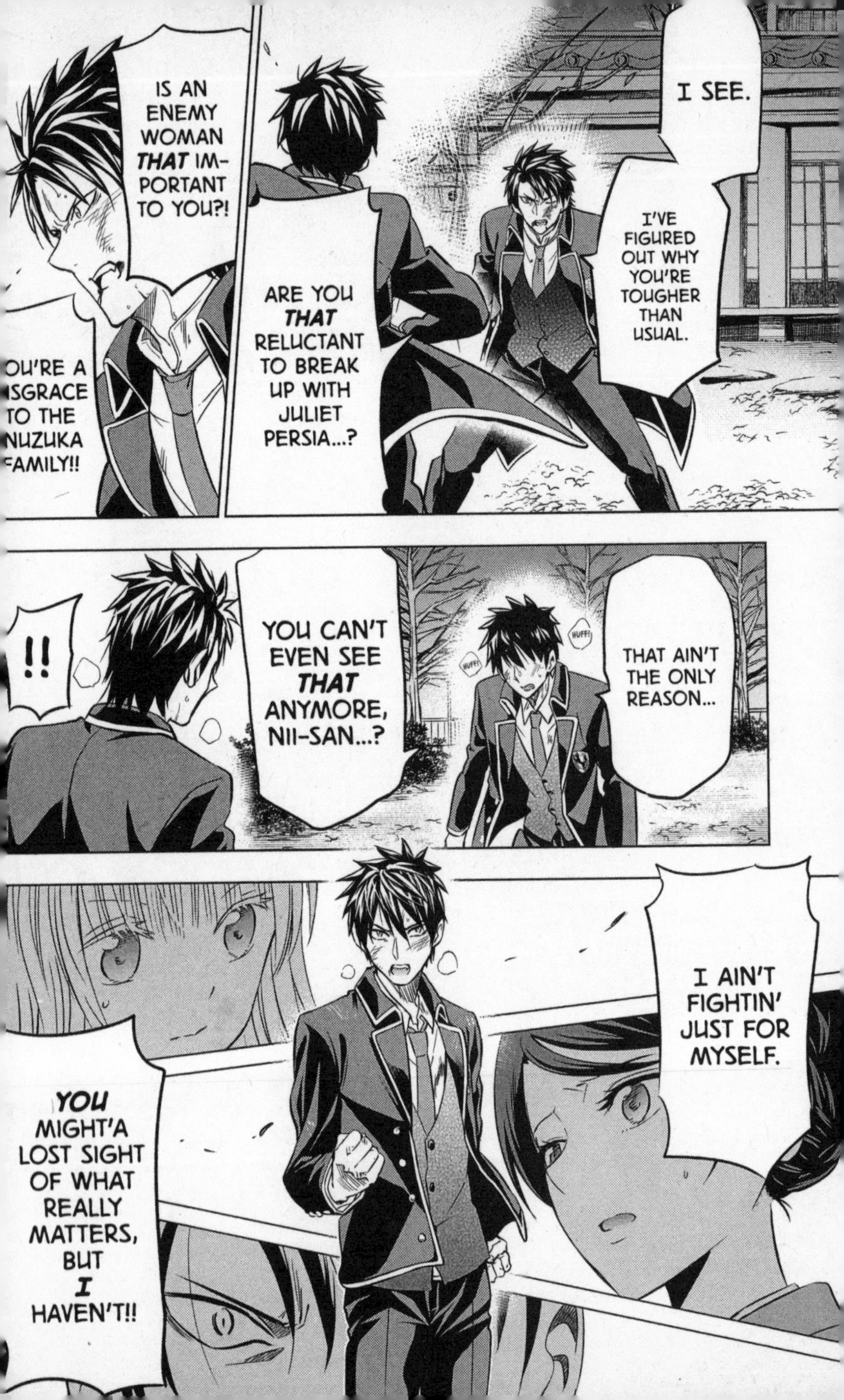
I SEE.
I'VE FIGURED OUT WHY YOU'RE TOUGHER THAN USUAL.
ARE YOU *THAT* RELUCTANT TO BREAK UP WITH JULIET PERSIA...?
IS AN ENEMY WOMAN *THAT* IMPORTANT TO YOU?!
OU'RE A ISGRACE TO THE NUZUKA FAMILY!!
HUFF! HUFF!
THAT AIN'T THE ONLY REASON...
YOU CAN'T EVEN SEE *THAT* ANYMORE, NII-SAN...?
!!
I AIN'T FIGHTIN' JUST FOR MYSELF.
YOU MIGHT'A LOST SIGHT OF WHAT REALLY MATTERS, BUT *I* HAVEN'T!!

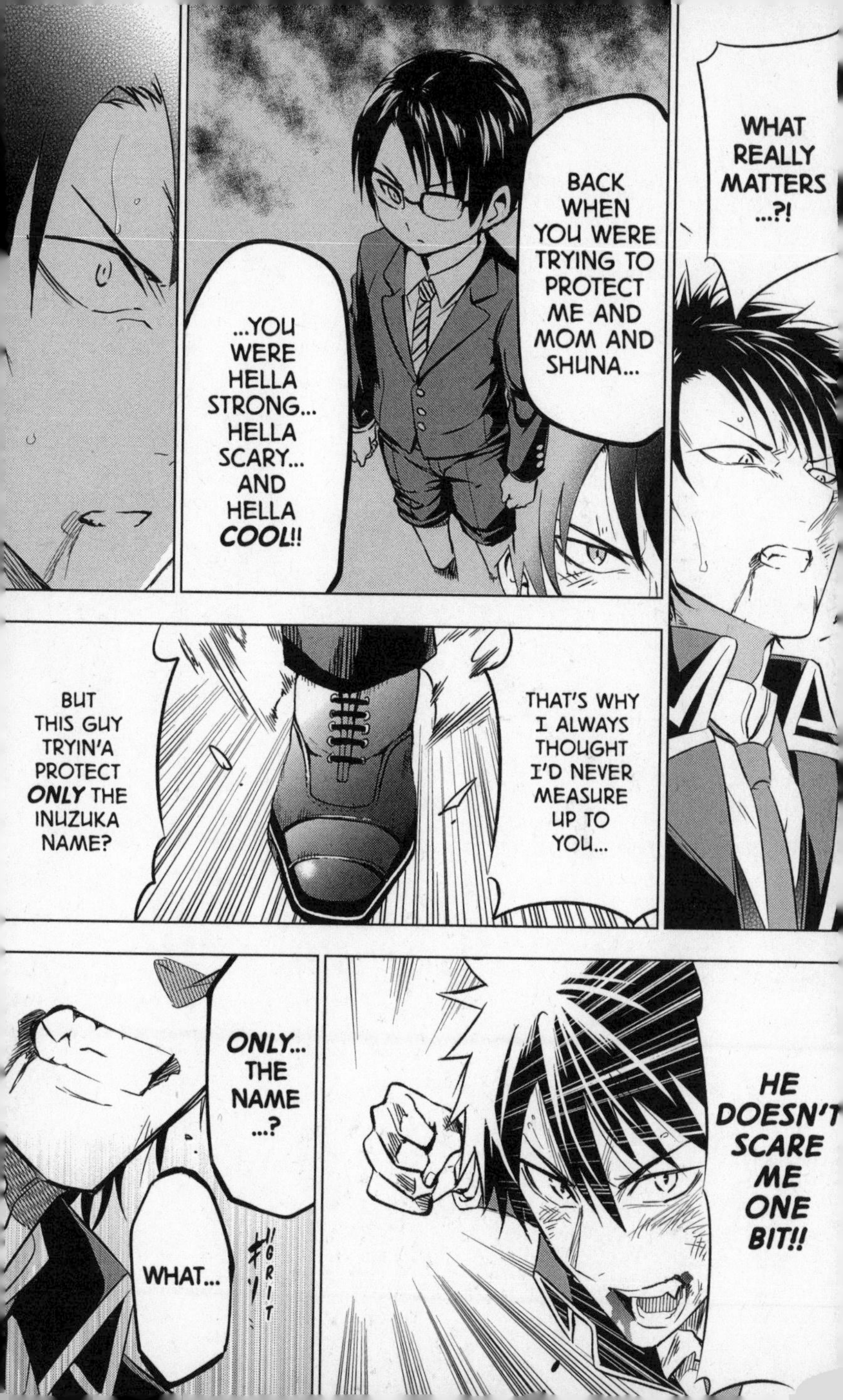
WHAT REALLY MATTERS ...?!
BACK WHEN YOU WERE TRYING TO PROTECT ME AND MOM AND SHUNA...
...YOU WERE HELLA STRONG... HELLA SCARY... AND HELLA *COOL*!!
THAT'S WHY I ALWAYS THOUGHT I'D NEVER MEASURE UP TO YOU...
BUT THIS GUY TRYIN'A PROTECT *ONLY* THE INUZUKA NAME?
HE DOESN'T SCARE ME ONE BIT!!
ONLY... THE NAME ...?
GRIT
WHAT...

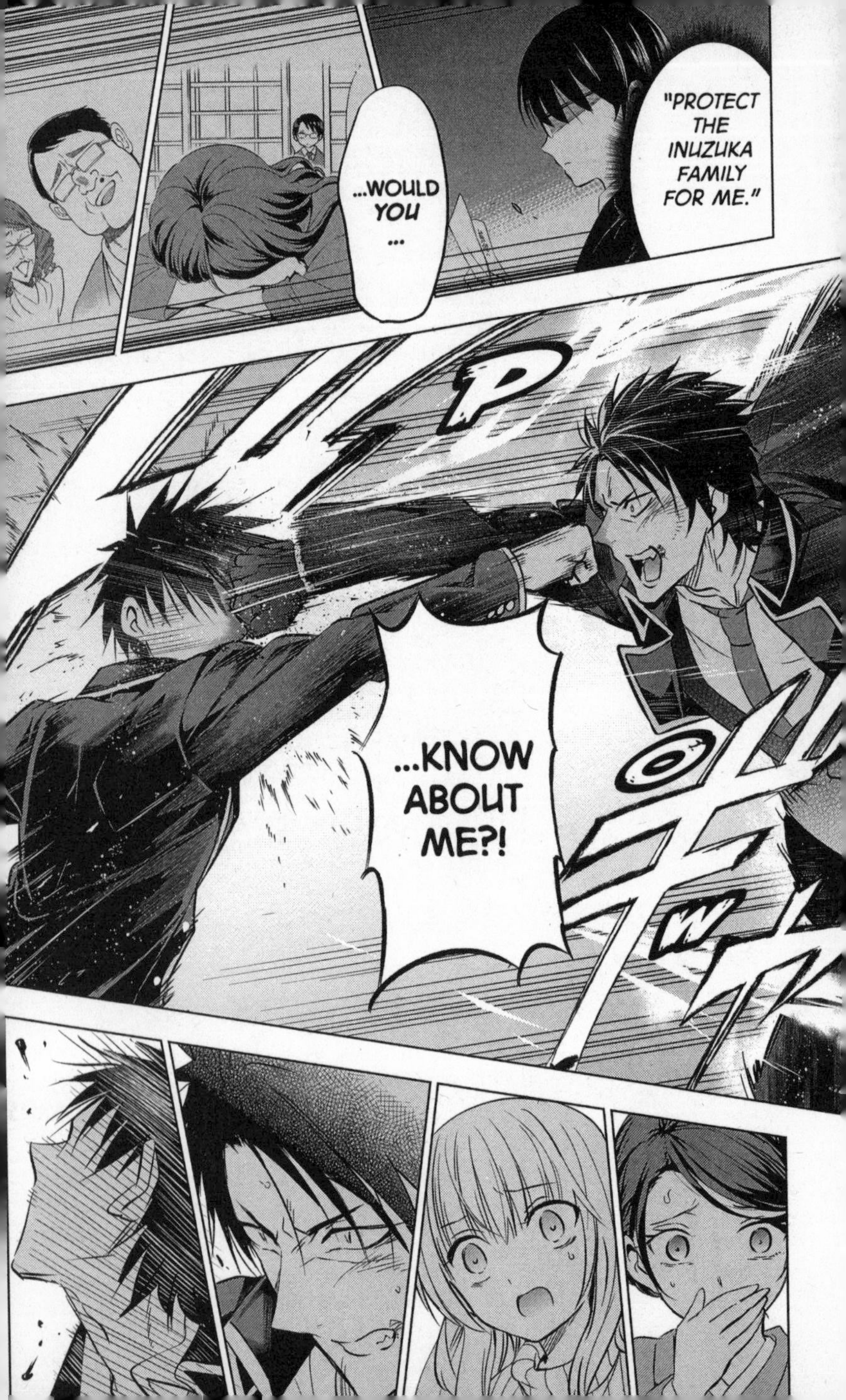
"PROTECT THE INUZUKA FAMILY FOR ME."
...WOULD YOU ...
...KNOW ABOUT ME?!

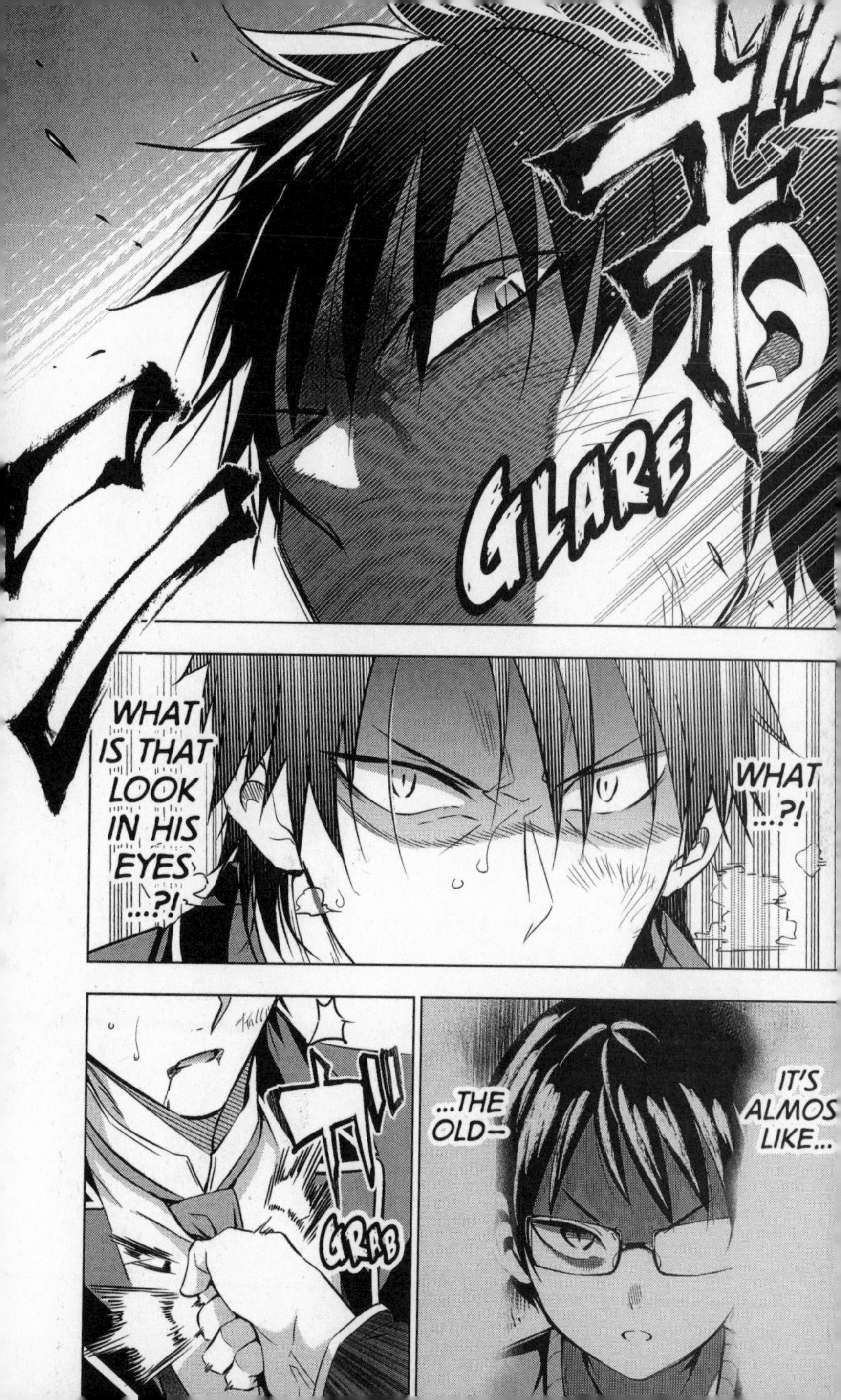
GLARE
WHAT ...?!
WHAT IS THAT LOOK IN HIS EYES ...?!
IT'S ALMOS LIKE...
...THE OLD–
GRAB

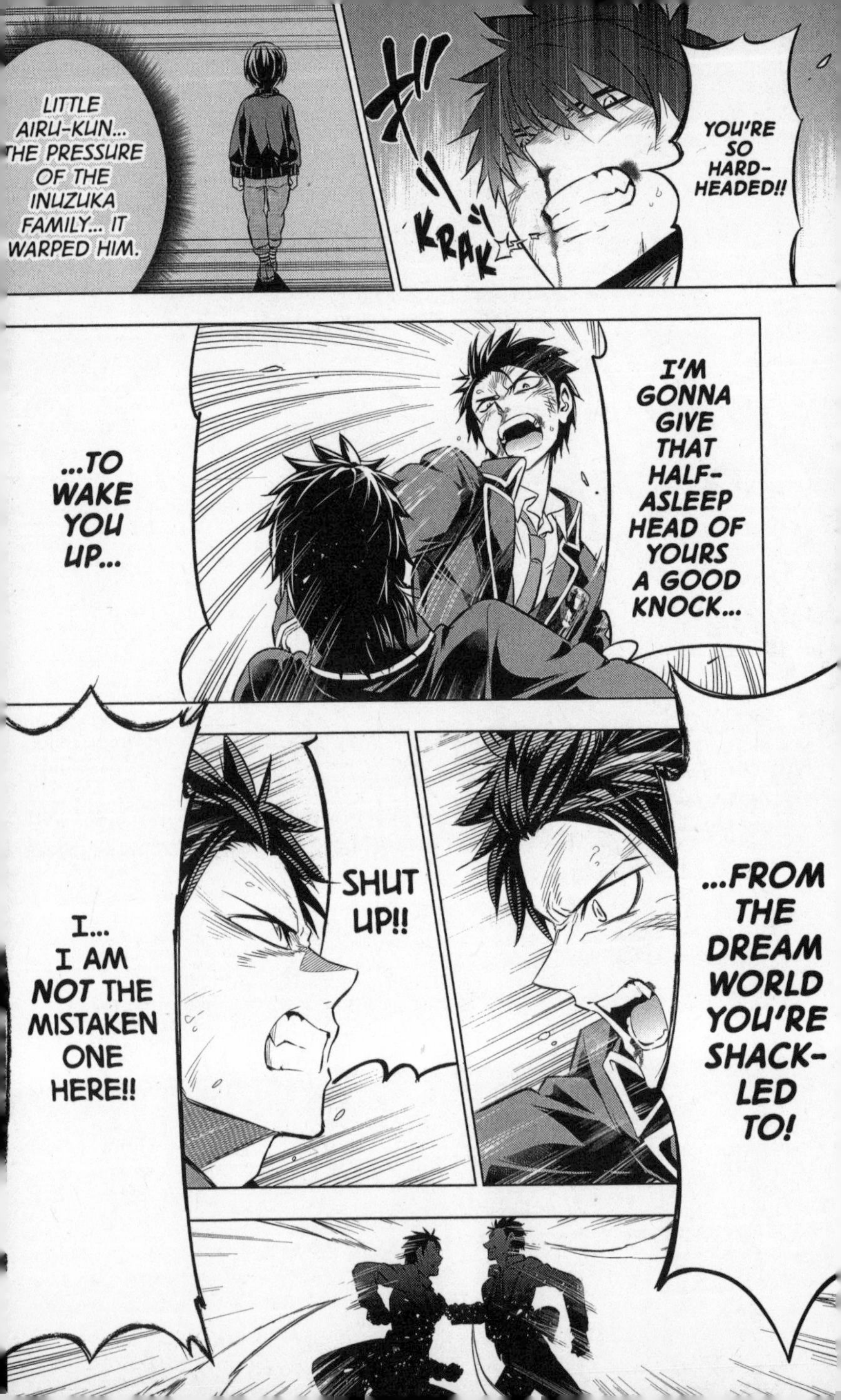
KRAK
YOU'RE SO HARD-HEADED!!
LITTLE AIRU-KUN... THE PRESSURE OF THE INUZUKA FAMILY... IT WARPED HIM.
I'M GONNA GIVE THAT HALF-ASLEEP HEAD OF YOURS A GOOD KNOCK...
...TO WAKE YOU UP...
...FROM THE DREAM WORLD YOU'RE SHACKLED TO!
SHUT UP!!
I... I AM *NOT* THE MISTAKEN ONE HERE!!

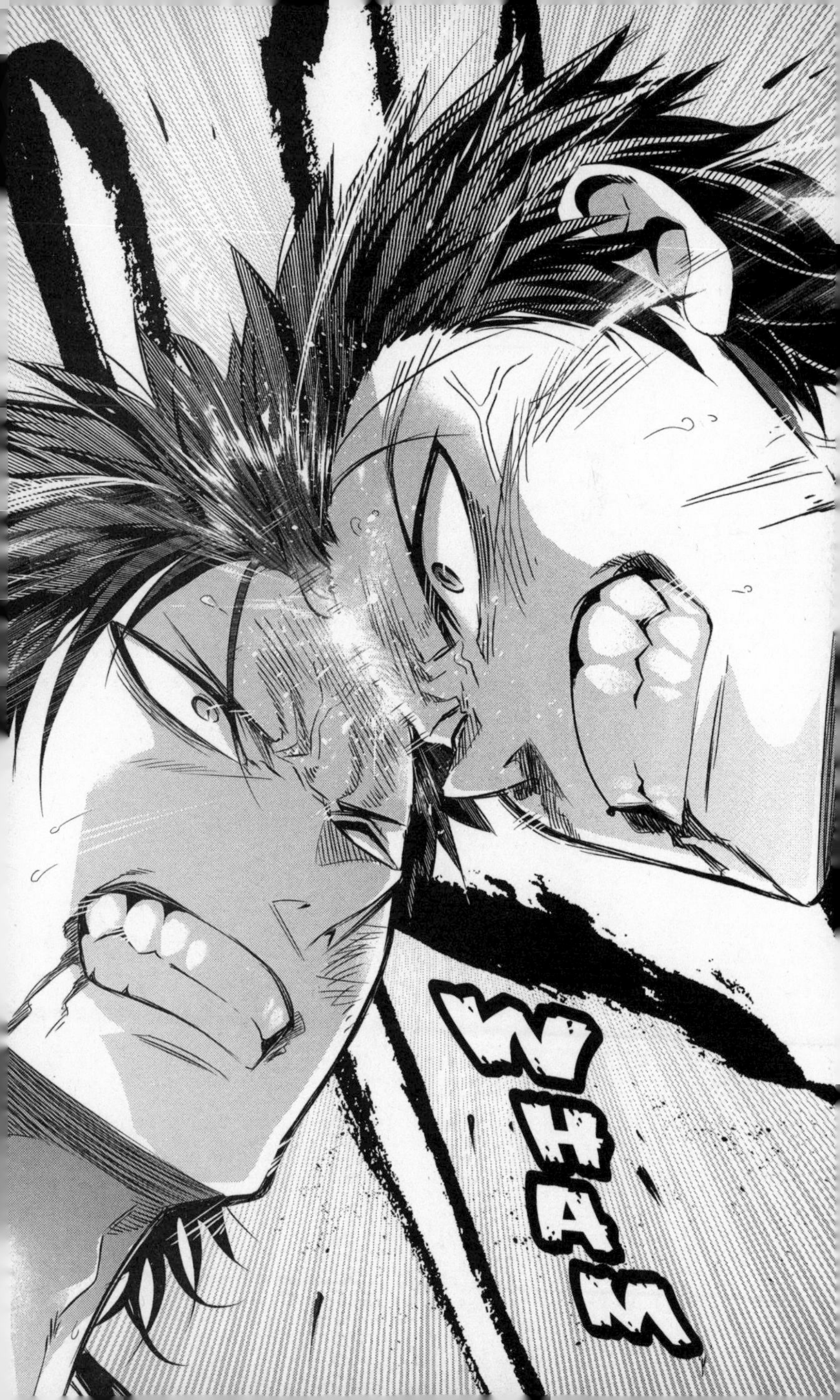
WHAM

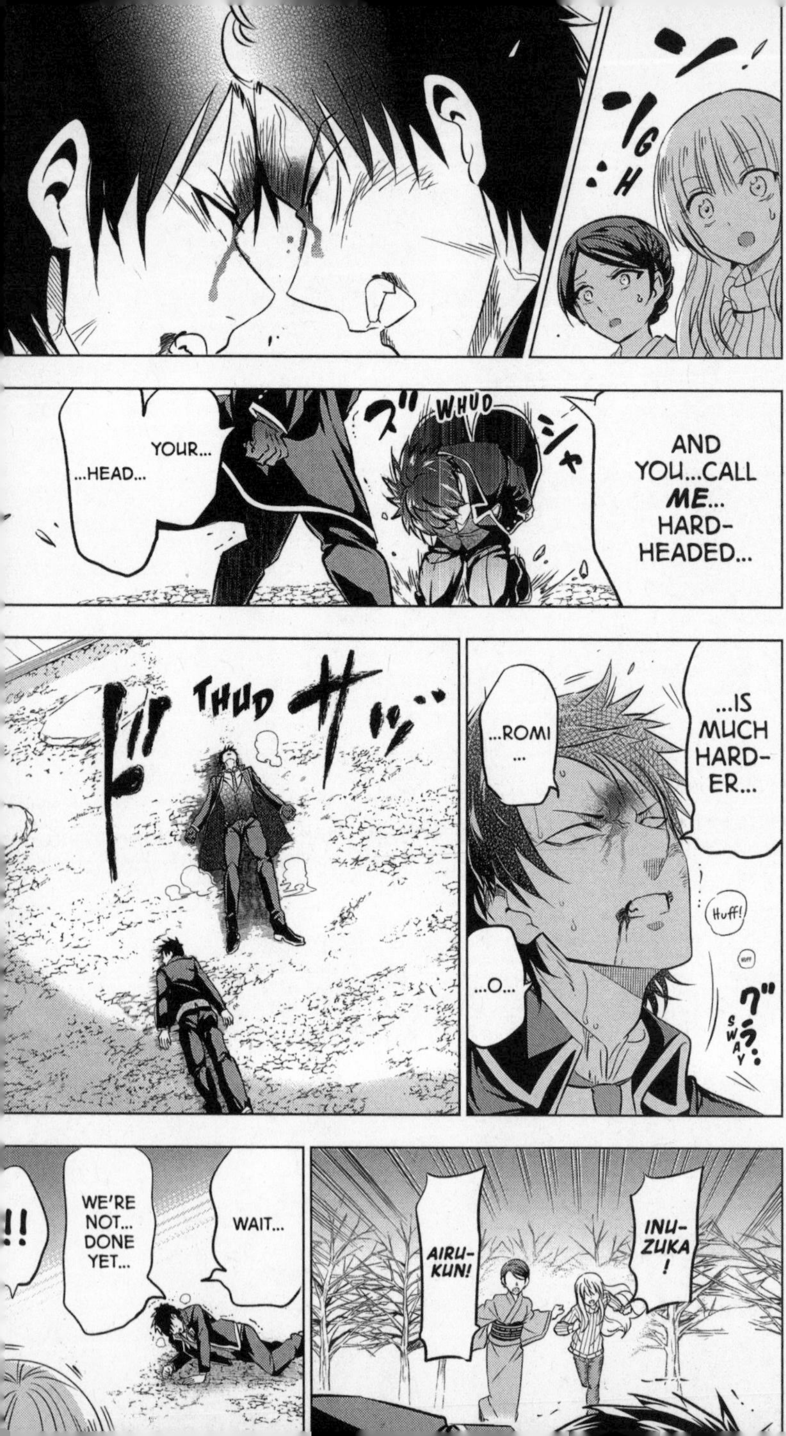
AND YOU...CALL ME... HARD-HEADED...
WHUD
YOUR...
...HEAD...
...IS MUCH HARDER...
...ROMI ...
Huff!
...O...
SWAY
THUD
INU-ZUKA!
AIRU-KUN!
WAIT...
WE'RE NOT... DONE YET...
!!

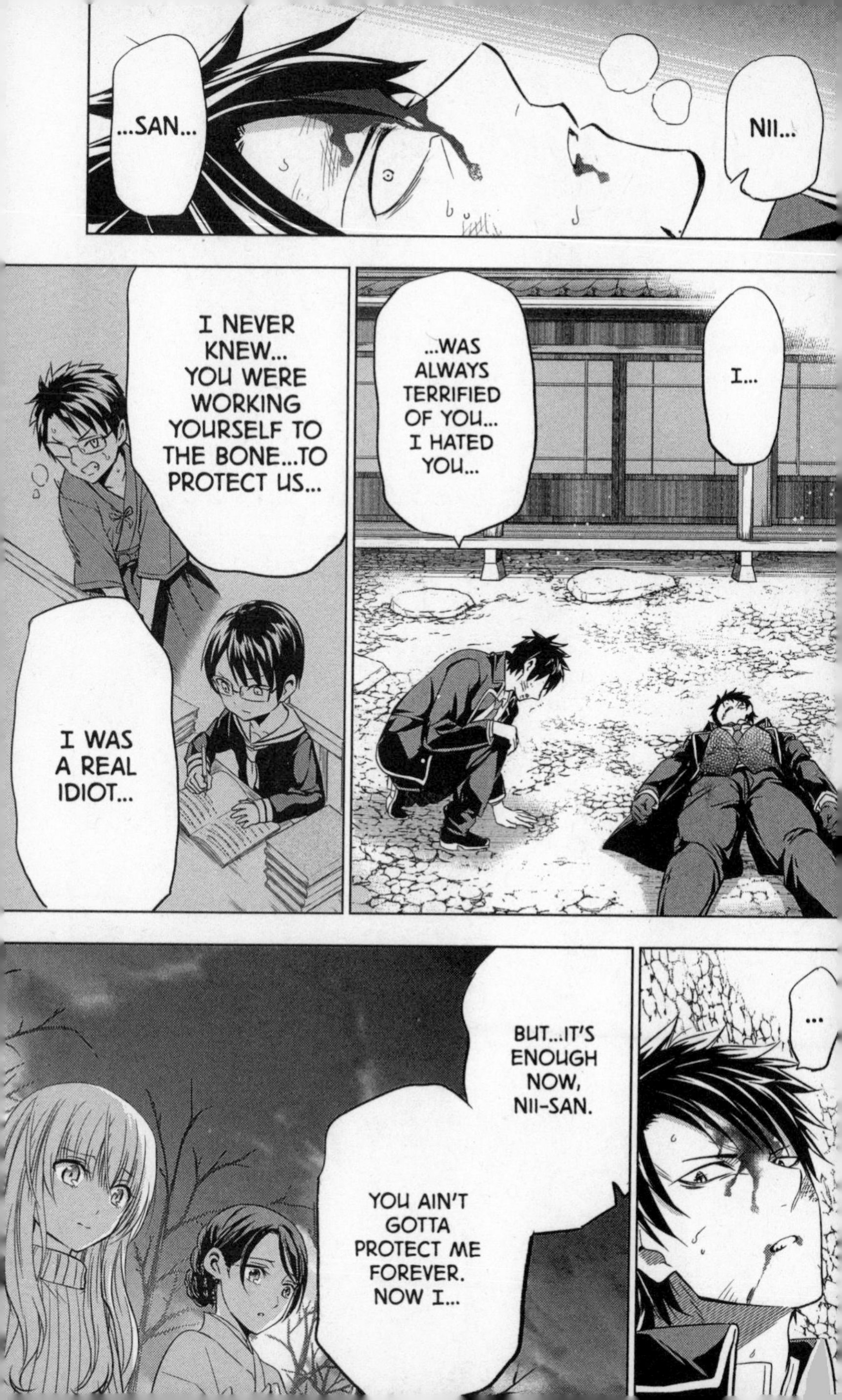
NII...
...SAN...
I...
...WAS ALWAYS TERRIFIED OF YOU... I HATED YOU...
I NEVER KNEW... YOU WERE WORKING YOURSELF TO THE BONE...TO PROTECT US...
I WAS A REAL IDIOT...
...
BUT...IT'S ENOUGH NOW, NII-SAN.
YOU AIN'T GOTTA PROTECT ME FOREVER. NOW I...

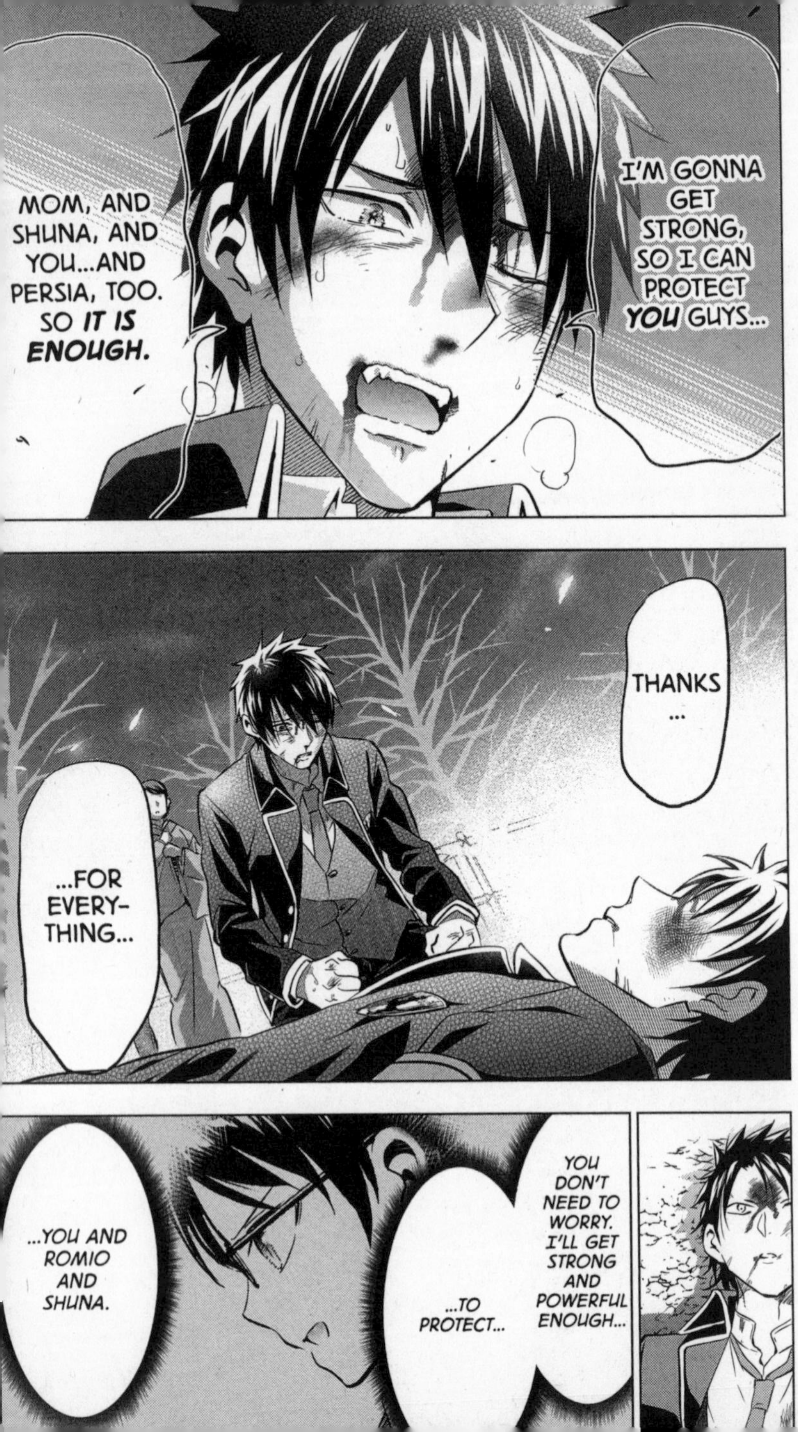
I'M GONNA GET STRONG, SO I CAN PROTECT YOU GUYS...
MOM, AND SHUNA, AND YOU...AND PERSIA, TOO. SO IT IS ENOUGH.
THANKS ...
...FOR EVERY-THING...
YOU DON'T NEED TO WORRY. I'LL GET STRONG AND POWERFUL ENOUGH...
...TO PROTECT...
...YOU AND ROMIO AND SHUNA.

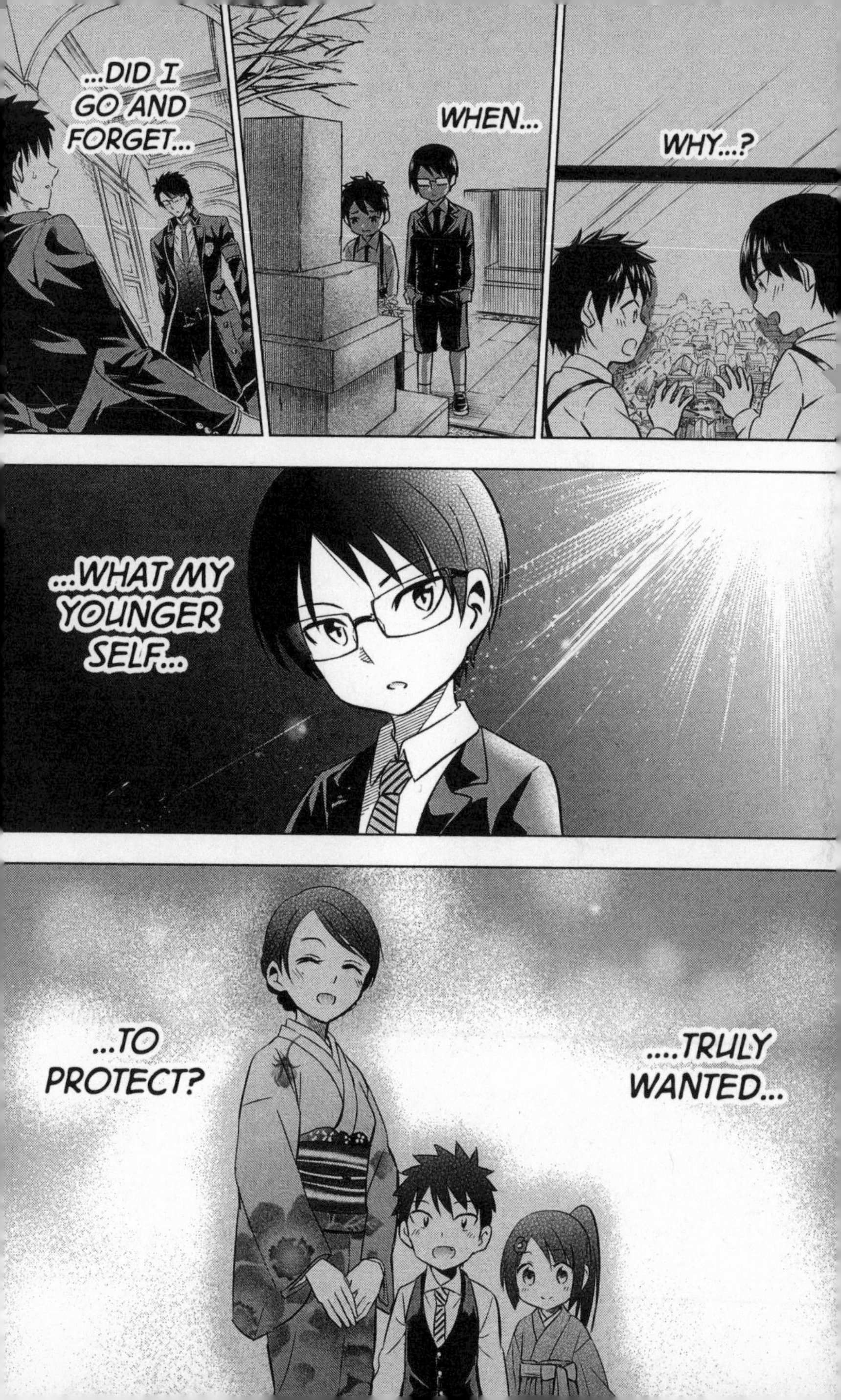
WHY...?
WHEN...
...DID I GO AND FORGET...
...WHAT MY YOUNGER SELF...
....TRULY WANTED...
...TO PROTECT?

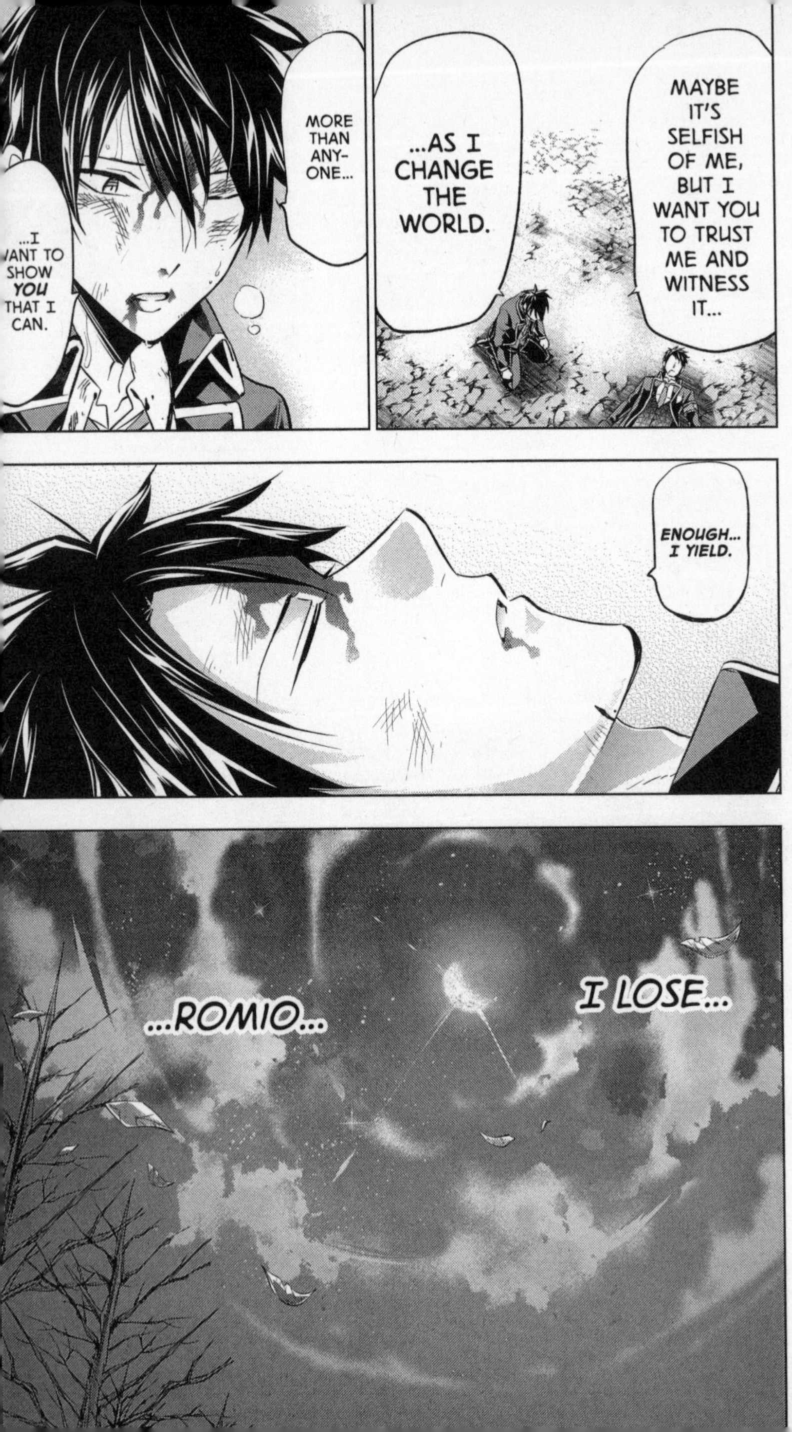
MAYBE IT'S SELFISH OF ME, BUT I WANT YOU TO TRUST ME AND WITNESS IT...
...AS I CHANGE THE WORLD.
MORE THAN ANY-ONE...
...I WANT TO SHOW *YOU* THAT I CAN.
ENOUGH... I YIELD.
I LOSE...
...ROMIO...

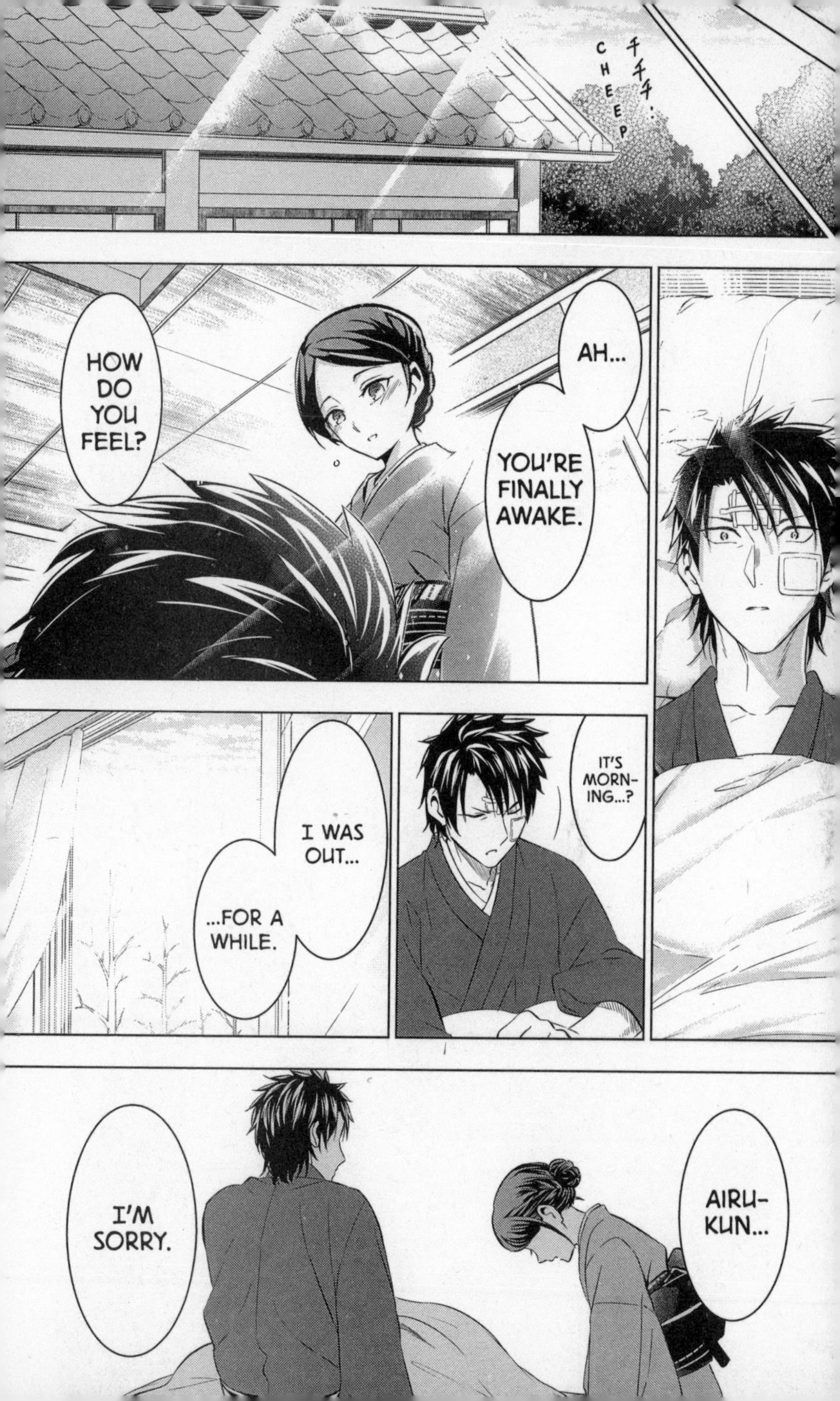
チチチ…
CHEEP
AH...
YOU'RE FINALLY AWAKE.
HOW DO YOU FEEL?
IT'S MORNING...?
I WAS OUT...
...FOR A WHILE.
AIRU-KUN...
I'M SORRY.

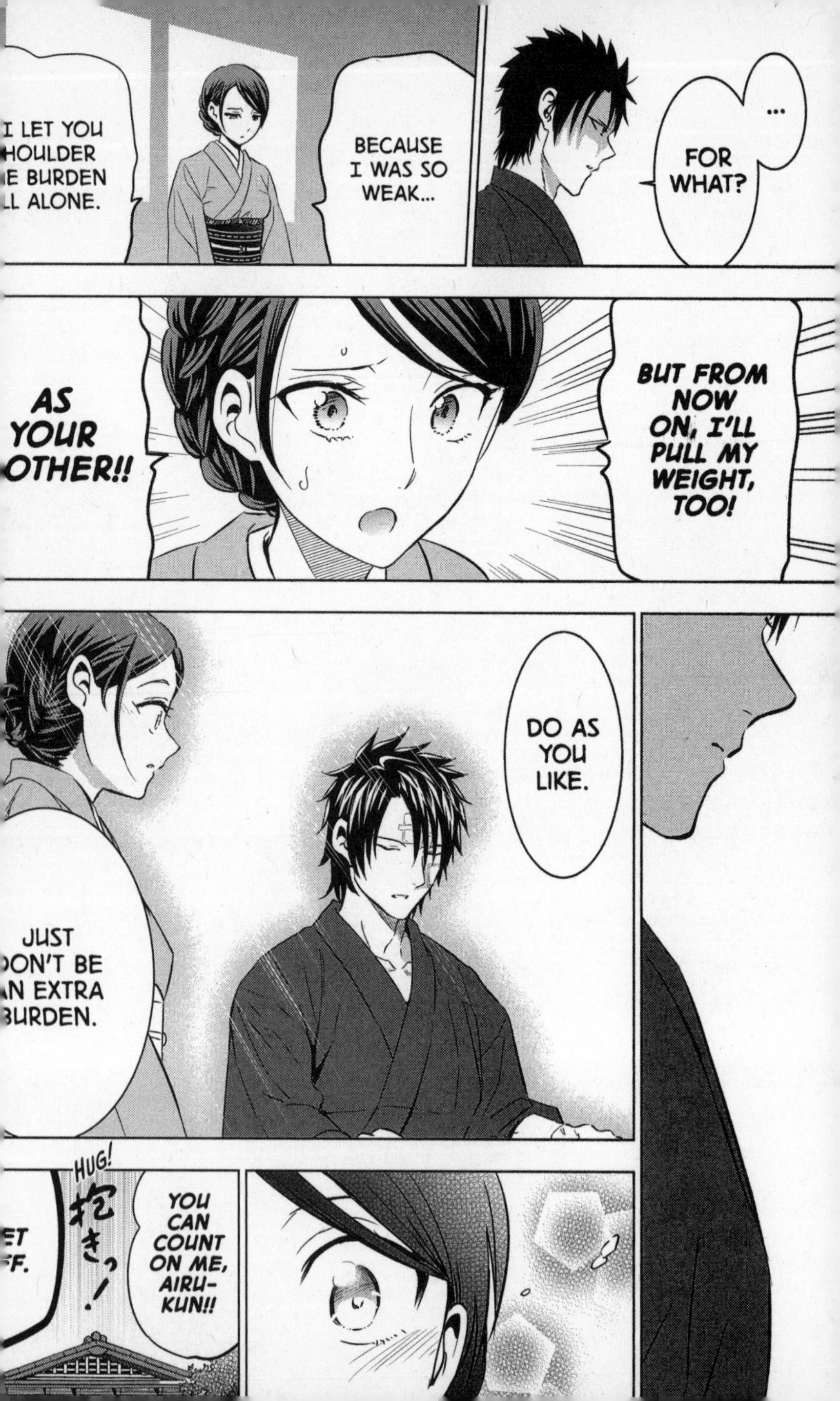
...
FOR WHAT?
BECAUSE I WAS SO WEAK...
I LET YOU HOULDER E BURDEN LL ALONE.
BUT FROM NOW ON, I'LL PULL MY WEIGHT, TOO!
AS YOUR OTHER!!
DO AS YOU LIKE.
JUST ON'T BE N EXTRA URDEN.
YOU CAN COUNT ON ME, AIRU-KUN!!
HUG!
抱きっ!
ET FF.

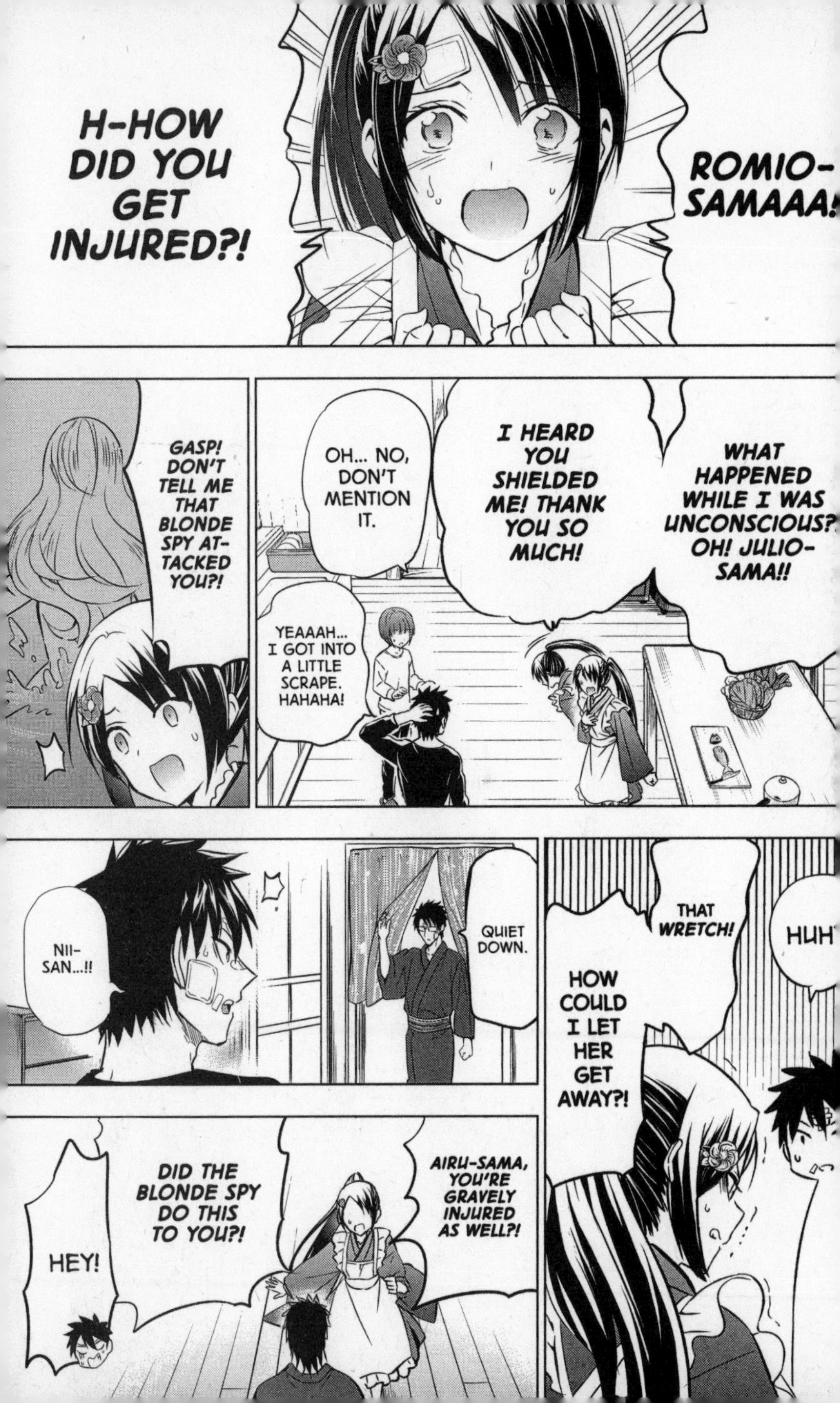
ROMIO-SAMAAA!
H-HOW DID YOU GET INJURED?!
WHAT HAPPENED WHILE I WAS UNCONSCIOUS?! OH! JULIO-SAMA!!
I HEARD YOU SHIELDED ME! THANK YOU SO MUCH!
OH... NO, DON'T MENTION IT.
YEAAAH... I GOT INTO A LITTLE SCRAPE. HAHAHA!
GASP! DON'T TELL ME THAT BLONDE SPY AT-TACKED YOU?!
HUH
THAT WRETCH!
HOW COULD I LET HER GET AWAY?!
QUIET DOWN.
NII-SAN...!!
AIRU-SAMA, YOU'RE GRAVELY INJURED AS WELL?!
DID THE BLONDE SPY DO THIS TO YOU?!
HEY!

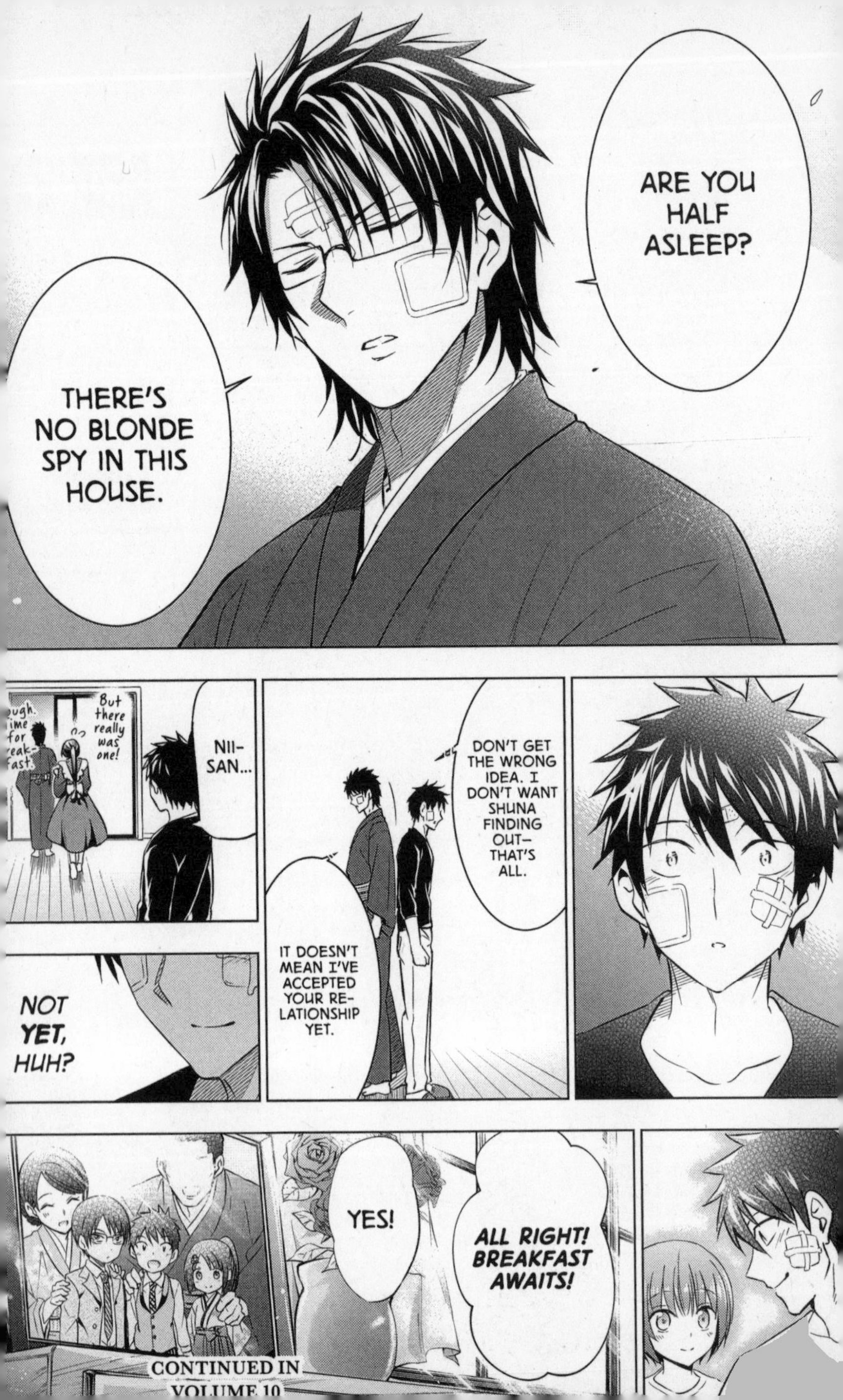
ARE YOU HALF ASLEEP?
THERE'S NO BLONDE SPY IN THIS HOUSE.
DON'T GET THE WRONG IDEA. I DON'T WANT SHUNA FINDING OUT—THAT'S ALL.
IT DOESN'T MEAN I'VE ACCEPTED YOUR RE-LATIONSHIP YET.
NII-SAN...
But there really was one!
NOT YET, HUH?
ALL RIGHT! BREAKFAST AWAITS!
YES!

CONTINUED IN VOLUME 10

BONUS MANGA: AIRU'S PROBLEM

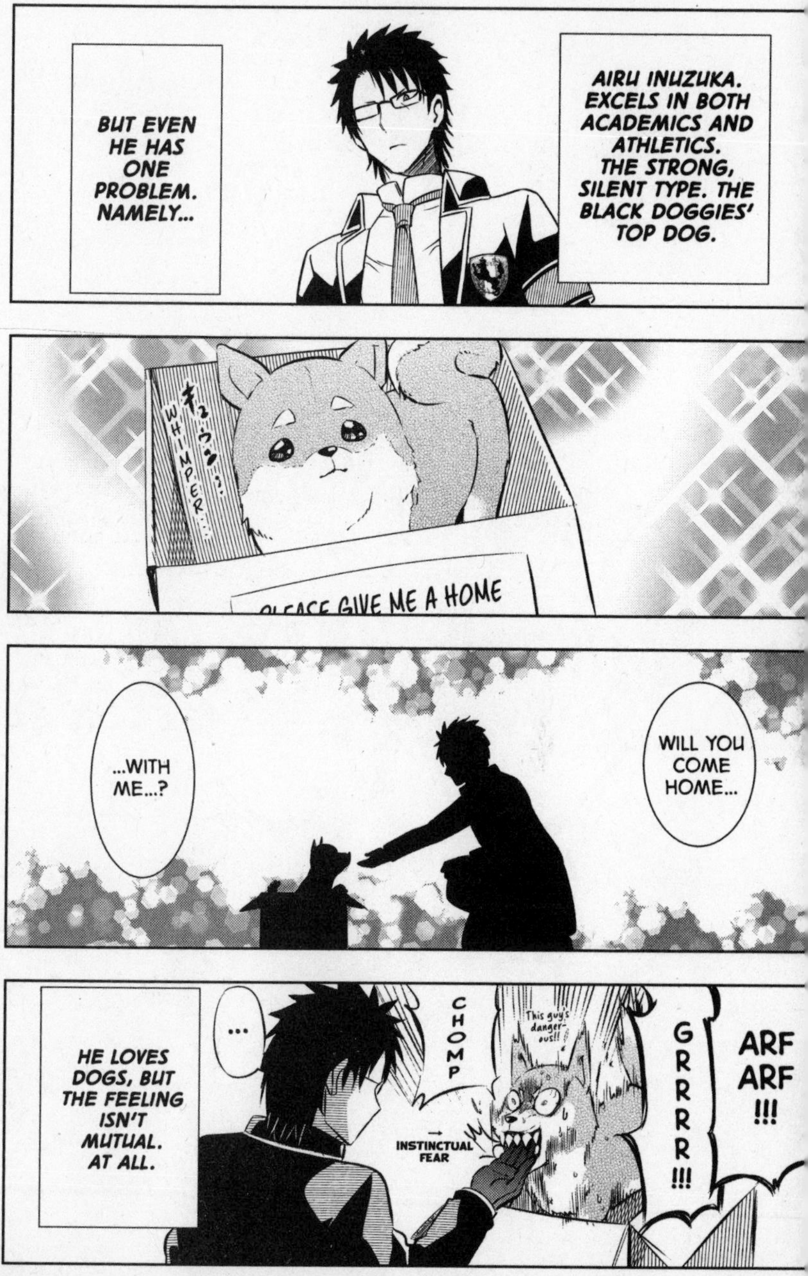
AIRU INUZUKA. EXCELS IN BOTH ACADEMICS AND ATHLETICS. THE STRONG, SILENT TYPE. THE BLACK DOGGIES' TOP DOG.
BUT EVEN HE HAS ONE PROBLEM. NAMELY...
WHIMPER...
GIVE ME A HOME
WILL YOU COME HOME...
...WITH ME...?
ARF ARF !!!
GRRRR!!!
This guy's danger-ous!!
CHOMP
INSTINCTUAL FEAR
...
HE LOVES DOGS, BUT THE FEELING ISN'T MUTUAL. AT ALL.

AFTERWORD

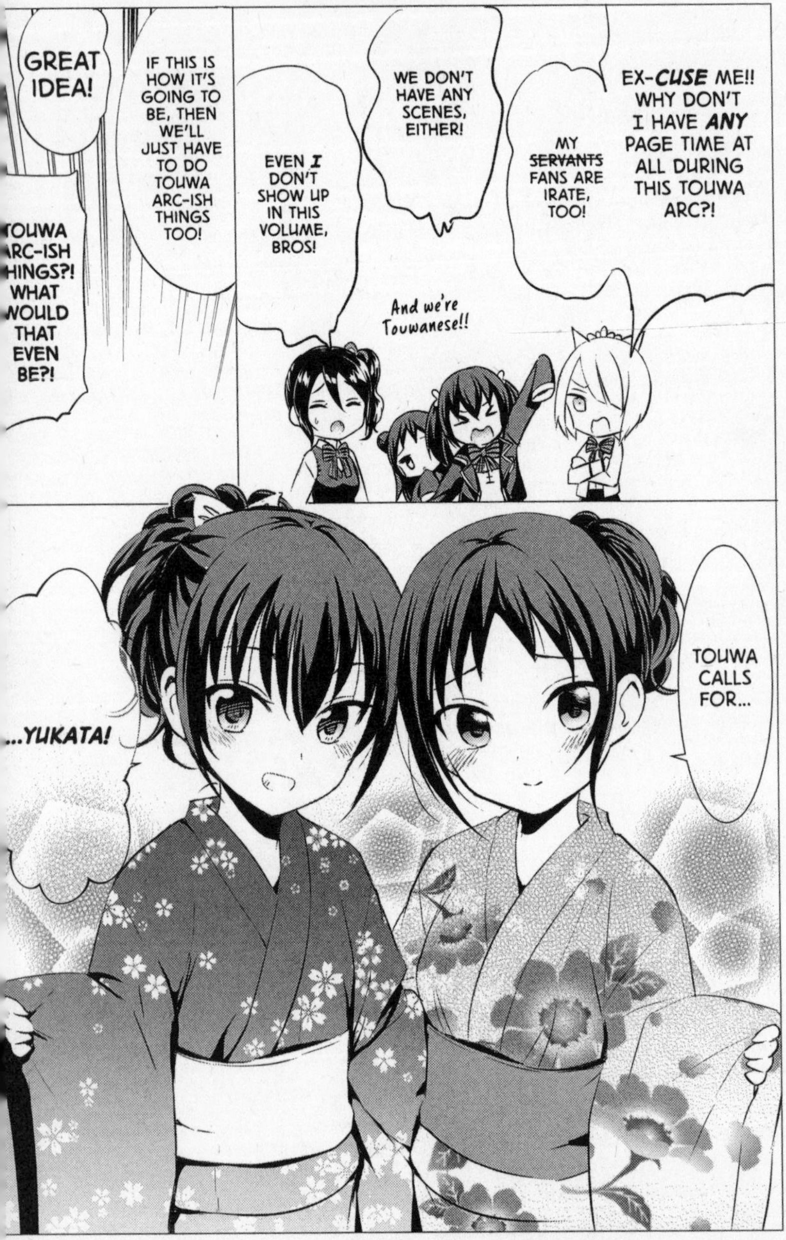

EX-*CUSE* ME!! WHY DON'T I HAVE ***ANY*** PAGE TIME AT ALL DURING THIS TOUWA ARC?!
MY ~~SERVANTS~~ FANS ARE IRATE, TOO!
WE DON'T HAVE ANY SCENES, EITHER!
EVEN *I* DON'T SHOW UP IN THIS VOLUME, BROS!
And we're Touwanese!!
IF THIS IS HOW IT'S GOING TO BE, THEN WE'LL JUST HAVE TO DO TOUWA ARC-ISH THINGS TOO!
GREAT IDEA!
TOUWA RC-ISH HINGS?! WHAT WOULD THAT EVEN BE?!
TOUWA CALLS FOR...
...YUKATA!

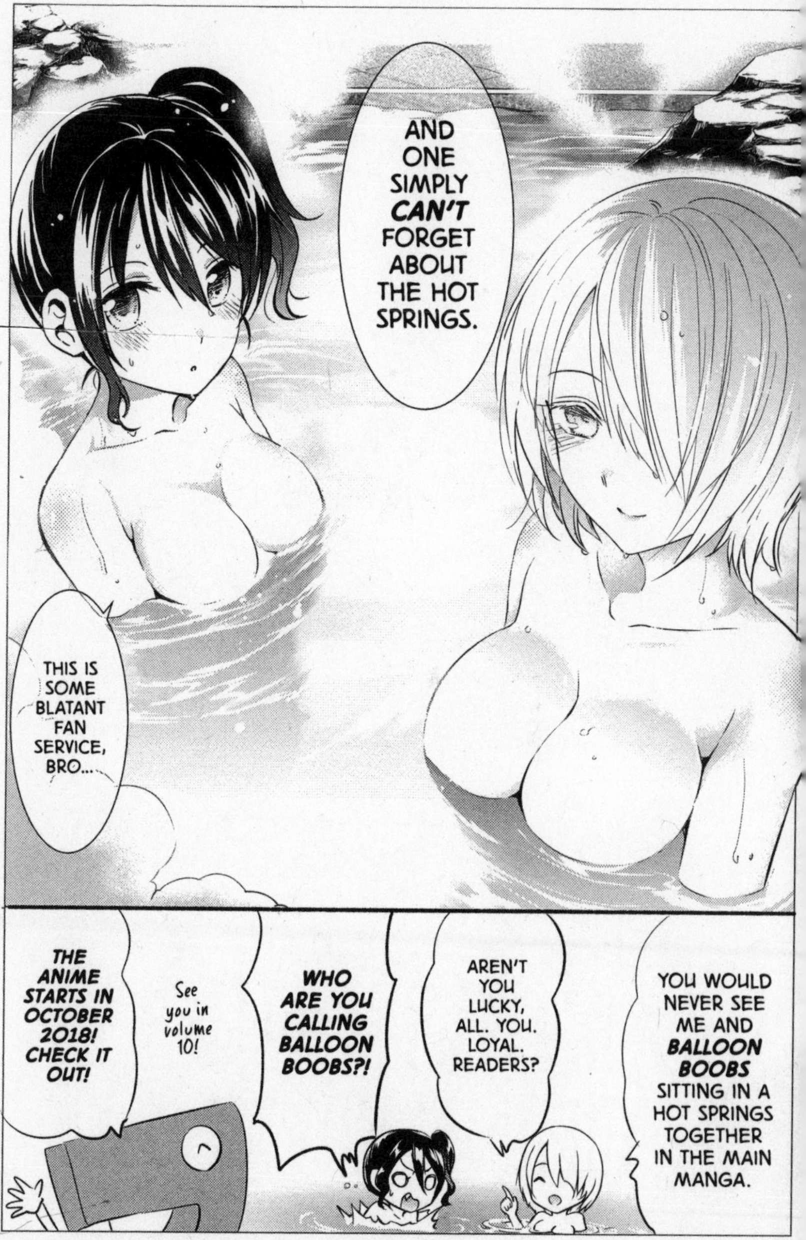
AND ONE SIMPLY CAN'T FORGET ABOUT THE HOT SPRINGS.
THIS IS SOME BLATANT FAN SERVICE, BRO...
YOU WOULD NEVER SEE ME AND BALLOON BOOBS SITTING IN A HOT SPRINGS TOGETHER IN THE MAIN MANGA.
AREN'T YOU LUCKY, ALL. YOU. LOYAL. READERS?
WHO ARE YOU CALLING BALLOON BOOBS?!
See you in volume 10!
THE ANIME STARTS IN OCTOBER 2018! CHECK IT OUT!

Futaro Uesugi is a second-year in high school, scraping to get by and pay off his family's debt. The only thing he can do is study, so when Futaro receives a part-time job offer to tutor the five daughters of a wealthy businessman, he can't pass it up. Little does he know, these five beautiful sisters are quintuplets, but the only thing they have in common...is that they're all terrible at studying!

THE QUINTESSENTIAL QUINTUPLETS

negi haruba

ANIME
T NOW!

KC
KODANSHA
COMICS

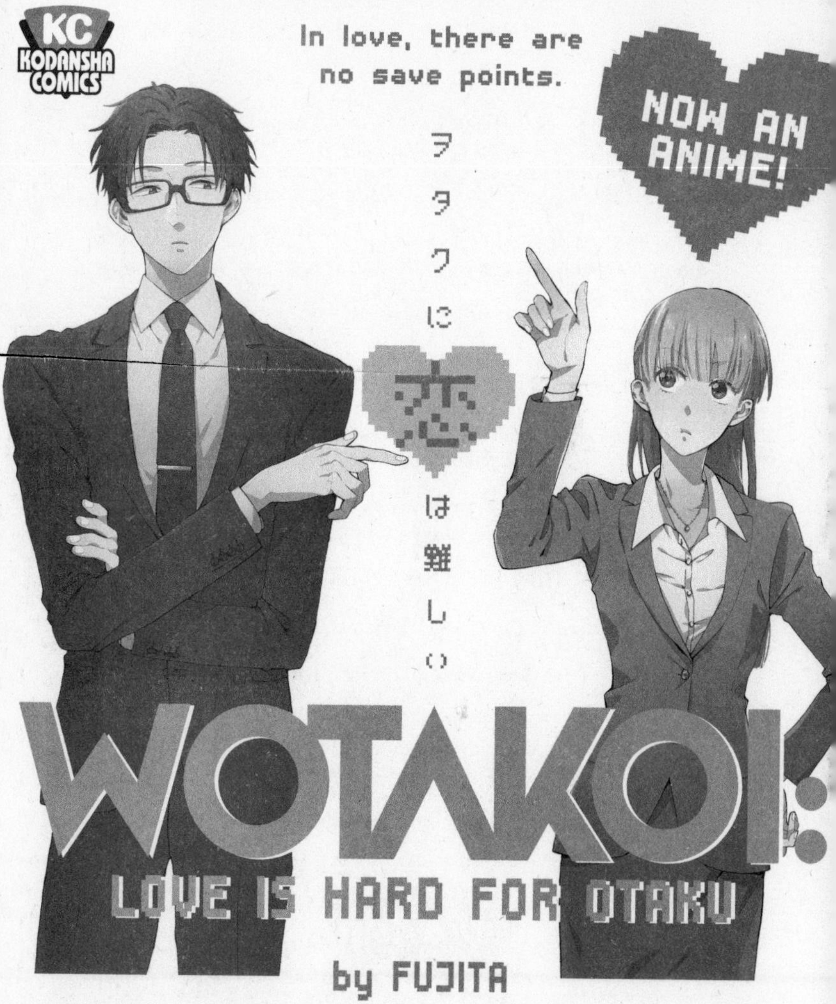
KC KODANSHA COMICS
In love, there are no save points.
NOW AN ANIME!
ヲタクに恋は難しい
WOTAKOI:
LOVE IS HARD FOR OTAKU
by FUJITA

Narumi has had it rough: Every boyfriend she's had dumped her once they found out she was an otaku, so she's gone to great lengths to hide it. At her new job, she bumps into Hirotaka, her childhood friend and fellow otaku. When Hirotaka almost gets her secret outed at work, she comes up with a plan to keep him quiet. But he comes up with a counter-proposal: Why doesn't she just date him instead?

CEYA

Boarding School Juliet volume 9 copyright © 2018 Yousuke Kaneda
English translation copyright © 2019 Yousuke Kaneda

Published in the United States by Kodansha Comics, an imprint of Kodansha USA Publishing, LLC, New York.

Publication rights for this English edition arranged through Kodansha Ltd., Tokyo.

First published in Japan in 2018 by Kodansha Ltd., Tokyo as *Kishuku Gakkou no Jurietto*, volume 9.

ISBN 978-1-63236-831-7

Printed in the United States of America.

www.kodanshacomics.com

9 8 7 6 5 4 3 2 1
Translation: Amanda Haley
Lettering: James Dashiell
Editing: Erin Subramanian and Tiff Ferentini
Kodansha Comics edition cover design by Phil Balsman

Publisher: Kiichiro Sugawara
Managing editor: Maya Rosewood
Vice president of marketing & publicity: Naho Yamada

Director of publishing services: Ben Applegate
Associate director of operations: Stephen Pakula
Publishing services managing editor: Noelle Webster
Assistant production manager: Emi Lotto